Red and Yellow, Black and Brown

Red and Yellow, Black and Brown

Decentering Whiteness in Mixed Race Studies

EDITED BY JOANNE L. RONDILLA,
RUDY P. GUEVARRA JR., AND
PAUL SPICKARD

RUTGERS UNIVERSITY PRESS

NEW BRUNSWICK, CAMDEN, AND NEWARK, NEW JERSEY, AND LONDON

Cataloging-in-Publication data is available from the Library of Congress
978-0-8135-8730-1 (Book/Paperback)
978-0-8135-8731-8 (Book/cloth)
978-0-8135-8732-5 (Epub)
978-0-8135-8733-2 (Web PDF)

A British Cataloging-in-Publication record for this book
is available from the British Library.

www.rutgersuniversitypress.org

Manufactured in the United States of America

In loving memory of Angela and Rudy Guevarra

For Jose Ureta, whose thirst for knowledge inspires

To Anna

CONTENTS

Red and Yellow, Black and Brown

1

Introduction

About Mixed Race, Not about Whiteness

PAUL SPICKARD, RUDY P. GUEVARRA JR., AND JOANNE L. RONDILLA

Hines Ward is an American success story. He played fourteen seasons for the Pittsburgh Steelers in the National Football League, which employs many outstanding African American athletes. He played in four Pro Bowls and three Super Bowls, and was named Super Bowl Most Valuable Player in 2006. He is the Pittsburgh Steelers' all-time leading pass receiver and doubtless will someday be enshrined in the Hall of Fame. As his football career was winding down, he competed in and won season 12 of the American TV dance competition *Dancing with the Stars*. He has appeared in several TV shows and movies, including *The Dark Knight Rises*, *The Walking Dead*, and a cooking show. Recently he has embarked on a second career as a studio football analyst for NBC Sports.[1]

Hines Ward was born in Seoul and came to the United States at the age of one. He grew up for a time as a Black boy in America, living in his early years with his father in Georgia and Louisiana. But he also had a Korean immigrant mother who was his sole day-to-day parent from the age of seven. As a boy in the American South, Hines felt ashamed of his mother:

> I was almost embarrassed to talk about my own upbringing. To me, it was tough. It was never like the upbringing my friends had. At first, I was embarrassed that I had a Korean mom. I was embarrassed that my friends all had to take off their shoes before coming into my house. It was tough when my mom spoke broken English to my friends and their parents and people couldn't understand what she was saying or she couldn't understand what they were saying. . . . I remember one day I got in trouble at school. The principal called my mom, and my mom told the school that she would be right there. My mom walked straight into my classroom, all maybe 4-foot-10 of her, and she paddled me right in front of all my

> classmates. My mom didn't play. She wanted to teach me a lesson I would
> never forget, and I have never forgotten it since.[2]

In time, Hines came to appreciate the Korean-style upbringing that his mother
provided.

> My mom is my hero. She is the reason why I am who I am today. When
> other kids were doing all the wrong things, I was doing all the right things
> because my mom wouldn't have it any other way. She taught me to never
> quit on anything in life. She taught me the value of hard work, sacrifice
> and perseverance. Although she is a little woman, she ruled our house
> with a big presence. She is my rock. . . . I will always love, respect and
> honor my mom. She left everything she knew, that she called home in
> South Korea to come to a foreign country where she didn't even speak
> the language to give me a better life. So she sacrificed her entire life,
> relationships, worked three jobs, kept the house, and took care of me, so
> that I wouldn't have to suffer or experience the discrimination that she
> suffered in Korea.

Now a father himself, Hines Ward values the Korean upbringing: "I have one
son, and. . . . My philosophy on parenting is similar to what my mom taught me.
I will teach my son to be tough, hard working, never quit, stay humble, no matter what. I will teach him the importance of self-sacrifice. I guess you could say
I will teach my son the Korean way when it comes to discipline and education.
It worked well for me. And I'm sure it will work well for him. I will always show
him that I love him by being there for him as he grows up."

Still later, Hines and Kim Young came to terms with Korea. Kim Young had
taken her baby to America because of anti-Black and antiforeign discrimination she and Hines had experienced in Korea. But after Ward won the Super
Bowl MVP trophy, he received an unexpected outpouring of praise from Kore-
ans. Some of this may have been a manifestation of what Cynthia Nakashima
calls the "claim-us-if-we're-famous syndrome"[3]—mixed race people of con-
spicuous achievement being acknowledged by racial communities that would
have ignored them if they were less accomplished. But the Korean wave of
appreciation for Hines Ward in 2006 and after also derived from his display
of Korean values.

> I didn't really associate with any Korean people growing up because of
> how my mom was treated in her own country. So when I won the Super
> Bowl XL MVP, that's when I heard that Korean people were calling out my
> name and cheering me on. I was really confused and shocked at this. . . .
> Everyone from little kids to the mayor of Seoul to the president of the
> country came out to thank me. And all I could think of was, "Thank me

for what?" Then I was told . . . that the entire country of Korea was very proud of me, as a Korean, for the way I accepted the Super Bowl MVP trophy. He said when I dedicated it and all I had accomplished to my mom, the entire country of South Korea cheered because of the humility and gratitude I gave to my mom, the parent who raised me. . . . He said that I brought the entire nation back to the days when kids would show complete respect and honor to their parents. And for that, he thanked me. I was really humbled by what he said. I was beginning to see how my Korean heritage and culture saw things. And I began to start feeling pride in my Korean side.

Hines Ward is a Black American, but he is also a Korean American. It is an open question whether Ward's athletic achievements owe more to the size, speed, and coordination some may think he inherited from his father, or to the incredible work ethic he undoubtedly learned from his mother. More important for the purposes of this book is the identity journey that Hines Ward has taken, from being a Black American man in a highly visible professional position, to marking himself as also a Korean American immigrant with ongoing ties to the land of his birth. He is a complicated guy.

Ariana Miyamoto is complicated too. Born in Sasebo, Japan, to a Japanese mother and a Black American father who soon returned to the United States, she grew up experiencing discrimination and abuse from other Japanese people. "There was pretty much a spasmodic vomit of racial abuse heaped upon me," said the twenty-year-old. "I was called n****r by some of my peers. Some of them threw trash and even a blackboard duster at me. I'm Japanese through and through, but in Japan if you look 'foreign' you are often not accepted as Japanese. But I am Japanese—100 percent."[4] Japanese is Miyamoto's first and most fluent language, although she does speak English and attended high school for two years in Arkansas while getting to know her father's family. She holds a fifth-level degree in Japanese calligraphy, a high level of mastery.

Although Japan thinks of itself as a very homogeneous country, lots of models and actors these days are *haafu*—"half." Miyamoto began a modeling career and soon was approached about being a candidate for Miss Nagasaki. Initially she refused, but she changed her mind when a haafu friend killed himself. "He could not find his identity. He committed suicide a few days after he told me, 'I don't have any idea where I should be located.' . . . To ensure that such a tragedy is never repeated and to eliminate prejudice and discrimination, I decided to enter the contest. I hope that Japanese society will become more open by accepting not only *haafu* but also LGBT people and others. I hope to make Japan and the world a livable place for anyone."[5]

Miyamoto won Miss Nagasaki and in March 2015 was crowned Miss Universe Japan. She went on to represent Japan in the 2015 Miss Universe pageant, the first haafu to represent Japan in that contest. The title brought her accolades from mixed race communities at home and abroad, but it also exposed deep-rooted racism in her country. Almost immediately, negative comments flooded social media and Internet sites questioning her victory. Negative comments from Japanese websites such as Byokan Sunday and Naver Matome questioned whether she was qualified to represent Japan since she is haafu. These included "Is it okay to select a *haafu* to represent Japan?" and "Because this is Miss Universe Japan, don't you think *haafu* are a no no?"[6] She was also criticized for not *looking* traditionally Japanese—she is tall (five feet, eight inches) and slim—and her very presence challenged what defines beauty in Japan. However, not all comments were negative. Haafu documentary filmmaker Megumi Nishikura said, "The selection of Ariana Miyamoto as this year's Miss Universe Japan is a huge step forward in expanding the definition of what it means to be Japanese. The controversy that has erupted over her selection is a great opportunity of us Japanese to examine how far we have come from our self-perpetuated myth of homogeneity while at the same time it shows us how much further we need to go."[7]

The study of multiracial people is the fastest-growing segment of ethnic studies.[8] By far the majority of the writing and teaching about multiraciality concerns people who are part White: Black and White, Mexican American and Anglo, Caribbean and English, Japanese and White American, and so on and on.[9] This book is not about such people. It is about people like Hines Ward and Ariana Miyamoto, who are racially mixed but have parents from multiple minority backgrounds. Historically, multiraciality has been limited to examining Whiteness in relation to non-White ethnic minorities. However, scholars such as Velina Hasu Houston, Karen Leonard, Rudy Guevarra, Vivek Bald, and others have illustrated that the histories of people who are of multiple minority descent should be given serious scholarly attention.[10] We crafted this collection to continue the groundbreaking work of scholars such as these. In putting these works together we expand the current conversations about multiraciality beyond the very limited scope of Black and White, inspire more work that continues to broaden our knowledge of multiracial communities, and explore conversations that reflect the changing racial landscape of the United States and other parts of the world where mixing is common.

It is of historical importance that we turn the center of attention of race relations scholars away from a focus on White/non-White binaries and direct them to a broader inquiry into relationships among different communities of color. Beginning in 2011, non-White births began to outnumber White births in the United States every year.[11] Demographers anticipate that by 2042, the

United States will become what some have called a "majority-minority" country (in fact, the term "minority" may even fall out of use).[12] The US Census Bureau recorded an increase in the mixed race population of 32 percent between 2000 and 2010. Of the people who identified as having multiple racial ancestries, 92 percent reported two different races. Approximately 21 percent of mixed race people reported being multiple minority, while 79 percent had ancestry that was part White.[13]

There is a persistent myth—an assumption built into eighteenth- and nineteenth-century science—that there once existed discrete, pure races on the face of the earth. This idea has a history.[14] Swedish botanist Carolus Linnaeus did humankind the estimable service of organizing all the visible living organisms conceptually into a vast pyramid of nested categories: kingdom, phylum, class, order, family, genus, species, and race. At each level of the hierarchy, he supposed the categories to be separate and distinct. His taxonomy sorts out a lot of material, but it creates the illusion of purity in each category. Johann Friedrich Blumenbach decided there were four, then five races of humankind: Negroid, Mongoloid, Amerind, Malay, and Caucasian. Arthur Comte de Gobineau ranked them according to their beauty, intelligence, character, and overall wonderfulness, with Whites at the top and Blacks at the bottom. Madison Grant elaborated distinctions within the White race and contributed to the popular acceptance of the idea of improving that race by selective breeding and sterilization.[15]

These schemas presented the human races as distinct and pure, each with its own separate ancestry, physical morphology (now we might say genotype or field of DNA), intelligence, character qualities, and potential for success. None of the schemas had a place for mixed or in-between peoples like Egyptians, Samoans, Uyghurs, Mexicans, and Filipinos. Insofar as racialist pseudoscience even acknowledged the existence of mixed people, it treated them as defective and inferior to their separate and supposedly pure parent stocks, and predicted weakness, ugliness, infertility, and tortured self-doubt in successive generations of mixing.[16]

In fact, there are not now, nor ever have there been, any pure races. Every human population—indeed, every human being—is racially mixed. If there is one undisputable fact of human history it is that just about everybody has been moving around the globe and mating with just about everybody else. There are patterns to the moving and the mating, but there are no pure races. Nonetheless, there remains plenty of racialized abuse. By that we mean that racial distinctions are drawn and rhetorically laid onto the body and into the gene pool of individuals and groups. Quanta of intelligence and character are assigned to them. Particular life chances are assigned to them. So if we are not actually (racially, biologically) distinct from one another, we are still distinct in the

opportunities we have and the abuse we may have to endure. Race may be a
false category—a social construction—but racism is a social fact.

The dominant voice among scholars and activists in mixed race studies has
contended that the assertion of a multiracial identity is a positive move that
has the potential to undercut racist structures.[17] Maria Root, the foremother of
multiracial studies, wrote in the introduction to her canonical edited volume,
Racially Mixed People in America,

> Why has the United States suppressed the historical reality that a sig-
> nificant proportion of its citizenry has multigenerational multiracial
> roots? . . . The silence on the topic of multiraciality must be understood
> in context. In the not-so-distant past . . . antimiscegenist sentiments
> were profound. . . . The history of antimiscegenist laws and attitudes
> combined with rules of hypodescent, a pseudoscientific literature on
> race mixing . . . and the internalized oppression still evident in commu-
> nities of color have unquestionably contributed to the silence on this
> topic. . . . Whereas one of the breakthroughs of the civil rights move-
> ment was empowerment of American racial minority groups by self-
> naming . . . , this process is just beginning among multiracial persons.
> In essence, to name oneself is to validate one's existence and declare
> visibility. This seemingly simple process is a significant step in the
> liberation of multiracial persons from the oppressive structure of
> the racial classification system that has relegated them to the land
> of "in between."[18]

Harvard law professor Randall Kennedy joined the chorus:

> Americans are becoming increasingly multiracial in their tastes, affec-
> tions, and identities. The rates of interracial dating, marriage, and
> adoption, are inching, and in some places rocketing, upward. This
> trend is, in my view, a positive good. It signals that formal and infor-
> mal racial boundaries are fading. . . . Against the tragic backdrop
> of American history, the flowering of multiracial intimacy is a pro-
> foundly moving and encouraging development, one that lends support
> to Frederick Douglass's belief that eventually "the white and colored
> people of this country [can] be blended into a common nationality,
> and enjoy together . . . the inestimable blessings of life, liberty, and
> the pursuit of happiness."[19]

Ronald David Glass and Kendra R. Wallace were less sanguine than Kennedy
about an imagined happy future that would come from embracing the multiracial idea, but they did see multiraciality as a potent platform from which to
attack racism.

Race cannot be ignored as a conceptual framework because of its theoretical inadequacy for capturing the phenomenon of race, nor because of its simplistic use of reified notions for historically dynamic meanings and practices. Nor can the politics of race be transcended by a mental act of some sort (like a change in belief, or an act of will) nor wished away in a fantasy of color blindness. Race matters . . . , and we argue for a focus of attention on the continuing significance and changing meaning of race . . . to be linked with projects engaged in contesting that very significance and meaning. . . . But an even stronger challenge to race can come from people at the margins to all racial centers; that is, from people expressive of multiracial existence and evident human variation, who resist efforts to be subdued and brought within racial orders.[20]

Some critics of the multiracial idea have suggested, to the contrary, that the assertion of a mixed race identity is a move on the part of people of mixed ancestry to flee Blackness and to claim a measure of Whiteness.[21] Jon Michael Spencer saw monoracial Black and White as the only races in American society.[22] He contended that the assertion of a multiracial identity was an attempt by White parents of part-Black children to construct a third race, "The New Colored People," between Black and White, in imitation of the oppressive tripartite racial system that had until recently obtained in South Africa. Citing Afrocentrist Molefi Asante, Spencer wrote, "In the context of a racist society . . . white parents want their mixed children to have the same privileges they enjoy, but these children are by tradition considered black. Because in this racist society blackness is viewed as negative, . . . the multiracialists attempt to minimize the effects of this negativity by claiming they are neither black nor white, but multiracial."[23] He continued,

We are faced again with this inescapable reality: black is the bottom line with regard to social caste. So mixed-race blacks, no matter what their mix, are always niggers. No wonder many mixed-race people choose to identify with blacks—revolutionary attitude or not, "black and proud" or not. With the racism mixed-race blacks face . . . in the United States (and elsewhere in the world), it makes sense that the one-drop rule would be viewed by blacks and many mixed-race blacks as a necessity . . . for the sake of the black community being able to maintain a healthy cohesiveness. . . . Any suggestion of changing the one-drop rule at this point would impair rather than enhance black unity and racial progress.[24]

This criticism of the multiracial movement—that it is a form of seeking after Whiteness—has theoretical validity: it points to a real danger. There are at least some people who advocate a multiracial identity as a way station toward not talking about race at all.[25] However, whatever the merits of Spencer's critique (and some of our contributors think it has considerable merit, at least in the case of some people who are part Black), it depends on the assumption that the multiraciality in question involves people of part-White ancestry.

This volume seeks to understand the often very different dynamics that exist for mixed people who are not part White. The project brings together scholars who study the multiraciality of people who cannot be construed as engaged in a Whiteness move. It draws on research into the social, psychological, and political situations of people of mixed race who have links to two or more peoples of color—Chinese and Mexican, Asian and Black, Native American and African American, South Asian and Filipino, Black and Latino, and so on. It also opens up theoretical questions surrounding the meanings and communication of racial identities in multiple minority situations. It even considers the implications for current racial understandings of prehistoric mixing between Neanderthal and other human populations. It brings together the intellectual perspectives of several disciplines: historians, sociologists, ethnic studies scholars, an anthropologist, a playwright, and a poet.

We seek to create an intellectual momentum that prompts scholars, writers, and others who are invested in multiracial studies to pay better attention to multiple minority communities, couples, and individuals. While these histories are not new, their presence in the field must be granted more attention than they have gained heretofore. In doing so, we also declare the relevance of *decentering Whiteness in multiracial studies.* In race and ethnic studies, scholars are often coerced into giving Whiteness (and, in turn, White people) more consideration than their numbers or social position warrant. This makes race talk inordinately limiting. When there is an overemphasis on including Whiteness in every discussion, or on taking extra steps to avoid offending White people, we lose out on essential, though difficult, conversations about race. We make absolutely no apologies for envisioning race talk without having to consider the feelings of White people or include consideration of Whiteness. This is not meant to exclude such communities from the conversation. Rather, we are centering the experience of non-White groups who have been historically silenced (and have been expected to accept that silence).

The Shape of This Volume

Part I charts the individual journeys of identity transited by playwright Velina Hasu Houston and poet Janet Mendoza Stickmon. Houston is one of the founding figures of the multiracial movement and the internationally acclaimed author of more than thirty plays. In chapter 2 she recounts her self-fashioning and struggles for acceptance among monoracial Blacks and Asians, and also among multiracial people whose parentage is Asian and White. She presents herself as culturally Japanese, spatially located in California, and frequently profiled as Black. As she says, "Mixed race people are The Other. Mixed race people of African descent are The Other's Other." She writes eloquently not just of her own pain at misrecognition by others, but also of quiet triumph among the women of Rising Soul, an organization of Black Japanese women.

Mendoza Stickmon's essay, "Blackapina," reflects on her experience of being a biracial woman of African American and Filipino American descent. It is divided into five movements, much like a musical composition: (1) "The Intersection," (2) "Multiple Families," (3) "Disconnection Exposed," (4) "Transformative Impact of Theology School," and (5) "The Blend." Through these movements, she explores her progression from identifying as "half African American and half Filipino American" to embracing hybridity as a Blackapina. She describes pivotal moments in her life, from the death of her parents to the birth of her child, that have shaped her understanding of herself as a multidimensional human being, specifically drawing upon the concept of psychosynthesis and its application to multiracial people.

Part II offers three studies of mixed marriage and parenting in multiple minority families and racially mixed communities. In "Intermarriage and the Making of a Multicultural Society in the Baja California Borderlands," Verónica Castillo-Muñoz takes us back in time. At the dawn of the twentieth century, a boom in mining and agribusiness brought thousands of single men from Mexico, Europe, and China to Baja California. The Mexican government initially required that workers be divided by race. Agriculture and mining companies maintained separate housing for Chinese, European, and Mexican workers—ostensibly for public health reasons but likely to divide the workforce ethnically and tamp down labor resistance. However, by the 1920s there was a big change in demographics: most families in Baja California were racially mixed, and people in Baja California spoke at least fourteen different languages and eight different dialects. Castillo-Muñoz's chapter examines what led to this transformation and how men and women undermined government efforts to selectively deny mixed race marriages and unions between Chinese men and Mexican women, mestizo men and indigenous women, and other multiple-minority unions.

Jessica Vasquez-Tokos writes in chapter 5 about the dynamics that occur in cross-minority intermarriages. She analyzes the marital choices, orientations to mainstream society, and parenting strategies of six non-White interracial couples. She finds that a minority-minority connection—where being a racial minority transcends identification with any particular racial category—facilitates non-White racial intermarriage. Emotional bonding is based on occupying a shared marginalized non-White racial status. A consequence of this minority-minority connection is the tendency to read contemporary racial politics through the lens of racial history in the United States. While most of these intermarried minority couples feel excluded from mainstream society and critique it from an "outsider-within" position,[26] those who claim to feel *included* in the mainstream do so by citing their middle-class status. Those who are parents rear their multiracial children with an instructional emphasis on racial identity, ethnic culture, immigration history, and awareness of racial inequality. In sum, evidence suggests that cross-racial non-White couples see their partnerships not as a panacea to racial and ethnic inequality in the United States, but instead as a viewpoint from which to critique US racist structures and processes, both past and present.

Research that focuses on racial socialization in multiracial families has been extremely helpful in advancing the field, but there has been an overwhelming focus on the racial socialization of multiracials who have one White parent. In chapter 6, Cristina Ortiz concentrates on the racial socialization practices of multiple-minority multiracial families. Based on extensive interviews and lengthy observations of one multiple-minority family, along with comparisons to several other such families, Ortiz exposes the methods by which these parents help their children learn to navigate race in the world.

Part III presents two studies of individuals who have African American parentage as well as ancestry from another racial group. In "Being Mixed Race in the Makah Nation," Ingrid Dineen-Wimberly starts from the ethical commitment that lies at the heart of the mixed race movement: that we must honor every person's right to identify as he or she chooses. She describes the history and memory of mixing between Native American peoples and non-Indians. Then she unfolds the stories of Landon, a Makah Indian who has a rich bouquet of racial ancestries—Black, White, Filipino, and Quileute as well as Makah—and his racially complex extended family. In particular, she illuminates the ways that Landon experiences the limits to and possibilities of his membership in Makah society on account of his father's Blackness, and the hurdles he has had to jump in order to succeed in claiming an Indian identity, along with Black and mixed identities.

In "'You're Not Black or Mexican Enough!'" Rebecca Romo reports on Blaxicans, multiple-minority multiracial individuals who are the offspring of one Mexican American parent and one African American parent. She explores how Blaxicans blend and borrow from both African American and Mexican American cultural and historical sources to formulate identities that are multiracial and multiethnic and that are resistant to monoraciality and Whiteness. She finds that Blaxican identities and experiences are influenced by the socialization provided by their parents, class, gender, and peer groups. While Blaxican identity is fluid and situational, Blaxicans reject the one-drop rule that labels them as Black on an intrapersonal level. Chapter 8 show Blaxicans existing in a borderland space that is in between African American and Mexican American identities.

In part IV, three scholars examine the lives of people who have part Asian ancestry. In "Bumbay in the Bay," Maharaj Raju Desai explores the identities and experiences of those of mixed South Asian and Filipino heritage, whom he calls Indipinos. He examines how racialization by both the Filipino American and Indian American communities, as well as the larger American community, affects their identity formation and cultural affinity. He uses interviews of four Indipino women from the San Francisco Bay Area to explore how the intersections of institutional, interpersonal, and internalized constructions of race affect the identities of double-minority mixed women. Desai's goal is to give visibility to the Indipino experience. The South Asian diaspora is not generally discussed in studies of mixed heritage outside of a few Indian mixes such as Black/Indian and Mexican/Indian. Furthermore, there is little scholarship on the South Asian diaspora in the Philippines and the mixing that occurs there and in communities of South Asian immigrants from the Philippines in the United States. Desai fills in these gaps.

Kaori Mori Want takes her analysis to Japan in chapter 10, "Hypervisibility and Invisibility of Female Haafu Models in Japan's Beauty Culture." Japan is usually considered to be a racially and ethnically homogeneous nation, but it has racial and ethnic diversity, and haafu have lived in Japan for a long time. Haafu—mixed race people—first emerged in the public imagination in the 1960s when many haafu singers, actors, and athletes were active in the media, and that time is called the first haafu boom. The new century has witnessed the second haafu boom, and we can see many haafu celebrities in the media today. Japanese girls worship the faces of haafu female celebrities, which are characterized as having big double-lidded eyes, long eyelashes, tall noses, and full lips. The cosmetics industry takes advantage of the haafu boom among Japanese girls and produces "haafu cosmetics," which allegedly make a typical Japanese face look haafu. Magazines also feature articles on how to use makeup to achieve a haafu-like appearance. What is problematic about this popularity of haafu is that the worshiped haafu face is half White and half Japanese. Half Black, half Brown, and half Yellow haafu are invisible in this phenomenon. Mori Want argues that the invisibility of the non-Caucasian haafu faces in the media and cosmetics industry has inadvertently contributed to stereotypes about haafu. She introduces the voices of non-Caucasian haafu and shows them challenging the stereotype.

Lily Anne Welty Tamai takes us back and forth across the Pacific in "Checking 'Other' Twice: Transnational Dual Minorities." She focuses on the narratives of mixed race American Japanese who were fathered by Black and Latino soldiers, who grew up in Japan, and who came to the United States as young adults. Leaving Japan to cross the Pacific Ocean meant arriving in their fathers' land to deal with a new set of rules surrounding race and the flux of a migrating identity. Welty Tamai connects the importance of oral history methodology with transpacific border crossing to address the issues of mixed race transnational adoption, migration, and citizenship.

Part V, "Reflections," extends the analysis in two very different directions. Terence Keel is a historian of science who contemplates what it may mean to various peoples to have a distant ancestor who was a member not of *Homo sapiens* but of *Homo neanderthalensis.* Since 2010 geneticists have found that Eurasians and Neanderthals mixed roughly thirty thousand years ago, leaving non-African groups with as much as 8 percent Neanderthal DNA in their genome. Keel explains that the story of how humans had children with Neanderthals should push scholars who study mixed race people to evaluate critically their preference for working within human timescales that tend to go no further into the past than the European colonial expansion of the eighteenth and nineteenth centuries, and are most often limited to twentieth-century American history. Thus Keel uses the case of human-Neanderthal hybrids to explore forms of mixing that predate the emergence of Whiteness as a racial category. His essay also draws attention to how being mixed is the baseline, not the exception, for what it means to belong to our species. He argues that if scholars of mixed race people take this seriously then they must confront the tension between knowledge of our biological selves as always already mixed and the pragmatic and political goals of mixed race scholarship in its attempt to highlight the experience of multiethnics—and especially first-generation mixed race people—as if they are social and biological exceptions to what it means to belong to our species.

The collection ends with an analytical postscript. Nitasha Sharma reflects on the eleven essays that constitute the body of this volume.

Taken together, the essays in this volume reveal that there are both thematic similarities and great differences between the experiences of multiracial people who are from multiple minority backgrounds and those who are part White.

This collection is only a beginning. One of the many challenges in putting together an anthology like this is the matter of representation. Throughout the process of producing this book, we were acutely aware of not only the voices that we were bringing to our audience, but also the other voices that were missing. We have assayed the lives and identities of a dozen kinds of multiple-minority multiracial people: Black and Mexican, Indian and Filipino, Chinese and Latino, Native and African American, even *Homo sapiens* and Neanderthal. This does not exhaust the range of possibilities in the realm of people who possess multiple ancestries that have little or nothing to do with White people. Most Pacific Islanders have knowledge of being mixed—Samoan and Tongan, Fijian and Indian, Hawaiian and Chinese, and so on.[27] In Central Asia, there are people who are mixed Kazakh and Korean, Uzbek and Tajik, and so on and on.[28] As Terence Keel points out in chapter 12, mixedness is the default condition of the human race; it is the very mark of our humanity.

NOTES

1. Information for this section is taken from Brian Han, "Hines Ward: The Legend Goes On," *Korea Times* (October 23, 2014); Jerry Crowe, "Ward Learned by Mom's Example," *Los Angeles Times* (February 4, 2006); Paul Wiseman, "Ward Spins Biracial Roots into Blessing," *USA Today* (April 10, 2006); John Branch, "Ward Helps Biracial Youths on Journey toward Acceptance," *New York Times* (November 9, 2009); Ji-Hyun Ahn, "Rearticulating Black Mixed-Race in the Era of Globalization: Hines Ward and the Struggle for Koreanness in Contemporary South Korean Media," *Cultural Studies* 28.3 (2014): 391–417.

2. All the quotations here are taken from Han, "Hines Ward."

3. Cynthia L. Nakashima, "An Invisible Monster: The Creation and Denial of Mixed-Race People in America," in *Racially Mixed People in America*, ed. Maria P. P. Root (Newbury Park, CA: Sage, 1992), 162–178.

4. Michael Fitzpatrick and Tim Macfarlan, "'I've Been Called N****r and Had Trash Thrown at Me': First Mixed Race Miss Japan Hits Out at the 'Spasmodic Vomit of Racial Abuse' She's Suffered Because Father Is African-American," *Daily Mail* (April 1, 2015). Other sources for this section include "Beauty Queen Brings Light to Japan's Racial Issues," *CBS News* (April 13, 2015); Traci G. Lee, "Biracial Miss Universe Japan Faces Backlash," *MSNBC* (March 26, 2015), http://www.msnbc.com/msnbc/biracial-miss-universe-japan -faces-backlash; Martin Fackler, "Biracial Beauty Queen Challenges Japan's Self-Image," *New York Times* (May 29, 2015).

5. Kosuke Takahashi, "Multiracial Miss Universe Japan Symbolizes the Country's Trans-formation," *Huffington Post Japan* (May 8, 2015), http://www.huffingtonpost.com/2015/05/08/multiracial-miss-universe_n_7205026.html.

6. http://www.huffingtonpost.com/2015/03/25/miss-universe-japan_n_6938584.html.

7. Ibid.

8. In 1995, to our knowledge, there were three university courses on multiraciality, taught by G. Reginald Daniel at UCLA, by Teresa Williams at UC Santa Barbara, and by Paul Spickard at Brigham Young University–Hawai'i. Two decades later, mixed race courses numbered at least 144: UC Santa Barbara (five courses in four depart-ments), University of Hawai'i Manoa, University of Colorado, Brown University (two courses), UCLA (courses in three departments), University of Southern California, University of Michigan (two courses), Arizona State University (two courses), Uni-versity of Wisconsin–Milwaukee, University of Virginia, Juniata College, Portland State University, Hamilton College, University of Maryland, University of Calgary, Huron University College, California State University, Fullerton, Princeton University (two courses), Rutgers University, Carnegie Mellon University, the London School of Economics, California State University, Los Angeles, Berklee College of Music, George Mason University, University of Warwick, Simmons College, Pennsylvania State

University, Vassar College, San Francisco State University (three courses), UC Berkeley (three courses), University of Buffalo, New York University (four courses), Rice University, UC Davis, Appalachian State University, Sonoma State University, University College London, UC San Diego, Bowdoin College, Edgewood College, University of North Carolina, University of Maryland Baltimore County (two courses), California State University, East Bay, Williams College, University of Vermont, Gerlind Institute for Cultural Studies, Athabasca University, George Mason University, Cornell University, Trinity College (Hartford), Indiana University of Pennsylvania, Fordham University, Lawrence University, Saint Louis University, Yale University, International Christian University (Tokyo), Shibaura Institute of Technology, University of Illinois at Urbana-Champaign (three courses), College of Wooster, Creighton University, Cal Poly Pomona, University of North Carolina Charlotte, DePaul University, UT Austin (three courses), University of San Francisco, Southern Methodist University, Macalester College, Dalhousie University, Amherst College (three courses), Lehman College, University of Virginia (two courses), Emory University, St. Lawrence University, University of Nebraska Omaha, Duke University (two courses), Pomona College, University of Miami, Castleton State College, St. Mary's College of Maryland, Wesleyan University, UC Santa Cruz, University of British Columbia, Kenyon College, Northwestern University (two courses), St. Joseph's University, University of Denver, Barnard College, Antioch University Los Angeles, University of Pennsylvania (two courses), Stanford University (three courses), Hampshire College, Goucher College, The New School (two courses), Oberlin College (two courses), Dartmouth College, University of Connecticut, Kent State University, University of North Texas, Mills College, University of Oregon, Antioch University Midwest (two courses), University of Washington, California State University, Northridge, UC Irvine, Scripps College, University of Nevada, Las Vegas (two courses), the College of Saint Rose, University of Toronto, Sacramento State University, and Harvard University (source: http://www.mixedracestudies.org).

9. See, for example, Katya Gibel Azoulay, *Black, Jewish, and Interracial* (Durham, NC: Duke University Press, 1997); Edward Ball, *Slaves in the Family* (New York: Ballantine, 1998); Lauren L. Basson, *White Enough to Be American? Race Mixing, Indigenous People, and the Boundaries of State and Nation* (Chapel Hill: University of North Carolina Press, 2008); Mary Beltrán and Camilla Fojas, eds., *Mixed Race Hollywood* (New York: New York University Press, 2008); Bliss Broyard, *One Drop: My Father's Hidden Life—A Story of Race and Secrets* (New York: Little, Brown, 2007); Greg Carter, *The United States of the United Races: A Utopian History of Racial Mixing* (New York: New York University Press, 2013); Emily Clark, *The Strange History of the American Quadroon: Free Women of Color in the Revolutionary Atlantic World* (Chapel Hill: University of North Carolina Press, 2013); Penny Edwards, Debjani Ganguly, and Jacqueline Lo, eds., "Mixed Race around the Globe," special issue of *Journal of Intercultural Studies* 28.1 (2007): 1–155; Kip Fulbeck, *Paper Bullets* (Seattle: University of Washington Press, 2001); Lise Funderburg, *Black, White, Other: Biracial Americans Talk about Race and Identity* (New York: Morrow, 1994); Annette Gordon-Reed, *The Hemingses of Monticello: An American Family* (New York: Norton, 2008); Shirlee Taylor Haizlip, *The Sweeter the Juice: A Family Memoir in Black and White* (New York: Free Press, 1995); Patricia Penn Hilden, *When Nickels Were Indians: An Urban, Mixed-Blood Story* (Washington, DC: Smithsonian, 1995); Kevin R. Johnson, *How Did You Get to Be Mexican? A White/Brown Man's Search for Identity* (Philadelphia: Temple University Press, 1999); Andrew J. Jolivette, ed., *Obama and the Biracial Factor: The Battle for a New American Majority* (Bristol: Policy Press, 2012); Bernie D. Jones, *Fathers of Conscience: Mixed-Race Inheritance in the Antebellum South* (Athens: University

of Georgia Press, 2009); Lisa Jones, *Bulletproof Diva: Tales of Race, Sex, and Hair* (New York: Doubleday, 1994); Jane Lazarre, *Beyond the Whiteness of Whiteness: Memoir of a White Mother of Black Sons* (Durham, NC: Duke University Press, 1996); Kent Anderson Leslie, *Woman of Color, Daughter of Privilege: Amanda America Dickson, 1949–1893* (Athens: University of Georgia Press, 1995); James McBride, *The Color of Water: A Black Man's Tribute to His White Mother* (New York: Riverhead, 1996); Robert S. McKelvey, *Dust of Life: America's Children Abandoned in Vietnam* (Seattle: University of Washington Press, 1999); Barack Obama, *Dreams from My Father: A Story of Race and Inheritance* (Tokyo: Kodansha, 1995); Jill Olumide, *Raiding the Gene Pool: The Social Construction of Mixed Race* (London: Pluto Press, 2002); Kerry Ann Rockquemore and David L. Brunsma, *Beyond Black: Biracial Identity in America* (Lanham, MD: Rowman & Littlefield, 2002); Clara E. Rodríguez, *Changing Race: Latinos, the Census, and the History of Ethnicity in the United States* (New York: New York University Press, 2000); Philip Roth, *The Human Stain* (New York: Houghton Mifflin, 2000); Danzy Senna, *Caucasia* (New York: Riverhead, 1998); Daniel J. Sharfstein, *The Invisible Line: Three American Families and the Secret Journey from Black to White* (New York: Penguin, 2011); Sui Sin Far, *Mrs. Spring Fragrance and Other Writings* (Urbana: University of Illinois Press, 1995); Barbara Tizard and Ann Phoenix, *Black, White, or Mixed Race?* (New York: Routledge, 1993); Dorothy West, *The Wedding* (New York: Doubleday, 1995); Henry Wiencek, *The Hairstons: An American Family in Black and White* (New York: St. Martin's, 1999); Gregory Howard Williams, *Life on the Color Line* (New York: Penguin, 1995); Joel Williamson, *New People: Miscegenation and Mulattoes in the United States* (New York: Free Press, 1980); Marguerite Wright, *I'm Chocolate, You're Vanilla: Raising Healthy Black and Biracial Children in a Race-Conscious World* (San Francisco: Jossey-Bass, 1998).

10. Velina Hasu Houston, *Tea* (New York: Dramatists Play Service, 2007); Nina Revoyr, *Southland* (New York: Akashic, 2003); Karen I. Leonard, *Making Ethnic Choices: California's Punjabi Mexican Americans* (Philadelphia: Temple University Press, 1992); Rudy P. Guevarra Jr., *Becoming Mexipino: Multiethnic Identities and Communities in San Diego* (New Brunswick, NJ: Rutgers University Press, 2012); Vivek Bald, *Bengali Harlem and the Lost Histories of South Asian America* (Cambridge, MA: Harvard University Press, 2013).

11. Jeffrey S. Passel, Gretchen Livingston, and D'Vera Cohn, "Explaining Why Minority Births Now Outnumber White Births" (Washington, DC: Pew Research Center, May 17, 2012), http://www.pewsocialtrends.org/2012/05/17/explaining-why-minority-births-now-outnumber-white-births/.

12. Sam Roberts, "Minorities in the US Set to Become Majority by 2042," *New York Times* (August 14, 2008).

13. Nicholas A. Jones and Jungmiwha Bullock, "The Two or More Races Population: 2010" (C2010BR-13; Washington, DC: US Census Bureau, September 2012).

14. Places to begin on scientific racism include C. Loring Brace, *"Race" Is a Four-Letter Word: The Genesis of a Concept* (New York: Oxford University Press, 2005); Stephen Jay Gould, *The Mismeasure of Man*, rev. ed. (New York: Norton, 1996); Jonathan Marks, *Human Biodiversity: Genes, Race, and History* (New York: Aldine de Gruyter, 1995); Paul Spickard, *Race in Mind: Critical Essays* (Notre Dame, IN: University of Notre Dame Press, 2015); Robert Wald Sussman, *The Myth of Race: The Troubling Persistence of an Unscientific Idea* (Cambridge, MA: Harvard University Press, 2014); Michael Yudell, *Race Unmasked: Biology and Race in the 20th Century* (New York: Columbia University Press, 2014).

15. Carolus Linnaeus, *Systema naturae per regna tria naturae, secundum classes, orgines, genera, species, cum characteribus, differentiis, synonymis* (Stockholm: Holmiae, 1758); Johann Friedrich Blumenbach, *The Anthropological Treatises of Johan Friedrich*

Blumenbach (London: Longman, Green, Longman, Roberts and Green, 1795); Arthur Comte de Gobineau, *The Inequality of Races* (1853–1855; repr., New York: Howard Fertig, 2010); Madison Grant, *The Passing of the Great Race; or, The Racial Basis of European History* (New York: Charles Scribner's Sons, 1916).

16. This line of thinking owes much to Gobineau, *Inequality of Races*. See Edward Byron Reuter, *The Mulatto in the United States, Including a Study of the Role of Mixed-Blood Races Throughout the World* (1918; repr., New York: Negro Universities Press, 1969); Reuter, *Race Mixture: Studies in Intermarriage and Miscegenation* (1918; repr., New York: Negro Universities Press, 1969); Everett V. Stonequist, *The Marginal Man: A Study in Personality and Culture Conflict* (1937; repr., New York: Russell and Russell, 1961). For analysis of this thinking, see Nakashima, "Invisible Monster." Sadly, this misbegotten kind of thinking is with us still; see Allyson Hobbs, *A Chosen Exile: A History of Racial Passing in American Life* (Cambridge, MA: Harvard University Press, 2014).

17. E.g., G. Reginald Daniel, *More Than Black? Multiracial Identity and the New Racial Order* (Philadelphia: Temple University Press, 2002); G. Reginald Daniel and Hettie V. Williams, eds., *Race and the Obama Phenomenon: The Vision of a More Perfect Multiracial Union* (Jackson: University Press of Mississippi, 2014); Jayne O. Ifekwunigwe, ed., *"Mixed Race" Studies: A Reader* (New York: Routledge, 2004); Kevin R. Johnson, ed., *Mixed Race America and the Law* (New York: New York University Press, 2003); Jolivette, *Obama and the Biracial Factor*; Gary B. Nash, *Forbidden Love: The Secret History of Mixed-Race America* (New York: Holt, 1999); Maria P. P. Root and Matt Kelly, eds., *Multiracial Child Resource Book: Living Complex Identities* (Seattle: MAVIN Foundation, 2003); Paul Spickard, Rowena Fong, and Patricia L. Ewalt, "Undermining the Very Basis of Racism: Its Categories," *Social Work* 40.5 (1995): 725–728; Teresa Williams-León and Cynthia L. Nakashima, eds., *The Sum of Our Parts: Mixed Heritage Asian Americans* (Philadelphia: Temple University Press, 2001).

18. Maria P. P. Root, ed., *Racially Mixed People in America* (Newbury Park, CA: Sage, 1992), 7. Root's book is the founding volume in the canon of mixed race studies.

19. Randall Kennedy, *Interracial Intimacies: Sex, Marriage, Identity, and Adoption* (New York: Pantheon, 2003), 36–37.

20. Ronald David Glass and Kendra R. Wallace, "Challenging Race and Racism: A Framework for Educators," in *The Multiracial Experience: Racial Borders as the New Frontier*, ed. Maria P. P. Root (Thousand Oaks, CA: Sage, 1996), 341–358.

21. Lewis Gordon, *Her Majesty's Other Children: Sketches of Racism from a Neocolonial Age* (Lanham, MD: Rowman & Littlefield, 1997); Rainier Spencer, *Spurious Issues: Race and Multiracial Identity Politics in the United States* (Boulder, CO: Westview, 1999); Rainier Spencer, *Challenging Multiracial Identity* (Boulder, CO: Lynne Rienner, 2006); Eduardo Bonilla-Silva and David Embrick, "Black, Honorary White, White: The Future of Race in the United States?," in *Mixed Messages: Multiracial Identities in the "Color-Blind" Era*, ed. David Brunsma (Boulder, CO: Lynne Rienner, 2006), 33–48; George Yancey, "Racial Justice in a Black/Nonblack Society," in Brunsma, *Mixed Messages*, 49–62; Hayward Derrick Horton, "Racism, Whitespace, and the Rise of the Neo-Mulattoes," in Brunsma, *Mixed Messages*, 117–121; Heather M. Dalmage, ed., *The Politics of Multiracialism: Challenging Racial Thinking* (Albany: State University of New York Press, 2004); Jared Sexton, *Amalgamation Schemes: Antiblackness and the Critique of Multiracialism* (Minneapolis: University of Minnesota Press, 2008); Michele Elam, *The Souls of Mixed Folk: Race, Politics, and Aesthetics in the New Millennium* (Stanford, CA: Stanford University Press, 2011); Minelle Mahtani, *Mixed Race Amnesia: Resisting the Romanticization of Multiraciality* (Vancouver: University of British Columbia Press, 2014). Paul Spickard has explored this critique in

more detail in reviews of Sexton's book in *American Studies* 50.1–2 (2009): 125–127, and of Jon Michael Spencer's in the *Journal of American Ethnic History* 18.2 (1999): 153–156.

22. Jon Michael Spencer, *The New Colored People: The Mixed-Race Movement in America* (New York: New York University Press, 2000). Spencer is not thoroughly consistent on this point, as he does make a few references to people who are part Asian and part Black, but analytically he throws the Asians by implication into the White category.

23. Spencer, *New Colored People*, 32–33. See also Molefi Kete Asante, "Racing to Leave the Race: Black Postmodernists Off-Track," *Black Scholar* 23.3–4 (1993): 50–51.

24. Spencer, *New Colored People*, 57.

25. Paul Spickard analyzes their positions in "Does Multiraciality Lighten? Me-Too Ethnicity and the Whiteness Trap," in *New Faces in a Changing America: Multiracial Identity in the 21st Century*, ed. Loretta I. Winters and Herman L. DeBose (Thousand Oaks, CA: Sage, 2003), 289–300.

26. Patricia Hill Collins, "Learning from the Outsider Within," *Social Problems* 33.6 (1986): 14–32.

27. Paul Spickard, "Pacific Islander Americans and Multiplicity: A Vision of America's Future?," in *Race in Mind*, 235–260.

28. Adrienne Lynn Edgar, *Tribal Nation: The Making of Soviet Turkmenistan* (Princeton, NJ: Princeton University Press, 2004); Saule K. Ualieva and Adrienne L. Edgar, "In the Laboratory of Peoples' Friendship: Mixed People in Kazakhstan from the Soviet Era to the Present," in *Global Mixed Race*, ed. Rebeca Chiyoko King-O'Riain et al. (New York: New York University Press, 2014), 68–90; Karina Mukazhanova, "The Politics of Multiple Identities in Kazakhstan," in *Multiple Identities: Migrants, Ethnicity, and Membership*, ed. Paul Spickard (Bloomington: Indiana University Press, 2013), 265–289.

PART I

Identity Journeys

2

Rising Sun, Rising Soul

On Mixed Race Asian Identity That Includes Blackness

VELINA HASU HOUSTON

Take a good look at me.

I am the woman on the right. The woman on the left is my biological mother, Setsuko Okazaki Takechi (see fig. 2.1).

It is likely that you have met someone who is an Asian of African descent. If, however, they are under the age of fifty-five, they may differ from me culturally. I am one of the last of my kind—a person of Japanese, Black, Native American Indian, and Cuban descent with a Japanese grandmother born in Japan's Meiji era, Japanese aunts born in the Taisho era, and a Showa-era Japanese mother. Those eras and the cultural traditions that ruled them are bygone, but they are entrenched in my DNA and spiritual muscle, embodying such concepts as

FIGURE 2.1. Setsuko Okazaki Takechi (*left*), circa 1952; Velina Hasu Houston (*right*), circa 1990. Photograph by Peter Szipal Martin. Used by permission of the Velina Avisa Hasu Houston Family Trust.

honor, the upholding of loyalty, discipline, integrity, and courage; sometimes (often) even the inability to be at ease in Western cultures. They affect my behavior in critical, subterranean modes. I grew up in the United States, but my cultural consciousness is a product of those eras and their perspectives. As the title of my collection of my plays indicates, I am a *Green Tea Girl in Orange Pekoe Country*. This culture of mine is ill fitted to Western ways beyond ideological perspectives. It also challenges facial expressions. Mine are usually misunderstood by Westerners because they define them in the context of Western comprehension. Contemplation, for example, often is read as sorrow, inquiry as anger, assertiveness as aggression, reflection as fatigue, and so on. The ways I move, think, and even gaze often are misconstrued by the Western world as it seeks to define me based on its viewpoint. If I looked like one specific monoethnicity, I might fare better, with Western assumption adjusted to its views of that specific monoethnicity. Often, however, those adjustments are askew because of a Western inability to come to grips with the actualities of any non-White ethnicity, especially a mixed ethnicity; or perhaps it is a lack of desire or a subconscious understanding that that energy need not be expended.

Such a cultural consciousness is even more challenging to possess when one does not look the part. How often I have heard the statement "But you don't look Japanese." In fact, many contemporary persons of Japanese descent may "look the part" but have little intrinsic Japanese culture. I also think about the parallel statement, which is, "But you don't look American." I have been told that, too. Whatever one thinks I may look like, I am nearly extinct. Once my generation is gone, the only mixed race Japanese will be those with

FIGURE 2.2. Setsuko Okazaki Takechi (*left*), Velina Hasu Houston (*right*), circa 2007. Used by permission of the Velina Avisa Hasu Houston Family Trust.

a Heisei (or later era) Japan-born parent or a Nikkei parent born and raised in a country that is not Japan such as a Japanese American or Japanese Canadian. Their outlooks, being more contemporary and often Western, will be 180 degrees from mine. That, of course, is as it should be because humanity must evolve. Think twice, however, when you meet someone who is mixed race but is not part White, especially if you are mixed race yourself. They may be more culturally integrated than you regardless of what they look like. They may be the short-grain rice and not the converted. Converting, in fact, may be out of the question. After all, what does it mean to look "Japanese" or "American"? Does it mean to have the same visage as someone in a magazine advertisement? Does it mean to look like the empress of Japan or the first lady of the United States? Does it mean to look like someone that can wear a kimono "properly" or look "correct" in clothing designed for the all-American being? Blue jeans and kimonos are both uncomfortable.

Looking the part is always an interesting experience for the mixed race person. What is she? Where is she from? Where are her parents from? That experience is even more interesting when the mixed race person's ancestry includes Blackness. Anti-Blackness remains an issue in US society, and I daresay many other societies, such as Japanese society. Consumer racial profiling (the former Kitson's in Santa Monica, Montana Avenue boutiques in Santa Monica, every store in Junction City, Kansas, when I was living there), police racial profiling (officer Joseph Bohr, Beverly Hills police department), the actions of non-Blacks who believe that they are superior to those of African descent—all are still there, usually subterranean or institutionalized so that there is nothing or very little to take a picture of. Sometimes. These actualities, all of which I have experienced personally, complicate mixed race. Everything that mixed race people who are not part Black experience as mixed race people, and everything that monoracial people feel and experience is tenfold for mixed race persons with African ancestry. Mixed race people are The Other. Mixed race people of African descent are The Other's Other.

The filmmaker Vincent Ward said, "To map someone else's territory is the first step in possessing someone else's land." I believe that he meant two things: the mapping of what is now Alaska by Westerners (in his film *Map of the Human Heart*) and also the mapping of the territory of a mixed race identity by monoracial people. Mixed race is race that does not embody or boast a singular ethnicity or race, but that signifies individuals who are amalgams of multiple consciousnesses that blend races and ethnicities (and sometimes cultures and nations as well). In the progressive sense, a mixed race person is an individual who embodies and embraces two or more races or ethnicities (with at least one being of color) in a *composite* identity; an inclusive rather than excluding approach to identity. The artificial European and European American construction of race demands falsification of the total genealogical ethnic actualities of the mixed race individual by attempting to constrain membership into a single, government-sanctioned racial category, thus ignoring (and invalidating) one or more of the other races or ethnicities of which the mixed race is composed. I am a progressive individual of blended ethnicities. I use the term "mixed race" to hail such an identity politically.

I employ the term "multiple consciousnesses" to describe the nature of mixed race. W.E.B. Du Bois's theory of double consciousness for African Americans provides an apt (but, of course, not perfect) parallel for mixed race identity: "It is a peculiar sensation, this double-consciousness, this sense of always looking at one's self through the eyes of others, of measuring one's soul by the tape of a world that looks on in amused contempt and pity. One ever feels his twoness . . . two souls, two thoughts, two unreconciled strivings; two warring ideals in one dark body, whose dogged strength alone keeps it from being torn asunder."[1]

Du Bois's biographer, David Levering Lewis, extended the double consciousness theory to include the natural path that a double consciousness must travel. The doubly conscious self was an infinitely spiritually and socially evolving being that, through struggle, was "destined to cohere and to merge," in time becoming stronger for being doubled, "the sum of its parts, not the dividend."[2] In its progressive incarnation, mixed race owns multiple consciousnesses that coalesce. The mixed race individual exists in a multitude of racial, ethnic, cultural, and/or national consciousnesses that she attempts to meld together organically into an authentic hybrid identity that may transcend the limitations of racial concept and code, and extend into a racially noncategorical humanity. The cohered sum has arrived.

The Western view of race is shackled by plantation-era race theory. Traditional race is presented as, in effect, monorace, for example, "White" or Caucasian being only "White" (and no longer Irish American, Norwegian American, German American, etc.—and certainly nothing else of non-White ethnicity) and "Black" or African American being only that and nothing else, and so on. In so doing, traditional race is defined as a hypodescent theory of race that reflects a one-person, one-race ideology. This obsession with the presentation of race as monorace—which has its foundations in the entrenched Black-White binary created during slavery by the European American power base of plantation owners—seeks to preserve, distinguish, and privilege what is White from anybody and everything that is not, "the dominant culture's tendency to collapse all racial groups into one undifferentiated mass which serves as the 'Other' of White society."[3]

Interestingly, this tool for the preservation of White elitism is wielded just as powerfully by people of color (especially monoracial people of color) as it is by Whites. The binary dictates that what is White is White, and everything else is Black; that, whenever the majority of the United States talks about race, it talks about Black versus White as if no other races of people existed on the continent or at least they do not matter in the large scheme of things (witness former President Bill Clinton's racial advisory panel's largely Black-White composition and its internal conflicts about whether its agenda needed to move beyond Black-White issues and embrace concerns of other groups of color as well).

Awareness of the context of racial politics related to my birth and growing up is useful. Progressive mixed race culture is relatively new, born into US discourse in the late 1970s and continuing with fortitude to the present day. Within this period, several textual constructs emerged including scholarly books and articles, dissertations, documentary cinema, popular periodical literature, mixed race organizational literature, popular media discourse, dramatic literature, poetry and prose, as well as visual expressions in art and performance art. These works have initiated public discourse that is reconfiguring the way that mixed race individuals are identified, and is attempting to dispel the myths and stereotypes that have plagued mixed race identity in the United States since the days of the plantation. Because of its bicultural and binational aspects that can complicate society's efforts to categorize it racially, the Hapa ethnicity has lent credence and support to the growth of the overall mixed race community's movement with the United States and its project: to allow those of multiple ethnicities to embrace and identify with all of their cultures, and to identify themselves as mixed race. The immigrant-kindred nature of some Hapa individuals can enrich the mixed race landscape. Some Hapas who are born in Asian nations or who have mothers who were born in Asian nations claim a sense of nationness within established nation-states with regard to "nation-ness, as well as nationalism . . . [being] cultural artifacts of a particular kind . . . [that] command such profound emotional legitimacy" and "deep attachments." Such attachments and the striving for emotional legitimacy that they catalyze enhance the project of the mixed race movement in the United States. The collective culture of progressive mixed race is what Benedict Anderson describes as a "sub-nationalism" within the borders of old nationalisms "once thought fully consolidated."[4]

My curiosity about the different phenotypes of my internationally, interracially married parents began early in life. I was five when I asked my parents why my mother was "vanilla" and why my father was "chocolate." My parents felt compelled to teach me about the realities of my roots. My father went to the store and bought Neapolitan ice cream. He returned home, opened the carton, and told me that the vanilla stripe was similar to my mother because she was Japanese. He

FIGURE 2.3. Utamaro, *Waitress Okita from the Naniwaya Tearoom.* http://www.japan-zone.com/culture/ukiyoe.shtml.

said the chocolate and strawberry stripes were kind of like him. He stirred the three flavors together into a brown mixture and showed it to me. "That's you," he said. Then he asked me if I could take that mixture and turn it back into the three stripes. Of course I could not, no more than I could take myself and divide myself into my various ethnicities. My father instructed me to remember that and to live my life that way. I have and I do. I take great pleasure in knowing that my father's actions have inspired others. Recently, I read another mixed race person's account of having this same experience with her parents in the 1990s. Legacy. Important.

Living one's life as a mixed race person wasn't always an easy thing in a small Kansas town in the 1960s and 1970s. Most things, including televisions in the early years, were black-and-white. To most Kansans, if you were not White, you were Black. When the US military brought nearly seven hundred US-Japanese couples to the area, the Kansans were dumbfounded. How were they to categorize the immigrant Japanese women and their mixed race children? Were Japanese White or colored? What if two partners in a couple were different colors? But their puzzlement was brief with regard to the mixed race offspring because, after all, they had to categorize us in order to feel safe, comfortable, and in control. They perceived those who were married to Whites and those who were ethnic blends of Japanese and White as White, and those who were married to Blacks or who were ethnic blends of Japanese and Black as Blacks. I can only assume that such people saw violet as red and blue, and not as a new color that looked different and therefore required a new name. Based on pre-judgment stemming from narrowly acquired assumptions, ignorance can present itself in many gradations.

Ethnic misinterpretations have abounded in my life. When I lived in Kyoto, Japanese people frequently told me that I was from "Ceylon," supplementing their declarations with information about how much they loved Ceylon tea and cinnamon. At the wedding of a Cuban friend, I was assumed to be a part of the Cuban family and immediately put to work helping with last-minute details. In

Tokyo, I have been asked more than once if I am from Colombia. I have been asked if I am from Mexico, Puerto Rico, Baghdad, Egypt, Sri Lanka, India, Pakistan, Hawai'i, Cambodia, Micronesia, Tonga, Bali, Thailand, and so on. I have sat on committees where White European Americans perceived Japanese Hapas of White extraction to be Japanese (or White), but did not perceive me as having any relationship to my own cultural origins. Furthermore, the Japanese Hapas of White extraction did not recognize me as anyone remotely akin to their experience. I have been dragged into a Tongan church group because a Tongan mother thought I was one of her relatives. I have been scrutinized by a White European American anthropologist who thought I was Micronesian. In Hawai'i, White European American tourists think I am Polynesian and ask me for directions to different sites on the islands. Never mind just trying to navigate the routine of life; ethnic inquiry and misinterpretation require a bit more navigation and maneuvering just to get through the day. Once when at the gym, a woman said to me, "Are you Korean and Black?" "No," I answered, "wrong war."

In my home while growing up, ethnic pigeonholing had no bearing. As far as my mother was concerned, the inside of the house was Japanese and the outside was the United States. Inside of the house, shoes were taken off, baths were taken at night, and Japanese food was prepared. It was a means of surviving in the midst of a United States that at that time felt hostility toward the Japanese due to the sociopolitical residue of World War II. It also was a means of my mother ensuring that her children would be steeped in her culture, despite growing up in the United States.

So that was my world. I saw it as the norm. I thought it was abnormal for people to have two parents of the same color. Didn't everybody have a Japanese immigrant mother and a father who was American? Didn't everybody eat short-grained rice and drink leaf green tea from Japan? And what was this Mother Goose that everybody at school seemed to know about? My mother shared with me the only children's literature that she knew, Japanese stories such as *Momotaro* and *Issunboshi*. How fortunate I was because those tales of natural and supernatural worlds coexisting and of fantastical elements that never gandered with Mother Goose came to be a tremendous influence on my artistry. I felt sorry for any mixed race Japanese who fiercely tried to acculturate, especially those who chose to pass for White or Black because, I suppose, it was easier—to fit in, to belong, to be in the mainstream. I felt that several worlds belonged to me ethnically and that I should not have to compromise who I was to be a part of any of them. I still feel that way. My mother used to say, "I was born Japanese, I die Japanese." I say, "I was born mixed race, I die mixed race."

In Kansas, the only Japanese Americans who I knew were like me, mixed race. The first time that I met a Japanese American that was not (at least to the best of his knowledge) was in Los Angeles in 1980. I remember thinking that he was not Japanese at all. He looked Japanese, in the historical sense of what it means to look Japanese, but he was entirely American. He was proud of that fact, and said that his family had fought hard to separate themselves from all things Japanese and to be fully, patriotically American. It was then that I realized that I was an anomaly ethnically. Not looking Japanese in the historical sense of what it means to look Japanese but being culturally Japanese, I realized that I was more Japanese than "Japanese Americans." I had not ever had to sidestep my heritage for the benefit of the US government or anybody else. My cultural idiosyncrasies, tastes in food, and cultural possessions were foregrounded in my life and would never take a backseat in the face of any threat. I also did not look like the average non-plantation racial perception of an African American. Some might ask if I was Black, but I knew that they long had been indoctrinated in the one-drop hypodescent theory that was a relic from US plantations. Even in Hawai'i, where being a racial mélange is commonplace, racial perspective is shifting: mixed race is so White that it is sometimes hard to identify who is mixed race. The native Hawaiians look more like people of African descent than like the majority of people born in Hawai'i today, not only phenotypically but also with regard to their cultural artifacts on display at the Bishop Museum, Honolulu.

Life is constant diplomacy. Coming to California posed other ethnic discoveries, too.

- I saw signs for sushi bars and was astonished to learn that Americans ate what they called sushi, what my family had always called o-sushi.

FIGURE 2.4. *Left to right:* Queen Kaahumanu of Hawai'i, King Kamehameha I, Princess Victoria Kaiulani Cleghorn, and Queen Kamamalu. *Sources*: John W. Perry, "Conquering the Conqueror." Art courtesy John W. Perry Archival Images. *Hana Hou*, the Magazine of Hawaiian Airlines. "Top Ten Events in Maui," *Pride of Maui*, http://www.prideofmaui.com/blog/maui/best-maui-celebrations.html. *The Affiliate*, Smithsonian Affiliations, http://blog-affiliations.org/?p=6922. "Queen Kamamalu," *Wikipedia*, https://en.wikipedia.org/wiki/Kamāmalu.

- When I was invited to a meeting for the UCLA Asian Pacific Alumni Association, I was appalled when I overheard a Japanese American judge telling another Japanese American that they had to do whatever they could to keep anybody who was part Black out of the organization.

- When I was an invited speaker at a mixed race studies conference, a Chinese and White scholar dismissed Blackness as part of Hapa culture.

- At another mixed race conference, a Japanese and White Hapa remarked that Afro-Asians would "do just fine if they stuck to sports and entertainment."

- At a National Black Journalists Association convention, as an invited panelist I spoke about mixed race identity and was booed and hissed at; several spectators threw wadded up paper and spit balls.

- In graduate school when my play *Asa Ga Kimashita* won several national first prize awards from the Kennedy Center including the Lorraine Hansberry Award for the best new play about the Black experience, several Black student union groups protested, resenting the choice of the play on racial grounds, saying that the play, which was set in 1946 Japan and included the representation of a mixed race Afro-Japanese couple, was in fact not a Black play.

I quickly learned that multiple-minority mixed race is different from mixed race that includes a White element. We are, in essence, seeking the same thing in challenging society to accept a person of multiple ethnicities, but we differ in that White mixed race often practices the same discrimination against mixed race that includes Black ancestry that it experiences from the monoethnic majority. Indeed, Afro-Asian identity can be peculiar not only to Whites, but also to other Asian Americans and other Hapas, not to mention Blacks. Many felt that they didn't need to understand it; many in the Hapa movement wanted Afro-Asians to be a part of the movement but did not address their marginality within the overall landscape of mixed race. Often at Hapa events, Afro-Asian programming was peripheral or nonexistent. Like Native American Indian identity, Hapa identity was foregrounded as an exclusive, non-Black arena. Mixed race persons with African ancestry were marginalized into an intellectual ghetto, just as the dominant population marginalizes the mixed race discussion in general. Such color against color discrimination diminishes the integrity of political movements of color, especially mixed race ones. This, I daresay, racist perception is part of the movement's foundation, despite the fact that two out of the three landmark dissertations that are the mixed race Asian movement's theoretical underpinnings were authored by non-White mixed race individuals, both being Japanese and Black; and the first mixed race Asian conference (ironically at UCLA) as well as the first mixed race Asian nonprofit organization were founded by someone of Japanese and Black heritage.

But still, like air, I'll rise. It is a line from a Maya Angelou poem that I also think speaks volumes about anti-Blackness, particularly for mixed race persons of African descent within and outside of the mixed race community. I have had many try to silence my mixed race transnationalism. I have had two death threats, and threats of violence from Asian Americans and African Americans. I have had statements made such as *Why don't you write for a Whiter audience* or *Why do you write that "stuff."* The poem coalesces the rising sun with the souls of Black folk, to borrow a term from W.E.B. Du Bois's seminal work of US literature and sociological history.

> Just like moons and like suns,
> With the certainty of tides,
> Just like hopes springing high,
> Still I'll rise.
> You may shoot me with your words,
> You may cut me with your eyes,
> You may kill me with your hatefulness,
> But still, like air, I'll rise.
>
> —Maya Angelou

Mixed race individuals live constantly with racial misrecognition, not necessarily and not usually self-misrecognition, but invariably from others. It is akin to what Judith Butler calls the "uneasy sense of standing under a sign to which one does and does not belong."[5] As Butler suggests, to stand under a sign that promises to be a site of hope for articulation or rearticulation of identity and experience failure may itself be "the point of departure for a more democratizing affirmation of internal difference."[6] Historically, mixed race individuals stood under signs of monorace and experienced failure of identification. As time moved into present day, they learned to use this failure to name their difference and to articulate their progressive mixed race identity in and on their own terms. While I have existed in a mixed race site all of my life, others have tried to place me under signs that reduced my ethnic identity to a singular that was comfortable to them, sometimes one that had nothing to do with my actual ethnic background such as the Sri Lankan gift shop owner, the Cambodian donut shop clerk, the Ecuadorian market manager, or the Pilipino gentleman on the plane full of White people who spoke to me in their respective native tongues, elated to find what they believed to be a face of a native of their motherland; and sometimes an attempt to reduce me to one monorace for the sake of (their) political imperatives. With such failure and misrecognition, is it any wonder that I depart from convention and avow my difference?

I am not the first person, and certainly will not be the last, to talk about race. European Americans often have diagnosed me as being "obsessed" with race, but I know that they are the only ones who have the luxury of not discussing race—and also the luxury or arrogance to believe that they have the right and wisdom to diagnose me, and to believe that their diagnosis is sacrosanct. Trina Grillo and Stephanie M. Wildman have pointed out that many European Americans take such a position toward people of color and cannot fathom why we invest so much "emotional and intellectual energy" into the issue of race. They note precisely that "white supremacy [domination of society] privileges Whiteness as the *normative* model," a stance that "allows Whites to ignore race, even though they have one"; and that the only time Whites do not ignore race is "when they perceive race (usually someone else's [someone else of color]) as intruding upon their lives."[7]

Noting that many people in the United States have trouble "accepting that you can be two things [racially/culturally] at once—that you can be 'double,'" Regge Life says that Japanese people, while not always accepting of Japanese Hapas, think more internationally and recognize that Japanese Hapas, while not being fully Japanese, have "a Japanese part" and allow them access to "even the subtlest elements of Japanese culture."[8] Rocky Kiyoshi Mitarai contends that mixed races of Japanese heritage often relate well with Japanese natives (in Japan or in the United States) because they are "raised with many of the same cultural values that exist there [in Japan]."[9] Life believes that the transnational and multicultural aspects of Japanese Hapas are definitely a benefit for them. I know, however, that this can be compromised when dealing with Japanese Hapas who are not part White.

NOTES

1. W.E.B. Du Bois, *The Souls of Black Folk* (Chicago: A. C. McClurg, 1903; repr., New York: Dover, 1994), 2.
2. Ibid.
3. Tania Modleski, *Old Wives' Tales and Other Women's Stories* (New York: New York University Press, 1998), 175–176.
4. Benedict Anderson, *Imagined Communities: Reflections on the Origin and Spread of Nationalism*, rev. ed. (London: Verso, 1991), 3–166.
5. Judith Butler, *Bodies That Matter: On the Discursive Limits of "Sex"* (New York: Routledge, 1993), 219.
6. Ibid.

7. Trina Grillo and Stephanie M. Wildman, "Obscuring the Importance of Race," in *Critical White Studies: Looking behind the Mirror*, ed. Richard Delgado and Jean Stefancic (Philadelphia: Temple University Press, 1997), 623, emphasis added.

8. Stewart Wachs, "Reel Life & Real Life: Film-maker Regge Life on Identity & the Joys and Trials of Being Intercultural," *Perspectives on Asia: Kyoto Journal*, no. 40 (Spring 1999): 14–19.

9. Rocky Kiyoshi Mitarai, "Hate Crime in Japantown," *Mavin* 1.3 (1999): 41–42.

3

Blackapina

JANET C. MENDOZA STICKMON

First Movement: The Intersection

People of multiethnic backgrounds are accustomed to existing at the intersections of multiple worlds and multiple identities, holding and juggling those
spaces in tension.[1] We become adept at navigating in and out and through numerous ethnoracial and ethnocultural contexts. The more one enters and exits these
contexts, and the more one critically examines racial hierarchy and essentialism
and their impact on the dynamics between racial groups, the more pronounced
one's experience of multiraciality and multiethnicity becomes. An understanding
of critical race theory coupled with the experience of existing within the interstices of life—surviving and thriving in a world dominated by binary thought and
then being inspired to rise above the surface unfragmented—are vital for multiethnic people who seek to live out the fullness of their humanity. It requires a
creativity that is prompted by the mere existence of the intersection in the road,
as well as the time taken to reflect upon the ramifications of that intersection.

As a Blackapina, a woman of African American and Filipino American
descent, I regularly reflect upon how truly I am embracing both sides of my heritage and how well I am serving the populations on both sides of my bloodline.
Existing in this in-between space of ethnicities and critically examining this
intersectionality informs and strengthens my ability to recognize the complexities and nuances that characterize life's mosaic. We, as multiethnic people, have
the potential to navigate this world of complexity and nuance. We have the
potential to create unconventional solutions for the intersections of life and
inspire deep, reflective transformation. Living in the intersection forces us to
deal with the multiple paths that come together; if those paths never meet, if

the crossroads don't exist, there is almost no reason, no opportunity for creative outcomes to arise.

So what does it mean to be at the crossroads? It means to stand at any intersection, any meeting of multiple paths, and ask the question: So what do I do now? It is to welcome transition.

Binary thinking would suggest selecting one of two paths. Perhaps a more nuanced way of thinking that informs the experience of many multiethnic people would suggest entertaining or exploring the possibility of taking multiple paths simultaneously. It means daring ourselves to believe that it is possible to walk multiple paths at the same time, embracing the transition, defying the conventional, the orthodox, the hegemonic and actively walking all of those paths—becoming a living, breathing mosaic. And as one bravely walks the multiple paths, one can clear the way, knocking down all obstacles that obstruct the flow of understanding, of compassion, of cooperation. This strengthens the ability of humanity to cocreate a world predicated on our capacity to remain in dialogue and allow our ideas to build upon each other as opposed to being combative in nature. Consequently, any collaboration among human beings should reflect this spirit of interdependence, manifesting in a force that brings healing wherever there is brokenness.[2]

Second Movement: Multiple Families

Having a Filipino American mother and an African American father, I juggled both ethnic backgrounds throughout my childhood and adolescence. Momma was from the *barangay* of Labangon in Cebu and left a clerical job to come to the United States—the country she considered the "land of milk and honey." Da'y (Daddy for short) was from Shreveport, Louisiana, and hopped freight trains to California—one of approximately six million African Americans who fled the oppression of the South during what came to be known as the Great Migration.[3] My biracial experience began with the very basic influences of food and language, eating Momma's *biko* and *bijon* and Da'y's hoe cakes and hot cakes, hearing Da'y sound "country" and Momma speak Cebuano.

It was 1989 when Momma died and Da'y was put in a convalescent hospital; I was fifteen years old. Three years later, Da'y died, and I officially became an orphan, continuing to juggle my dual heritage along with the meaning of life in the absence of parental love. I was tossed around from one social worker to the next, telling my story over and over again, becoming attached to no one. Though the most immediate lifelines to my history were gone, my sense of self was informed by the memories my parents left behind, the Filipino relatives I moved in with, the holidays spent with my African American relatives, and close high school and college friends. In the public sphere—school, church,

work, commerce, etc.—I learned what was acceptable and unacceptable according to Eurocentric standards. Though my family was from a poor, working-class
background, I quickly learned how to operate effectively within a social environment that was predominantly White, middle-class, and Christian-centered. For
example, I recall dropping my voice and speaking in a very formal fashion that
appeared to command the respect and attention of middle-aged Whites. There
were also many times I chose to stay quiet about living in a run-down house
that my parents rented for $150 per month or how my mother and I picked cans
in the park; I remained silent because I did not want to be judged for being
poor. While I received messages about how certain ways of speaking and behav-
ing commanded respect from those who lay at the intersection of these social
categories, I had to also remain socially fluent within predominantly Filipino
and African American environments. I gradually learned to do this by educating
myself about the respective histories of Filipino and African Americans, as well
as the contemporary issues most relevant to or that had the greatest impact on
each community.

Death. New family. New school. More death. These were my adolescent
years. And out of all of this, I was trying to figure out who I was and what purpose
I had. I was a fairly quiet and private person to begin with, but losing Momma
and Da'y drove me into a deeper silence where lethargy coiled around my spirit,
making hope seem hilarious. I always planned for the worst so I could be prepared for disappointment. I cried and cried until I had no tears left; it wasn't as
though the pain stopped—a raw ache always lingered, but tears brought only
partial relief, and I was sick of crying. I developed a callousness toward life,
promising myself I'd never get hurt again. Little did I know that when you shut
off one emotion, you end up shutting off others; so as I became numb to pain, I
became numb to joy and all my laughs were hollow.

When I was around people I could trust—people who knew how to be gentle
with me, but also recognized my strengths and knew how much I hated pity—I
was vibrant, playful, and vocal. Some of these angels were relatives like my
cousin Alison Rodriguez on my Filipino side, her husband Martin, and their
two children, JoAnna and Chris. Alison became a lifeline to my Filipino family
and implicitly reminded me that indeed there was a time when Momma did
exist. Martin embodied the meaning of letting go of the past as he embraced
members of our family who initially didn't accept him because he was Mexican. Eventually, his family in Cuernavaca became my family and introduced a
third culture into my upbringing. I felt a special connection to JoAnna and Chris
partly because they were biracial like me. I assumed the responsibility of being
the best *tia* I could be, which included nurturing their Mexipina(o) identity.

Most of the angels in my life were friends, teachers, and mentors—or a
combination. In my adulthood, a period in life when I thought I wouldn't need

parents, I found a new mother and father amid this group of angels. It took me over twenty years before I was able to embrace new parents and not feel as though I was betraying my birth parents. Many adults struggle to express their new "grown-up" needs to parents who've always known them, but never completely understood or accepted them. I have somehow been spared this experience; instead, I am able to choose the new parents of my adulthood not only according to how well they suit my emotional and spiritual needs, but also based on how well we relate to one another. Today, I am blessed with their love and blessed with opportunities to share my love with them.

My new father, Tom Shepardson, is my former high school history teacher. He is White of Italian, English, Scottish, German, Austrian, Dutch, and Native American ancestry. His gentleness and patience have been priceless. Observing his comfort with being an introvert allowed me to accept my own introvert side. His ability to listen to me and affirm me throughout my adolescent and adult life is the reason why I believe I am a sane and loving person today. I consider Tom, his wife Diana, and their three children Katie, Anna, and Louis to be blood. Together, Tom and Diana continuously remind me that they love me for all that I am, including my determination, optimism, intelligence, and generosity, and my African American and Filipino American backgrounds.

Vangie Canonizado Buell, a Filipino African American woman and mother to many (including three loving daughters of her own), has become my mom, auntie, confidant, mentor, and the *lola* to my daughter. We share a common ethnic mix and complex family history. She modeled how one could actively embrace one's African American and Filipino American heritages at the same time with depth and integrity. This woman is an activist and a "connector," taking great pleasure in introducing good people to good people.[4] She is a patient, good listener, with a keen awareness about the various systems of oppression and privilege that exist in the United States. Whenever I confide in Mama Vangie, she always draws from one of her own personal experiences that directly relates to whatever I am sharing. Often the parallels are so eerily similar that I sit in awe and immense gratitude that God has blessed me with a new mother who understands me so well. I can rest in her spirit and find inspiration there—a feeling I thought I'd never experience again after my mom died.

Mama Vangie and Dad have never met, yet they have me in common. My new parents have been a constant source of support and guidance. Their warmth and wisdom have sustained and strengthened me. They've always believed in my integrity, generosity, intellect, and strength of character, and never doubted that my African American and Filipino American heritages were integral to my beauty as a human being.

Third Movement: Disconnection Exposed

During the summer between my second and third years in undergraduate school, I went to UCLA for a research program. There I met a number of students of color who were conducting research in some way related to their ethnic heritage. Through our conversations, I became more aware of myself as a Black and Filipino woman, but also discovered all the things I didn't know about both cultures. I didn't know how to speak Cebuano or Tagalog and knew very little about the history of the Philippines and the history of Filipino Americans. The few Filipinos I knew as a child were the children of Mom's closest friends; some of them were also Black and Filipino. Other than that, I didn't have many Filipino friends or classmates but was still proud to tell everyone I was half Filipino. The few second-generation Filipinos I met in college were disconnected from their roots like me.

As far as my Black side, I had the same problem. I barely knew anything about African and African American history. I knew about slavery, Booker T. Washington, and Martin Luther King Jr., but that was about it. During my adolescent years and early twenties, I remember feeling uncomfortable with other Black people because I was insecure about my own Blackness, afraid they'd think I wasn't "Black enough." Even though it was never blatant, I think this stems partly from some members of my family who didn't view me as "Black enough" back then.

The more I became aware of what I didn't know and the connection I didn't have with my people, the more difficult it was to learn what I was missing. What was holding me back? Embarrassment clung to every admission I made to not knowing my cultural histories. If other Filipinos discovered I didn't know who Lapulapu was, I knew I'd be judged. I'd embarrass myself if I began spending time at the Black Student Union, and people discovered I didn't know who Angela Davis, Marcus Garvey, and Maulana Karenga were. To save myself the public embarrassment, I avoided these circles and never placed myself in situations where I was a "learner" of my own cultures. I feared being vulnerable to criticism.

Because of this fear, I gravitated toward Mexican American students who were fellow science and engineering majors. They had not assimilated into mainstream White culture, but they weren't exactly militant revolutionaries either.

Being with them was comforting. My mother was an immigrant to this country like many of their parents. We understood what it meant to be the descendents of those in search of the "American Dream," and thus knew what it meant to be among the first in our families to graduate from college. With them, I was never held accountable for what I didn't know about my Black and Filipino backgrounds. Since I was not Mexican, there was never any pressure to be an expert in their Mexican heritage. I was free to learn without being stigmatized. And I enjoyed that luxury. However, something needed to change.

I was between races and between homes, clinging to a culture that felt safe, but was not my own. Although the Black side of my family fully acknowledged my Filipino side and never insulted it, I still felt viewed as less Black, due to my speech, my light skin, my education, and my quiet nature. When I was with the Filipino side of my family, my Blackness was insulted and I became less Filipino because of that Blackness; I didn't want to be accepted as a full-fledged Filipino, if it was gained at the expense of my Black side. It was distressing not feeling at home in places that were supposed to be home.[5]

Fourth Movement: Transformative Impact of Theology School

There were many mentors who helped me understand various aspects of my identity. Some were family members. Some were dear friends. However, one who embodied multiplicity and fluidity and helped me to feel whole when existing within the in-between spaces of ethnicities was Fr. Elias Farajajé-Jones, now known as Baba Ibrahim Abdurrahman-Farajajé. I met Ibrahim while I was a graduate student at the Graduate Theological Union in Berkeley.

Ibrahim's wealth of knowledge and experience challenging social divides carried wisdom and courage. His passion and command of the subject matter were incredible. He knew Hebrew, Greek, Aramaic, Latin, German, French, Spanish, Portuguese, Italian, Russian, Old Slavonic, and Arabic. As an esteemed scholar, he also stayed in touch with pop culture. At the time, he was an Eastern Orthodox priest, a bisexual and multiracial (African American, Native American, and Irish) man, a father, and a husband, and how he seamlessly wove all aspects of his identity into one living tapestry was a great inspiration to me.

During Ibrahim's "Interrupting Conversations: Race-ing The(a)ologies" course, it didn't matter if he was standing before us delivering a lecture or sitting with us facilitating circle discussions, I soaked in every word. With each lesson, he explained the complexities of historiography, exposing lies passed down as truth; he taught us about the demonization of Blackness and African religions, the value of racial purity during the Enlightenment, the discrimination experienced by the lesbian, gay, bisexual, transgendered, and questioning community (LGBTQ), the importance of maintaining agency as people of color, and the construction of Whiteness and White privilege.

Through his courses, my mind was gradually reshaped. In our readers, we had texts from *The Colonizer and the Colonized* by Albert Memmi, *White* by Richard Dyer, *Killing the Black Body* by Dorothy Roberts, *White on Black: Images of Africa and Blacks in Western Popular Culture* by Jan Nederveen Pieterse, and *The*

Philippines Reader edited by Daniel Schirmer and Stephen Shalom.[6] Each reading assignment forced me to question everything that I was taught and (not taught) in history and catechism classes since childhood. When I had the urge to cross-reference and verify the assertions Ibrahim or these texts made, I asked myself why I questioned these texts when I never questioned, researched, or attempted to verify ideas posited in more mainstream texts.

In Ibrahim's courses, my education in critical race theory began; at the same time, I was also learning to recognize myself as a biracial woman—someone who could embrace both sides of my heritage while also understanding the ways I, having light skin, benefit from the misconceptions people have about light-skinned Black people. Conversations with him, attending mixed race conferences, and reading articles he recommended all taught me that being biracial didn't mean I had to view myself as a racially fragmented person condemned to a lifetime of confusion.

Ibrahim recommended I read the work of Rita Nakashima Brock, who outlined the concept of "interstitial integrity." As a woman raised by an Okinawan mother and a White American stepfather, Nakashima Brock defined "interstitial integrity" in the following manner:

> Integration brings many diverse parts together, the way a collection of ingredients finally makes a dish. Integrity is how we know ourselves and make choices that sustain our values in relationship with others. It is a complex, evolving process over time, captured in moments of self-awareness and self-acceptance—brief interludes of consciousness that appear within the tossing turbulence of many people and places.
>
> "Interstitial" comes from interstium, and it is used in biology to describe tissue situated in vital organs. The tissue is not organ tissue, but, rather, it connects the organs to one another. Interstitial tissue lives inside things, distinct but inseparable from what would otherwise be disconnected. It is a channel of life in and out of things separated and different. It makes a living, pulsating unity, both many and one. Without interstitiality, parts of my life would wither and die, unnourished by the connective tissues of memory that constantly flow in and out of my consciousness. Interstitial integrity is how I improvise a self, recognizing the diverse cultures and experiences that have made me who I am. It is how I mix a life together from myriads of ingredients.[7]

I began to understand myself as that "interstitial tissue" who serves as a "channel of life" that moves in and out of African American and Filipino American contexts; I was that "pulsating unity" who was made of many and yet still whole. Up until that point, for most of my life, I tended to switch on and off my two ethnicities. Depending on whose company I was in, I turned into a chameleon, blending in as best I could, sometimes unaware of how clumsy and awkward my shape shifting was; if I was in predominantly Filipino environment, I used the few Cebuano and Tagalog phrases I knew or talked about Filipino dishes I cooked or initiated conversations about the latest issues in Filipino politics; if I was in an all-Black environment, I used Black vernacular and made sure to discuss the latest issues relevant to Black life and politics. Sometimes, in both blatant and subtle ways, I was asked to choose, hearing questions like, "Are you more Black than Filipino or more Filipino than Black?" As people spent hours staring at me trying to figure me out, asking, "What are you?" I learned quickly how uncomfortable people become if they cannot place me in one racial category. Noticing Ibrahim embrace every aspect of himself, I gradually understood that it was okay to embrace both sides and be Black *and* Filipino all the time, creating my own fluid, multidimensional state of being. Beginning to reject my compartmentalized lifestyle and become whole helped me draw from the well of that unique space between ethnicities.[8]

As I drew from this well, I also continued to draw from the insights of Nakashima Brock as she elaborated upon the notion of interstitial integrity: "Interstitial integrity is this spirit in us, our struggle to hold the many in the one. We endeavor to make sense and meaning out of the multiple social locations, the hybrid cultures, and the many powers of death and life that are placed before us. Interstitial integrity is our ability to lie down, spread-eagled, reaching to all the many worlds we have known, all the memories we have been given, tempered in the cauldrons of history and geography in our one body."[9]

Her insights revealed a greater, redemptive meaning behind my struggle to stretch myself out to reach and touch all that had informed my being. Reading Nakashima Brock's words and being mentored by Ibrahim Abdurrahman-Farajajé represented a pivotal, transformative moment in my life, prompting me to make modest attempts toward synthesizing the various complexities of my life: my two ethnic backgrounds, the loss of my parents, the love of new and old family members, and more.

Fifth Movement: The Blend

Being both African American and Filipino American means having the benefit of drawing from the richness of both ethnicities and bearing the responsibility of sharing both ethnicities with all I come in contact with. It means not just having an intellectual understanding of the histories and contemporary issues relating to each ethnicity, but also an intuitive understanding—an ability to feel and sense the rhythm and curves that give shape and life to the reality of being African American and Filipino American. It means understanding and living out the complex interplay between culture, race, and ethnicity on a daily basis and being in regular contact with each side. It means that the knowledge about my African American and Filipino American backgrounds in concert with the act of remaining socially connected to both sides served as two anchors that not only prevented me from succumbing completely to the pressures of assimilating into a White-dominated society, but also provided me with double the arsenal to confront, combat, and defy hegemonic notions of being.

Throughout my life, I was constantly searching for a word or label that would communicate my pride in both sides. Identifying as only African American or Filipino American never felt right because it just wasn't true. College and scholarship applications told me "Please choose one," but categories like African American and Asian/Pacific Islander felt too constraining. Friends, family, and strangers frequently asked me, "Are you more Filipino than Black or more Black than Filipino?" anticipating that I would select one—perhaps the one they feared the least or perhaps the side to which they belonged. Such questions reflected a dangerous polarization and discomfort with nuance. By such questions, it seemed some people were attempting to determine my authenticity or use my response to justify how "nice" of a Black person I was. The binary thinking embedded in how the question was framed reflects how many of us operating in a Western context tend to approach people and ideas; we are conditioned to choose between or identify with one of two extremes—Black and White, rich and poor, good and evil—suggesting that one couldn't possibly (1) identify with more than one thing at the same time, (2) embrace a perspective or state of being somewhere in between, or (3) have multiple options to choose from other than the two presented.

Though racial categories and questions reflecting binary thought were limiting, I never longed to identify only as "just human." This didn't fully capture what I was about either, especially since being both Black and Filipina shaped my human experience. My humanity was not something that could be extracted from its ethnic milieu. I was one who valued the unique histories of both sides and wanted to celebrate how being African American and Filipina American have shaped my human experience.

For many years I identified as half Black and half Filipino, figuring this was a way I could declare to the world that I was both. However, identifying in terms of fractions reinforced a fragmented self-perception; it signified my silent insecurity about believing I was a diluted or counterfeit version of each ethnicity. Since my Filipino features weren't immediately noticeable to most people in Lancaster, California, I became aware that phenotypically I looked Black and therefore regularly reminded others that I was also Filipino, being sure to use the few Cebuano words I knew. This was done partly to show pride in my Filipino side, but also to show myself off as not-your-average-Black-person—someone with an "interesting" twist. So as early as elementary and junior high school, long before I had the language for it, I had done what many had done to me: I exoticized myself. In addition to spewing out the few Cebuano words I knew, I often told my friends stories about Mom's family in the Philippines, explaining to them that the reason why I was a quiet person was because my mom was Filipino. I did all these things because it was a part of myself that I felt wasn't so obvious. Since the average person saw me as Black, telling these stories and using Cebuano words at the time made me feel as if I was more interesting and exotic. Being mixed drew the attention and envy of many, and I knew it.[10]

I continued to do things like this until I became aware of some direct consequences of exoticization, like men openly expressing how they were more attracted to me as soon as they discovered I was part Filipino while at the same time expressing little to no interest in my intellect or personality. In such instances, I didn't always feel so special and unique in a positive sense, but instead felt objectified and less human.

During my late teens and early twenties, I noticed that I felt pressured to believe I had to turn on and off each side of my ethnic identity depending on who was around. I thought that in order to be accepted as Black within an all-Black social environment, I had to turn on my Black side (i.e., using Black vernacular and speaking only about issues most relevant to African American life) and leave behind or downplay my Filipino side; when I was in an all-Filipino environment I felt that I had to turn on my Filipinoness (i.e., speaking in Cebuano or Tagalog, speaking English with a Filipino accent, and speaking only about issues most relevant to Filipinos and Filipino Americans) and downplay my Black side.[11] I felt like I was contextualizing; however, this wasn't satisfying, and I continued to search for a way to contextualize without denying my other half. I wanted to bring all of me wherever I went, and I wanted all of me to be accepted regardless of whose company I was in.

Making attempts to be in touch with both sides, learning about the history of both and remaining socially connected to each community, I eventually became comfortable saying I was 100 percent African American and 100 percent Filipino American and devised various combinations of these terms. I was and am fully both. Identifying as such seemed to be a defiant response to the questions, "Are you more Filipino than Black? More Black than Filipino?" Not only was I proud to be both, but I was also proud to be a woman. So, beginning in my late twenties, I found ways to embrace my womanhood as I bounced between several ways of identifying: Filipino African American woman. African Filipino American woman. Filipina African American. African Filipina American. These names communicated the ideas of "together" and "distinct" at the same time.

Around this time, while working on my master's thesis on precolonial West African and Filipino tricksters at San Francisco State University, I came across *Heirs of Prophecy*, a fantasy novel by Lisa Smedman, whose main character,

Larajin, was half elf and half human. I was fascinated with how she invoked the deities from both her human and elven sides. This caused me to stop thinking of being biracial as a deficit or an impurity. I began to wonder if instead I had the potential to be emotionally and spiritually stronger and more capable of facing life's challenges because I could call upon the assistance and guidance of deities on both sides of my ethnic heritage. From that point on, I've expanded the circle of deities that I address and thank during prayer, calling out to God, Eshu, Oshun, Yemaya, and Bathala. Consequently, I have learned more about the multidimensionality of the Divine, gaining greater clarity about the multiple ways the Divine manifests itself on Earth.

In early 2007, the possibility of identifying as "Blackapino" or "Blackapina" crossed my mind. The term floated around in my head for a bit, but didn't seem to get concretized for quite some time. I didn't have the courage to use it, but I couldn't completely articulate why. In retrospect, I know some of this had to do with my discomfort with blending terms, as if the process of blending would corrupt the ethnic essence of each side. This was an indication that I was still afraid of being viewed as a diluted version of a Filipina or African American. I was also hesitant to use the term because to untutored ears it evoked only laughter and was never taken seriously; hidden in the laughter, I could almost hear people say, "Aw, that's cute and catchy. But is that real? Is that a real, lived experience?"

Folded into this transition were memories of a number of scholars who researched and published articles on multiracial identity. Such scholars either used blended terms or used concepts that involved blending. I remember the early writing of Rudy Guevarra Jr. in which he explored the experiences of multiethnic people of Mexican and Filipino descent, becoming the first to use the term "Mexipinos" in a published work.[12] From his clothing line, Multiracial Apparel, I bought some shirts for my niece and nephew that read "Mexipino" and "Mexipina."[13] Shortly following the release of my memoir in 2005, I also met an undergraduate student and scholar, Matthew M. Andrews, who attended one of my writing workshops on biracial identity that year. Through his work with the McNair Scholars Program, Andrews became the first to conduct research focusing on multiracial identity specifically among those of both African American and Filipino American descent.[14]

A few years later, during the summer of 2007, I delivered a presentation at the Loving Decision Conference on precolonial West African and Filipino tricksters being empowering, decolonizing role models for biracial people of African American and Filipino American descent. There, I had the pleasure of listening to Rebecca Romo present her research about biracial people of African American and Mexican American descent and remember how freeing it was to hear her use the label "Blaxican."[15] Susan Leksander presented research on applying the concept of psychosynthesis to multiracial clients. Leksander described psychosynthesis as a process within Western psychology that drew from various traditions including an African worldview describing how each human being is "seen as a community in and of itself, including a plurality of selves."[16] She pointed out the normalcy of each person having many subpersonalities and stated the following:

> Subpersonalities are thought to form in response to a "unifying center," a center of meaning that evokes a deep response in us. Different subpersonalities might arise in relationship to many different unifying centers—"parents, siblings, school, profession, philosophical systems, religious environments and the natural world."[17] I would add to this cultural and ethnic communities. A unifying center can be contacted at any age, from our earliest relationships to experiences late in life. What one experiences as outside of oneself, with enough exposure and meaning, eventually becomes internalized as a subpersonality. This new identity internalizes and consolidates the skills, gifts, drives, qualities, beliefs and values activated and gained in response to the unifying center.[18]

Her research put my complex relationship with my African American and Filipino American backgrounds into perspective. At various times throughout my life, different aspects of each ethnicity seemed to be "outside" of myself since I had fashioned my life after the White-dominant paradigm. In order to fully understand what it meant to live out my African American and Filipino American identity with depth and integrity, I consciously exposed myself to the people, language, arts, and history of each side to the point where each ethnicity gradually became internalized as one of my subpersonalities.

My nucleus of subpersonalities was and will continue to be strengthened by my continuous immersion in social circles consisting of African Americans, Filipino Americans, women, introverts, extroverts, artists, athletes, theologians, healers, the various subgroups lying within each circle, and the intersection of all these and more. This nucleus is a tight, yet fluid, ever-expansive, ever-evolving blend housed within my spirit. I possess an authenticity that laughs in the face of essentialism. I am "Blackapina."[19] Black. Filipino American. Woman. I am an African American unafraid of identifying as Black because it hearkens back to the Black Power Movement when Black, the color and the culture, were embraced with pride. I also use it because *bibi*, the word for "black" among the Sonay of Mali, referred only to "the essential goodness of things"—a definition predating the distortion and demonization of the color.[20] I am a second-generation Filipina American, holding my mother's immigrant dreams and sacrifices; as my *utang na loob*, I offer Momma and Da'y the fruits of my work as professor of Filipina(o) American Heritage and Africana Studies. I am a woman who menstruates and gives birth and nurses and nurtures and fights. I am each of these and more. I am all these at the same time. I live at the crossroads, straddling multiple worlds. Hybridity is my home where transition and nuance are always welcome. At the interstices, you'll hear my breath. When I walk, listen for the sound of ancestral spirits and deities hailing from the African continent and the Philippine islands; hear them pulse and drift, cry and whisper, laugh and pray as they clear the way for their children to walk the world protected, guided, and strengthened. *Ashe.*

NOTES

1. The term "multiethnic" is used to denote a person who is composed of more than one ethnicity. Based on the work of sociologist G. Reginald Daniel, I use "multiethnic," as opposed to "multiracial," considering the notion that ethnicity includes the concepts of both race and culture. Daniel states, "Ethnicity generally refers to a segment or subset of a larger society whose members are thought by themselves and/or others to share a common culture (beliefs, ideals, values, meanings, customs, artifacts), which sets them off from other groups in the society. However, these individuals also share a common ancestry or origin (real or imagined)—and thus may have similar or common geno-phenotypical traits—that distinguish them from other members of society as well. In addition, they may more or less participate in shared activities in which that common origin and culture are significant ingredients. Considering that ethnic formation includes notions of both race and culture, it might seem more appropriate in this book to use the term multiethnic, rather than multiracial." See G. Reginald Daniel, *More Than Black? Multiracial Identity and the New Racial Order* (Philadelphia: Temple University Press, 2002), xv.

2. "First Movement: The Intersection" was adapted from an introduction originally written in my article "Barack Obama: Embracing Multiplicity—Being a Catalyst for Change," in *Race and the Obama Phenomenon: The Vision of a More Perfect Multiracial Union*, ed. G. Reginald Daniel and Hettie V. Williams (Jackson: University Press of Mississippi, 2014).

3. Isabel Wilkerson, *The Warmth of Other Suns: The Epic Story of America's Great Migration* (New York: Random House, 2010), 9.

4. Malcolm Gladwell, *The Tipping Point: How Little Things Can Make a Big Difference* (New York: Little, Brown, 2000), 38–48.

5. "Third Movement: Disconnection Exposed" was adapted from an excerpt originally written for my book *Crushing Soft Rubies—A Memoir* (Oakland: Broken Shackle Publishing, 2014), 78, 81–82, 143–146.

6. See Albert Memmi, *The Colonizer and the Colonized* (Boston: Beacon Press, 1967). See also Richard Dyer, *White—Essays on Race and Culture* (New York: Routledge, 1997); Dorothy Roberts, *Killing the Black Body: Race, Reproduction, and the Meaning of Liberty* (New York: Vintage, 1999); Jan Nederveen Pieterse, *White on Black: Images of Africa and Blacks in Western Popular Culture* (New Haven, CT: Yale University Press, 1995); and Daniel Schirmer and Stephen Shalom, eds., *The Philippines Reader* (Boston: South End, 1987).

7. Rita Nakashima Brock, "Cooking without Recipes—Interstitial Integrity," in *Off the Menu—Asian and Asian North American Women's Religion and Theology*, ed. Rita Nakashima Brock, Jung Ha Kim, Kwok Pui-lan, and Seung Ai Yang (Louisville: Westminster John Knox Press, 2007), 126.

8. This portion of "Fourth Movement: Transformative Thought and Lives in Theology School" was adapted from an excerpt originally written for my book *Crushing Soft Rubies*, 198–200.

9. Nakashima Brock, "Cooking without Recipes," 140.

10. This portion of "Fifth Movement: The Blend" was adapted from an excerpt originally written for my book *Crushing Soft Rubies*, 83–84.

11. Since phenotypically I appear African American to most people, it was more difficult to "turn off" my Black side than "turn off" my Filipino side.

12. Rudy P. Guevarra Jr., "Burritos and *Bagoong*: Mexipinos and Multiethnic Identity in San Diego, California," in *Crossing Lines: Race and Mixed Race across the Geohistorical Divide*, ed. Marc Coronado, Rudy P. Guevarra Jr., Jeffrey Moniz, and Laura Furlan Szanto (Santa Barbara: University of California, Santa Barbara, Multiethnic Student Outreach, 2003), 74.

13. Guevarra recently released *Becoming Mexipino: Multiethnic Identities and Communities in San Diego* (New Brunswick, NJ: Rutgers University Press, 2012).

14. Matthew M. Andrews, "(Re)examining (Multi)racial Identity: Black-Filipino Multiracials in the San Francisco-Bay Area," *Berkeley McNair Research Journal* 13 (2005): 27–38.

15. Rebecca Romo, "Blaxican Identity: An Exploratory Study of Blacks/Chicanas/os in California" (paper, National Association for Chicana and Chicano Studies Annual Conference, San Jose, CA, 2008), 64.

16. O. A. Ogbonnaya, "Person as Community: African Understanding of the Person as an Intrapsychic Community," *Journal of Black Psychology* 20.1 (1994): 75, quoted in Susan Leksander, "Psychosynthesis and Multiracial Clients: Diversity and Integration of Multiple Selves" (San Francisco: California Institute of Integral Studies, 2007), 2.

17. John Firma and Ann Gila, *Psychosynthesis: A Psychology of the Spirit* (Albany: State University of New York Press, 2002), 12, 73.

18. Leksander, "Psychosynthesis and Multiracial Clients," 12.

19. The first Blackapino I met was Lance Adderly. Our mothers, Lucrecia Adderly and Lucrecia Stickmon, and our fathers, John Adderly and Fermon Stickmon, became friends in the 1970s and consequently we became childhood playmates. Thanks to his mother, he and I were recently reunited. It is only in my adulthood that I understand how those early years of playing together prevented me from feeling like the lone Blackapino in the world. Beginning in 2004, I began meeting other multiracial people of African American and Filipino American descent like Vangie Canonizado Buell, Tony Robles, Matthew M. Andrews, Dennis Calloway, and Teresa Hodges. Thanks to the work of Myrna and Carlos Zialcita, I learned about jazz artists who were also Black and Filipino like Sugar Pie DeSanto, Bob Porlocha, Elizabeth Ramsey, Joe Bataan, Lena Sunday, and Anna Maria Flechero. In 2011, I learned that long before I identified as Blackapina, Joe Bataan used a blended term, "Afro-Filipino," to describe himself. Bataan released an album in 1975 called *Afro-Filipino*, which included a song titled "Ordinary Guy (Afro-Filipino)."

20. Wade Nobles, *Seeking the Sakhu: Foundational Writings for an African Psychology* (Chicago: Third World Press, 2006), 329.

PART II

Multiple Minority Marriage and Parenting

4

Intermarriage and the Making of a Multicultural Society in the Baja California Borderlands

VERÓNICA CASTILLO-MUÑOZ

Maria Librada Wong Duarte was born in La Paz, Baja California, in 1915. The daughter of a Chinese immigrant man and a Mexican mestiza woman, she was raised speaking both Spanish and Cantonese. Her younger brother, Alejandro Vicente Wong Duarte, used his bilingual abilities to secure a job as a sailor in La Paz, facilitating communication between Mexican and Chinese commercial interests.[1] Maria Librada and Alejandro Vicente's bicultural identities were not unique to the region. Indeed, they formed part of a new generation of Chinese Mexican children in Baja California. The boom of US and European mining enterprises and

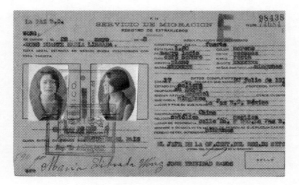

FIGURE 4.1. Maria Librada Wong Duarte, 1933, immigration form F14. Courtesy of the Archivo General de la Nación, Mexico City, Registro del Departamento de Migración.

agribusinesses spearheaded a large migration of Chinese, Japanese, and European single men to the Baja California peninsula. Agribusiness and mining companies had initially relied on local indigenous and Mexican labor, but when the scarcity of workers threatened production, managers recruited additional skilled and nonskilled laborers from central Mexico, Japan, China, and Europe.

Historians have previously attributed the success of settlements in Baja California to mining, fishing, and agribusiness, as well as to colonization projects sponsored by the Mexican government.[2] While these factors were important, they do not explain fully why more single men, who were highly transient in the past, began to settle permanently, leading to the formation of culturally and racially diverse communities in Baja California.

By 1921, more than 93 percent of Baja California's population was racially mixed, according to Mexican census records. People there spoke at least fourteen different languages and eight distinct dialects.[3] Thirty years earlier, the region consisted primarily of Mexican and local native peoples. Census records and oral testimonies reveal that migration and mixed race unions contributed to the increase of permanent settlements in the region. For example, in the Mexicali Valley, mestizo, European, Japanese, and Chinese men intermarried and cohabitated with mestizo and Indian women.[4] Chinese and Japanese last names then, became widespread in agricultural communities in the Mexicali Valley, while Chinese and European surnames became commonplace in coastal communities where they settled.

In the past ten years, more historians have published important works on the Chinese experience at the US-Mexico borderlands.[5] These authors examine the transnational lives of the Chinese living in the Southwest and northern Mexico since the Chinese Exclusion Act took effect in the United States in 1882. For example, Julia Schiavone Camacho has demonstrated that Chinese Mexican families pushed the boundaries of mestizaje in Sonora, Mexico, by claiming *Mexicanidad* (Mexican identities) at a time of exclusion.[6] This chapter contributes to this larger historiography by examining how migration and mixed race marriages complicate our understanding of race and ethnicity in northern Mexico. As Paul Spickard notes, intermarriage and ethnicity can be useful theoretical tools to examine social relations and how societies change over time.[7] This chapter examines why ideologies of mestizaje took precedence over ideologies of Whiteness (*criollo*) in twentieth-century Mexico and how mestizaje both incorporated and excluded people of different ethnic and racial backgrounds in Baja California.

The Santa Rosalía Mines

Five hundred miles south of the US-Mexico border in Santa Rosalía, the Compagnie du Boleo, a French mining company, recruited Chinese and Japanese workers, most notably after 1892, when the Mexican government prevented the company from hiring indigenous people during the Yaqui Wars. President Por-firio Díaz prohibited the Compagnie du Boleo from hiring Yaqui Indians because he feared they would spend their earnings on arms and ammunition.[8]

Boleo managers recruited Mexican mestizos from the nearby states of Sinaloa, Sonora, and Nayarit, but they departed after only a year, largely because competing recruiters from the United States traveled to Santa Rosalía to hire mestizos with the promise of higher wages. Between 1895 and 1899, the Santa Rosalía mestizo population declined from 4,115 to 2,975 (see table 4.1), while the European population remained under 300. These foreigners represented a skilled class that occupied managerial positions as supervisors, engineers, and merchants.[9] Indeed, French newspapers advertised jobs for young engineers interested in work outside the country with the company. To entice them, the Compagnie du Boleo offered them free transportation from France to Santa Rosalía and covered all their housing expenses.[10] Santa Rosalía also served as an important port of entry for Chinese and Japanese migrant workers. The approval of the 1899 Treaty of Amity, Commerce, and Navigation between Mex-ico and China facilitated the migration of thousands of Chinese men to north-ern Mexico. In fact, the Compagnie du Boleo, a French-owned mining company, built its own port in Santa Rosalía and recruited workers directly from China.

Chinese migration to Mexico was part of a larger transpacific migration to Latin America, Canada, and the United States that took place during the second half of the nineteenth century, when about 113,000 Chinese workers emigrated to the United States and Canada, and about 80,000 went to Latin America.[11] According to historian Robert Chao Romero, Chinese immigrants numbered about 24,000 by 1924, making them the second largest group of immigrants in Mexico.[12] The Mexican government benefited from the Chinese Exclusion Act enacted in the United States in 1882.[13] In contrast, Mexico signed treaties with

TABLE 4.1

Workers in the Santa Rosalia Mines

Year	Mexican mestizos	Indians	Europeans
1893	3,706	805	281
1895	4,115	600	212
1899	2,975	200	140

Source: Boleo Company census records, 1893, 1895, and 1899.
Archivo Pablo Martínez, La Paz, Baja California Sur.

Japan in 1889 and with China in 1899 to facilitate efforts to bring Asian men to work in Mexico.[14]

To transport Chinese workers who had embarked in Hong Kong or Vladivostok, a Russian port city near the Chinese border, the Compagnie du Boleo contracted German and French vessels.[15] Ten years later, in 1900, the company contracted with the Tokio Imin Gaisha (Oriental Immigration Co.) to bring Japanese workers to Santa Rosalía.[16] Within ten years, Boleo had recruited approximately three thousand Chinese and one thousand Japanese workers. This trend coincided with the discovery of large deposits of copper in Baja California that had the potential to produce an average of eleven thousand tons of copper per year.[17] Company records indicate that the Mexican Department of Development approved every single petition to bring Chinese workers to Santa Rosalía over objections from the Mexican Department of Health, which cited the threat of highly contagious diseases among Chinese workers as its rationale. For example, in 1907, when agents from the Department of Health denied Boleo's request to bring more workers from Hong Kong to Santa Rosalía, Pablo Macedo, the company's manager, wrote to both departments to ask them to approve his petition. He argued that it would "jeopardize" the company if Chinese workers could not come to Santa Rosalía. As expected, the Department of Development overruled the Department of Health's decision, and the company continued to bring workers to Santa Rosalía from China and Japan.[18]

In an effort to reduce dependence on Chinese workers, the Compagnie du Boleo turned to mestizo laborers and their families, offering them free transportation from Sinaloa and Sonora to the mines. Mestizo and Indian workers lived in the communities of Providencia, Purgatorio, Soledad, and Santa Rosalía. To accommodate employees, the company established three different communities in Santa Rosalía: Mesa Francia, Mesa Mexicana, and Arroyo. Reflective of the racial, cultural, and skilled hierarchies at the company, Mesa Francia housed European administrators and engineers, while Mesa Mexicana housed families of government employees and Mexican administrators. Both settlements had two-story homes with separate patios and fantastic views of the Sea of Cortes. In contrast, Arroyo, the settlement for Mexican workers and their families, was located far down the hill, away from Mesas Francia and Mexicana. These workers' dwellings were similar to homes in Purgatorio, Soledad, and Providencia: small wooden boxes or shacks with a diminutive kitchen and running water, but no electricity.[19] They also had a church, but it was a prefabricated metal structure that Boleo purchased at an exhibition in France in 1894, most likely built by Gustave Eiffel, the famous French engineer.[20] It was shipped to Santa Rosalía, erected between Mesa Francia and Arroyo, and named Santa Barbara. It was the only church in town. Most marriages between Mexican women and European men were celebrated there.[21] Outside the church was a large plaza with cafes, restaurants, and bars where women and men could stroll and mingle. Even though the space was considered a segregated area for workers, French engineers and administrators frequented the public square, where they met and sustained romantic relationships with Mexican women.

By 1920, approximately 71 percent of the French single male immigrants who had been hired at the company married Mexican women.[22] These Mexican women, in turn, specifically the ones who had married engineers and administrators, gained better housing with electricity and running water in Mesa Francia. As the wives of administrators and engineers, they also enjoyed the benefits of upward mobility. Table 4.2 offers a small sample of intermarriages celebrated in Baja California's coastal region. Marriage records reveal that Mexican women were usually the daughters of migrant mestizo workers or politicians from Baja California (see table 4.2).

Engineers and managers who married Mexican women eventually applied for Mexican citizenship, which the government granted after they had been in the country for more than five years.[23] In 1897, Nicolas Minar, a Greek mechanic at the Compagnie du Boleo, married María de Jesús Serrano, a widow from Mulege, Baja California. One year later, thirty-one-year-old Mathiot Pierre, a French engineer at Boleo, married twenty-three-year-old Agustina Mejia, also from Mulege. Polish and German Jews emigrated from California to Ensenada to work for British and American investment companies. In 1887, Maximiliano Bernstein served as director for the International Mexican Co. in Ensenada. He later invested in mining and cattle in San Rafael, near Ensenada. Bernstein married

TABLE 4.2.

Sample of Intermarriages in Coastal Regions of Baja California

Husband's full name	Place of birth	Wife's full name	Place of birth
Pierre Mathiot	France	Agustina Mejia	Baja California
Francisco Bragg	United States	Lupe Serrano	Sonora
Barbieri Julio	Italy	Trinidad Espinosa	Baja California
Gray Thomas	England	Domitila Garcia	Sinaloa
Ulbrich Frank	Austria	Carolina Legaspy	Sinaloa
Gustavo Strickroth	Germany	Flavia Guzman	Sinaloa
Nicolas Minar	Greece	Jesus Serrano	Baja California

Source: Pablo Martínez, *Guía familiar de la Baja California 1700–1900: Vital Statistics of Lower California* (1870–1900).

a mestizo woman, Guadalupe Riveroll, and they had five children. His business partner, Luis Mendelson, also Jewish, came to Baja California to work as a broker for the Lower California Development Co. He married Carmen La Madrid, a mestizo woman from Baja California. Both Bernstein and Mendelson settled permanently in Baja California and became Mexican citizens.[24] Mendelson later served as attorney general of Ensenada.

In contrast, marriages between Chinese men and Mexican women were scarcely recorded in the Boleo census. Later population documents show that even though they were not recorded, such marriages did occur, but based on the company's experience with the Department of Health, the company managers probably did not want to disclose that Mexican women intermarried or cohabited with Chinese laborers. Only three marriages appeared in the census. Perhaps the company survey excluded Chinese workers cohabitating with Mexican mestiza women outside of marriage. The Chinese men who married Mexican women left the bachelor housing provided by Boleo, and moved into the emerging towns of Santa Rosalía and Mulege, away from the company. By 1926, Chinese people composed 26 percent of the population of Santa Rosalía, and civil records show that twelve out of twenty-nine Chinese men living in Santa Rosalía had married Mexican women.[25] Based on the few records available, we do know that Chinese merchants were the first people to settle outside the company town. As in Mexicali, Chinese stores sprouted up in Santa Rosalía outside the Boleo mines. Some stores sold vegetables, shoes, and staples at lower prices than the company store. Jobs at Chinese stores and restaurants provided alternative employment options for Chinese workers from the Compagnie du Boleo.

In the Mexicali Valley, similar migration patterns emerged in agricultural communities where there was a burgeoning demand for laborers as the native population began to decline. In 1912, the Colorado River Land Co. (CRLC) introduced labor-intensive cotton to the Mexicali Valley, aggressively leasing and developing 676,024 acres of land near the Colorado River.[26] The need for seasonal farm labor led to a jump in population from 462 to 11,700 people during the cotton season. At the same time, census takers noted a remarkable decline in the Indian population in Baja California. According to a 1921 census report, Indians represented only 6 percent of the population in Baja California.[27] The Cocopah population declined from 5,000 in 1890 to 1,817 in 1920.[28] The census also revealed that many Indian women intermarried or lived in consensual unions with Mexican mestizo men, thus accounting for a substantial increase in the mestizo population in the Mexicali Valley.[29]

Initially, indigenous and mestizo families lived in separate communities. While Mexican workers lived on CRLC farms, indigenous farmers were displaced by the 1906 damming of the Colorado River. In response, indigenous people moved closer to the US-Mexico border. Yet, they did not leave willingly, and they resisted the settlement of immigrant mestizo workers. Zaragoza Contreras, one of the first mestizo migrants, described the Cocopah as "wild Indians who did not speak a word of Spanish. We could not live in peace because they would shoot at us every time we went outside in the evenings."[30] His narrative reveals the tensions between the native population (trying to survive under new conditions) and the mestizo newcomers (who viewed the Cocopah as foreigners because they did not speak Spanish). Ethnic tensions increased after the CRLC opened additional land to European American farmers and mestizo workers.

Many mestizo men first came to the Mexicali Valley by themselves, and then brought their families a few years later. Between 1901 and 1907, the Sumaya, Villarino, and Barrios Arias families were among the thirty mestizo families who migrated to the Mexicali Valley from nearby states.[31] Leaving his wife and family, Ramón Sumaya came in 1901 from the Ensenada mining camps. Seven years later, Bernarda Sumaya joined her husband in Mexicali, bringing her widowed *comadre*, Delfina Moreno. These two women were among the first mestizas who worked as temporary farm laborers for the CRLC, clearing land and planting trees along the Colorado River. Still, CRLC preferred to hire men over women for labor-intensive tasks such as clearing the land and the installation of irrigation works. By 1909, the Sumayas saved enough money to purchase a vacant lot from A. J. Flores, and they opened a small shop that supplied goods and staples to mestizo migrant workers in the valley.[32] The two women probably ran this shop, while Sumaya continued working as a seasonal laborer at different CRLC farms. The 1910 census reported 989 men and 428 women living in Mexicali.[33] They made homes out of *cachanilla* and other native plants that provided protection from the extreme climate.

CRLC farmers did not offer permanent housing for farmhands, making it difficult for farmers to retain farmhands and build a stable workforce. Workers built improvised structures (known as *ramadas*) out of grass, loose boards, and wood. The farmers did not want to invest in worker housing, and the CRLC did not provide them with any incentive to do so.[34] In fact, the CRLC contract stated that all improvements by the renter (including the construction of housing and fences) would become property of the CRLC after the lease expired. No extra compensation would be provided for these upgrades.[35] After their contracts ended, many workers left the farms voluntarily to find other agricultural jobs in Mexico, while others migrated to the United States. The CRLC investors feared that the permanent settlement of Mexican workers on the farms would lead to the confiscation of substantial portions of their property if those workers stayed for more than one year. This seemed to be the policy after the company had a difficult time evicting indigenous and Mexican tenants who claimed to have permanent lease and work agreements with (former owner) Guillermo Andrade.[36]

With a cotton boom in 1914, more male laborers were contracted from the nearby states of Sonora, Sinaloa, and Nayarit. Mestizos and Indians worked side by side in the cotton fields. Daily interactions between Indians and mestizos changed their perceptions of one another. Mestizos, who formerly viewed indigenous people as "savages," started to appreciate the Cocopah people's knack for building homes resistant to the extreme heat. In turn, Cocopah people, who had grown up listening to their parents' stories about "evil" mestizos, found their own perspectives changing as they spent time working with them on CRLC farms.[37] Indeed, previously Cocopah children believed in a mestizo "boogie" man who would come at night to take them away if they misbehaved, and Cocopah adults perceived the mestizos as "evil" foreigners not worth trusting.[38]

In spite of these common misconceptions, indigenous women continued to marry mestizo men in greater numbers than they had done so in the past. In fact, marriage and consensual unions became central to the survival of women in the Mexicali Valley. More than 80 percent of women between the ages of sixteen and sixty were married or lived in consensual unions with migrant men, while about 20 percent were widows or single mothers.[39] For single mestizo men, finding wives or women with whom they could cohabitate was one way to get their domestic needs met. Women not only provided homemade meals but also contributed financially to the household. In 1927, 537 out of 1,006 civil marriages celebrated in Baja California's Northern Territory were between Indian women and migrant men.

The nature of seasonal labor reinforced gender and labor inequalities in the Mexicali Valley. In spite of the flourishing cotton industry, single women struggled to find permanent jobs in the valley. Between 1910 and 1920, the majority of women were identified as part-time workers and only during the cotton-picking season.[40] Cotton farms and ranchos offered housing and year-round work to male heads of household and single men under the assumption that men were better equipped to perform physical labor and were responsible for maintaining dependents. Indeed, cotton farms had a skewed population of 8,237 men to 4,675 women.[41] Women were usually offered only part-time work, and only during the cotton-picking season.

Oral testimonies of indigenous women reveal that as strategies of survival, single mothers and widows often agreed to live in consensual unions with mestizo men to escape extreme poverty and hunger. Juana Portillo Laguna, for instance, lived in a consensual relationship with Estanislao Sandoval, a mestizo who worked as a cowboy near Sierra Juarez. When Sandoval left Juana for another woman, she shortly moved in with Juan Valenzuela, a worker from Guaymas Sonora. Valenzuela helped raise her children, and they had more children together. Because he was well connected in the Mexicali Valley, Valenzuela had steady work even in the off-season. The couple stayed together for many years until their children became adults.[42]

In some cases, single mothers who lived in consensual unions with mesti-zos endured domestic abuse, for many had few other recourse for survival. The experience of Delfina Cuero provides a glimpse in to the lives of Indian single mothers. A Diegueño Indian, she was widowed when her four children were young. To provide for her children, she lived with different mestizo men, even if it meant great harm. In her autobiography, Cuero describes her traumatic experience with different mestizo men:

> I tried to live with several different men, each one said he would take care of me but each time it was always the same. I did all the cooking, wash-ing, ironing, and everything, all the work I had always done, but it wasn't enough. I had to clear land and cut fence posts. I had to work like a man, as well as the house and garden work, hard, heavy work. If I didn't do enough to suit him, he would beat me. I have been black and blue so many times because there was still more work to do. Even with all that, each man would get mad about feeding my children and beat me for that. When the man would not let me feed my children, I would have to find someone else to work for.[43]

Cuero's narrative demonstrates how unmarried native women faced enor-mous challenges in the countryside. Life for Cuero and her children became even more precarious as she moved around with her children to work tem-porary jobs. In between relationships, she worked as a part-time farmhand, took in laundry, and begged for food when she was unemployed. Her perilous situation forced her to ask her *comadre*, Matilda, to help her raise Eugenia, one of her younger daughters. Left with no other recourse, given the gender discrimination at the worksites, she also negotiated consensual unions for her two teenage daughters, Lupe and Lola, hoping each would find a better life with a male partner. Meanwhile, her two older sons had found well-paying jobs on nearby farms.

As more men and women moved around to work on different farms in Baja California, the Mexican government began looking for ways to motivate sea-sonal workers to stay permanently in Baja California. To do so, Subjefe Politico Esteban Cantú approved land colonization projects in Mexicali. Cantú's strat-egy was to populate the valley with Mexican residents in order to ward off the constant threat of US annexation. Indeed, between 1910 and 1920, the US gov-ernment, represented by the US Senate, three times attempted to approve the purchase of Baja California.[44] In 1919, Elwood Mead, a former professor from the University of California and the appointed chairman of the California Commis-sion on Colonization and Rural Credit, advocated for the US purchase of the Mexican territory. His idea: to shift the boundary line far enough south to place the Colorado River wholly within the borders of the United States.[45]

Cantú's strategies included expropriating approximately 6,500 hectares from the Compañia de Terrenos y Colonizacion (an English company) and the Compañia de Terrenos y Aguas de la Baja California (a US company) to form Mexican colonias.[46] These companies had purchased the land from the CRLC, but because they had defaulted on their property taxes, Cantú targeted them. Cantú's support for the settlement of Mexicans in new colonias proved successful. By 1919, there were four thousand Mexicans living in the Mexicali Valley who owned or leased an average of 10 hectares per family. Colonia Herradura had approximately 240 hectares for twenty-four families; Abasolo had 129 hectares for twelve families; and Sonora (among the largest colonias) had 685 hectares for sixty-five families.[47] As a result, the number of Mexicans in Mexicali tripled between 1910 and 1919 (see table 4.3).

Families living in colonias (such as those in table 4.3) had only enough land for subsistence farming, so they still needed to work on CRLC farms to make ends meet. The Mexicali government designed an optional plan where a tenant could either purchase the lot or lease it for three years or more.[48] In an effort to increase the size of the Mexican army at the border, Cantú offered men (women were excluded) the option to stay in colonias at no cost as long as they served in the army.[49] Cantú was clearly concerned about the region's US-dominated agribusiness model, and fearful of losing the Mexicali Valley to the United States.

The boom in cotton production during World War I led to a labor shortage. CRLC farmers complained about the high turnover of Mexican laborers as most of those recruited as seasonal cotton pickers did not return. Instead, they crossed the border and worked for agricultural enterprises in Arizona

TABLE 4.3.

Colonias in the Mexicali Valley

Colonia	Hectares	Individual lots
Abasolo	129	12
Benito Juarez	640	64
Herradura	240	24
Sonora	685	63
Grupo Oriental	580	50
Grupo Occidental	50	40

Source: Pablo Herrera Carrillo, *Reconquista y Colonización del Valle de Mexicali y Otros Escritos Paralelos* (Mexicali: Universidad Autónoma de Baja California, 2002), 162–163.

and in California's Imperial Valley. Imperial Valley growers proved more successful than their counterparts in Mexicali at attracting and retaining workers because they offered higher wages.[50] According to Lawrence Cardoso, Mexicans earned an average of $0.12 per day in Mexico, while they earned between $1.00 and $3.50 per day in the United States for the same type of work.[51]

From 1910 to 1920, irrigation development transformed the Colorado Desert into the Imperial Valley, giving rise to some of the most fertile farmland in the United States. By 1920, the Imperial Valley was called "America's Amazing Winter Garden" and the "American Valley of the Nile."[52] Growers increased significantly the cultivation of cantaloupe, lettuce, cotton, and alfalfa. The cantaloupe industry alone yielded $9.5 million in profits in one year.[53] Imperial Valley farmers were desperately in need of labor, as the regular sources of workers had decreased in different years. The Chinese Exclusion Act that went into effect in 1882 prohibited US farmers from hiring Chinese laborers.[54] Consequently, they hired Mexicans in greater numbers. In 1917, the US secretary of labor was pressured to omit the required literacy test for the contracting of foreign labor at the US-Mexican border. As a result, more than 750,000 Mexicans migrated to the US Southwest to work in agriculture, transportation, and mining between 1910 and 1930.[55] Historian Vicki Ruiz writes that by 1920, Mexican migrant workers and Mexican Americans emerged as the primary labor force in the mining, agricultural, and railroad industries in the US Southwest.[56] In order to attract more workers, CRLC managers employed recruiters known as *enganchadores* to hire Mexican, Chinese, and Japanese workers from mining towns in Santa Rosalía and Ensenada. CRLC recruiters used deceiving tactics to attract Chinese and Japanese workers from Santa Rosalía to work in the Mexicali Valley. Recruiters told them that they would own land and get paid higher wages if they worked for the CRLC. Some Chinese and Japanese workers left the mines in search of better opportunities. Mariano Ma, for example, left his job at the mines near Ensenada to go to the Mexicali Valley, only to find out wages there were actually lower.[57]

The labor shortage persisted, and the CRLC could not attract enough Chinese or Japanese immigrants. By 1912, the CRLC began formal talks with the Mexican government to contract Chinese workers. Some renters with the CRLC were actually wealthy Chinese American farmers from California who recruited their own labor force from Canton, China.[58] Cantú approved the contract of Chinese laborers, under the condition that each one pay a $100 tax when they entered the territory.[59] But not all Chinese workers arrived through the ports of Baja California; many arrived at the port of San Francisco in California, where they were sent on a "sealed" South Pacific train to Calexico.[60] At the CRLC, there were two basic labor agreements. Some farmers paid an hourly wage for time on the job cultivating and picking cotton, while others divided the profits among the workers after the harvest. While Chinese laborers who belonged to transnational

Chinese associations based on regional, family origin, or political associations chose the latter agreement, Mexican workers preferred a set wage.

Workers with management skills, such as Mariano Ma, eventually scored better jobs in the Mexicali Valley. His story provides an example of how Chinese workers moved into leadership positions at the CRLC. In 1884, Mariano Ma emigrated from China to work at the Ensenada mines. In 1906, the CRLC recruited him to clear land for farms. Between 1884 and 1906, Ma learned to speak English and Spanish, which allowed him to ascend the company's ranks, first working as a contractor, later as a supervisor for the company's irrigation projects. As a supervisor, Ma managed thousands of men from different backgrounds: "As a supervisor I oversaw men from different countries: Mexican, Chinese, Japanese, and Anglo workers. There were some occasions where I had to supervise and mobilize 2,000 men as if they were soldiers."[61] His trilingual abilities were the key to his upward mobility from seasonal worker to supervisor. Ma later became a Mexican citizen, and worked for the company until 1937.

As more Asian American farmers from San Francisco subleased medium-size parcels from the CRLC, the Asian working population increased in Baja California. Farmers subleased an average of 100 to 3,000 hectares known as ranchos.[62] According to historian Evelyn Hu-DeHart, there existed approximately 125 Chinese-operated ranchos on CRLC land that employed 1,314 Chinese men.[63] Some Chinese cotton ranchers invested in other enterprises in Mexicali as well. Wong Kee, a well-respected cotton rancher, had stores and other business ventures in Baja California.[64] In 1915, two Japanese farmers, K. Lato and Ben Kodama, leased a medium-sized parcel from the CRLC and employed about 30 Japanese laborers on their ranch; they also opened stores in Mexicali.[65] From 1914 to 1920, the ongoing influx of Chinese laborers into Mexicali surpassed that of Mexican workers. Approximately 5,000 Chinese and 500 Japanese workers lived in the valley.[66] Chinese laborers worked in fields other than agriculture; some of them even had jobs in Mexicali's red light district. As historians Casey Christensen and Eric Schantz note, gaming houses and bars emerged in Baja California in 1909 and became part of the border economy.[67] In the 1920s, when alcohol was prohibited in the United States under the Eighteenth Amendment to the US Constitution, or the Volstead Act, US and Chinese investors opened gaming houses, restaurants, and bars in Mexicali and Tijuana, where many Chinese men worked in these red light districts as cooks, bartenders, and waiters.

At the same time, US-owned land companies in Baja California continued to rely on Asian and Mexican laborers. By 1910, intermarriage between mestizas and Asian men was changing the racial makeup of the Mexicali Valley. Census records show that after 1910, more Chinese and Japanese workers married or lived in consensual unions with Mexican women. In 1927, approximately 300 out of 1,006 weddings in Baja California took place between Asian men and mestiza women.[68] This seems to be consistent with the mixed race marriages recorded in Chihuahua and Sonora, where they also had a large migration of Chinese workers.[69] As Grace Peña Delgado and Julia María Schiavone Camacho noted, Mexican wives could help their Chinese husbands establish social ties within the local community.[70]

The testimonies of local Mexican and Asian merchants reveal, as well, the close connections they had with agricultural workers. For example, Henry Wong was an agricultural worker in the Mexicali Valley who came from Canton, China, as a teenager. At the age of twenty-nine, Wong filed a petition for Mexican citizenship in the municipality of Mexicali.[71] Wong Luen, a merchant from Mexicali, testified that he had known Wong since he was *chiquito* (young), and that he was worthy of Mexican citizenship because he was a decent man. Similarly, Mexican merchants Carlos Saracho and Enrique Uribe testified on behalf of Luis Ma Chu, and José Lim, and Antonio Foy. Luis Ma Chu came to Baja California Norte from Canton in 1917. He worked on farms in Baja California for six years.[72] After he married a Mexican woman in 1922, he applied for Mexican citizenship. His application was approved and he became a naturalized Mexican citizen. Chinese men, previously confined to CRLC farms, moved to the northern part of Mexicali, which they called Chinatown, while other people moved onto CRLC lands rented by Chinese farmers.

Over time, marriages between Mexican women and Chinese men transformed segregated neighborhoods assigned to Chinese bachelors into diverse Chinese Mexican communities. In 1913, Manuel Lee Chew immigrated to the Mexicali Valley to work for Rancho del Pacífico, a CRLC cotton farm. Lee Chew had two older brothers who had worked in the valley since 1910, and they had arranged the job for him. In 1920, while working as a supervisor at Rancho del Pacífico, he met Flavia Mancilla Camacho, a mestiza migrant from Santa Rosalía who worked part time on the ranch during cotton-picking season. Her father had come to Mexicali a few years prior from Santa Rosalía, where he had worked at the Compagnie du Boleo. Lee Chew asked Mancilla Camacho to marry him after a long courtship. She loved him and was determined to marry him, although her father opposed. Her father finally gave his consent, and in 1920 Lee Chew arranged a big wedding celebration at Casa Blanca, one of the most expensive restaurants in Mexicali's Chinatown. The bride's family and Chinese and Mexican workers from the farm all attended the wedding. Lee Chew borrowed a new Cadillac from a friend (a Chinese merchant from Tijuana), and he drove his new bride back to Rancho del Pacífico.[73]

Mixed Race Children and the State

By the 1920s, mixed race marriages became part of a larger public debate in postrevolutionary Mexico. President Alvaro Obregon envisioned a new government that incorporated rural indigenous people into the mainstream of Mexican society through education and by emphasis on mestizo roots. In 1921, Alvaro Obregon appointed José Vasconcelos, a noted scholar and politician, as head of Mexico's Department of Education. His mission was to overhaul the educational system. Vasconcelos changed the school curricula and launched a campaign to send teachers to rural communities to educate indigenous people, with the goal of incorporating them into what he called the *Raza Cosmica* (Cosmic Race).[74] Vasconcelos was a critic of US segregation policies on Indian reservations and believed that the incorporation of Indians (not segregation) would modernize the Mexican countryside. According to Vasconcelos, people of mixed race origins (*mestizaje*) were the race of the future, or what he called "the fifth race."[75] At the same time, Vasconcelos and Mexican politicians began to politicize civil marriages increasingly condemning marriages between Mexican women and Chinese men.

The children of mixed race mestizo and indigenous couples went along with this new image of postrevolutionary Mexico. Growing up in the 1920s, Cocopah mestizos forged new identities in Baja California. The local government categorized the children of mestizo and Cocopah parents as "Cucapá-Mestizo" because most of these children spoke both Yuma and Spanish. Locally, the second Cocopah mestizo generation was known as *cuarterones* because they spoke more Spanish than Yuma. Interviews with Cucapá-Mestizo children reveal that their identities where shaped according to the place where they grew up.

For example, the sons and daughters of Felix, a Mexican mestizo cowboy from New Mexico and Petra Portillo, a Cocopah Indian from El Mayor, identified themselves as Cocopah.[76] When their parents worked as seasonal laborers in the United States, the children stayed with their maternal grandparents in El Mayor. The children grew up around Cocopah people, learned indigenous cultivation techniques, spoke mainly Yuma, and frequently traveled to visit relatives in Yuma, Arizona.[77] Still, when the Portillo Laguna children got older, they worked on US farms with mestizos and formed intimate relationships. Adelina, María de Jesús, Felipa, and Juana Portillo, for instance, all married mestizo migrant men.[78] Cucapá-Mestizo families who moved near the Mexicali municipality spoke more Spanish than Cocopah, and their children attended local schools with mestizo children.

As a symbol of their integration to mestizo culture, only 457 reported that they spoke an indigenous language by 1921.[79] Most Cucapá-Mestizo men dressed like their mestizo fathers in pants and shirts, but wore their long hair braided. Women chose dresses instead of Indian attire and, like the men, wore their long hair braided.[80] Mestizo children visited relatives in El Mayor, Yuma, and Somerton, but only a few learned Yuma language or fishing and farming techniques. Adela Sandoval Portillo, granddaughter of Petra Laguna and Felix Portillo, lamented that the second generation of Cucapá-Mestizos did not want to learn indigenous fishing techniques, and instead chose to work as seasonal laborers on irrigation projects and cotton farms, much like mestizo migrant workers.[81]

Chinese Mexican children had similar experiences as Cocopah mestizo children. Most spoke both Cantonese and Spanish because their fathers spoke to them in Cantonese and their mothers spoke to them in Spanish. As Julian Lim has observed, the testimony of Manuel Lee Mancilla provides a window to examine how Chinese and Mexicans lived and challenged daily live on the border.[82] As the son of Flavia Mancilla Camacho and Manuel Lee Chew, he spoke both languages fluently. Manuel Lee Mancilla recalls how his mother, Flavia, taught him how to write and speak in Spanish to prepare him for elementary school.[83] But Manuel felt more comfortable speaking Cantonese, the language spoken at the farm where his father worked as a manager, and where he and his siblings spent most of their time. As a young child, his favorite foods were those given to him by the Chinese cook who prepared meals for the workers and maintained a vegetable garden near the cotton farms. On the farm, young Manuel got to know the vegetables and meat used to prepare authentic Chinese meals. He and his siblings ate with the Chinese workers, who often talked about various dishes from their villages back in China. But as Manuel and his siblings got older, they spent their days in school rather than the ranch. The Lee Mancilla children spoke Spanish at school and Cantonese at home. As an adult, Manuel Lee Mancilla volunteered as an interpreter for Chinese workers in the Mexicali Valley. Like his father, he married a Mexican mestizo woman, Enriqueta Sandoval from Tecate. Lee Mancilla and Sandoval later opened a restaurant called La Paloma Oriental that fused the flavors of Chinese and Mexican cuisines.

Nevertheless, as intermarriage between Chinese men and Mexican women became more common in northern Mexico, xenophobia and anti-Chinese sentiment were also on the rise. In Sonora, merchants and politicians pressured the Mexican government to pass laws banning marriages between Mexican women and Chinese men.

Anti-Chinese zealots scorned Mexican women who dared to marry Chinese men, whom the zealots considered genetically inferior.[84] They argued that the Chinese were of a lesser race, and that such marriages jeopardized the future of the Mexican nation.[85] During the 1920s, the states of Sonora and Sinaloa passed laws prohibiting intermarriage between Mexican women and Chinese men.[86] In 1923, Sonora passed Law 31, prohibiting marriage not only between Mexican women and Chinese men, but also between Mexican women and Chinese Mexican men, even naturalized Mexican citizens of Chinese descent.[87] Violators

were fined from 100 to 500 pesos. Women who married Chinese men were categorized as Chinese and were forced to register as foreigners. In addition, the
newspapers published the names of Mexican women married to Chinese men
to bring shame upon the wife and her extended family.[88]

In Baja California, there was no law prohibiting marriages between Mexican women and Chinese men, but the Department of Immigration enforced
the registration of Mexican women who were married to Chinese men. Isabel
Barrera Wong, a mestiza woman from El Triunfo, Baja California, had to register
as a foreigner because she married Mr. Wong, a migrant merchant from southern China (see figure 4.2).[89] The children of the Wong Barrera family were also
registered as foreigners, even though they were born in Baja California. Maria
Librada Wong Duarte and her brother, Alejandro Wong Duarte, mentioned earlier, were forced to register with the Department of Immigration as Chinese
nationals.[90] These immigration cards issued to Chinese Mexicans reveal the
contradictory nature of exclusion. The identifications defined their ethnicity as
mestizos of Chinese nationality.

Conclusion

As these stories attest, intermarriage played a central role in shaping Baja California
cultural, racial, and ethnic borderlands. Government plans to separate workers by
race and ethnicity were initially supported by land developers and mine managers.
For example, the Compagnie du Boleo designed a company town with strict boundaries segregating Asian and Mexican workers, and also separating workers from
managers. In the Mexicali Valley, Chinese workers lived on CRLC ranchos while
mestizos and Indian workers lived in Mexican colonias. Over time, intermarriage

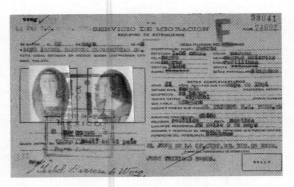

FIGURE 4.2. Isabel Barrera Wong from El Triunfo,
Baja California, immigration form F14. Courtesy of the
Archivo General de la Nación, Mexico City.

and cohabitation challenged these racial boundaries. Contrary to previous scholarship, my research demonstrates that Chinese, Japanese, and French workers did not live in what would be described as solely bachelor communities. Many intermarried with local mestizo and Indian women and settled permanently in Baja California. In Santa Rosalía, 70 percent of the European engineers who came to work at the Compagnie du Boleo married Mexican women. Chinese workers from Boleo also intermarried and cohabitated with Mexican women, and they moved out of company housing to settle in mixed race communities with their families.

In the Mexicali Valley mixed race families moved to Mexicali's downtown near the international border with Calexico, California, an area initially occupied by displaced Indians. After 1910, Mexicali became a booming town with Mexican, Chinese, and mixed race colonias. New government buildings were built in Mexicali's downtown after Cantú moved his post from Ensenada to Mexicali, near to the Mexican customs office. Mexicali became a municipality in 1914, and by 1917 government offices were relocated from Ensenada to Mexicali. Between 1917 and 1920, Chinese merchants and farmers purchased more than twenty lots in downtown Mexicali (for $100 to $1,000 per lot) to open casinos, restaurants, stores, and hotels. In 1917, Wong Wa Fey purchased two lots, which later became the first Chinese Association in Mexicali, later known as Chineseca (Chinatown).[91]

This essay also shows how indigenous and Mestizo women enabled migrant men to succeed in Baja California. The changing racial and ethnic landscape did not go unnoticed. The anti-Chinese movement led to policing of mixed race marriages marginalizing of Chinese Mexican families in northern Mexico during the 1920s and 1930s. When President Lázaro Cárdenas redistributed land in Baja California, it excluded Asian and Asian Mexican people from petitioning for communal farmland. Asian and Asian Mexican farmers were the first targeted during CRLC land expropriations in 1937. However, in spite of Mexico's efforts to exclude them, Asian men still benefited from land reform policies. Asian men who married Mexican women benefited from land distribution through their wives. Similarly, Asian Mexican farmers purchased private land in the Mexicali Valley where they continued to plant cotton and vegetables on a smaller scale. Asian Mexicans who did not purchase farms either migrated to the United States or lived in the city of Mexicali, where they worked for Chinese and Chinese Mexican merchants, restaurateurs, and casino owners in Mexicali's Chinatown.

By the 1940s, Asian and Asian Mexican people who remained in Mexicali continued to participate in the Chinese Association, which promoted the interest of the region's Chinese community throughout the twentieth century. To this day, the association offers Spanish and English classes for recent immigrants and sponsors Chinese schools for Chinese Mexican children. The association's continuity exemplifies that, in many ways, Asian and Asian Mexican workers in Baja California succeeded at challenging marginalization and discrimination by appropriating and shaping their own conceptions of *Mexicanidad*. Multiracial border towns like Mexicali extended across transnational borders and shaped communities by influencing labor practices, border politics, and migration patterns in the US-Mexico borderlands.

NOTES

1. "Registro de Extranjeros Chinos," Departamento de Migracion/Chinos/Caja 1/ Extranjeros, Exp. 150, Archivo General de la Nación, Mexico City.

2. Celso Aguirre Bernal, *Compendio Histórico Biográfico de Mexicali 1539–1966* (Mexicali: Mexicali, B. CFA, 1966); Dorothy Pierson Kerig, "Yankee Enclave: The Colorado River Land Company and Mexican Agrarian Reform in Baja California, 1902–1944" (PhD diss., University of California, Irvine, 1989); Everardo Garduño, *La Disputa Por La Tierra . . . La Disputa por La Voz: Historia Oral del Movimiento Agrario en el Valle de Mexicali* (Mexicali: Universidad Autónoma de Baja California, 2004); Rachel St. John, *Line in the Sand: A History of the U.S.-Mexico Border* (Princeton, NJ: Princeton University Press, 2011).

3. Censo General de Habitantes (Instituto General de Estadística y Geografía, 1920).

4. In colonial Mexico, the Spanish Crown created a caste system dividing racially mixed families into different categories. Initially, the word "mestizo" applied to the offspring of indigenous women and Spanish men, but by the nineteenth century it had evolved into a term used to indicate a broader range of racially mixed families, such as the children of African and Indian parents. Douglas Cope, *The Limits of Racial Domination in Colonial Mexico City* (Madison: University of Wisconsin Press, 1993); María Elena Martínez, *Genealogical Fictions: Limpieza de Sangre, Religion and Gender in Colonial Mexico* (Palo Alto, CA: Stanford University Press, 2008). These two sources offer more information on the concept of mestizo.

5. Robert Chao Romero, *The Chinese in Mexico* (Tucson: University of Arizona Press, 2010), 67; Evelyn Hu-DeHart, "China Towns and Borderlands: Inter-Asian Encounters in the Diaspora," *Modern Asian Studies* 46.2 (2012): 425–451; Julia María Schiavone Camacho, *Chinese Mexicans: Transpacific Migrations and the Search for a Homeland 1910–1960* (Chapel Hill: University of North Carolina Press, 2012); Grace Peña Delgado, *Making the Chinese Mexican: Global Migrations, Localisms and Exclusion in the Mexico-U.S. Borderlands* (Stanford, CA: Stanford University Press, 2012); Freddie González, "Chinese Dragon and Eagle of Anahuac: The Local, National, and International Implications of the Ensenada Anti-Chinese Campaign of 1934," *Western Historical Quarterly* 44.1 (2013): 48–68; Elliot Young, *Alien Nation: Chinese Migration in the Americas from the Coolie Era to World War II* (Chapel Hill: University of North Carolina Press, 2014); Jason Oliver Chang, "Racial Alterity in a Mestizo Nation," *Journal of Asian American Studies* 14.3 (2011): 331–359; Julia Lim, "Chinos and Paisanos: Chinese Mexican Relations in the Borderlands," *Pacific Historical Review* 79.19 (2010): 50–85.

6. Schiavone Camacho, *Chinese Mexicans*; Schiavone Camacho, "Crossing Boundaries, Claiming a Homeland: The Mexican Chinese Transpacific Journey to Becoming Mexican, 1930–1960," *Pacific Historical Review* 78.4 (2009): 545–577.

7. Paul Spickard, *Mixed Blood: Intermarriage and Ethnicity Identity in Twentieth-Century America* (Madison: University of Wisconsin Press, 1989).

8. Edward H. Spicer, *The Yaquis: A Cultural History* (Tucson: University of Arizona Press, 1980); Edward H. Spicer, *Cycles of Conquest: The Impact of Spain, Mexico, and the United States on the Indians of the Southwest 1533–1960* (Tucson: University of Arizona Press,

1962); José Patricio Nicoli, *El Estado de Sonora: Yaquis y Mayos* (Mexico City: Imprenta de Francisco Díaz de León, 1885); Edith Gonzalez Cruz, "La Inversión Francesa en la Minería Durante el Porfiriato" (thesis, Universidad Veracruzana, Xalapa, Veracruz, 1985). These four sources offer more information on the Yaqui Indians.

9. Compagnie du Boleo census records, 1893, 1895, and 1899, vols. 306–315, document 330, expediente 31, Archivo Histórico Pablo Martínez, La Paz, Baja California.

10. León Diguet, "La Basse-Californie d'après," *Annales de Geographie* 9.45 (1900): 243–250.

11. Erika Lee, "The Yellow Peril: Asian Exclusion in the Americas," *Pacific Historical Review* 76.4 (2007): 537–562; Hu-DeHart, "China Towns and Borderlands"; Schiavone Camacho, *Chinese Mexicans*; Peña Delgado, *Making the Chinese Mexican*.

12. Romero, *Chinese in Mexico*, 67.

13. The Chinese Exclusion Act prohibited unskilled Chinese workers from immigrating to the United States.

14. Trev Sue-A-Quan, *Cane Reapers: Chinese Indentured Immigrants in Guyana* (Vancouver: Riftswood, 1999); Clarence E. Glick, *Sojourners and Settlers: Chinese Migrants in Hawaii* (Honolulu: University of Hawai'i Press, 1980); Young, *Alien Nation*. These three sources offer more information on transpacific migration to the Caribbean, Hawai'i, and Latin America.

15. Memorias de Gobernación, 1907–1908, grupo Gobernación, Sección Colonización, pagina XIV, Archivo General de la Nación, Mexico City; Ramo de Gobernación, Jefatura Política del Distrito Sur de la Baja California, 1903–1911, Archivo Pablo Martínez, La Paz, Baja California Sur.

16. María Elena Ota Mishima, *Siete Migraciones Japonesas en México 1890–1978* (Mexico City: El Colegio de México, 1982), 53–54; Daniel Marterso with Funada-Classen, *The Japanese in Latin America* (Urbana: University of Illinois Press, 2004); Andrea Geiger, *Subverting Exclusion: Transpacific Encounters with Race, Caste and Borders, 1885–1928* (New Haven, CT: Yale University Press, 2011).

17. Ignacio Rivas Hernandez, "La Industria," in *Historia General de Baja California Sur I. La Economia Regional*, ed. Deni Trejo Barajas and Edith Gonzalez Cruz (La Paz: Universidad Autónoma de Baja California, 2002), 303.

18. In 1904, a vessel arrived from Japan with 400 Japanese workers. Historical document, July 21, 1904, vol. 383, document 570, expediente 5, Archivo Histórico Pablo Martínez, La Paz, Baja California. In 1908, a vessel arrived from Vladivostock with 473 Chinese workers contracted by the company. Ramón Corral, December 28, 1908, letter to government indicating vessel en route, Fondo Gobernación, vol. 469, document 460, expediente 74, Archivo Histórico Pablo Martínez, La Paz, Baja California; p. XLVII, 1907, Archivo General de la Nación, Mexico City.

19. Compagnie du Boleo meeting minutes, March 2, 1893, grupo gobernación, vol. 250, expediente 139, Archivo Histórico Pablo Martínez, La Paz, Baja California.

20. There is still some debate about who built the church. The Compagnie du Boleo did not keep a receipt of the purchase.

21. Registry of weddings and baptisms, 1895–1900, Iglesia de Santa Barbara, Santa Rosalia, Baja California.

22. Mexican census records from 1900, 1920, and 1930, vol. 919, expediente 33, Archivo Histórico Pablo Martínez, La Paz, Baja California.

23. File of applications for naturalization (Aplicaciones de Naturalización Mexicana a Extranjeros), 1917–1924, Juzgado Primero del Distrito, Casa de la Cultura Juridica, Mexicali, Baja California.

24. Norton B. Stern, *Jewish Refuge and Homeland* (Los Angeles: Dawson's Book, 1973).

25. Historical document, vol. 919, expediente 33, Archivo Histórico Pablo Martínez, La Paz, Baja California.

26. Out of the 823,620 acres owned by the CRLC, 146,596 acres were categorized as mountains, riverbeds, or lakes. Allison, "Reclamation of the Lower Colorado."

27. Mexican census records from 1910 and 1921, Baja California, Instituto Nacional de Estadística y Geografía.

28. Mexican census records from 1890 and 1910, Northern Territory of Baja California, Instituto Nacional de Estadística y Geografía.

29. In 1917, some Cocopah families left the Mexicali Valley for Yuma, Arizona, after receiving reservation land grants approved by US President Woodrow Wilson the same year. Inter Tribal Council of Arizona, "Cocopah Tribe: Introductory Information," www.itcaonline.com; Otis Tout, *The First Thirty Years in Imperial Valley California* (San Diego: Otis Tout Publisher, 1931), 273; Alvarez de Williams, *The Cocopah People* (Phoenix: Indian Travel Series, 1974), 42; St. John, *Line in the Sand*, 79.

30. "Indios broncos que no hablaban ni jota de español y que no nos dejaban vivir en paz, pues a cada rato nos balaceaban, principalmente cuando pretendíamos salir después de la puesta del sol." Pablo Herrera Carrillo, *Reconquista y Colonización del Valle de Mexicali y Otros Escritos Paralelos* (Mexicali: Universidad Autónoma de Baja California, 2002), 112.

31. Oral statements, "Pioneros y Fundadores de Mexicali," box V, expediente 47, fondo Pablo Martínez, Archivo Histórico del Gobierno del Estado, Mexicali, Baja California; José Alfredo Gómez Estrada, *La Gente del Delta del Rio Colorado: Indigenas, colonizadores y ejidatarios* (Mexicali: Universidad Autonoma de Baja California, 2000).

32. A. J. Flores to Ramón Sumaya, report of purchases and sales, February 12, 1909, Office of the Notary of the State of Baja California, book 10, Protocolo de Primera Instancia, Mexicali, Baja California.

33. Aguirre Bernal, *Compendio.*

34. Harrington W. Cochran, report on Baja California, 1919, 130-E and 38, box 001, Special Collections, University of California, Irvine; Herrera Carrillo, *Reconquista y Colonización*, 147.

35. CRLC rental agreement, 1933, box 67, Sherman Library, Corona del Mar, California.

36. Aguirre Bernal, *Compendio*; Kerig, "Yankee Enclave."

37. Adela Sandoval Portillo, oral interview in Gómez Estrada, *La Gente del Delta.*

38. Ibid.

39. Mexican census records from the Northern Territory and Southern Territory of Baja California, 1910 and 1921, Instituto Nacional de Estadística y Geografía.

40. Mexican census records from the Northern Territory of Baja California, 1910 and 1921, Instituto Nacional de Estadística y Geografía.

41. Mexican census records from the Northern Territory of Baja California, 1921, Instituto Nacional de Estadística y Geografía.

42. Adela Sandoval Portillo, interview in Gómez Estrada, *La Gente del Delta*; Mexican census records from the Northern Territory of Baja California, 1910 and 1921, Instituto Nacional de Estadística y Geografía.

43. Florence C. Shipek, ed., *Autobiography of Delfina Cuero* (Menlo Park, CA: Ballenas Press, 1991), 62.

44. Elwood Mead, "The Southwest International Problems," 1919, *San Francisco Chronicle*, in Jas. D. Schuyler Papers, Water Research Archive Center, University of California, Berkeley.

45. Ibid.; quote from Eric Boime, "Beating Plowshares into Swords: The Colorado River Delta, the Yellow Peril, and the Movement for Federal Reclamation, 1901–1928," *Pacific Historical Review* 78.1 (2009): 49.

46. Herrera Carrillo, *Reconquista y Colonización*; Kerig, "Yankee Enclave," 162.

47. Cochran, report on Baja California; María Eugenia Anguiano, *Agricultura y Migración en el Valle de Mexicali* (Tijuana: El Colegio de la Frontera Norte, 1995), 77; Herrera Carrillo, *Reconquista y Colonización*, 162.

48. Cochran, report on Baja California.

49. Kerig, "Yankee Enclave," 162.

50. Mexican laborers who migrated to the United States faced precarious living and labor conditions. Gilbert González explains how Mexican families lived in poor, segregated enclaves throughout the Southwest. Gilbert G. González, *Labor and Community: Mexican Citrus Worker Villages in Southern California County 1890–1950* (Chicago: University of Illinois Press, 1994), 8.

51. Lawrence A. Cardoso, *Mexican Emigration to the United States, 1897–1931: Socio-economic Patterns* (Tucson: University of Arizona Press, 1980).

52. "Imperial America's Fertile Winter Garden," *Los Angeles Times*, January 1, 1920.

53. Ibid.

54. Chinese people continued to go to the United States illegally, but their rate of immigration slowed. Romero, *Chinese in Mexico*, 1–16.

55. US Department of Agriculture published report (1917), 18; González, *Labor and Community*, 7.

56. Vicki Ruiz, *From Out of the Shadows: Mexican Women in Twentieth-Century America* (New York: Oxford University Press, 1998), 11–12; David Gutiérrez, *Walls and Mirrors: Mexican Americans, Mexican Immigrants, and the Politics of Ethnicity* (Berkeley: University of California Press, 1995); George J. Sánchez, *Becoming Mexican American: Ethnicity, Culture, and Identity in Chicano Los Angeles, 1900–1945* (New York: Oxford University Press, 1993).

57. Mariano Ma, statement in Herrera Carrillo, *Reconquista y Colonización*, 439.

58. Almost all Chinese immigrants and merchants who applied for Mexican citizenship between 1917 and 1924 declared that they were from Canton, China. File of applications for naturalization, 1917–1924, Juzgado Primero del Distrito, Casa de la Cultura Juridica, Mexicali, Baja California.

59. Cochran, report on Baja California; Kerig, "Yankee Enclave," 157.

60. Robert H. Duncan, "The Chinese and the Economic Development of Northern Baja California, 1889–1929," *Hispanic American Historical Review* 74.4 (1994): 623; Romero, *Chinese in Mexico*, 35.

61. "Como contratista o como mayordomo y teniendo bajo mis ordenes a hombres de numerosas nacionalidades: Mexicanos, Chinos, Japoneses y Norteamericanos. . . . En ciertas temporadas llegué a tener bajo mis ordenes hasta 2,000 hombres que en ocasiones tenia necesidad de reclutar y movilizar como un ejercito." Herrera Carrillo, *Reconquista y Colonización*, 439.

62. K. Lato and Ben Kodama, court report, 1920, file of applications for naturalization, 1917–1924.

63. Evelyn Hu-DeHart, "La Comunidad China," *Revista Ciguatan*, no. 17 (1988): 16.

64. File of applications for naturalization, 1917–1924.

65. Ibid.

66. Cochran likely categorized indigenous people, Mexican mestizos, and Chinese Mexicans all as "Mexicans." Cochran, report on Baja California.

67. Casey Christensen, "Mujeres Publicas: American Prostitutes in Baja California, 1910–1930," *American Historical Review* 82 (May 2013): 215–247; Eric Schantz, "From the Mexicali Rose to the Tijuana Brass: Vice Tours of the United States-Mexico Border 1910–1965" (PhD diss., University of California, Los Angeles, 2001).

68. Calculated from marriage statistics in Abelardo Rodríguez, *Memoria Administrativa. Del Gobierno del Distrito Norte de la Baja California 1924–1927* (1927; repr., Mexico City: Universidad Autónoma de Baja California, 1993), 336.
69. Romero, *Chinese in Mexico*; Schiavone Camacho, *Chinese Mexicans*.
70. Peña Delgado, *Making the Chinese Mexican*; Schiavone Camacho, *Chinese Mexicans*, 31.
71. Ibid.
72. Ibid.
73. Manuel Lee Mancilla, *Viaje al Corazón de La Península: Testimonio de Manuel Lee Mancilla* (Mexicali: Instituto de la Cultura de Baja California, 2000).
74. José Vasconcelos, *La Raza Cósmica* (Los Angeles: California State University, Los Angeles, Centro de Publicaciones Department of Chicano Studies, 1979).
75. Ibid.
76. Adela Sandoval Portillo, interviewed in Gómez Estrada, *La Gente del Delta*, 110–111.
77. Statement by Portillo, Archivo Histórico del Gobierno del Estado, Mexicali, Baja California.
78. Adelina married Condrio Garcia. Juana married Stanislao Sandoval; after he abandoned her, she cohabitated with Juan Valenzuela, a migrant mestizo worker from Guymas Sonora. Agrarian Census, expediente, Ejido Cucapá, 1937, Registro Agrario Nacional, Baja California.
79. Mexican census data on languages, 1921, Northern Territory of Baja California, Instituto Nacional de Estadística y Geografía.
80. Secretaria de la Economia Nacional, Mexican census data on population, 1910 and 1921, Northern Territory of Baja California.
81. Statement by Portillo.
82. Lim, "Chinos and Paisanos."
83. Lee Mancilla, *Viaje al Corazón de La Península.*
84. Letter to Governor Agustín Olachea, Baja California Norte, in José Gómez Izquierdo, *El Movimiento Antichino en México 1871–1934: Problemas del Racismo y del Nacionalismo Durante la Revolución Mexicana* (Mexico City: Instituto Nacional de Antropología e Historia, 1991), 146.
85. José Angel Espinoza, *El Ejemplo de Sonora* (Mexico: Edicion Privada, 1932); Rodríguez, *Memoria Administrativa*, 58.
86. Catalina Velázquez Morales, *Los Imigrantes Chinos en Baja California, 1920–1937* (Mexicali: Universidad Autónoma de Baja California, 2001), 191.
87. Espinosa, *El Ejemplo de Sonora*, 35.
88. Camacho, "Crossing Boundaries."
89. See Registro de Extranjeros, Caja 46, Expediente 64, Archivo General de la Nación, Mexico City.
90. Maria Librada La Paz, Baja California Registration Immigration Form (F14), 1933, Alejandro Vicente Wong, Baja California Registration Immigration Form (F14), 1933, Registro de Extranjeros Chinos, Departamento de Migracion/Chinos/Caja 1/Extranjeros, Exp. 160, Archivo General de la Nación, Mexico City.
91. Registro de la Propiedad, Ensenada, Baja California, 1917.

5

Cross-Racial Minority Intermarriage

Mutual Marginalization and Critique

JESSICA VASQUEZ-TOKOS

In 1959 Judge Leon Bazile defended Virginia's prohibition against interracial marriage by opining, "Almighty God created the races white, black, yellow, malay and red, and he placed them on separate continents. And but for the interference with his arrangement there would be no cause for such marriages. The fact that he separated the races shows he did not intend for the races to mix."[1] Using an essentialist view of race, Judge Bazile convicted the trial court defendants, Mildred Loving, a Black woman, and Richard Loving, a White man, of violating Virginia's Racial Integrity Act of 1924 designed to prevent interracial relationships.[2] This court opinion not only suggests that racial mixing is anathema but in so doing upholds the racial hierarchy—in particular White supremacy—through essentializing race and demanding racial separation. By ruling to uphold the racial order, the orating judge implies a fear over such pairings. In interviewing non-White cross-racial married couples, my study puts the margin at the center.[3] By using this vantage point—of centering the periphery[4]—I argue that the ramifications of non-White romantic partnerships that are founded upon an experience of mutual marginalization are not the production of "a mongrel population and a degraded civilization" but instead generate a critique of racial and gender inequality in the United States.

Patricia Hill Collins argues that being an "outsider within"—someone who is marginal to and oppressed by the larger social structure—allows for a poignant critique of the system.[5] In this chapter, the notion of outsiders within comes alive as a lived experience for non-White racially heterogeneous couples.[6] The orienting questions for this chapter are threefold: How might being an outsider within motivate cross-racial minority marriage? How do interracial minority couples—who are similar in their marginality but dissimilar in their racial status—experience race? How does race operate within cross-racial families?

This chapter draws from twelve individuals (six heterosexual couples) who represent a portion of a larger project on racial endogamy and exogamy. These married pairs include one US-born Latino (or, if foreign-born, a person who arrived in the United States by age twelve) and a non-Latino racial minority (Asian, Black, or Native American). Of the six Latinos, five are US-born and one is Mexican-born; five are Latina women and one is a Latino man. The non-Latino racial minority side of the pair includes Chinese American (2), Native American, multiracial Black/White (2), and Japanese American. Interviews were conducted in California and Kansas, the intent in the larger project to compare a border state with high racial diversity to an interior state that is predominately non-Hispanic White. Of the six couples, three reside in California, three in Kansas. I recruited participants through Latino-serving organizations, high schools, professional contacts, and snowball sampling where I asked interviewees for referrals. The interviews lasted one to two hours and were conducted at a location chosen by the interviewee. The interviews took a life history approach, beginning with early life, moving through schooling and dating experiences, and culminating in questions about marriage choices, marital life, cultural practices, and child rearing. I used Dedoose, an online qualitative data analysis software program, to assist in the coding process. I engaged in inductive analysis of interview material, reading verbatim interview transcripts and field notes for pertinent themes around issues of race, gender, marriage, and family dynamics.[7]

Prior scholarship has not shed much light on *dual-minority* couples, most work to date focusing on Black/White,[8] Asian/White,[9] and Latino/White couples.[10] Intermarriage scholarship tends to ask questions concerning social distance or changing rates of intermarriage over time. This chapter uses cross-racial minority pairings, an overlooked demographic reality, to delve into the reasons behind marriage trends as well as the ramifications of them. The chief reasons my respondents gave for intermarriage with a member of another minority group are a non-White minority-minority connection and women's desire to escape patriarchy through out-marriage. As far as consequences of cross-minority marriages, sharing a non-White status but belonging to different racial groups opens the possibility of overt race-oriented discussions. Race and culture are discussed in these homes, with both historical and contemporary issues transported into everyday conversations. Most couples were race-conscious and cultivated both an American identity and racial minority pride; those who stressed American identity did so out of recognition of race as a salient social feature. Couples who were parents hoped they were harbingers of a multicultural and multiracial American future, this stance an effort to preserve their culture(s) as well as a critique of rigid racial categories and hegemonic Whiteness.

Making Marriage Choices

Minority-Minority Connection: Mutual Marginalization as a Bond

Dual-minority partnerships are often founded on a non-White connection that facilitates a race-conscious critique of US racial history and race relations. While this minority-minority bond can occur among people who are mixed with Whiteness, this finding was prominent among racial minorities and mixed race individuals without White heritage, non-Whiteness lending itself to a marginalized perspective that craves consensus. Three couples were passionate about the comfort they feel with a marital partner who shares their racial subordination. To understand each other fully, these couples feel they need to share an outsider-within status. Moreover, the way that these pairs draw links between their racially disparate but similarly oppressed backgrounds demonstrates how "racial categorizations constantly evolve, and groups may develop a panethnic consciousness that transgresses 'official' designations."[11]

Penelope Rio, who is Mexican American and Native American (Ojibwa, otherwise known as Chippewa), and Travis Strong, who is Native American (Lakota), felt cultural commonality because they are both non-White. Speaking from his racially peripheral status, Native American Travis expressed a deep and dear connection with Mexican people, saying, "We are all Brown people," as he rubbed his index finger along his arm to indicate his tan skin color. He is highly sensitive to the historical oppression, including forced removal, of Native Americans, and this subjugation is the primary reason why he feels a bond with Mexican Americans who were similarly dispossessed of land,[12] and nowadays face the threat of deportation.[13] Travis grew up off-reservation in Colorado and South Dakota, where Native/Mexican mixed families were part of the racial landscape: "A lot of Lakota families married into Mexican families. A lot of Lakotas have Mexican last names. . . . But they were . . . a big part of the Native community, too. . . . They mingle in like that, marriage-wise." Travis took cues about the compatibility between Native Americans and Mexican Americans not only from his own observations of marriage patterns, but also from community leaders such as medicine men: "Talking with a lot of the medicine men—the spiritual leaders—we are all the same. We don't . . . call Mexicans 'them.' In *our* eyes, the Lakota eyes, they are our brothers and sisters, they are no different—they're Indians too. That's why a lot of our medicine men treat spiritually the Mexicans now, for healing. . . . So we look at them as the same, there's no difference."

One reason for Natives' acceptance of Mexicans as "brothers and sisters" is historical. "They're Indians too" harkens back to the historic origins of indigenous oppression at the hands of the Spanish conquering forces of Hernán

Cortés in Montezuma's Aztec empire in the 1530s. First, Aztecs and other tribes in present-day Mexico are indigenous to the Americas, just as Native Americans are to the United States. Second, both Mexicans and Native Americans suffered deterritorialization and diaspora as a result of conquest. Significant parts of Mexico were ceded to the United States due to provisions of the Treaty of Guadalupe Hidalgo (1848) that ended the Mexican-American War. This move echoes the forced removal of Native Americans instituted by US government legislation such as the Indian Removal Act of 1830 that was the genesis of the Trail of Tears.[14] Conquest and deterritorialization are common themes between Native Americans and people of Mexican descent, making Mexicans "Indians too," in Travis's eyes. The shared experience of colonization is central to this cross-racial minority couple's bond.

Being historically marginalized from the mainstream offers a basis of critique, Travis juxtaposing White culture with non-White ethnic culture: "You don't get stuck in this everyday rut of 'dog eat dog world' if you've got culture. You can always activate the culture button and everything will be okay after that." By culture, Travis means song, dance, and ethnic celebrations. Travis draws a comparison with his White brothers-in-law who do not "share about who they are" and whose "culture seems like to be just basketball." Judging this lack of culture as "sad," Travis's narrative reflects a pattern whereby Mexican Americans and Native Americans discursively valorize minority culture and critique White society in order to reinvest their derogated groups with esteem.[15]

Penelope Rio agrees with Travis that their mutual marginalization is a bond. She was raised in Horton, Kansas, knowing only the simple fact that she was half Native on her mother's side. Oppression of Native Americans kept Penelope's mother ashamed of her Native heritage until she reclaimed it (through Penelope and Travis) at the end of her life. Due to poverty, Penelope's maternal grandparents sent her mother to a boarding school in South Dakota, retrieving her in the eighth grade when she threatened to commit suicide. Indian boarding schools were established in the United States during the late nineteenth and early twentieth centuries to educate Native American youth according to Euro-American standards. The schools were originally established by Christian missionaries, but the Bureau of Indian Affairs created the assimilation-model schools that over a hundred thousand Native Americans were forced to attend.[16] Native American children were immersed in Euro-American culture: they were forbidden to speak their native languages, their traditional dress and haircuts were changed, and their given names were replaced by Anglophone names. Boarding schools were a heavy-handed approach to Anglo-conformity, forcing abandonment of Native American identity.[17] Penelope's Mexican American father also suffered racism: despite being a high school "big basketball stud," he was forced to "stay in the boiler room" at state championships because "the hotel . . . wouldn't allow him a room."

For those minorities sensitive to their history of oppression, finding another minority partner with whom they share a *racialized affinity* was a clear preference. Trinity and Rodrigo Valencia gravitated toward one another because racial subordination (and class disadvantage) played a large role in their lives and they needed to share this foundation in order to feel intimately understood. Trinity Valencia, a biracial Black/White woman, says relative to her dating history, "I was always attracted to men of color—even though I was surrounded by White men. . . . My choices had always been . . . men of color." I asked, "What draws you to them?" Trinity links her experience of being a racial outsider to her preference for men of color: "Just feeling like [men of color] would understand what it's like to be an 'other.' Not always feeling comfortable in the White culture. . . . Yeah, shared experience and someone who understands being an 'other.'" The experience of being a racial "other" is so fundamental that it was essential to share this experience with a loved one.

Rodrigo Valencia, Trinity's Mexican American husband, preferred the company of Mexican Americans or Blacks because of their "life experience" similarities. Rodrigo and Trinity met working for a college preparatory program that serves high school students from low-income families and families in which neither parent holds a bachelor's degree. Even their place of meeting, a summer job helping disadvantaged students gain admission to and succeed in college, reveals the extent to which they care about racial and class inequality. Rodrigo explains his desire for a racial minority life partner: "The people I was *interested* in . . . [were] either Mexican American/Hispanic or . . . Black. . . . [When I met Trinity] I thought, 'She's biracial . . . [we] have similarities in . . . life experiences.'" "Life experiences" captures both race- and class-related subordination. For my respondents, it was not critical to mirror one another's racial background in order to be on the racial periphery together and share that marginal perspective.

In cross-minority pairs, racial subordination was a unifying transcendent theme. In "half and half" pairs that are biracial and share Whiteness, the experience of non-Whiteness overriding Whiteness facilitated bonding. Caroline and Bryce Wu are both half Caucasian, yet despite having claims to Whiteness, they feel marginal to mainstream US society. Even calling themselves "half and half" suggests that they do not feel accepted by the US public, otherwise their mixed race status would go unmentioned.[18] This illustrates a similarity among mixed race individuals who do and do not include Whiteness: everyday racialization that telegraphs a subordinated status can render inconsequential a technical entitlement to Whiteness.

Caroline Wu is a thirty-one-year-old woman who was born to an Ecuadorian mother and a White father. Like Penelope Rio and Travis Strong, Caroline feels a comfort in discomfort, taking solace that she and her husband Bryce are mixed race. She describes her first reaction to her half White, half Chinese husband: "[What] I did like about him right away . . . right off the bat . . . was that he was half just like me. . . . I really latched onto that [as] something that we had in common. . . . We have this one major thing in common, which is growing up . . . with one foot in each culture in Kansas." The experience of being "half" was so central to Caroline's life experience that she instantly felt a visceral connection to Bryce. They share an experience of not fitting into neatly bounded racial categories or cultures.

Dual-minority couples make creative connections with one another, as Travis Strong did by referring to himself and his wife as phenotypically Brown people. Caroline made similar inventive links: "My cousins say he looks more Latin than I do. . . . [Laughter.] It's the Black hair. . . . Besides the obvious, like physical characteristics, there's the food . . . eating things that aren't . . . part of the regular day to day American diet . . . things that are steamed or . . . wrapped. . . . Often we joke . . . that Chinese and Ecuadorian people really are the same race. [Laughter.]" Understandings of racial identity evolve, as we see among cross-racial minority respondents who perceive and assert similarity where others would not. Anthony Ocampo observes this with Filipinos who see greater cultural affinity with Latinos than Asians based on a history of Spanish conquest: "despite linguistic, socio-economic and cultural differences, ethnic groups develop panethnic consciousness . . . emphasizing cultural commonalities or highlighting shared racial experiences."[19] This process of identifying and underscoring commonality that underlies apparent differences reveals mechanisms behind panethnicity and cross-racial coalitions.

Bryce, too, feels comfort with a spouse who shares his half White and half minority experience. He feels a bond with Caroline because she struggled with issues of race and acceptance as he did: "[Caroline's] mom . . . spoke Spanish, she was from Ecuador . . . and her dad was [from] Texas, Oklahoma, Kansas. [That] kind of mix . . . I think really . . . was intriguing for me. It's like, 'oh, here is someone who . . . went through some of the same self-realization that I went through, but not the same culture.' . . . There were common experiences with a different twist. . . . She understood going to family reunions and having all the older generation speaking . . . Spanish. I would go and they'd all be speaking Chinese." Being mixed race with immigrant ancestors is qualitatively different from being monoracial with native-born forbearers, and sharing this experience with a spouse is a source of connection. Many interracial minority couples echoed Bryce's comment that "support and understanding [comes from] having gone through some of the same things." While outsider-within experiences can be discomforting, sharing that experience is grounds for bonding.

Critique of Gender and Racial Inequality

The dual-minority marriages also had a gendered aspect to them. The Latinas I interviewed who had domineering fathers generalized that quality to all Latino men and excluded Latino men from their prospective long-term romantic partners. This moratorium on Latino men freezes masculinity in the image of one's father and forecloses the opportunity to become familiar with men who enact different forms of masculinity.[20] Latinas who out-married with non-Latino, non-White men did so for two chief purposes: to find a heterosexual partner whose gender ideology was more egalitarian and to avoid racial othering they associated with Whites.

Penelope was unhappy with her natal family's patriarchal structure and the gendered division of labor: "I have three brothers: they didn't have to do any of the work hardly. The girls all took care of all the other kids, did all the laundry, helped in the kitchen, and I just didn't think that was very fair. . . . I really rebelled against that thinking." Part of Penelope's rebellion was to reject Latino men as potential marital partners. She dated men from various backgrounds, yet she "never dated a Mexican man" because she "just didn't want it," referring to the male authority she associated with her father. "It was by choice," a racialized affinity, that she preferred to associate with Native Americans and learn more about her Native heritage. Penelope chose to "put [herself] in that . . . scene," including attending powwows, which led to meeting her husband. Penelope escaped the brand of masculinity she resisted in her youth through both shifting *away from* Latino culture and *toward* Native culture: "I . . . turned off the Mexican side and the *macho-ism*. . . . I just feel a lot more comfortable in the Native culture. . . . I just feel better, identifying and raising my family as Native." Her reaction to generalize her father's dominance to his entire ethnic group has intergenerational consequences, as she raises her daughter not as Mexican American, a defamed category in her mind due to gender inequality, but as Native American.

Inez Korteweg, a Mexican immigrant, also preferred an out-group member, hoping to find a partner who was not patriarchal and abusive like her father. Inez explained why she married outside of the Latino category: "I married out of my culture . . . because I didn't feel that I could work out with someone born [in Mexico] or have the mentality of a [Mexican] man. I don't fit that traditional role. My dad always said I needed to learn to cook and clean . . . so that my husband would be happy with me. I hated it. . . . I didn't want to be my mom. . . . I didn't want to be submissive. I didn't want to be taken advantage of. I wanted to have a voice." Critical of both her parents, Inez resisted her father's "mentality" and the "traditional role" he socialized her to fulfill and her mother's position as "submissive." Not wanting to turn into her mother—"taken advantage of" and without a "voice"—meant avoiding a man like her father who enforced a narrow definition of femininity. Inez's father "was very abusive emotionally, physically, psychologically," getting "really upset" and "smacking her mother if she neglected to put an appropriate utensil on the table." Inez summarized, "I guess you call it *machismo*. . . . I didn't want that disrespect."

As a stay-at-home mother, Inez stressed that this was her "choice," her husband Darnell's egalitarian gender ideology allaying her concerns about being controlled by him. Darnell conveyed his gender egalitarian perspective: "I'm not a *Machista* [macho man]. . . . I wash dishes and . . . I'll carry my wife's purse. . . . I don't see it as a male role or a female role. I'm not raising my boys to think that cutting the lawn is a male thing and washing the dishes is a female thing. . . . It's not like I'm going to trump her because I'm the man." Darnell and Inez cocreate an emotionally stable and gender egalitarian household that is in stark contrast to Inez's natal family. Yet, as prominent as gender ideologies are in motivating Inez and Darnell's partnership, race is not entirely absent. Rejecting racial descriptors, they both stress they are "human." Leveraging rhetoric of humanity, this couple tries to dislocate the racial classification system. Significantly, this move comes from non-White (and immigrant, in Inez's case) people who, despite their focus on humanity, recognize their disadvantage in the racial order. It is their very awareness of racial (and immigrant status) inequality that catalyzes their discourse of humanity, this race-minimizing rhetoric a strategy for inclusion in American identity.[21]

Being on the non-White side of the White/non-White divide, minority respondents did not experience their race as the taken-for-granted standard as Whites typically do.[22] Not being situated at the top of the social hierarchy affords a type of situated knowledge derived from a particular vantage point.[23] For intermarried minority men and women, connection on racial minority grounds is important. For Latina women previously subjugated or abused by Latino fathers, avoiding Latino men influenced their marriage decision. Yet, why not marry White men? For the Latinas in this chapter, Whites lacked a perspective they valued: that of a minority man who comprehends the power of race. In this formulation, the Latina women critiqued both Latino men for aggression and White men for lacking a perspective on race and power. Marriage with a non-Latino minority man is the answer, provided that he is also nonviolent and race-conscious. Intermarried minority men and women valued their non-White commonality and the awareness of race it entailed, while women also sought non-overbearing men.

Intermarried minority pairs view their relationships as racial havens. Within these relationships where both partners had experienced racial marginality from society at large, couples can grieve racial wounds, rail against racial inequities, and ponder potential racial futures. As these pairs coconstruct a home life together, they create a racial and cultural environment that they perceive to be safe, shared, and liberatory.

Voices of Outsiders Within: Living Interracial Lives

Relationship to Mainstream Society

While the mainstream is remade by immigration,[24] the extent to which minorities feel included in the mainstream is debatable. Of the twelve people represented in this chapter, six felt that they were peripheral to mainstream society, four said they fit within mainstream society, and two gave inexact answers.

All six people (50 percent of respondents) who said they were peripheral to mainstream society were immigrants to the United States, children of immigrants, or Native Americans. All were very familiar with their family's immigrant narrative or their oppressed group history. Five of the six respondents were from Kansas, and one was from California. Being a racial minority in a dual-minority relationship has a different social meaning in predominately White Kansas than in racially heterogeneous California. People perceive themselves to be on the periphery of mainstream society if immigration is a generationally recent memory and if they reside in a predominately White social context. As a consequence of feeling like an outsider, four of these six people used their occupations related to racial diversity to offer social critique and remedy. Turning to the private realm, those who felt peripheral preferred to marry a fellow minority, and they anticipated that racial marginality would be a basis for bonding.

Four intermarried interviewees (one-third of respondents) said that they fit comfortably within mainstream society, whatever they envisioned that term to mean. Two (both Asian American men) of the four who said they fit mainstream society cited their middle- or upper-class status to justify their answer. Leveraging both birthright and socioeconomic status, Russ Cheng remarked, "I'd say that we're Americans. Besides both born here, both of us worked and are retired, have a good retirement plan. That's what mainstream America is." Socioeconomic status is used here to compensate for a racial minority status and legitimate why he and his wife belong to mainstream society.

All four people who felt they were part of mainstream society lived in California. Living in a racially diverse environment like Los Angeles County normalizes both multiraciality and interracial romantic relationships. Two respondents called on multiraciality to justify their sense of belonging. Russ Cheng qualifies his statement of fitting in by saying that he fits in "multiethnic environments." Darnell Korteweg says that as mixed race and intermarried he is a harbinger of a multiracial society: "I'm . . . what the world is becoming." For both of these men who say they are part of mainstream US society, their vision of "mainstream" is specifically *multiracial*, not Anglo-dominant. Their local heterogeneous environment of Los Angeles County bolsters their claims of a racially mixed society. All four of the non-White respondents who do not feel outside of mainstream US society use justifications—either multiracial society as a the new norm or high class status—to *qualify* their belonging to mainstream society.

Racial Awareness Connects the Past to the Present

Oppression is remembered and discussed frequently among cross-racial minority pairs. Not only does conversation concerning historical eras of racial injustice produce a bond among interracial minority couples, it also lays the groundwork to connect past oppression to contemporary inequality. In cross-minority pairs we see an evaluative process of comparative subordination wherein individuals identify parallels with other non-White groups, underscoring how the power of race transcends the historical moment.

History was alive in the present in cross-minority couples due to their overt discussion of historical racial oppression. Historical events and power differentials informed interracial minority couples' views on contemporary racial issues. Among couples with different racial backgrounds, group histories of race-based domination are a connective theme. Cross-racial minority couples, including half Whites, are outsiders within who possess two *different* racial minority perspectives, and they cast a bright light on how the nation has systematically used race as a tool to privilege some and oppress others.

Travis Strong, who works in building maintenance at Haskell Indian Nations University in Lawrence, Kansas, offers a striking example of how history is alive in the present. Operating since 1884 and originally a residential boarding school for American Indian children, Haskell attracts students from various tribal nations in the United States. Travis illustrates how Native experience with colonialism at the hands of the US federal government is alive in, and casts a pall on, the present day:

> There was a person that came to Haskell, a White guy. He had something in a box and he said, "I'm lost, can you direct me to somebody? I need to give these to somebody." Well, what is it? . . . He unveils it. He goes, "My grandfather gave me these years ago. He used to use these. . . ." It turned out to be a little kids' handcuffs. Handcuffs. His grandfather would gather all these Indian kids and bring them to boarding schools. Forcefully. It just tore you apart because they were made for little wrists, they were scaled down. He said he couldn't live with those handcuffs no more. . . . Man, we freaked out. We had to have [cleansing] ceremonies. It just tore everybody up. . . . It's a good reminder, though, of what went on.

Haskell began as a boarding school for Native Americans where they were forcibly taken to undergo cultural stripping and retraining in the name of

"Americanization." A harsh brand of Anglo-conformity assimilation, Americanization programs were not unique to Native peoples but also targeted other immigrant groups such as Latinos and Asians.[25]

Travis continues, "Haskell is still Haskell from years ago. It is very much alive. What I mean by that is the past still makes its presence." He cited a recent example of an apparition caught on camera that the Cultural Center director confirmed wore the dress and haircut of the boarding school days. The past being very much alive is seen in Haskell's concerted effort to preserve history, such as maintaining a graveyard on Haskell land and nearby wetlands and safeguarding historical records at the Cultural Center. For his part, Travis participates in the restoration of racial memory through race-conscious conversations with his family and his intentional transmission of Native culture.[26]

Travis sees the similarities between the Native and Mexican group histories as a reason for interracial coalition. His concluding remark reemphasizes interracial connections: "We consider the Mexicans as our brothers and sisters now. . . . A lot of boundaries went down: we need each other as allies. This is our Mexican and Native lands, you know. . . . We are coming back as Brown people." Using the term "Brown people," which refers more to skin color than political movements (which were two distinct movements, Brown Power and Red Power, during the civil rights era) rhetorically *unifies* Natives and Mexicans. By highlighting their similar dispossessed histories, their non-White phenotype, and other issues such as "violence, drug runs, land disputes, water rights . . . the 'haves' and 'have-nots,'" Travis enumerates the reasons to act as a coalition. Travis tacitly invokes the notion of linked fate,[27] a concept that refers to political action whereby group interests are seen as a proxy for self-interest. Multiple subordinated groups identifying as "Brown" due to their interconnections would be a powerful way to combat race-based inequality. At minimum, this interracial solidarity is a solid foundation for his marriage.

Trinity Valencia's ruminations on her intersectional oppression as a woman of color are also laced with history. When I asked about her experience as a woman of color, Trinity drew out the particular situation of Black women in America: "This entire nation was built on the backs of Black women. . . . Black women go through all this struggle and they still provide for their families and they're still this strong rock. . . . A lot of time people count me out because I am a woman of color. . . . I . . . really identify with the Maya Angelou poem 'Still I Rise.' . . . Sometimes when I'm feeling . . . marginalized or invisible, I recognize that . . . people before me have played a strong role in creating the country and getting us where we are today." Trinity has a sharply gendered racial consciousness, the long history of racial and gender inequality very real to her. Her narrative ushers history into the present moment, referring to Black women's "struggle" in slavery and yet their persistence as "strong rocks." Moving to the contemporary moment, Trinity says she is "counted out" as a minority woman, a modern slave of a gender and race hierarchy in which Black women are at the bottom. As a spokesperson for multiculturalism in her personal and professional life—she works in a multicultural office in higher education—Trinity credits historical figures who worked for equality. History is one way Trinity gauges the progress that has been made and the work still to be done. As we saw, Trinity selected her life partner based on their similarity of racialized and class-disadvantaged position. This motivation for marriage to a non-White is directly related to the consequence of cross-minority intermarriage: racist histories are alive in the present and intersecting oppressions are topics of concern.

Interracial Familial Relationships: Ethnic Culture and Racial Awareness

Revivification of non-White culture is a critical response to historical racial oppression and contemporary racial marginalization. By bringing to the fore positive aspects of racial minority culture, these couples reposition themselves from the margin to the center. Caroline and Bryce Wu are teaching their five-year-old daughter English, Spanish, and Chinese and acquiring Chinese culture for their daughter's benefit: "We had our first Chinese New Year party last year. . . . We [had] . . . some people over and [had] special foods." The birth of their daughter ignited Bryce's yearning to preserve his cultural roots. Bryce described being raised with a "behemoth of culture" and is trying to re-create that for his daughter: "I grew up . . . knowing . . . there was this . . . behemoth . . . of support and . . . culture and history and tradition. . . . It's one of the reasons why we really want . . . to pursue the whole trilingual language thing." A consequence of child rearing is the revivification of culture among adults as they acquire cultural knowledge to pass on to their children. Bryce and Caroline are learning Chinese to support their daughter's ability to communicate with Chinese speakers, a move that honors global linguistic and cultural diversity.

We typically think of teaching and learning running across channels within the same generation (between friends, peers, or spouses) or from older to younger generations (from parents to children). However, knowledge can also move from younger to older generations.[28] While people often intentionally pass cultural knowledge to their children, they can also act as conduits for their parents. This is a powerful, if unintended, consequence of marriage. In the Strong-Rio family, recall that Penelope's Native American mother was taught by widespread anti-Indian policies that Native American was a shameful status. Through Penelope and Travis, Penelope's mother revived a positive sense of her Native heritage, an illustration of what families are *doing* to repair history in the present moment. In this example, we see how cultural transmission can work its way up the generations from younger to older. Recall that Penelope grew up with a dearth of Native culture due to her mother's aggrieved experience as a Native American during a time of high racial discrimination. Travis played an essential role in supplying both Penelope and her mother with information about their Native American history and culture. Penelope chokes up as she tells the story of how Travis introduced a positive image of Native American life to her mother:

> One of our first social events [as a couple] with the family was . . . my great niece's . . . first birthday party. Travis is a flute player, so . . . he took his flute out and played her a song. . . . My mom cried and said, "when I die, I want you to play at the funeral. . . ." She really clung on to Travis. And he brought so much to my mom during her last few years. . . . [Crying.] I think he's kind of woken up everybody in my family about it's okay to know things about your Native side and to celebrate it. . . . Right after that song he played, she was diagnosed with cancer, so she only lived two more years.

Near the end of her life, Penelope's mother received positive Native American cultural messages and information that assuaged her race-related wounds. In the Strong-Rio family, Travis, as a husband, father, and son-in-law, was a vital cultural resource who passed decolonized cultural knowledge and healing to all three generations.

Not everyone wants to communicate culture to relatives. Due to concerns about male domination and class status achievement, the Nakamura and Korteweg families did not transmit culture to their children beyond a few foreign-language words. The emphasis in these families is on upward mobility and achievement of an unqualified American identity. Even as families deemphasize race, society nevertheless keeps racial issues alive. Inez cited Arizona SB 1070, a proposition aimed to allow police to racially profile Latinos to check authorization status, as a current example.

The Kortewegs simultaneously want to fit in and yet challenge the boundaries of racial categories. Because Darnell thinks that race *should not* matter, he resists using racial labels, choosing "none" or "all" racial categories on official forms. When I asked how he racially identifies, he deferred by saying, "my ethnic background is whatever you say I am because it changes even in that our definition socially changed." He eventually answered using a hyphenated amalgam of his genealogy: Euro-Afro-Native-Asian-American. He was mindful of race when naming his son, citing his son as an example of multiracialism. Darnell suggests that his son is a racial mélange and harkens to the idea of a "cosmic race" whereby future racial admixtures combine admirable qualities of each contributing race.[29] Through naming choices, Darnell and Inez destabilize assumptions and meanings attached to racial categories:[30] "My oldest son's name is Enrique. . . . And his middle name is Alejandro. Then his last name is Korteweg. That's the part that I love. So his name is Enrique Alejandro, which is a beautiful Spanish sounding name, then Korteweg. I love that because it's like, 'Your name is Enrique Korteweg?' . . . His name represents a lot of what I stand for. It should throw you for a curve. If you think you know who he is because his name is Enrique, that's sad." Wanting to "throw you for a curve," Darnell, as a large, dark-skinned man and high school administrator in a low-income area of Los Angeles, is aware of racial disparities and uses his son's name to trouble assumptions about identity. Naming is an important cultural decision that signifies ethnic identity,[31] and, in this case, it is a political gesture toward toppling assumptions of monoracial families and racist assumptions.[32] Even as Inez encouraged Americanness ("it's important that you learn the [American] culture and you support your new country") and Darnell rejected racial categories, these strategies acknowledge that racial status and nationality filter people into either the center or the margins of the US national imaginary.

Conclusion

This chapter began with questions about whether racial minority status promotes dual-minority pairings and how race operates within those relationships. Most of my respondents, as outsiders within, have a strong racial consciousness and consider racialized affinity a desirable basis for romance, which, in turn, directs them toward a minority from another racial group. Being a racial minority in a racialized society may also be a catalyst for sociopolitical critique. Gender enters the equation in that Latinas with domineering fathers did not want to replicate that dynamic in their marital life. They rejected Latinos and also spurned White men whom they viewed as too racially different in favor of non-Latino minorities with a shared position of racial subordination. These race- and gender-sensitive Latinas experienced a Goldilocks moment where they saw Latino men as too macho, White men as too dissimilar, but other men of color as just right. This is not only a critique of Latino men but also a critique of White men as inappropriate partners. These Latina women expressed their strong concern over gender subordination and their preference for a minority-minority connection in their selection of a spouse.

Non-White cross-minority marriages are founded in part on experiences of racial subordination. Romantic racialized affinity is developed out of a common experience of marginality on the US racial scene. This minority-minority connection is founded on experiences with historical or contemporary oppression, which fosters emotional attachment and allows race-conscious partners to feel that they are understood in fundamentally important ways. The distinction that these cross-minority couples make in their marital lives centers on Whiteness versus non-Whiteness. These couples undergo a process of comparative subordination wherein they identify correspondences between their own racial group and another non-White group. This recognition underscores a dominant/subordinate power dynamic between Whites and non-Whites. These couples' non-White racial status influences their life experiences, and in order to be empathic with—and understood by—a mate, they pivot toward other non-Whites. Due to experiencing similar structures of discrimination and racial meanings within families and communities, these minorities prefer to marry other people of color. Most intermarried minority couples feel excluded from mainstream society and critique it from their racially marginal position. Yet those who assert they are part of the mainstream reveal split tendencies: those who justify their inclusion by virtue of their middle class status yield to conventional notions of the mainstream, while others who cite their racially diverse local environment expand the definition of mainstream.

These interracial minority relationships based on racialized affinity offer support, solace, and a like-minded perspective on race and are a home base for cross-racial coalitions. These cross-minority couples' marriage choices, cultural practices, and racial awareness all demonstrate that they are sensitive to their positions in intersecting axes of domination and conscientiously build their families as havens from racial and gender imbalances of power. As a retort to the opening vignette justifying bans on interracial marriage, these families demonstrate the very opposite of a "degraded civilization"— they point out that cross-racial intimacies offer *insight* into civilization. Yet the judge's fears about racial mixing destabilizing White supremacy may be well founded as these families with vibrant racial memories critique systemic racial inequalities.

NOTES

1. Randall Kennedy, *Interracial Intimacies: Sex, Marriage, Identity, and Adoption* (New York: Pantheon, 2003), 20.
2. In *Loving v. Virginia* (1967), the Supreme Court later ruled antimiscegenation laws unconstitutional.
3. Kevin J. Mumford, *Interzones: Black/White Sex Districts in Chicago and New York in the Early Twentieth Century* (New York: Columbia University Press, 1997), xii.
4. Renato Rosaldo, *Culture and Truth: The Remaking of Social Analysis* (Boston: Beacon Press, 1993).
5. Patricia Hill Collins, "Learning from the Outsider Within," *Social Problems* 33.6 (1986): 14–32.
6. While there is debate as to whether Latinos constitute a racial or ethnic group, I defer to my respondents' understandings of their identities and therefore refer to Latinos as "non-White."

7. Barney G. Glaser and Anselm L. Strauss, *The Discovery of Grounded Theory: Strategies for Qualitative Research* (Hawthorne, NY: Aldine de Gruyter, 1967); Kathy Charmaz and Richard G. Mitchell, "Grounded Theory in Ethnography," in *Handbook of Ethnography*, ed. Paul Atkinson et al. (Thousand Oaks, CA: Sage, 2001), 160–174.

8. Erica Chito Childs, *Navigating Interracial Borders: Black-White Couples and Their Social Worlds* (New Brunswick, NJ: Rutgers University Press, 2005); Heather M. Dalmage, *Tripping on the Color Line: Black-White Multiracial Families in a Racially Divided World* (New Brunswick, NJ: Rutgers University Press, 2000); Rachel F. Moran, *Interracial Intimacy: The Regulation of Race and Romance* (Chicago: University of Chicago Press, 2001); Maria P. P. Root, *Love's Revolution: Interracial Marriage* (Philadelphia: Temple University Press, 2001); Michael J. Rosenfeld and Byung-Soo Kim, "The Independence of Young Adults and the Rise of Interracial and Same-Sex Unions," *American Sociological Review* 70.4 (2005): 541–562; Werner Sollors, *Interracialism: Black-White Intermarriage in American History, Literature, and Law* (New York: Oxford University Press, 2000); Paul Spickard, *Mixed Blood: Intermarriage and Ethnic Identity in Twentieth-Century America* (Madison: University of Wisconsin Press, 1989).

9. Kelly H. Chong, "Relevance of Race: Children and the Shifting Engagement with Racial/Ethnic Identity among Second-Generation Interracially Married Asian Americans," *Journal of Asian American Studies* 16.2 (2013): 189–221; Jiannbin Lee Shiao and Mia H. Tuan, "'Some Asian Men Are Attractive to Me, but for a Husband . . .': Korean Adoptees and the Salience of Race in Romance," *Du Bois Review* 5.2 (2008): 259–285; Danielle Antoinette Hidalgo and Carl L. Bankston, "Blurring Racial and Ethnic Boundaries in Asian American Families: Asian American Family Patterns, 1980–2005," *Journal of Family Issues* 31.3 (2010): 280–300; Rosalind Chou, Kristen Lee, and Simon Ho, "Love Is (Color)blind: Asian Americans and White Institutional Space at the Elite University," *Sociology of Race and Ethnicity* 1.2 (2015): 302–316; Kumiko Nemoto, *Racing Romance: Love, Power, and Desire among Asian American/White Couples* (New Brunswick, NJ: Rutgers University Press, 2009); Jennifer Lee and Frank D. Bean, *The Diversity Paradox: Immigration and the Color Line in Twenty-First Century America* (New York: Russell Sage Foundation, 2010).

10. Tomás R. Jiménez, "Negotiating Ethnic Boundaries: Multiethnic Mexican Americans and Ethnic Identity in the United States," *Ethnicities* 4.1 (2004): 75–97; Sharon Lee and Barry Edmonston, "Hispanic Intermarriage, Identification, and U.S. Latino Population Change," *Social Science Quarterly* 87.5 (2006): 1263–1279; Edward Murguia, *Chicano Intermarriage: A Theoretical and Empirical Study* (San Antonio, TX: Trinity University Press, 1982); Zhenchao Qian and José A. Cobas, "Latinos' Mate Selection: National Origin, Racial, and Nativity Differences," *Social Science Research* 33.2 (2004): 225–247; Jessica M. Vasquez, *Mexican Americans across Generations: Immigrant Families, Racial Realities* (New York: New York University Press, 2011).

11. Anthony C. Ocampo, "Are Second-Generation Filipinos 'Becoming' Asian American or Latino? Historical Colonialism, Culture and Panethnicity," *Ethnic and Racial Studies* 37.3 (2014): 426.

12. Rodolfo Acuña, *Occupied America: A History of Chicanos*, 7th ed. (New York: Longman, 2011); Juan Gonzalez, *Harvest of Empire: A History of Latinos in America* (New York: Viking, 2000).

13. Tanya Maria Golash-Boza and Pierrette Hondagneu-Sotelo, "Latino Immigrant Men and the Deportation Crisis: A Gendered Racial Removal Program," *Latino Studies* 11.3 (2013): 271–292; Cecilia Menjívar and Leisy J. Abrego, "Legal Violence: Immigration Law and the Lives of Central American Immigrants," *American Journal of Sociology* 117.5

(2012): 1380–1421; Leo R. Chavez, *The Latino Threat: Constructing Immigrants, Citizens, and the Nation* (Stanford, CA: Stanford University Press, 2008); Nicholas De Genova, *Working the Boundaries: Race, Space, and "Illegality" in Mexican Chicago* (Durham, NC: Duke University Press, 2005).

14. Christopher Wetzel, *Gathering the Potawatomi Nation: Revitalization and Identity* (Norman: University of Oklahoma Press, 2015).

15. Jessica M. Vasquez and Christopher Wetzel, "Tradition and the Invention of Racial Selves: Symbolic Boundaries, Collective Authenticity, and Contemporary Struggles for Racial Equality," *Ethnic and Racial Studies* 32.9 (2009): 1557–1575.

16. David Wallace Adams, *Education for Extinction: The American Indian Boarding School Experience, 1875–1928* (Lawrence: University Press of Kansas, 1995).

17. Brenda J. Child, *Boarding School Seasons: American Indian Families* (Lincoln: University of Nebraska Press, 2000); K. Tsianina Lomawaima, *They Called It Prairie Light: The Story of Chilocco Indian School* (Lincoln: University of Nebraska Press, 1995).

18. Alejandro Portes and Rubén G. Rumbaut, *Legacies: The Story of the Immigrant Second Generation* (Berkeley: University of California Press, 2001); Tanya Golash-Boza, "Dropping the Hyphen? Becoming Latino(a)-American through Racialized Assimilation," *Social Forces* 85.1 (2006): 27–56.

19. Ocampo, "Are Second-Generation Filipinos 'Becoming' Asian American or Latino?," 441.

20. Jessica M. Vasquez, "Gender across Family Generations: Change in Mexican American Masculinities and Femininities," *Identities* 21.5 (2014): 532–550.

21. Julie A. Dowling, *Mexican Americans and the Question of Race* (Austin: University of Texas Press, 2014), 125.

22. Ruth Frankenberg, *White Women, Race Matters: The Social Construction of Whiteness* (Minneapolis: University of Minnesota Press, 1993). Even if interviewees were half White biologically, their non-White heritage carried significant social weight.

23. Donna Haraway, "Situated Knowledges: The Science Question in Feminism and the Privilege of Partial Perspective," *Feminist Studies* 14.3 (1988): 575–599.

24. Richard D. Alba and Victor Nee, *Remaking the American Mainstream: Assimilation and Contemporary Immigration* (Cambridge, MA: Harvard University Press, 2003).

25. Tomás Almaguer, *Racial Fault Lines: The Historical Origins of White Supremacy in California* (Berkeley: University of California Press, 1994); Gonzalez, *Harvest of Empire*; George J. Sanchez, *Becoming Mexican American: Ethnicity, Culture, and Identity in Chicano Los Angeles, 1900–1945* (New York: Oxford University Press, 1993).

26. Wetzel, *Gathering the Potawatomi Nation*.

27. Michael C. Dawson, *Behind the Mule: Race and Class in African-American Politics* (Princeton, NJ: Princeton University Press, 1994).

28. Vasquez, *Mexican Americans across Generations*.

29. José Vasconcelos, *The Cosmic Race/La Raza Cósmica*, trans. Didier T. Jaén (1979; repr., Baltimore: Johns Hopkins University Press, 1997).

30. Michael Omi and Howard Winant, *Racial Formation in the United States: From the 1960s to the 1990s*, 2nd ed. (New York: Routledge, 1994).

31. Christina Sue and Edward Telles, "Assimilation and Gender in Naming," *American Journal of Sociology* 112.5 (2007): 1383.

32. Childs, *Navigating Interracial Borders*.

6

Parental Racial Socialization

A Glimpse into the Racial Socialization Process as It Occurs in a Dual-Minority Multiracial Family

CRISTINA M. ORTIZ

We live in a racialized society where the social dimensions of race have real consequences. How children are racially socialized matters. Families, and specifically parents, are viewed as one of the most important socialization agents in children's early development. Research that focuses on racial socialization in multiracial families has been extremely helpful in advancing the research on racial socialization, but there has been an overwhelming focus on the racial socialization of multiracial individuals with one White parent.[1] In addition, the existing research frequently gathers data from the individual themselves highlighting the multiracial persons' perspectives on their parents' role in the racial socialization process rather than exploring parents' process directly.[2] Research has also overlooked how parents' own racial socialization contributes to the strategies they use to teach their children about race.

While the field has made substantial strides, the understanding of the range of parental contributions to a multiracial child's racial socialization remains limited. To address this limitation, this chapter presents a single case study that uses in-depth interviews to examine how the minority parents in this dual-minority multiracial family have navigated their own racial and ethnic differences and, in turn, taught their children about race. This chapter focuses on the first family to participate in this study. In doing so, it is able to provide an in-depth analysis of the range of factors that exist within a single family that influence how parents teach their children about race. Although the chapter focuses on this single family, it highlights how these factors were influential to the strategies used by other families in the larger study as well. This chapter represents a call for researchers to begin to attend to how parents' own racial socialization and awareness of race has significant implications for how they teach their children about race. In shifting our lens to examine the valuable role that parents play in this process, we may also begin to see how individual racialized experiences, or lack thereof, contribute to the types of messages parents send their children about race.

Shifting Demographics

A study conducted by the National Academy of Sciences predicted that by 2050 at least 20 percent of the country's population will identify with more than one race.[3] These predictions are well on their way to becoming true. In 2004, one in forty people identified with more than one race.[4] Studies have estimated that this number could soar to one in five people by 2050, if not sooner.[5] Of the 9 million people identifying in the 2010 US census with two or more races,[6] over 75 percent of this population indicated that they have a White parent. The four largest multiracial combinations—White/Black (1.8 million), White/Some other race (1.7 million), White/Asian (1.6 million), and White/American Indian and Alaska Native (1.4 million)—accounted for 6.8 million of those reporting to be multiracial.[7]

Although the multiracial population has received significant attention from the media and researchers in recent years, the focus has typically been on families with one White parent. The prevalence of studies on families that are White/Black is understandable given that White/Black multiracials make up the largest percentage (20 percent) of multiracials,[8] and given our society's obsession with understanding how families function when the parents are from different racial groups that have been constructed as being in polar opposite positions on the racial hierarchy.[9] By continuing to prioritize this group of multiracials in research, however, the opportunities to learn about and from other dual-heritage families are overlooked.

All multiracials, regardless of racial background, have the shared experience of being raised by parents who are unable to relate to being part of two different racial backgrounds; however, the White multiracial experience is much different from the dual-minority multiracial experience. Research suggests than some White multiracials who are not mixed with Black are racially designated as White by their parents, are able to identify as White, and are considered as sociologically White.[10] Based on their closeness or integration into Whiteness, their day-to-day experiences will be much different than dual-minority multiracials, who will more often than not be identified as a minority. Based on these experiences, parents of dual-minority multiracial children have a different set of responsibilities for teaching these children about race in a society where they will be racialized much differently than their White multiracial counterparts.

Race and Multiracial Families

The racial socialization process in multiracial families can be quite complex for the following two reasons: (1) children in multiracial families do not have a parent with whom they share a multiracial identity; and (2) parents do not share racial socialization experiences or identities with one another.[11] These children learn about race from their monoracial parents, and often have distinct racial experiences even from their siblings.[12] There is a great need for parents in multiracial families to be able to recognize and understand the types of race-specific life experiences that their children may have since these and other factors result in a racial socialization process that is distinct from that in monoracial families.[13]

The research on multiracial racial socialization addresses only some of the dimensions of the racial socialization process. By continuing to examine the racial identity and identification of multiracials, limited information exists on how racial identities are developed and the role that parents play in their child's development of self-identification. While an emphasis on specific aspects of the racial socialization process has provided a significant amount of information, research has overlooked the relationships that parents have with their children during the process and the importance of this parent-child role, and has limited our understanding to a specific group of multiracial families.[14] This is problematic, as it may signal to dual-minority multiracial families that their children's racial socialization process isn't of significant importance in comparison to families with a White parent.

Why Explore Dual-Minority Multiracials?

There are 308.7 million people in the United States, and multiracials account for only 2.9 percent of the total population.[15] The dual-minority multiracial population (which includes multiracial individuals whose parents are both racial minorities) consists of only 1.5 million people who report two races among ten different dual-minority racial combinations.[16] This population accounts for only 16 percent of the entire multiracial population, making them a minority within a minority group. Few studies have examined the familial processes of racial socialization as they occur in these types of families. With its focus on dual-minority multiracial families, this study represents a shift away from previously held monocentric assumptions that all families share a single racial heritage, identity, and experience.

All children will inevitably experience some type of racialization and will experience situations that contribute to their feeling negatively or positively about their racial heritage. Even persons with White heritage do not escape racialization. Scholars have long theorized how racialization positions Whiteness as a raceless social position with one's ethnicity being optional.[17] Opposition to the multiracial movement has often projected these understandings of Whiteness onto White multiracials, and has viewed the push for a multiracial identification as an attempt to escape out of minority racialization and into the racelessness of Whiteness.[18] The case of non-White multiracials provides an opportunity to examine the racial socialization of a group of multiracials whose multiracial identities are not linked to the identity politics embedded within constructions of Whiteness. By focusing specifically on a non-White interracial couple, this study moves beyond the White/Black focus that dominates the multiracial research.

There are potentially unique factors that influence racial socialization within dual-minority multiracial families. These families include parents who, although coming from different racial backgrounds, have a shared experience of being non-White and a racial minority. In American society, people of color frequently share common experiences of discrimination, racialization, and otherness.[19] This study focuses on dual-minority multiracial families, as opposed to monoracial or multiracial families with one White parent, because this population deals with racism and discrimination in distinct ways from their single-race and White multiracial peers.

While White parents of multiracial children may place an emphasis on developing their child's multiracial identity, findings from this study reveal that parents in dual-minority multiracial families are more attuned to developing their child's racial awareness of their single-race minority background rather than their multiracial identity. Given the absence of a White parent in these families, these families' approaches to racial socialization will be noticeably different from those of multiracial families with one White parent given their inability, as well as their multiracial child's inability, to pass as White in American society. In addition, the experience, or lack thereof, that each of the minority parents has had with racialized prejudice or discrimination may contribute greatly to their ideas about where they fall in the racial hierarchy,[20] and where their multiracial child may fall within it as well.

Parents in a dual-minority multiracial family share a common bond as racially stigmatized people, in that they are unable to negotiate Whiteness and the privileges that come along with being part of this racial group.[21] However, their individual experiences with regard to race, and how they teach their children about their own race, will not necessarily mirror one another. Research that focuses on dual-minority families can draw attention to the range of lived experiences that exist for minorities within American society. It can also demonstrate how the racialized experiences of each minority parent in a multiracial family, or the lack thereof, can contribute to how they teach, or are unable to teach, their child to understand each of their racial-minority backgrounds, and/or their multiracial background.

Minority parents in multiracial and/or multiethnic families may find them-selves teaching their children what they know about being a minority and leave the children to figure out how they will navigate their own multiraciality. Findings from this study indicate that these parents may use a range of strategies to teach their children about their background, such as (1) drawing on their own experi-ences to teach their multiracial child about their background, (2) having a lim-ited amount of racialized experiences and choosing not to teach their child about their background, and (3) immersing themselves in information about their spouse's background and aiming to teach their child about both backgrounds.

Racialization and Racial Socialization

Research suggests that by age three children are able to identify racial differ-ences and engage in racial discrimination.[22] This period in children's lives is crucial since stressors, such as being the subject of racial discrimination, can affect their long-term well-being, as well as brain development.[23] Parental racial socialization is critical to teaching children how to effectively navigate a racialized and racially biased society and has been identified as essential for well-being and health among racial-ethnic minorities across their life course.[24] While racial socialization has been identified as being important for teaching monoracial minority children how to cope with racism and for instilling beliefs that counter racial stereotypes, little is known about how parents in multira-cial families, especially dual-minority families, go about teaching their children about their different racial-minority backgrounds.

Children of color, both monoracial and multiracial, will inevitably experi-ence some type of racialization. Racial socialization is a central process to the development of minority children, who have an inherently different racial expe-rience than White children in America.[25] Although many scholars have written about racial socialization, there is no single or commonly accepted definition. Racial socialization has been conceptualized in a range of ways: as a protective process,[26] as a provision of tools for coping with racism and prejudice,[27] and as an instructive internalization process for countering racial stereotypes that exist within mainstream US society concerning a child's racial group(s).

Most of the research on parental racial socialization refers to the socializa-tion process as it occurs within monoracial families. The general assumption is that same-race couples tend to share childhood racial-ethnic socialization experiences, and that they may also share racialized experiences and beliefs about how to socialize their children.[28] Parents and children in these families will likely share similar racial experiences, although gender plays a complicat-ing role in their respective socialization experiences.

Multiracial Socialization

Researchers have suggested that the multiracial identity movement has been largely driven by multiracial families who are seeking to claim their Whiteness as opposed to their Blackness.[29] The racial hierarchy has real implications for life outcomes,[30] and White parents of Black/White multiracial children may not feel comfortable having their child positioned at the bottom of this hierarchy.[31] One can assume that the drive behind the development of a multiracial category was a result of White parents hoping to shift their child's position in the racial hierarchy, dispel the one-drop rule,[32] and at the same time feel included in their child's experience and identity. The development may also have occurred as a result of White parents not feeling like it is politically correct to teach their children about White pride, nor could they contribute anything culturally specific to their children, as a result of having divorced themselves from an ethnic-specific group.[33] The ability to have an optional ethnic identity may unintentionally teach White multiracials about White privilege and how they have the ability to pick and choose what they want to racially and ethnically identify with.

In contrast, minority parents in dual-minority multiracial families cannot pick and choose what part of their racial and ethnic background they want to emphasize. Findings in this study indicate that these parents want their dual-minority multiracial children to be proud of their specific single-raced minority backgrounds. In teaching their children about each of their racial or ethnic backgrounds, they may actually be more at risk for socializing their children monoracially than multiracially. Consequently, racial socialization strategies of parents in dual-minority multiracial families tend to be more similar to those used by monoracial minority families and less like those used in multiracial White families. Further research can highlight how dual-minority parents place an emphasis on monoracially socializing their children, whereas White multiracial families may be leaning more toward racially socializing to multiraciality.

The Nature of the Study

Research Design

The overall goal of this study was to understand how parents in dual-minority multiracial families racially socialize their children. In order to accomplish this goal, I chose a qualitative research design. Qualitative researchers are known for studying phenomena in their natural setting.[34] They are also known for building a complex and holistic picture of what they are studying, and reporting the detailed views of their informants.[35] The research design consisted of process-oriented interview questions, which were helpful for obtaining information about the racial socialization behaviors of study participants. Although there was some preplanned structuring of questions, the questions were exploratory and open, providing the parents with opportunities to share in detail information about their past, present, and future—all of which have implications for how they racially socialize their children. Descriptive questions were also used to gain an understanding of participants' past and current experiences and their day-to-day environment. The incorporation of all of these various types of questions was important in determining parents' existing methods of racial socialization, as well as understanding their past experiences and how those experiences currently influence and potentially will influence their future racial socialization practices.

I used a constructivist grounded theory approach in order to gain an alternative understanding of the process of parental racial socialization. This method provides useful strategies for studying the experience of parents in dual-minority multiracial families by aiding in the discovery and understanding of study participants' meaning-making processes, as well as their social processes.[36] The goal of constructivist grounded theorists is to construct theory from data on the lived experiences of study participants to see how they construct their world. These lived experiences shape how the researcher approaches the analysis.[37]

Data Analysis

For the constructivist grounded theorist, the process of coding goes beyond merely describing the topic.[38] I began by identifying and coding processes, actions, and assumptions line by line on a PDF document in order to identify emerging ideas. By pulling apart the data and framing analytic questions about it, I was able to eliminate any preconceived assumptions I had about the data by examining only the data I had collected.

Sample and Data Collection

Purposive sampling was used to recruit non-adoptive families who self-identified as dual-minority multiracial families.[39] Families who have a White parent were excluded from the study. I sought out families with children of all ages and conducted in-depth interviews with parents and children over the age of twelve. Interviews took place at the participants' homes, their places of work, and a local coffee shop. Each interview lasted from one to two hours. Parent interviews focused on participants' upbringing and experience with racial socialization and discrimination. The interviews also focused on their experiences as an interracial couple, their collective plan for teaching their children about race, and their individual parenting strategies for communicating to their children about race. The child interviews focused on the children's understanding of race, their background, and how they have learned about race. The interviews were audio-recorded and transcribed verbatim. I developed pseudonyms for all participants that were consistent with their real name. If names were ethnic toward a specific heritage, I went online and looked up names that were specific to that ethnic group and chose one of those.

The Thomas/Brown/Lewis Family

This study focuses on the Thomas/Brown/Lewis family. This family was recruited through word of mouth and was the first family to participate in the study. The family is blended and consists of an Indian mother (Alina Thomas), Black father (Harold Brown), Guyanese/Black father (Lance Lewis), twelve-year-old son (Indra Thomas-Brown), and two-month-old daughter (Celeste Lewis). Indra is the biological son of Alina and Harold, and Celeste is the biological daughter of Alina and Lance. Alina and Harold have equal joint custody of Indra. Indra spends half of the week living with his mother, stepfather, and newborn sister, Celeste, and the other half of the week living with his father, Harold, and his wife and newborn daughter.

Each of the parents in the family has a unique upbringing. Lance and Alina have the shared experience of growing up in predominantly White areas, with Alina living in the suburbs of Detroit and Lance living in a small town in southern Maryland. Harold grew up in a neighborhood in west Michigan that had a balance of White and Black people. Today, most of Alina's friends are Black and Lance's are Indian.

The common parenting link that all of these parents share is their twelve-year-old son, Indra. All of them talked in depth about how they have, are, and plan on racially socializing Indra, who they all believe will be perceived as Black. Although they all have had discussions with Indra about his racial background, each of them is uncertain about whether or not he is "getting it" yet and concerned about his current ability to understand the impact that race will have on his life. While Alina and Harold both openly doubt whether or not they are adequately racially socializing Indra, their comments indicate they are teaching him more about his racial background than they are aware of. Because most of their strategies are focused on the development of his racial identity, less time has been spent on developing his Indian and multiracial background.

Findings

The Black Experience of a Multiracial "Blindian"

At the age of five, Indra's mother taught him a unique way to embrace both sides of his heritage. She recalled this lesson vividly, stating, "he's said before, 'I am the Blindian King,' like Black and Indian . . . we made up this song with his little djembe drum: 'From India and Africa, India and Africa that's where my family is from.'"[40] The development of this song was a racial socialization technique used by Indra's mother to help him grasp the concept of having two heritages. This technique contributed to Indra using the term "Blindian" in his younger years to identify himself. The endearing combination of a multiracial child's heritage labels has become more popular with the rise of the multiracial population. Both multiracial individuals and scholars who study the multiracial population have developed identity labels such as Mexipino, Blaxican, Blasian, Chicanese, Korack, and Nigganese.[41] Although the "Blindian" label developed for Indra was a fun way to incorporate both of his backgrounds, his mother wasn't sure of what the label really meant to a five-year-old. The use of the label alone played a role in building his awareness of having two distinct backgrounds, but wasn't able to provide him information about what it meant to be from each of these groups.

Indra is identified by each of his parents as Indian and Black. Indra also identifies himself as Indian and Black. Although his mother is Indian, she admits to not cooking Indian food often and questions the quality of her cooking. Her use of the Malayalam language with her son has been limited since she doesn't have a Malayali community around her to practice the language and her husband has concerns about not being able to understand what they are saying. Indra's exposure to the Indian community and culture has become more infrequent as he has gotten older, and his mother expressed doubt about how successful she has been at teaching her son about his Indian background. As a brown-skinned male living in two predominantly Black neighborhoods, his physical appearance has contributed to a shift between the way his parents identify him and the way they racially socialize him. The social perception of Indra as a Black male and the experiences they are anticipating him having have contributed to the parents' prioritization of the need to prepare him for his Black experience rather than his Indian or multiracial experience.

The experience that Black people have in American society was the most frequently discussed topic across each of the interviews. While I conceptualized the "Black experience" to be broad and inclusive of both positive and negative experiences, participants' discussions tended to focus on the negative aspects of the Black experience. The argument can be made that there are disproportionately more negative messages about Blackness than about any other minority group identity, contributing to the need to prepare these children for these types of messages.

Being unable to personally relate to the Black experience, Alina expressed her concern and worry for her son: "The concern, as for Indra, navigating the world as a Black male . . . with everything that's been happening with Ferguson, the Trayvon Martin, all of this is sad and I have talked to Indra about that. . . . I am just like, 'You have to be really careful because the way the world works—this is the unfortunate . . . reality for Black males in the United States.' And it pains me to have a conversation like that with my son, but he also needs to be aware . . . there is unfortunately a lot of racism and prejudice and stereotypes that exist, but you can't be defined by those stereotypes and you have to know how to operate with it."[42] Although Alina has not lived the Black experience herself, having a Black husband, a significant number of Black friends, teaching in a predominantly Black classroom, and raising a son who is racially perceived as Black provide her with a level of awareness that other Indians who are not in an interracial relationship with a Black partner may not have. Although she described on several occasions how she has talked to her son about race, how it will impact his life, and his need for caution, she still doubts whether what she has done is enough, or if she has really done anything to racially socialize her son.

In contrast, both Lance and Harold use their personal experiences to identify how they will go about teaching Indra about race. For these men, a large part of the Black experience is coming to terms with a set of unfortunate realities for Black males. These unfortunate realities include the need to accommodate non-Black people to make them less fearful, to wear clothes that don't seem threatening (i.e., not wearing hooded sweaters with the hood over their head), and to be knowledgeable about appropriate ways to interact with police. Their own recollections of their earliest memories of racial awareness give them the impression that their awareness of being Black is inherent and part of their birthright responsibility. This sense of responsibility motivates them to teach Black youth, especially Black males, how to combat discrimination and to survive and navigate the world as a Black male in an oppressive society.

Parent-to-Parent Differences

The existing research has introduced the notion that minority parents in interracial relationships will inevitably have different individual experiences, different beliefs, and different overall racial lenses. While the parents in this study have some commonalities (e.g., Alina and Lance are both the first generation in their families to be born in America, and both Lance and Harold have the common experience of growing up as Black males), their distinct individual upbringings contribute greatly to how all of them navigate their day-to-day life and incorporate their experience as a minority into their strategy for teaching their children about race.

American: To Be or Not to Be

Within the Thomas-Lewis household reside two parents who, although they have the similar life experience of growing up in predominantly White neighborhoods, have had distinctly different racialized experiences. For Alina, growing up in an Indian household, socialization messages about culture were transmitted more often than messages about race. On the rare occasions when race was discussed in her home, Alina recalls her father using her desire to self-identify as Indian American as a point of reference for how she would be racially perceived in American society.

> I remember my dad made me write an essay about what it means to be Indian-American. . . . I grew up with this message of "You're Indian American, but other people are going to see you as Indian. They're not going to see you as American." And I grew up with that message. And then I did not believe that—like really see how that manifested until post–September 11th. There was this incident . . . I was walking home from the train and there's this group of—they were maybe older boys. . . . They were like, "You terrorist, you killed all those people." And I was scared. . . . I'd never been so fearful. . . . When that happened I was like, "My dad was right. I am not American." . . . And that was a like a turning point in my life I think.[43]

Alina's recollection of this experience speaks to the fact that although one may receive racial socialization messages from one's parents during one's teenage years, it is possible that a significant amount of time can pass before one's self-awareness of being a racialized minority in American society is developed. Although Alina didn't speak about whether her father defined "American" as synonymous with "White," his lesson about the perception of Indian people demonstrates the otherness that is experienced for those in American society who are perceived as immigrants or minorities, or whose identity is not clear-cut. Her father's point of reference may have come from his own experience as an immigrant to the United States and being treated as less than American.

Both Alina and Lance were raised by parents who had immigrated to the United States as adults. Their parents held similar ideas about what their children needed to do to be successful in America. For both families, there was an ongoing concern about their child's Americanness and how they would prepare their children for what that entailed. While Alina struggled with the idea of not being perceived as American by outsiders, Lance received specific messages from his family about making sure he didn't do anything that might contribute to his being perceived as American. When asked about the point at which he became aware of his family's Afro-Guyanese background, his response was as follows:

> It was like from birth . . . literally. . . . It was very pervasive. . . . My parents had no qualms about telling me . . . that we were not expected to act like Americans. . . . "Your family is Guyanese and there are certain expectations associated with that." My parents made that very clear . . .

something else that they made very clear was the racial inequalities, the history of the United States. . . . Most kids learn to read on like Dick and Jane books. . . . When we were growing up, my mother would read my sister and I like "Native Son" and "Kaffir Boy" and the "Autobiography of Malcolm X." . . . My parents made it very clear like from as early as possible that you are Black. Moreover you are Guyanese, and there are things that we expect from you and there are going to be expectations from outside that we don't, that you are not allowed to meet those expectations. . . . [You are] not supposed to fit into any of these stereotypes that people will have of you.[44]

Lance's recollection of his upbringing demonstrates how he, too, received messages about his culture growing up. It also speaks to how his mother's view of "American" was different from Alina's father's view. Lance's mother used the term "American" term to refer to Black Americans, whom she perceived as lazy, disconnected from their history, and not understanding the need to excel. It can be assumed that being identified as American was a bigger identity threat to Lance than to his Indian wife, for whom identifying as American may have been beneficial.

Point of Racial Awareness

Although Alina grew up in a predominantly White neighborhood, her family's strong connection to the Indian Catholic community may have served as a source of insulation for her awareness of racialized experiences prior to her post–September II experience that occurred when she was twenty-three. Alternatively, her self-identification as Asian may have also contributed to her limited awareness of racialized experiences, given that the negative connotations and racialized ideas about who is Asian in American society may not have been inclusive of individuals with Indian heritage during her upbringing.

Lance's discussion about the development of his racial awareness highlights the similar experience that he and Harold have had as Black males in American society. For each of them, there was no clear point in time when they learned about their racial background. Both men were immersed in environments where they were able to see firsthand the disparities within the Black community. Each of them learned about the complexities of the Black experience, and how the social environment shapes and contributes to it, through discussions about the inequalities that exist for Black people as well as through exposure to people who had life experiences of segregation in a pre–civil rights era. These experiences contrast with Alina's. She didn't recall any racial socialization messages about what it means to be Asian, and remembered her first racialized encounter as occurring when she was an adult. While Alina's experience contributed to her ability to see more clearly how the society we live in is highly racialized, both Lance and Harold have had a lifetime of experiences that have prepared them for how to navigate being Black.

Discussion and Implications

The findings of this study suggest that there are elements to the racial socialization process for dual-minority multiracial families that are both similar to and different from what research has implied to be specific to monoracial families or for families with one White parent. This study draws attention to three of these similarities and differences: (1) the racialization of minority children, (2) the process of overlooking the need to develop each of the child's racial backgrounds, and (3) parents' own racial socialization and the influence it has on the racial socialization strategies they employ with their children.

While some may believe that multiracial individuals have transcended the color line and are representative of a postracial America, the experiences that many of them have as minorities challenge this assumption. This is especially the case for dual-minority multiracials. Although these individuals are part of two distinct racial groups, their physical appearance and societal perception can contribute to their parents socializing them to only one of their heritages. This is especially true for dual-minority multiracials who have a Black parent. For these multiracials, the one-drop rule—which was initially used to maintain White supremacy—impacts these families so much that they are more focused on preparing their child for how they will be perceived in society. Instead of being able to teach their child about each of the child's backgrounds, their child's Blackness is prioritized because it has a range of negative connotations attached to it. This contributes to the non-Black parent in dual-minority families being forced to teach his or her multiracial child about a racialized group that is different from the parent's own.

The parents in this family were only three of numerous parents in this study who had been influenced by society's racialized perception of their children. Society's racialization of the children in this study contributed to many of the parents' strategies for teaching their children about race. Although the children in this study are multiracial, like many of the families in this study, the Thomas/Brown/Lewis family's approach to racially socializing Indra is similar to the strategies used in monoracial Black families. As his biological father states, "The reality is that although Indra is biracial, he will be perceived as a Black boy, and that is something that I am very aware of. . . . I'm not sure to what degree he thinks about it and understands it . . . it's certainly something I know I need to talk with him more about, sort of the navigation and the survival skills, whether in Chicago or outside of Chicago."[45]

The research on the racial socialization process as it occurs in monoracial Black families discusses in depth the range of messages that are geared toward preparing children for racial bias and for encounters with racial discrimination and prejudice, helping them to develop coping mechanisms, and fostering resilience for occasions when they will encounter negatives experiences as a result of discrimination and prejudice based on their appearance and status as a minority.[46] Indra has the benefit of having two Black men with whom he can relate and from whom he can learn. Both of them were taught how to navigate the world as Black men and are able to draw upon these lessons, how these lessons were transmitted, and what they wished they had learned more of or sooner. Although Indra's parents are taking proactive steps to prepare him for the experiences he will have as a Black male, they are hopeful that there will be a time in his life when he will be in an environment where he can get more connected to his Asian American and Indian background. His mom identified college as such an environment.

According to Diane Hughes and Lisa Chen, as a child's age increases, so does the frequency of messages about preparation for bias. While the child's age can serve as an antecedent for these types of messages, so can the parents' own experience with racism.[47] All of the parents talked briefly about what they have taught Indra thus far about his racial background, and talked more in depth about what they need or plan to teach him. While the parents' experiences influence their view on the type of information that Indra will need in order to navigate a world where he is perceived as Black, his age and their uncertainty of whether or not he is able to comprehend what exactly all of this means right now have stalled their racial socialization process.

Research suggests that around the age of twelve, children are able to understand historical and geographical aspects of racial identity. However, knowledge and feelings about personal struggles against racism become more complex.[48] At the age of twelve, Indra is uncertain about how his parents have taught him about race, but does recall conversations with his mother and paternal grandmother about the need for him to be careful given his skin color. His most recent memory of learning about race was a conversation that his mother had with him about the tragedy that occurred in Ferguson, where an unarmed eighteen-year-old Black male was fatally shot by a police officer.[49] The takeaway that was easiest for him to recall from this conversation was the need to be careful with how he approaches and speaks to police officers.

The need for this family, and many of the families in this study, to prepare their child for being perceived as Black demonstrates how the racialization of minority children, regardless of if they are monoracial or multiracial, is real and ongoing. The way that these families prioritized the development of only one of their child's racial backgrounds speaks to the abundance of negative stereotypes and perceptions that exist for Black people in American society. It can be argued that the need to prepare a child for adversity in our society can overshadow the need to teach the child about how to be proud and to embrace other aspects of his or her background. The segregation and racialized climate that Chicago is notorious for may also contribute to the need to prepare any child who may be perceived as Black for the negative experiences that he or she may have in society. In addition, there is a strong likelihood that the current climate of America in general has increased these parents' already heightened levels of awareness of the perception of Black males.

Parents' own experiences with racial socialization and racialization play a significant role in how they teach their child about race. Although the parents in Thomas/Brown/Lewis family have different upbringings, identities, and understandings of race, they all have a familiarity with the Black experience. Lance and Harold are living the Black experience and preparing to teach their son how to navigate American society as a Black man. It can be assumed that Alina's disconnect from her Indian background and her experience of having a secondary connection to the Black experience, which includes living in a predominantly Black neighborhood, provide her with the ability to approach her racial socialization strategies in a distinct way from Harold and Lance. Although she claims to have had a limited amount of personal experience of discrimination, she has a heightened awareness of the types of experiences her son may have, and her fear and desire to communicate to him to be cautious guide her racial socialization techniques.

Minority parents are assumed to inherently have a connection to their background and know how to teach their child about it. This study begins to challenge this assumption by drawing attention to the fact that minority parents have their own distinct experiences, which may or may not have been racialized. Even without such experiences, however, parents have the ability to be sensitive to someone else's racial experience. Instead of assuming that minority parents know how to handle all matters of race that their child will encounter, we can begin to see that parents who may not have a significant amount of racial awareness may be learning about race at the same rate as their child. This influences how they racially socialize their children and whether their approach is proactive or reactive.

The role of parents in their child's development of racial awareness is not something that is specific to or relevant only for dual-minority multiracial families. Parents in both monoracial and multiracial families contribute to their child's understanding of race, or lack thereof. Parents with a limited awareness of race can't be expected to teach their children something that they don't know or don't have any experience with.

To date, parental racial socialization research has provided us with insight into how researchers, parents, and children think of the racial socialization process. This study draws attention to additional dimensions of the racial socialization process that exist for dual-minority multiracial families and the challenges that these families have when trying to teach their children about their distinct racial-minority backgrounds. While this study has focused on dual-minority parents, it has revealed how the racial socialization strategies used for this population are similar to and distinct from those used in other populations.

NOTES

1. Brett Coleman, "Being Mixed and Black: The Socialization of Mixed-Race Identity" (PhD diss., University of Illinois at Chicago, 2012); Nicolette De Smit, "Mothering Multiracial Children: Indicators of Effective Interracial Parenting" (PhD diss., McGill University, 1997); Iyabo A. Fatimilehin, "Of Jewel Heritage: Racial Socialization and Racial Identity Attitudes amongst Adolescents of Mixed African–Caribbean/White Parentage," *Journal of Adolescence* 22.3 (1999): 303–318; Rebecca R. Hubbard, "Afro-German Biracial Identity Development" (PhD diss., Virginia Commonwealth University, 2010); Ja'Nitta Marbury, "Racial Socialization of Biracial Adolescents" (PhD diss., Kent State University, 2006).

2. Coleman, "Being Mixed"; Susan Crawford and Ramona Alaggia, "The Best of Both Worlds? Family Influences on Mixed Race Youth Identity Development," *Qualitative Social Work* 7.1 (2008): 81–98; Rebecca Romo, "Blaxican Identity: An Exploratory Study of Blacks/Chicanas/os in California" (paper, National Association for Chicana and Chicano Studies Annual Conference, San Jose, CA, 2008).

3. Reynolds Farley and John Haaga, eds., *The American People: Census 2000* (New York: Russell Sage Foundation, 2005).

4. Elizabeth M. Grieco and Rachel C. Cassidy, "Overview of Race and Hispanic Origin, 2000," vol. 8 (Washington, DC: US Census Bureau, 2001).

5. Farley and Haaga, *American People*; Barry Edmonston and James P. Smith, *The New Americans: Economic, Demographic, and Fiscal Effects of Immigration* (Washington, DC: National Academies Press, 1997).

6. Nicholas A. Jones and Jungmiwha Bullock, "The Two or More Races Population: 2010" (C2010BR-13; Washington, DC: US Census Bureau, September 2012).

7. Ibid.

8. Ibid.

9. Miri Song, "Introduction: Who's at the Bottom? Examining Claims about Racial Hierarchy," *Ethnic and Racial Studies* 27.6 (2004): 859–877.

10. Pew Research Center, "Multiracial in America: Proud, Diverse and Growing in Numbers" (June 11, 2015), http://www.pewsocialtrends.org/2015/06/11/multiracial-in-america/; David Brunsma, "Interracial Families and the Racial Identification of Mixed Race Children: Evidence from the Early Childhood Longitudinal Study," *Social Forces* 84.2 (2005): 1131–1157. The racial identification and designation of those mixed with White is a particularly complicated process, and appearance and phenotype are critical components to this process. Although research may lead one to assume the process of passing or being identified as White is a simple one, several autobiographies have discussed the complexity of moving to Whiteness. See Mary Crow Dog and Richard Erdoes, *Lakota Woman* (New York: Harper Perennial, 1990); Kip Fulbeck, *Part Asian, 100% Hapa* (San Francisco: Chronicle Books, 2006); Kevin R. Johnson, *How Did You Get to Be Mexican? A White/Brown Man's Search for Identity* (Philadelphia: Temple University Press, 1999).

11. Kerry Ann Rockquemore and Tracey A. Laszloffy, *Raising Biracial Children* (Lanham, MD: AltaMira, 2005).

12. Maria P. P. Root, "Experiences and Processes Affecting Racial Identity Development: Preliminary Results from the Biracial Sibling Project," *Cultural Diversity and Mental Health* 4.3 (1998): 237–247.

13. Laurie McClurg, "Biracial Youth and Their Parents: Counseling Considerations for Family Therapists," *Family Journal* 12.2 (2004): 170–173; Rockquemore and Laszloffy, *Raising Biracial Children*.

14. Chase L. Lesane-Brown, "A Review of Race Socialization within Black Families," *Developmental Review* 26.4 (2006): 400–426.

15. US Census Bureau, "Population Estimates, American Community Survey, Census of Population and Housing, State and County Housing Unit Estimates, County Business Patterns, Nonemployer Statistics, Economic Census, Survey of Business Owners, Building Permits" (December 2, 2015), http://quickfacts.census.gov/qfd/states/00000.html.

16. Jones and Bullock, "Two or More Races Population."

17. Mary Waters, *Ethnic Options: Choosing Identities in America* (Berkeley: University of California Press, 1990).

18. Rainier Spencer, *Challenging Multiracial Identity* (Boulder, CO: Lynne Rienner, 2006).

19. Marc Bendick et al., "Discrimination Against Latino Job Applicants: A Controlled Experiment," *Human Resource Management* 30.4 (1991): 469–484; Major G. Coleman, "Job Skill and Black Male Wage Discrimination," *Social Science Quarterly* 84.4 (2003): 892–906; Harriet Orcutt Duleep and Seth Sanders, "Discrimination at the Top: American-Born Asian and White Men," *Industrial Relations* 31.3 (1992): 416–432.

20. Song, "Introduction."

21. Peggy McIntosh, "White Privilege: Unpacking the Invisible Knapsack," in *Race, Class, and Gender in the United States*, ed. Paula Rothenberg (New York: Macmillan, 1988), 188–192.

22. Joe Feagin and Debra Van Ausdale, *The First R: How Children Learn Race and Racism* (Lanham, MD: Rowman & Littlefield, 2001).

23. Margaret O'Brien Caughy, Patricia J. O'Campo, and Carles Muntaner, "Experiences of Racism among African American Parents and the Mental Health of Their Preschool-Aged Children," *American Journal of Public Health* 94.12 (2004): 2118–2124.

24. Carolyn B. Murray, Julie E. Stokes, and Jean Peacock, "Racial Socialization of African American Children: A Review," in *African American Children, Youth and Parenting*, ed. R. L. Jones (Hampton, VA: Cobb and Henry, 1999), 209–230.

25. Diane Hughes et al., "Parents' Ethnic-Racial Socialization Practices: A Review of Research and Directions for Future Study," *Developmental Psychology* 42.5 (2006): 747–770.

26. Diane Hughes, "Correlates of African American and Latino Parents' Messages to Children about Ethnicity and Race: A Comparative Study of Racial Socialization," *American Journal of Community Psychology* 31.1–2 (2003): 15–33; Howard Stevenson, "Validation of the Scale of Racial Socialization for African American Adolescents: Steps toward Multidimensionality," *Journal of Black Psychology* 20.4 (1994): 445–468.

27. Tiffany Brown and Ambika Krishnakumar, "Development and Validation of the Adolescent Racial and Ethnic Socialization Scale (ARESS) in African American Families," *Journal of Youth and Adolescence* 36.8 (2007): 1072–1085; Lesane-Brown, "Review of Race Socialization"; A. Wade Boykin and Forrest D. Toms, "Black Child Socialization: A Conceptual Framework," in *Black Children: Social, Educational, and Parental Environments*, ed. Harriette Pipes McAdoo and John Lewis McAdoo (Thousand Oaks, CA.: Sage, 1985),

33–51; Murray, Stokes, and Peacock, "Racial Socialization of African American Children"; Anita Jones Thomas and Suzette L. Speight, "Racial Identity and Racial Socialization Attitudes of African American Parents," *Journal of Black Psychology* 25.2 (1999): 152–170.

28. Cheryl Crippen and Leah Brew, "Intercultural Parenting and the Transcultural Family: A Literature Review," *Family Journal* 15.2 (2007): 107–115.

29. Rainier Spencer, *Spurious Issues: Race and Multiracial Identity Politics in the United States* (Boulder, CO: Westview Press, 1999); Spencer, *Challenging Multiracial Identity*; Eduardo Bonilla-Silva and David Embrick, "Black, Honorary White, White: The Future of Race in the United States?," in *Mixed Messages: Multiracial Identities in the "Color-Blind" Era*, ed. David Brunsma (Boulder, CO: Lynne Rienner, 2006), 33–48; George Yancey, "Racial Justice in a Black/Nonblack Society," in Brunsma, *Mixed Messages*, 49–62.

30. Song, "Introduction."

31. Wendy Roth, "The End of the One-Drop Rule? Labeling of Multiracial Children in Black Intermarriages" (paper, Sociological Forum, 2005).

32. Ibid.

33. Waters, *Ethnic Options*.

34. Norman K. Denzin and Yvonna S. Lincoln, *The Qualitative Inquiry Reader* (Thousand Oaks, CA: Sage, 2002).

35. John W. Creswell, *Qualitative Inquiry and Research Design: Choosing among Five Approaches* (Thousand Oaks, CA: Sage, 2012).

36. Kathy Charmaz, *Constructing Grounded Theory* (Thousand Oaks, CA: Sage, 2014).

37. Kathy Charmaz, "'Discovering' Chronic Illness: Using Grounded Theory," *Social Science and Medicine* 30.11 (1990): 1161–1172.

38. Ibid.

39. Jennifer Mason, *Qualitative Researching* (London: Sage, 2002).

40. Alina Thomas, interview by author, Chicago, September 8, 2014, tape recording.

41. Rudy P. Guevarra Jr., *Becoming Mexipino: Multiethnic Identities and Communities in San Diego* (New Brunswick, NJ: Rutgers University Press, 2012); Romo, "Blaxican Identity"; Donna M. Talbot, "Exploring the Experiences and Self-Labeling of Mixed-Race Individuals with Two Minority Parents," *New Directions for Student Services*, no. 123 (2008): 23–31.

42. Thomas interview.

43. Ibid.

44. Lance Lewis, interview by author, Chicago, September 22, 2015, tape recording.

45. Harold Brown, interview by author, Chicago, September 2, 2014, tape recording.

46. Hughes et al., "Parents' Ethnic-Racial Socialization Practices"; Diane Hughes and Lisa Chen, "The Nature of Parents' Race-Related Communications to Children: A Developmental Perspective," in *Child Psychology: A Handbook of Contemporary Issues*, ed. Lawrence Balter and Catherins S. Tamis-LeMonda (Philadelphia: Psychology Press, 1999), 467–490.

47. Diane Hughes and Lisa Chen, "When and What Parents Tell Children about Race: An Examination of Race-Related Socialization among African American Families," *Applied Developmental Science* 1.4 (1997): 200–214.

48. Louise Derman-Sparks, Carol Tanaka Higa, and Bill Sparks, "Children, Race and Racism: How Race Awareness Develops," *Interracial Books for Children Bulletin* 11.3–4 (1980): 3–15.

49. NBC News, "Michael Brown Shooting," May 13, 2015, http://www.nbcnews.com/storyline/michael-brown-shooting.

PART III

Mixed Identity and Monoracial Belonging

7

Being Mixed Race in
the Makah Nation

Redeeming the Existence of African Native Americans

INGRID DINEEN-WIMBERLY

As scholars of the mixed race experience, we pride ourselves on recognizing the shortcomings of racial categories. For the most part, we agree that the constructed quality of race and ethnicity renders them inaccurate as markers of identity. These markers, by definition, are essentially incapable of portraying an individual's or a community's experiences. Necessarily, the emerging field of multiracial studies embodies sensitivity to racial erasure, which occurs all too frequently in the maintenance of a monoracial order common to the United States and elsewhere.[1] For students and scholars of multiracial studies, to honor one's right to identify as one chooses represents a key ideological commitment.[2]

Erasing Race

It is with this self-celebratory claim in mind that I call attention to sanctioned acts of erasure taking place within the field. Simply put, when an African American asserts indigenous ancestry, glares of disbelief and giggles often accompany such identification. This rejection of identity is rooted in the assumption that many African Americans are misguided by fantastical tales of Indian princesses serving as the matriarchal heads of their families.[3] Other, more critical assumptions include the belief that some African Americans are engaged in a move to betray Blackness. Refusing to recognize as authentic the progeny of such a union between Black and Red has become increasingly acceptable, particularly at the intersection of academia and popular culture.

Henry Louis Gates Jr., on his show *Finding Your Roots*, frequently offers crude commentary regarding the prevalence of African Americans who affirm Native ancestry. Gates suggests that most African Americans are duped by the belief that they have Native ancestors.[4] In a conversation with White House Senior Advisor Valerie Bowman Jarrett, he sarcastically quipped, "Well, you and every other Negro I know claim to have Native ancestry." Jarrett responded, "But we really do." Gates explained that her case was in effect exceptional because she actually was 5 percent Asian/Native, as quantified by the pseudo-scientific genetic testing upon which his show relies.[5] More generally, the use of genetic testing to identify racial or even ethnic identity has reemerged with a capitalistic rigor. At-home genetic test sets from 23andMe, which promise to let consumers know their true race, are flying off the shelves. As scholars who research matters of race and ethnicity, we have yet to grapple with, much less agree upon, a pedagogical path forward. For decades scholars of ethnic studies have stood before students insisting that race is not biological—it is social. Yet here was a Harvard professor pretending it was biological.[6]

It is no surprise that Gates would feel so free to dismiss the existence of African American Natives. Studying multiracial identity within the context of the African American experience is frequently met with resistance, even suspicion.[7] The record of US slavery and Jim Crow segregation (or the reverence that history commands) often prevents mixed race African Americans from embracing multiplicity, as they might consider themselves as caretakers of a legacy. In some cases the assertion of a monoracial identity signals a loyalty to the complexity of the African American experience, both triumphant and oppressive. In other words, for some "being Black" is a calling to safeguard the historical record of the African American experience.

The Historiographical Path Forged

Met with resistance, historians and sociologists have nevertheless researched and profiled African American Indians. In the 1970s, historian Gary B. Nash's *Red, White and Black* set ablaze this field of inquiry with his watershed analysis of colonial-era relationships between African Americans and Natives in North America. Since then historians like William Loren Katz, Jack Forbes, Circe Sturm, James F. Brooks, Theda Perdue, and Claudio Saunt have gone on to produce comprehensive histories specific to various eras and regions of the United States.[8]

In 2009, in collaboration with the Smithsonian's National Museum of the American Indian, Gabrielle Tayac edited a beautiful anthology of the often-hidden histories of blended African American and Indian families: *IndiVisible: African-Native American Lives in the Americas.*[9] Theda Purdue, author of the landmark book *"Mixed Blood" Indians*, contributed a chapter to Tayac's anthology, which directly informs this chapter. In her chapter, "Native Americans, African Americans and Jim Crow," Perdue explained that African American and Native relationships were "neither inevitable nor uniform." Particularly germane to my research among mixed race Makah of African descent, she stressed that during the height of Jim Crow "most Indians did not make common cause with African Americans . . . [but rather] police[d] their own racial boundaries [and] discourage[ed] unions with African Americans but generally not whites."[10]

When I began this project I imagined I'd find two sets of racial rules: one set of norms functioning on the reservation and the other operating outside those territorial boundaries. Historian Carey McWilliams spoke to this phenomenon when he wrote, "there are always two nations in every nation: the dominant ongoing nation, enchanted with its self-proclaimed virtues . . . and another nation that exists . . . half-buried, [and] seldom surfacing."[11] Instead, my research of mixed race Makah in Neah Bay, Washington, dismissed an oversimplistic focus on borders and replaced those related binary assumptions with a racial system that more closely resembled concentric circles of race hierarchy.

This chapter is based on interviews with several members of a racially complicated family—mainly Black, Indian, and Filipino—though it is centered on an account of the racial experiences of one individual: Landon Zendell Wimberly. The people I interviewed navigated various racial spaces as they maintained complex racial and ethnic consciousness. Indeed their experiences were impacted by racial norms within and beyond various geographic boundaries, but were also ameliorated by the interactions they had with different racial or ethnic groups. On the Makah Reservation ("the rez") in Neah Bay, mixed race Natives of African descent in particular grappled with tribal relations and racism from within. Beyond the rez extending to the larger communities of the Olympic Peninsula, they confronted racism not exclusively related to their Native ancestry but as a result of their African American heritage as well.[12] Each of the mixed race Makah I interviewed had previously lived in Oxnard, California, for a significant amount of time. In California, the increased presence of Black and Brown people rendered both positive and negative receptions, which became more welcoming over time.[13]

While conducting the interviews, I was quite surprised to learn how prominent the calculation of "blood quantum" remained in their everyday lives.[14] Landon Wimberly, an enrolled member of the Makah nation, has African American roots, which extend to the states of New Jersey and Georgia. According to family records and his testimony, Landon's Makah mother, Jo Ann Della, was one-eighth Makah, one-eighth Quileute, one-quarter Irish, and one-half Filipino. Landon's father, Ritchie Wimberly, who identifies as African American, has a family lineage that includes ancestors from Portugal, Germany, and the Cherokee Nation. Landon's maternal cousin Natalie Aguirre, who is also an enrolled member of the Makah Nation, shared the same maternal heritage but indicated that she was half Puerto Rican. She explained that when she visits her family in Puerto Rico the racial norms are further complicated by a language barrier.

This study is not about two nations, one on the rez and one off. Rather it is about the ways in which these mixed race Makah experienced the multiple points of identity formation and reinforcement, as they interacted with different peoples in different regions of the world. One can think of their identities as a series of concentric circles having one central space in common. At the center of this layered system stands the consciousness of successful mixed race Makah cousins whose commitment to family trumps loyalties to race, class, nation, or tribe.

Interviewing Landon

I waited to interview Landon in Daleena's Wellness Center. Daleena, the mother of Landon's three children and his life partner, is also an enrolled member of the Makah Nation. Her Wellness Center, which is attached to their very large two-story home, smelled of lemon grass, lavender, Himalayan salt, and smoke from the wood burning in their potbelly stove. As I readied my voice recorder, notes, and questions I felt mesmerized by a picture of Daleena's great-grandmother taken in 1915 by Edward Curtis, who titled the photo, "Makah Maiden." The same picture adorns the main entrance of the Makah Cultural and Research Center, a museum located on the rez.[15] The Makah are one of the few tribes that host and control their own museum.[16] The museum houses artifacts collected during the 1960s and 1970s from the Ozette archeological excavation project, which unearthed over fifty-five thousand artifacts from a five-hundred-year-old Makah village. It is the pride of the fourteen hundred Makah who live in Neah Bay today.[17]

The Trouble with Being Mixed while Black

Landon and I immediately began joking about the unique considerations endemic to maintaining a mixed race identity. We talked about the old joke that serves as a sort of caveat to mixed folks of African descent, which warns, "When the revolution comes, you better know where you stand! You're Black"! As a mixed race woman of African American and Irish descent, I laughed and said, "But when the revolution comes, what am I going to do with my White father? Hide him in the basement? These are real people we're talking about." We identified with each other and homed in on a key theme of this chapter: the notion that both internal and external pressures to maintain monoracial identity may indeed result in a sort of intellectual racial erasure, but more importantly it discounts the relevance of really important people—our loved ones, our families.[18]

Ethical Considerations

At this point, the reader may question the familiar tenor between Landon and me. He is my stepson. The fact that I am married to his father might raise ethical concerns in some readers' minds. Could I be an unbiased observer in a family of which I am a part? In stark contrast to my work, anthropologist Elizabeth Colson stayed with the Makah in 1941, she said, to "collect life histories."[19] Colson expressed no remorse when she admitted to interviewing the Makah under false pretenses. She admitted to conducting phony "'formal interviews' to maintain the fiction that [she] was interested in the old times."[20] She had no problem lying to the Makah while paying informants. It's no wonder that she did not feel that she "was ever in complete confidence of any member of the group."[21]

By contrast, I sensed strongly that both Landon and Natalie felt completely comfortable to be honest with me. This project was not necessarily about the Makah per se; it was about giving voice to people who lived as a minority within a minority. To ensure integrity, they each maintained complete control over which parts of the interviews would make it into this chapter. I follow the lead of Janine Bowechop, director of the Makah Cultural and Research Center, who explained, "I always felt it was more meaningful to offer criticism from within than to wage a blind war from afar."[22] As a member of this Makah family, I am telling their story from within.

Landon's Background

Landon has a cornucopia of ethnic possibilities. His mother, Jo Ann Della, was born to Beverly Violet Daniels Della and Eulalio Della in 1953. Beverly's mother, Lucille Kallappa, was half Makah and half Quileute and her father was Irish. Beverly's husband Eulalio was Filipino. Lucille's intermixture of Makah and Quileute is not out of the ordinary, as coastal Natives practiced intermarriage oftentimes to reinforce peace treaties and tribal alliances. The Makah and Quileute also shared what Makah elder Melissa Peterson-Renault calls "resource acquisition areas."[23] The seas and land of the Olympic Peninsula fed and supported various groups governed by intertribal arrangements. One can perceive a kind of *identity agency* operating among Native peoples. That is, individuals with complicated ancestry may assert Indian identity even while they also may have non-Native ancestors. This assertion may bring a measure of social and economic mobility to mixed race Natives.

Nonetheless, my suggestion of the potential power of Indian or Native identity in no way diminishes the decimation or destructive reeducation suffered by the vast majority of indigenous peoples in North America. Like many other states, Washington instituted compulsory "Indian Education," and Beverly was forced into an Indian Boarding School as a young teenager. The conditions were so horrible that Beverly ran away from school and eventually made her way to Seattle. Anthropologist Carolynn J. Marr conducted extensive research on the horrors Indians in the Pacific Northwest endured. In one interview she captured the type of brutality one would suffer if one attempted to run away from the Chemawa Boarding School in Salem, Oregon, where many of the Makah resided. A Makah woman named Helma Ward described such consequences to Marr: "Two of our girls ran away . . . but they got caught. They tied their legs up, tied their hands behind their backs, put them in the middle of the hallway so that if they fell, fell asleep or something, the matron would hear them and she'd get out there and whip them and make them stand up again."[24]

Beverly eventually met her considerably older, soon-to-be husband Eulalio Della, a Filipino sailor whom the US Navy recruited from Subic Bay, Philippines, in the early 1930s.[25] Eulalio was also a runaway of sorts as he had literally jumped ship to leave the Navy and settle in Seattle. The couple for a time moved back to the reservation, but, according to family lore, life proved terribly difficult there. While the federal government initiated restrictions on their fishing rights, the reservation's remote location hampered economic development. Moreover, the terrain was not suitable for commercial agriculture, like so many other reservations in the United States.[26] Despite the fact that the state constructed a public school at Neah Bay in 1932, the assimilation policy of Natives remained so abusive that the school forbade any expression of Makah culture, especially the use and retention of language.[27]

In addition, as the 1930s came to a close, war loomed in the Pacific. Members of another Filipino family, the Pasquals, who lived on the rez at that time, were often mistaken as Japanese men and as such were detained on the Air Force base located nearby.[28] By the early 1940s, out of frustration and fear, Eulalio and Beverly moved to Oxnard, California, a small agricultural town where Eulalio worked as an agricultural laborer for the remainder of his life.[29]

How did the lives of Makah and Filipinos intersect? From a macro-analytical view there are two key patterns that fostered relationships between Natives and Filipinos: agricultural migratory patterns from Southern California to the Pacific Northwest and land lease agreements, which allowed Filipinos to circumvent alien land laws.[30] Rick Baldoz explained how Indian "sovereignty over reservation land" in Washington provided a loophole through which Filipinos could experience potential economic and social mobility.[31] According to Baldoz, the incidents of Filipinos settling on reservations and leasing or buying Indian land raised two important concerns among those Whites interested in maintaining social and economic control. That is, the legal relationship between Indian tribes and Filipinos over the leasing of land alarmed White officials, who understood these "alliances as a threat to their domination over both populations."[32]

Essentially, land agreements had the potential to undo a monoracial order. Vigilantes, anti-immigrant Grange organizations, and elected officials in Washington accused Filipinos of "alien subterfuge," when Filipino men accessed land through intermarriage with Indian women.[33] In the case of the Della couple, leasing land may not have been the central issue. However, because of the Indian Citizenship Act of 1924, no matter what her other obstacles, Beverly enjoyed US citizenship whereas Eulalio did not.[34] In that sense, her Indian identity would provide Eulalio a legal position he would not enjoy otherwise. In other words, in comparison to Eulalio, she had identity power. Interwoven cultural traditions of Filipinos and Indians when banded together had the potential to create something stronger, something impenetrable. Like a tightly braided basket, an Indian and Filipino couple together might be better suited to bear the weight of restrictive US policy.

Rudy Guevarra Jr., in *Becoming Mexipino*, also explored the ways in which Filipino and Mexican labor migratory patterns (from the Pacific Northwest to San Diego) resulted in interethnic couplings. Guevarra described the relationship between Filipinos and Mexicans in twentieth-century California as one characterized by "cooperation and disagreement." Guevarra contends that an ethnic group's ability to selectively assert Whiteness is a powerful differential in terms of comparative power and mobility. In Guevarra's study Filipinos could not claim social power by asserting Whiteness, while those of Mexican descent could.[35] In this case study, it is the Makah who get to selectively assert Whiteness or Indianness, which directly impacts the social reception of African-descended, mixed race Makah.

My interview with Landon provided important insights into the cost of affirming a mixed identity in rez life and also revealed how the addition of African ancestry impacted the ways in which people received him both on and off the rez. Over the course of several days we explored his experiences of racial reinforcement as a child: the fear and courage he felt in the face of racism, the impact of his relationship choices, the importance of blood quantum in Makah life, and finally what he considers to be the "long-term genocide" of Native peoples. Landon is a successful commercial fisherman and does well financially. His work ethic is geared toward productivity, but not as a means of simple wealth accumulation. Rather, he prides himself on being a source of support for his family. Many of his extended family members rely on him as a paternal figure. As an educated man, he has put many of his younger Makah relatives through college. In his role as a football and basketball coach Landon works with Makah youth extensively. Landon is the provider for his family, but his most treasured role is that of a father to his two sons and daughter.

Landon's Story

Landon recalled his first recollection of his racial or ethnic self. "It had to be when I was really young. Probably kindergarten or first grade . . . when all the little Mexican kids [in Oxnard were] talking about 'Negroes.'" I asked if there was context to this memory. Was his class learning about some related issue like slavery or the civil rights movement? With humor in his heart he responded, *"No! I was like, I'm not one."* Landon first heard the term "Negro" while living in Oxnard with both his parents. He recalled being dropped off at school by his father: "That's when they started calling me that. It made me feel a little bit different. I was a little timid and shy of who would drop me off. [The students] didn't know I was Black. Maybe they thought I was Mexican. A lot of older guys called me 'choncho' because I could pass as a Spanish cat or a Mexican. So they made up their own little name."

Landon had moved to and from the rez several times during his life. He lived in Oxnard until he was about seven or eight years old, when he, along with his entire Makah family (with the exception of Eulalio who had died), moved up to the rez in the early 1980s. Landon explained that life in Oxnard became tough personally and the entire family considered the rez a safe haven. This is consistent with Paul Spickard and W. Jeffrey Burroughs's observation, which pointed to the data provided by the 1970 and 1980s censuses that demonstrated a huge increase in the number of people who identified as Indian. As a result of the political mobilization of the 1960s, native groups throughout the country began to win "substantial new benefits" that led to an increase of people who "flooded back . . . to reservations" while embracing the new "social cachet" of being Indian.[36] Landon returned to Oxnard while he attended the ninth and tenth grades, made his way back to the rez for eleventh grade, and then moved back yet again to Oxnard to complete his senior year. He stayed in Oxnard until 2005 and then made his final move back to Neah Bay, where he lives today. When I asked about what it felt like to be called "Negro" and about his identity, he emphasized the importance of location: "You know everywhere I went it was just different. Over here [in Washington] there's mixed Natives. In Cali there were a lot of Mexicans and Blacks that I hung out with. Everybody knew what I was. My mom would always tell me: 'This is what you are . . . and set me straight [as to] who I am.' She would tell me that I'm half Black, Filipino, Indian and Irish. She would tell me constantly. So I told everybody that. This is what I am. [However,] up here it's a little more racist."[37] Because of the racism in Neah Bay, Landon explained that as a child he was sometimes "scared of being Black." This is consistent with Claudio Saunt's study of mixed race Oklahoma Creek Indians. Saunt argued that Creeks mixed with Black ancestry "bore the heavier burden," when compared to those whose ancestors included Whites and Creeks.[38]

"When you moved back to the rez in the 1980s did you feel pressure to go one way or the other?" He replied, "No. I just came here [to the rez] and now it was Indians instead of Mexicans. The Indians were telling me the same thing. 'You're Black.' I always told everybody what I was." Landon didn't yearn for approval from the Makah so much because he had it from his parents. "I didn't need anybody else's approval as long as my mom and my grandmother told me I was good, I was good. But it was weird. Their generation would say 'niggers,' all while hugging me." Landon's temperament is extremely confident. One would be hard-pressed to find any evidence of self-pity. Rather than to internalize racism, Landon receives racial slurs as challenges to prove others wrong. But for this interview he was willing to open up about the harmful impact of racism: "I never liked being called a nigger. I got called it a lot. I used to tell my mom, 'I got called a nigger today.' It made me mad. She raised me to stand up for myself. It hurt. It always hurt but she'd say, 'You just got to be strong—be stronger than these guys.' . . . I got called it by grown people."[39]

As a young child Landon recalled being "scared to be Black because I didn't want the N-word coming." He recounted an exchange between himself and his PE teacher. "I was in third or fourth grade. We were playing hockey with my class and the PE teacher said, 'give me the ball, you little fucking nigger.' It stuck with me until today." He recalled another incident with a fourth grade substitute teacher from Crescent, Washington: "His name was Mr. Phillips and everybody was talking [while] it was quiet time and he just came and grabbed me by the back of my head and just hit it across the desk. He came all the way to me and just slammed my head. I thought, 'how do they let these guys teach?' The kid sitting next to me was crying and I just whispered [in a reassuring tone,] 'you're all right man. Be quiet.'"[40]

Landon gained his strength as a protector, a caretaker of his family, his tribe, and friends. I identified and shared that I too felt shielded from racism by becoming a protector. He responded, "I never liked bullies. I'd protect people. I always have." Another incident that occurred at a football jamboree, also in Crescent, proved to be a turning point for the remainder of Landon's life. From thence forward he committed to confronting racism directly. He recalled, "I had made varsity at the age of thirteen. We went to a jamboree at Crescent Loggers, which is a town (near Clallam) about fifty miles from the rez. It was the beginning of the season and everything was packed. There were four to six teams present." He was with his fifteen-year-old maternal cousin Jazz Aguirre, who also had an African American biological father. Landon reveled in the memory of having a very successful football showing. He was involved in a lot of tackles. "When I was running the ball I could hear players calling me 'nigger.' . . . I'd make a tackle and I'd hear, 'nigger.'" I asked him if hearing that slur bothered him, and he unequivocally said, "No. I just wanted to make another tackle. I wanted to feel my fire. Other team members were like seventeen or eighteen years old and I was an eighth grader." It was a sunny Saturday afternoon and as the games finished at two o'clock fights broke out: "All you heard was players [standing] by their parents yelling out 'nigger.' Jazz was on the sideline and when the game ended we walked over to the boys [and said] . . . 'Oh, you calling people "niggers"? You wanna do something.' These towns hate each other. They don't like Indians; they don't like niggers and we were both. Cooler heads prevailed and somehow the fights settled."

I asked if these sorts of exchanges happened frequently. He replied, "Yes, it still happens. They still call us names." Again, I sought clarification as to whether this was regional. He reasoned that it occurred more often in northern Washington "because there are not too many Black people up here." In contrast, he explained, "In Oxnard, you know them all. It's like you know all the Black kids in every school. You know them. It seems like there were a lot." What was most important about this story was Landon's ability to confront racism directly. "The football thing made me feel good because you hold people accountable for what they say." Landon would have plenty more opportunities to continue to hold people accountable. In both Washington and California he committed to confronting racism directly: "I was tired of everybody disrespecting Black people. So I was like what's up? I checked so many people . . . even up here."

Pride in Blackness

When Landon lived in Oxnard he lived with his father. I sensed that his father definitely modeled Black manhood for him. We discussed him watching his dad "shave" with Magic Shave, a lye-based powder used commonly in the Black community to remove facial hair. Landon traveled with his father frequently to the East Coast to visit the Black side of his family in Paterson, New Jersey. From Landon's perspective, his Black identity was deeply rooted in positive experiences, enough to combat those rumbles with racism. Nonetheless, I asked if he ever felt that he had to prove his Blackness. He answered, "No. I was very proud of being Black. [Especially in] Cali, I embraced my Blackness. All my friends were Black." You never had brothas test your Blackness? "Well, a couple of times, but I was told that I was the Blackest mixed kid anybody ever knew." He described it as sort of a state of mind. "It's like going to Africa and telling them, 'Yo, I'm Black.' They might say, 'Yeah right.' But I say, 'It's not how much you have in you [that matters], it's if you're proud of it. It's about how you walk [figuratively], and how you carry that thing.'" Here in the most elegant, concise manner Landon laid out the social constructedness of racial identity. However, his identity was also influenced by region. He explained that when he was in California "I'd be straight Negro there." His choice of the term "Negro" was not rooted in the lexicon of outdated, racist terms from the mid-twentieth century, but rather he spoke from a place of deep esteem and pride. It's difficult to convey this cultural cue in print, but it was clearly a term of endearment. His description of being "straight Negro" I understood as an uninhibited, unencumbered expression of identity, rather than some shift in racial consciousness. He made it clear that for all his various heritages—Black, Native, Filipino, White—"I consider myself to be 100 percent of each."[41]

Proving Native

"Over here there's something about it. I say, 'us Natives or us Indians . . . and they say, 'who you trying to fool?'" I asked Landon if he had ever been called a "paper Indian," a derogatory reference to those born off the reservation but who were enrolled later in life. He replied, "They've called me an adoptee." When Landon returned to the rez in the early 1980s his Aunt Susan included him in what is known as a "blanket adoption." He explained, "When I am here, I say 'I got Native in me.' Most people don't buy that I am Native." I asked if that were true off or on the rez. He answered, "On the rez." Despite the fact that the entire tribe knows the Della name, and that Landon is enrolled, with his BIA card tucked safely in his wallet, he admitted, "I still have to prove that I am Native. A lot of people still confuse me with Jazz. They've known us for thirty years." Jazz Aguirre is Landon's maternal cousin whose biological father is also African American but whose Dad is Puerto Rican. Earlier that same day, Natalie, Landon's maternal cousin and Jazz's sister, confirmed how racist it was on the rez, and that it was more difficult for Jazz and Landon, ostensibly because they both have Black fathers. In fact, she said, "It's like they're one."[42] Landon said with assurance, "It's just more comfortable saying that I am a Black man. That's what most people on the West Coast see me as. I get a different thing on the East Coast. [There,] I am a mixed Black man."

Pride in Mixedness, His "Allness"

We discussed how all Makah are mixed, but that only those who are conspicuously mixed, like himself, experience it as such. I asked him if he ever wished that there were more mixed Black people in Neah Bay. "No, I never wished it. I always thought I was special. That's what my mom always told me. Anything I did I approached it with extreme confidence. Everything came easy for me. That's because of my mixedness. That's because of my allness." With these types of studies on mixed race consciousness, it might be tempting to envision the people as psychologically divided. This is not the case with Landon. He is a well-rounded, whole person whose term "allness" captures that essence.

The Impact of Romantic Relationships

While interviewing Landon I wondered whether his racial identity influenced his choice of romantic partners. Apparently, he was quite the ladies' man, but identified three central romantic relationships. His first love was African American, his next love was Filipina, and his life partner, Daleena, is Makah. I asked if their ethnic or racial identities impacted his own identity, and he said "No" but explained that sometimes his mixed identity allowed a particular woman's family to accept him more easily. Thus, when his Filipino girlfriend's family found out that he was mixed with Filipino, they were much more approving of their relationship. However, at the end of the day, he explained, "In a way, I could relate with all of them: Black, Filipino and Indian." I asked if having children with a Makah woman reinforced his Makah identity. He responded, "I am what I am. With her it made it stronger because my kids have a little more blood quantum of Makah."

Circe Sturm examined the prominence of proving fractions of blood among Native peoples; however, it still shocked me that discussions of blood quantum were part of everyday conversations on the rez. It is ironic that fractions of blood were used to subjugate African Americans in the Jim Crow era and that Natives still rely so heavily on the same system. Landon offered some clarity: "They look at it as land and money. Who's more deserving? I know Natives here that were half Makah twenty years ago but now they are on the books as five-sixteenths. It's politics. It's who's working the books. . . . [It's] who has the [authority] to change things." I asked if council members change the numbers. He said, "They are not supposed to but record keepers can change things."

Trying to get a better sense of the logic, I proposed that if someone were to alter a Makah's ancestral record, wouldn't it behoove the tribe to increase "blood quantum"? Landon elaborated on the complexity of "blood politics" and how class tensions impact the whole system. That is, financially insecure Makah tend to tout having more Makah blood. Those, like Landon, who are financially stable don't really think about it as often. This was more than some esoteric conversation we were having. He recently tried to get his brother adopted by the tribe and class jealousy derailed the adoption. At the tribal council meeting when Landon and other supporters attempted to advocate on behalf of his brother getting adopted and thereby enrolled, another Makah man "showed up and argued that you have to have one-quarter Makah blood to vote at council." A tribal elder shut the man down, but the tribe still voted to not adopt David. Landon is convinced that class jealously was the main reason for the denial.

Genocide

While discussing the requirement to prove Native identity and the significance of blood quantum we stumbled on a question: How does the Makah Nation continue to survive while members continue to intermarry with non-Makah? With a limited number of tribal members, could emphasizing one's mixedness threaten the survival of the Makah? We discussed Natalie's observation that "some people want you to be one-quarter Makah to vote at council." She warned, "What? Do you want people to go back to incest . . . to keep the blood line high?"[43] Many tribes have faced this conundrum and some have resorted to approving marriage among cousins. But for today's Makah that option is considered taboo.

Looking at the larger picture, Landon said, "It's not that complicated. It's genocidal here." He was definitely *not* advocating incest but went on to say, "The only way the Makah are going to survive is to stay with each other. It's long-term genocide unless Natives figure out a way to stay together. This is how it works for me: [We're] all Coastal Natives. In order to conquer people, you divide and then start giving them names: Makah, Quileutes, Quinaults, Hoh, etc. It's all the same thing. You just start dividing to say you're better." Landon went on to assert that tensions among tribes reduced intertribal marriages and then rhetorically asked, "How [do] you do that and keep your blood high? Once they gave us names, and we were no longer Coastal Indians, it became just long-term genocide. You could change a whole nationality in one generation."

He offered me a new perspective, one different from the widespread concern among academics who fear that using terms like "Native" or "Indian" suggests cultural homogeneity and results in panethnic cultural genocide. Here, Landon suggested that by identifying separate tribes, we unwittingly encourage competition and disunity. Eventually, each group is less apt to intermarry because of tensions between tribes, which ultimately results in shrinking populations among all Coastal Indians. He ended with, "Everybody is going to look like Sean Penn in another thirty years."

Nonetheless, both Landon and Natalie agreed that the irony of the Makah is that they are all mixed. Both insisted that there were no pure Makah. In terms of the cost of identifying as mixed, I asked if there existed a status hierarchy. Despite the fact that Natalie believed Neah Bay to be "very racist," she concluded that in terms of ethnic or racial status the order would be something like this: "mixed White-Makah, mixed Filipino-Makah, mixed Black-Makah, and mixed Mexican-Makah." Some of the race hierarchy may be based on tribal survival. For example, pitting the plight of Indians against African Americans was fairly common, particularly in the 1960s. The *Seattle Times* in 1968 ran an article titled "State Indians Worse Off Than Negroes."[44] It is tempting to conclude that influences from beyond the reservation were solely to blame for this stratification, but Melissa Peterson-Renault argued that status hierarchy is not new to the Makah social structure. She explained that "the Makah classes [of] chieftain, commoner, and slave [have long] established a specific hierarchy of duties and responsibilities."[45]

Concerns for tribal survival impacted whether one would or should emphasize one's mixed identity. Clearly, mixed race people have a more or less difficult time identifying as mixed depending on where they live and among whom. Among the Makah, emphasizing mixedness has higher costs. That is, if I identify as Black there's no loss, real or imagined, to the Irish. For the Makah, there are treaties depending on quantifiable population trends; their very survival as a people is at stake. Treaties governing land, residences, health care, education, fishing, and hunting rights are at stake. According to Makah elder Peterson-Renault, the "main goal of the tribe . . . is to protect treaty rights, as these rights are constantly being challenged."[46]

Peterson-Renault's interpretation is consistent with Alexandra Harmon's argument in *Indians in the Making* that "more than any other group, Indians . . . have had to defend their claims [of identity] with a frequency and rigor seldom demanded of people in other ethnic or racial classes."[47] Harmon explained that this phenomenon is of tremendous importance because the US government through its treaty obligations "reserves valuable resources to Indians but lacks a single definition of Indian."[48]

Conclusion

This chapter has examined the perceptions and experiences of some members of the Makah nation who identify as mixed race, and one man in particular who identities as both African American and Indian. He is a Black man, a mixed man, a Native, and an Indian. As researchers we might struggle with this sort of messy plurality of identity, but it is the voice of a real person who stands as an expert on his own life. My central focus in this chapter has been to examine and redeem the existence of the African Native American through the eyes of one man. We participated in the traditional sort of interview, but I was also able to peek in and enjoy what it means to be Makah and what it means to stay Black while being Native. When Landon first picked up my husband, our youngest son, our daughter, and me from the airport we were on a mission to get ham hocks. It was the day after Christmas, and we flew in for these interviews but more importantly we came to spend time with our family. Landon wanted collard greens and fried chicken. We laughed at this bizarre stereotype some might find offensive. I remember, out of ignorance, asking where on earth we could get ham hocks along the five-hour drive from Seattle to Neah Bay. Landon explained that it was no problem. We were going to "Tacoma, the Compton of Washington." In Tacoma, we found everything we needed and had a splendid southern New Year's Eve dinner: fried chicken, macaroni and cheese, and collards with ham hocks. I knew there were Black communities that settled all throughout the Pacific Northwest, particularly during the nineteenth century, but that fact resonated only in historical terms. I didn't consciously factor in the existence of contemporary Black communities located in various cities from Seattle to the rez.[49] When we arrived many hours later, we settled into our four-year-old granddaughter's room. The next morning as I awoke I realized we had slept in a little princess room, but it wasn't Disney's version of Pocahontas that I saw. Instead, the walls were adorned with Princess Tatiana, Disney's first African American princess. Despite the fact that Landon's children do not appear to be of African descent, he and Daleena have made it their business to teach them about their entire identity. When our eight-year-old grandson sees other Black children he just assumes they are related to him. Landon shared with me that his son often says, "Dad I want to get brown" and with pride he continues, "Dad, I'm browner than this cousin or that cousin." It seems that racial self-loathing is nowhere to be found in their home.

The days that followed on the rez were filled with cheer. Friends and family paraded through every day. Landon's Korean fishermen friends dropped by for the New Year's party, the children on New Year's Day broke out in a traditional Makah dance with a drum that beat in sync with their little feet and warrior poses. Daleena cooked Filipino adobo and rice and reminded me that Landon needed rice at every meal. All these cultures were ever-present, at every minute, and yet standing in relief was this larger, more important idea: the vital role of family. Landon's central identity was and remains rooted in the term family. In fact, he's tattooed with the word. This value transcends tribal, ethnic, or racial affiliation, but it is also a very Makah choice to make. As Peterson-Renault insisted, "family [is] the fabric of Makah life."[50]

ACKNOWLEDGMENTS

This chapter is dedicated to Jo Ann Della, Landon Zendell Wimberly, Ritchie Wimberly, Natalie Aguirre, and Jazz Aguirre. I am eternally grateful to the Makah Cultural and Research Center and to author, proprietor of Raven's Corner, and Elder Melissa Peterson-Renault.

NOTES

1. For a discussion of "monoracism," see Marc P. Johnston and Kevin L. Nadal, "Multiracial Microaggressions: Exposing Monoracism in Everyday Life and Clinical Practice," in *Microaggressions and Marginality: Manifestation, Dynamics, and Impact*, ed. Derald Wing Sue (Hoboken, NJ: John Wiley, 2010), 123–144.
2. Maria P. P. Root, "A Bill of Rights for Racially Mixed People," in *The Multiracial Experience: Racial Borders as the New Frontier*, ed. Maria P. P. Root (Thousand Oaks, CA: Sage, 1996), 3–14.
3. In this chapter I use the word "indigenous" as an umbrella term. Because I aim to refer to people in the manner in which they prefer, I employ the term "Indian" or "Native" interchangeably when recounting a story or when writing a general description. I use the term "Makah" when I refer to a self-described member of the Makah tribe.
4. Henry Louis Gates, Jr., "High Cheekbones and Straight Black Hair? 100 Amazing Facts about the Negro: Why Most Black People Aren't 'Part Indian,' Despite Family Lore,"

Root, April 21, 2014, http://www.theroot.com/articles/history/2014/04/why_most_black
_people_aren_t_part_indian.4.html.

5. "We Come from People," in *Finding Your Roots with Henry Louis Gates, Jr.* (KOCE, October 28, 2014, DVD). It is unclear which ethnicities constitute the so-called "Asian/Native" group.

6. Stephen Cornell and Douglas Hartmann, *Ethnicity and Race: Making Identities in a Changing World*, rev. ed. (Thousand Oaks, CA: Pine Forge Press, 2007); Michael Omi and Howard Winant, *Racial Formation in the United States: From the 1960s to the 1990s*, 2nd ed. (New York: Routledge, 1994); Paul Spickard and W. Jeffrey Burroughs, eds., *We Are a People: Narrative and Multiplicity in Constructing Ethnic Identity* (Philadelphia: Temple University Press, 2000); Audrey Smedley, *Race in North America: Origin and Evolution of a Worldview* (Boulder, CO: Westview, 1999); Jonathan Marks, *Human Biodiversity: Genes, Race, and History* (New York: Aldine de Gruyter, 1995); Paul Spickard, "The Return of Scientific Racism? DNA Ancestry Testing, Race, and the New Eugenics Movement," in *Race in Mind: Critical Essays* (Notre Dame, IN: University of Notre Dame Press, 2015), 142–173.

7. Jared Sexton, *Amalgamation Schemes: Antiblackness and the Critique of Multiracialism* (Minneapolis: University of Minnesota Press, 2008); Michele Elam, *The Souls of Mixed Folk: Race, Politics, and Aesthetics in the New Millennium* (Stanford, CA: Stanford University Press, 2011); Rainier Spencer, *Spurious Issues: Race and Multiracial Identity Politics in the United States* (Boulder, CO: Westview, 1999).

8. Gary B. Nash, *Red, White and Black: The Peoples of Early America* (Englewood Cliffs, NJ: Prentice Hall, 1974); Jack D. Forbes, *Africans and Native Americans: The Language of Race and the Evolution of Red-Black Peoples*, 2nd ed. (Urbana: University of Illinois Press, 1993); William Loren Katz, *Black Indians: The Hidden Heritage* (New York: Simon & Schuster, 1985); James F. Brooks, ed., *Confounding the Color Line: The Black-Indian Experience in North America* (Lincoln: University of Nebraska Press, 2002); Circe Sturm, *Blood Politics: Race, Culture, and Identity in the Cherokee Nation of Oklahoma* (Berkeley: University of California Press, 2002); Theda Perdue, *"Mixed Blood" Indians: Racial Construction in the Early South* (Athens: University of Georgia Press, 2010); Claudio Saunt, *Black, White, Indian: Race and the Unmaking of an American Family* (New York: Oxford University Press, 2005).

9. Gabrielle Tayac, Ed., *IndiVisible: African-Native American Lives in the Americas* (Washington, DC: Smithsonian, 2009). See also Theda Perdue, "Native Americans, African Americans and Jim Crow," in Tayac, *IndiVisible*, 21–33.

10. Perdue, "Native Americans," 21–25.

11. Carey McWilliams, "Introduction," in *America Is in the Heart*, by Carlos Bulosan (1946; repr., Seattle: University of Washington Press, 1973), xxi.

12. Here, my use of the term "Native" serves two functions. First, it reflects what the people of Neah Bay call themselves. Second, it reflects an inclusive impulse to recognize that many self-described Makah are a mixture of various tribes indigenous to the Olympic Peninsula, including the Quinault, Quileute, Hoh, Makah, etc. See Melissa Peterson-Renault, "'Makah': Melissa Peterson and the Makah Cultural and Research Center," in *Native People of the Olympic Peninsula: Who We Are, by the Olympic Peninsula Intertribal Cultural Advisory Committee*, ed. Jacilee Wray (Norman: University of Oklahoma Press, 2002), 151–167.

13. Landon Wimberly, interview by Ingrid Dineen-Wimberly, Makah Reservation, Neah Bay, WA, January 2, 2014; Natalie Aguirre, interview by Ingrid Dineen-Wimberly, Makah Reservation, Neah Bay, WA, December 30, 2013.

14. See Sturm, *Blood Politics* for a comprehensive examination of the prevalence of blood quantum politics among Native tribes in the United States generally and among the Cherokee in particular.

15. I employ the term "rez" when referring to the Makah reservation.

16. Greg Kolfax, Makah Cultural and Research Center, interview by Ingrid Dineen-Wimberly, Makah Reservation, Neah Bay, WA, January 3, 2014; Ann M. Renker, "Makah Tribe: People of the Sea and the Forest" (University of Washington Digital Collections), https://content.lib.washington.edu/aipnw/renker.html.

17. There are 2,303 enrolled members of the Makah Nation. Eighteen hundred people live in Neah Bay, but of those only fourteen hundred are Makah. See Peterson-Renault, "Makah," 159.

18. Wimberly interview.

19. Elizabeth Colson, *The Makah Indians: A Study of an Indian Tribe in Modern American Society*, 2nd ed. (Westport, CT: Greenwood, 1977), v.

20. Ibid., vii.

21. Ibid., vii.

22. Janine Bowechop, "Preface," in *Voices of a Thousand People*, ed. Patricia Erikson, with Helma Ward and Kirk Wachendorf (Lincoln: University of Nebraska Press, 2005), xi.

23. Peterson-Renault, "Makah," 151.

24. Carolyn J. Marr, "Assimilation through Education: Indian Boarding Schools in the Pacific Northwest" (University of Washington Digital Collections, n.d.), https://content.lib.washington.edu/aipnw/marr.html#bibliography.

25. Wimberly interview.

26. Marr, "Assimilation through Education."

27. By the 1960s and 1970s a move to reintroduce the Makah Language found its way back through elementary and secondary curricula; the movement flourishes today. See Peterson-Renault, "Makah," 160. For a thorough history of Indian assimilation, see David Wallace Adams, *Education for Extinction: The American Indian Boarding School Experience, 1875–1928* (Lawrence: University Press of Kansas, 1995).

28. Colson, *Makah Indians*, 27.

29. Wimberly interview. For a biographical examination of the migrant labor pattern from Washington to California, see Bulosan, *America Is in the Heart.*

30. Rick Baldoz, *The Third Asiatic Invasion: Empire and Migration in Filipino America, 1898–1946* (New York: New York University Press, 2011), 67, 108; Rudy P. Guevarra Jr., *Becoming Mexipino: Multiethnic Identities and Communities in San Diego* (New Brunswick, NJ: Rutgers University Press, 2012), 6–7.

31. Baldoz, *Third Asiatic Invasion*, 106–107.

32. Ibid., 108.

33. Ibid., 108.

34. Peterson-Renault, "Makah," 161.

35. Guevarra, *Becoming Mexipino*, 6.

36. Paul Spickard and W. Jeffrey Burroughs, "We Are a People," in Spickard and Burroughs, *We Are a People*, 11.

37. Wimberly interview.

38. Saunt, *Black, White, Indian*, 210.

39. Wimberly interview.

40. Wimberly interview.

41. Landon Wimberly, telephone interview by Ingrid Dineen-Wimberly, Chicago, November 16, 2014.

42. Aguirre interview.

43. Aguirre interview.

44. Don Hannula, "State Indians Worse Off Than Negroes," *Seattle Times* (July 26, 1968): 9, reprinted in Alexandra Harmon, *Indians in the Making: Ethnic Relations and Indian Identities around Puget Sound* (Berkeley: University of California Press, 1998), 222.

45. Peterson-Renault, "Makah," 156.

46. Peterson-Renault, "Makah," 161.

47. Harmon, *Indians in the Making*, 3.

48. Ibid., 252n7.

49. For excellent histories on Black settlement of the Pacific Northwest, see Esther Hall Mumford, *Seattle's Black Victorians, 1852–1901* (Seattle: Ananse Press, 1980); Quintard Taylor, *The Forging of a Black Community: Seattle's Central District from 1870 through the Civil Rights Era* (Seattle: University of Washington Press, 1994); Douglas Henry Daniels, *Pioneer Urbanites: A Social and Cultural History* (Berkeley: University of California Press, 1991). For films, see Shaun Scott, producer and director, "The End of Old Days" (Seattle Civil Rights & Labor History Project, January 3, 2015), http://depts.washington.edu/civilr/film_end_days.htm.

50. Peterson-Renault, "Makah," 156.

8

"You're Not Black or Mexican Enough!"

Policing Racial/Ethnic Authenticity among Blaxicans in the United States

REBECCA ROMO

Latinos growing up would call me nigger and stuff like that, *mayate*," said Andrea, a Blaxican woman whom I interviewed in Los Angeles.[1] Anti-Black sentiment coming from Latinas/os was a common theme in the interviews that I conducted with forty Blaxicans, or individuals with one African American parent and one Mexican or Mexican American parent in the United States. Simultaneously, Blaxicans like Andrea experienced rejection and prejudices directed toward them by African Americans. In Andrea's case, her African American peers in high school accused her of thinking that she was better than them for having "good" hair, and ridiculed her for speaking English with a Spanish accent. Blaxicans feel pressure to conform to the race, class, and gender expectations in both the African American and Mexican American communities. Indeed, individuals act at the risk of being evaluated with regard to their essential natures, presumably captured in categorical identities that gain meaning through everyday interactions.[2]

This chapter examines how authenticity policing enforces racial/ethnic boundaries that shape Blaxican identities. Scholars studying mixed race experiences have used different terms to describe the interactional power dynamics between monoracial people of color and mixed race people such as monoracism, monoracial microaggressions, borderism, and interethnic and intraracial discrimination.[3] I explore how racial/ethnic authenticity policing is at the core of many of these conflicting interactions, and how these interactions drive the development of new or post–civil rights hybrid racial/ethnic identities. I argue that Blaxican identities exist in a borderlands space between the socially constructed categories of African American and Mexican American, and emerge out of the contradictions that arise when claiming authenticity to both groups.

Blaxican identities diverge from White/minority multiracial identities. White/ minority multiracials tend to identify with their minority parent for several reasons: identifying with their minority parent as a means of associating with a history of oppression, for the simplicity of identifying as monoracial, and because they had contact only with their minority parent.[4] The way that White/minority multiracials identify is also influenced by phenotype. White/minority multiracials with darker physiognomy perceive more ethnic discrimination, and are more likely to self-identify as a minority race.[5] Blaxicans identify with both of their backgrounds regardless of phenotype or ethnic leanings favoring one group over the other. They articulate a connection to two separate histories of racial oppression. Rather than choose between two racial/ethnic minority identities, Blaxicans choose both.

This chapter raises the following questions: What racial realities do Blaxicans experience due to their intersectional identities? Also, how are Blaxicans held accountable to African American and Mexican American racial/ethnic authenticity? How do Blaxican men and women experience authenticity policing differently? And, what do narratives about skin color, hair, and other markers reveal about how authenticity is used as a source of intragroup power that marginalizes Blaxicans and pushes them to craft an in-between identity that embraces both of their backgrounds?

Intersectional and Borderlands Identities

I use intersectional frameworks to understand Blaxican lives and identities.[6] Intersectional theory underscores the complexities of lived experiences and focuses on situated knowledge. From an intersectional perspective, Blaxicans' experiences are unique and critical knowledge-producing spaces that inform how intersecting systems of power (i.e., race, class, gender, sexuality) maintain and reinforce different forms of oppression simultaneously. Intersectional frameworks argue that sociological theory should examine more than one variable (i.e., race, class, gender) at a time and that these variables work in concert to create inequality. According to Patricia Hill Collins's concept of the "matrix of domination," women will experience oppression differently depending on the way that social variables intersect with one another.[7] Andrea provides an example of how she experiences her identity the same as and different from African American and Mexican American women. She says, "All the drama and stuff that Chicanas have to go through and African American women have to go through, multiply that times two, and I go through that. All the strengths that Chicanas have and the strengths that African American women have, multiply that by two and I have that. I have all the struggles that women in general have. Now add Chicana and add African American and you multiply that times two and you have a situation where every day there are people wanting you to choose a side. That is a different thing you have to deal with than if you are just one race."[8]

Andrea discusses some of the elements that make up her identity: woman, African American, Chicana, and multiracial. One way that Blaxican identities and experiences are unique from those of monoracials and White-minority mixed race people is their position as dual minorities. Blaxicans' two racial/ethnic reference groups (African Americans and Mexican Americans) have been socially, economically, and politically disadvantaged for generations.[9] Because Blaxicans have two non-White parents, and Whiteness is not an option, choosing both is less likely to be viewed as trying to climb the racial hierarchy, and therefore appealing. Blaxicans choose both as a way of embracing a non-hierarchical valuation of one group over the other.

My analysis of Blaxican identities also draws on borderlands theory articulated by the late Chicana lesbian feminist theorist Gloria Anzaldúa. I situate Blaxicans' identities and experiences within the borderlands, a site for political, historical, and sexual consciousness for appreciating the coming together of different cultures.[10] Anzaldúa calls for a new "mestiza" consciousness that embraces the contradictions and ambiguity of those who live in more than one culture.[11] "The new *mestiza* copes by developing a tolerance for contradictions, a tolerance for ambiguity. She learns to be an Indian in Mexican culture, to be a Mexican from an Anglo point of view. She learns to juggle cultures."[12] Blaxican identities encompass tolerance for contradictions, ambiguity, and the juggling of two cultures consistent with what Anzaldúa articulates as the new mestiza consciousness.[13] Anzaldúa argues that the new mestiza turns ambivalence, or the state of having simultaneous conflicting feelings, into "something else."[14] Blaxicans' ambivalence toward not being viewed as authentically African American or Mexican American motivated their agency of crafting a hybrid racial/ethnic identity that borrows from multiple historical sources at the same time. This in-between state that Blaxicans experience can be juxtaposed to the concept of liminality, which captures the ambiguous periods between two relatively fixed or stable conditions.[15] The liminal person is "betwixt and between" all that is structurally fixed and recognizable by a society. To exist in a liminal or borderlands space means to contend with borderism, or a unique form of discrimination faced by individuals who transcend racial lines or attempt to claim membership in more than one racial group.[16]

Method and Data

I conducted forty in-depth interviews with Blaxican adults from the United States. I interviewed first-generation mixed race individuals who have one parent who is designated and identified as African American and one Mexican or

Mexican American parent.[17] I recorded, transcribed, and coded my interviews. Not surprisingly, more than half of the sample (twenty-seven) resided in California, which is among the top ten states in the United States with the highest percentage of "two or more races."[18] Other participants were from the following states: Texas, New Mexico, Maryland, Indiana, Arizona, Louisiana, New York, and Illinois. Twenty-two women and eighteen men participated in this study. The participants' age ranged from eighteen to seventy-one, and the majority (90 percent) was between the ages of twenty and forty. Thirteen of the participants have Mexican fathers (three born in Mexico) and mothers who are African American. The remaining twenty-seven participants have African American fathers and mothers that are Mexican (seven of the mothers were born in Mexico). I use "Blaxican" when talking about all of the participants. It is a self-designation that emerged organically among many participants and combines two familiar terms, "Black" and "Mexican," into one designation. There are other spellings and terms used to describe Blaxican individuals, including AfroMex, MexiBlack, Black-Chicana, and Afro-Mexican. However, most participants used "Blaxican" as the appropriate spelling for this designation and noted that Blaxican sounded phonetically better than the other terms.

In 2010, nine million people reported more than one race, 33 percent of whom were of Hispanic origin.[19] Determining the exact numbers of people with one African American parent and one Mexican or Mexican American parent in the population is not immediately apparent for two reasons. First, the designation of Mexican is treated as an ethnicity, not a race, on the census. Second, Blaxicans record themselves in the census in a variety of ways. For example, the majority of participants marked "Black" and "Some Other Race" and would be included among 314,571 people in the 2010 census who marked the same categories. Some selected "Black" as a race and marked "Hispanic" as an ethnicity, similar to 1.8 million people in the 2010 census.[20]

Policing Racial/Ethnic Authenticity

Blaxicans encounter authenticity policing, or social interactions that occur when an inside member of a racial/ethnic group challenges another's claim to authenticity and belonging through assumptions about their race, class, and gender. These social interactions occur in obvious and subtle ways through behaviors such as body language, gestures, and speech and involve power. Authenticity policing is often internalized and self-inflicted.

Authenticity policing indicates intragroup power dynamics such that the person being challenged to prove his or her authenticity is viewed as tentative or marginal. Not being viewed as authentic for people from racially and ethnically mixed backgrounds is insulting.[21] In this view, authenticity can be juxtaposed to microaggressions, which are offensive mechanisms that are designed to reduce, dilute, atomize, and encase subordinate groups into place.[22] In an American context that values monoraciality, multiracials often experience marginality because of their non-monoracial status and are viewed as non-normative. Thus, multiracials experience racial microaggressions in similar ways to monoracials, yet in unique ways due to their multiraciality.[23]

In my interviews with Blaxican participants, I found that their African American and Mexican American relatives and peers consistently policed the boundaries around the intertwined constructions of race, class, and gender that make up presumably "essential" racial categories. African American and Mexican American peers remarked on how Blaxicans were never Black or Mexican "enough." Hair texture, skin color, Spanish fluency, and hip-hop dancing were some of the markers of authenticity. Measurements of authenticity carried implications about gender, and I found that Blaxican women were policed more than Blaxican men. Authenticity policing does not occur every time Blaxicans are in the presence of other African Americans or Mexican Americans; however, these interactions occurred frequently throughout many participants' lives. Authenticity policing is situational and contextual, and is sometimes viewed as nonthreatening, depending on the interaction. An extreme example of confrontational authenticity policing that occurred was being asked on the spot to speak Spanish or to perform a hip-hop dance. The latter examples were viewed as offensive because of the messages conveyed about Blaxicans not being racially/ethnically authentic. Racial/ethnic authenticity is ranked such that the more an individual is perceived as authentic, the more power he or she has to claim membership within a specific group.

At the same time, Blaxicans experienced microaggressions from their own families, which is consistent with the multiracial experience.[24] Within Mexican American families, the act of policing boundaries was heavily located around their mother's experiences. Nicole, from Albuquerque, shared a story about how a Mexican border patrol agent questioned her mother crossing the border on one of their visits to Mexico. After looking at Nicole in the passenger seat, he asked her mother, "You slept with a Black guy? You have a Black child?"[25] Reminiscent of the 1960s Chicano Power Movement when men attempted to define women's role as maintaining the race through bearing and raising Chicana/o children, the policing of Mexican American mother's bodies was a common theme in interviews that reinforced the idea of boundary crossing as taboo.[26] Blaxicans reported that many of their Mexican American male relatives initially disapproved of their Mexican American mother's choice of having an intimate relationship with their African American father. Only one Blaxican participant reported that his African American grandfather disapproved of his African American mother's relationship with his Mexican American father. Some

African American relatives battled to enforce a Black identity over a Mexican American one. For example, against Gaby's wishes, her African American grandmother legally changed her Spanish-sounding name as a child, and maintained a conflicted relationship with her Mexican grandmother.

Policing Mexican American Authenticity

Mexican American authenticity was an important factor shaping Blaxican identities for all participants; however, it was experienced in different ways depending on gender and demographic makeup of the regions in which Blaxicans lived. Blaxican women and men had similar experiences in terms of how their Mexican American peers policed racial/ethnic authenticity. However, Blaxican women claimed that issues surrounding identity were more difficult and frequent for women than for Blaxican men. Blaxican women reported being exoticized by men in general, and by Latino and Black men specifically. Eliza, a woman from Los Angeles, says, "I have had experiences where Latino men would talk to me, and it would be like they are talking to me just regular, they have no interest. Then once it comes up that I am Chicana it's like a heightened level of interest comes out. If I am just Black then I am not interesting to you, however, if I then I say I am Black and Chicana then this whole world of possibility then opens up."[27]

Blaxican women's experiences with some men were such that their mixedness made them more sexually desirable. For Latino men, being more than Black made Blaxican women acceptable to pursue. In Latin America, and Mexico specifically, the mulata (or mixed race woman) is an icon of sexual desire and a symbol for the danger of racial contamination through miscegenation.[28] Blaxican women are sexually exoticized because they symbolically represent dangerous boundaries that have been crossed.

Mexican authenticity policing is also dependent on region. Blaxicans living in places such as Maryland knew few Mexicans or Mexican Americans outside of their own immediate families. Instead, Blaxicans on the East Coast were mistaken for Puerto Rican, Cuban, or Dominican, and many felt an affinity with these ethnic groups. In some regions there were many Mexican Americans, and in others a Mexican American population was virtually nonexistent. Some participants from Arizona described a racial context in which Native Americans, African Americans, and Mexican Americans made up the racial landscape, and how these groups influenced their identities. The degree of contact with other minority groups within a neighborhood influences the degree of felt closeness to one's racial reference group.[29] For the purposes of this chapter, I focus on participants' face-to-face experiences in social contexts that included Mexicans and Mexican Americans.

My interviews with Blaxicans revealed that the salient markers of Mexican authenticity included fluency in Mexican Spanish or ability to blend Spanish and English, known as Spanglish. Also important was knowledge of Mexican or Mexican American culture, a Brown phenotype, and ascribed working-class status. Class, racial, and ethnic signifiers are melded together in a way that authentic Black and Brown identities are imagined as urban and lower class.[30] Most importantly, not appearing mixed with African ancestry determined by skin color or hair was a phenotypical determinant. If Blaxicans appeared to be mixed with African Americans, they were viewed as Black, and many of their Mexican American peers assumed that they were not knowledgeable of Mexican American culture. Mexican Americans perceptions of Blackness are influenced by racial attitudes and ideas transmitted from Mexico and the United States.[31] Although Mexican-descent people have African ancestry and African-influenced cultures, the national rhetoric of *mestizaje*, or the process of racial mixing, has convinced many that they are all *mestizas/os* of one race, and African ancestry is often denied and ignored.[32] The monoracialization of Mexican American or Chicana/o identity was later exacerbated in the 1960s Chicano Movement, solidifying identification with a distinct Brown race.[33] In my interviews, not appearing mixed with African ancestry and knowing Spanish were the two most important factors in determining Mexican American racial/ethnic authenticity. Desire, a Blaxican woman from Las Cruces, New Mexico, whose mother is Mexican and father is African American, explained that she is culturally Mexican American yet appears African American. She says, "As far as looks, I feel more Black, but as far as culture, I feel more Mexican."[34] Desire understands and speaks some Spanish. She grew up surrounded by Mexican American culture, and even described how her African American father often cooks *menudo*.[35] She says,

> I feel more comfortable in a room full of Mexicans speaking Spanish with mariachi music and *corridos* in the background rather than in a room full of Black people where I felt awkward.[36] I worked at a restaurant where a lot of families only spoke Spanish. I was the only one in the night crew that spoke Spanish, so whenever there was a question they always directed them to me. I would talk to these people and they would be really confused. They would be like, "How do you know Spanish?" Or, "Where did you learn Spanish?" Then I would have to say from my mom's side of the family, and then I would tell them I'm a Blaxican. Then they would eventually be accepting and think it's really cool I speak Spanish.[37]

Mexican Americans had more positive reactions to Blaxicans if they demonstrated the ability to speak Spanish, even if they appeared Black. Speaking and/or understanding Spanish allowed Blaxicans to feel more connected to Mexican culture. However, oftentimes knowing and presenting Mexican American culture was not enough to prove authenticity if Blaxicans appeared to have

Black blood. Monica, a woman from Tucson, Arizona, was raised by her single Mexican American mother and is often perceived as Black. Monica feels very connected to Mexican American culture and traditions. As a young girl she danced *folklórico* with a group at her Catholic church.[38] Monica grew up around many of her Mexican American cousins, and for a long while she never thought of herself as anything other than Mexican American. It was not until the girls in her folklórico group excluded her because of her dark skin that she began to understand that people viewed her as Black. She recalled, "One time in third grade I was in folklórico and I went to a very Mexican church and the girls there were mean to me, they picked on me. I was on a folklórico team and I thought I was good, and my mom said I was good, and I performed, and I was on it for a couple years. One day I had to miss practice for a day and they told me, 'You can't perform in the next performance because you missed practice.' Then my friend that was on the team, told me that they really did not want me to be on the performance because I was Black. I wasn't Mexican enough for them."[39]

In the story that Monica recounted, the Mexican girls in the folklórico group informed her that she was not viewed as authentically Mexican American, despite her knowledge of folklórico dance, because her skin color and hair marked her as Black. Ironically, folklórico consists of Jarocho and Chilena dances that are heavily Afro-Mexican.[40] Dances originating from states like Veracruz, an African slave port state, are among the most popular. Authenticity policing forced Monica, similar to other participants, to reconsider her racial/ethnic identity. Monica refused to identify with one reference group to be accepted and, like other participants, embraced a blended dual-minority racial/ethnic identity as Blaxican. Thus, Blaxican as a borderlands identity embraces the contradictions of claiming authenticity in two recognizable and seemingly fixed groups. Blaxican identities include those that appear Black, Mexican, mixed, or ambiguous, with Mexican American, African American, or blended cultural backgrounds, and are complicated by class, sexuality, and gender identities.

Policing Black Authenticity

I found that Black authenticity was a constant factor that Blaxicans faced. Examples of Black racial/ethnic authenticity were available to participants through media and face-to-face interactions in their communities through strangers, peers, and family. Understandings about Black presence and identity are also informed by global media representations of African Diaspora peoples that come from television broadcasts.[41] The list of markers that determined Black authenticity was far more exhaustive than that for Mexican American authenticity. In the United States, Black people are relegated to the lowest position on the racial structure, and authenticity is equated to loyalty to Black liberation.[42] Therefore, for African Americans, the stakes are higher when determining racial/ethnic authenticity. Some of the markers of authenticity for African Americans include dress, talk, hip-hop culture, knowledge of African American history, dancing, "kinky," "afro," or "crinkly" hair, darker skin, and working-class status. When Blaxicans did not "act" Black according to their peers, their behavior was equated with acting White. If their hair was loosely curly or straight and long, they received double-sided compliments about having good hair, thus being complimented on their hair and insulted on their African ancestry. Dominant standards of beauty in the form of hair, skin color, and phenotype is one way that controlling images depreciate African American women.[43] Controlling images are often used to define authentic Black womanhood and reflect the dominant groups interests in maintaining the subordination of Black women and are powerful influences on Black women's relationships with one another.

During high school, Andrea, from Los Angeles, attended school in the city of Pasadena, which has a large percentage of African Americans. Andrea noted, "When I went to school in Pasadena, it was the reverse of what I experienced with Latinos in Highland Park. So it was like, 'You think you're better?' 'Why do you talk like that?' 'Why do you have that accent?' The hair thing came up. 'You think you're better because you have good hair.' So I got that. So I always experienced that type of racism or behavior from my own people."[44] While Black racism would require a widely accepted racist ideology directed at Whites with the power to systematically exclude others, the behavior that Andrea refers to is authenticity policing.[45] Authenticity policing is a form of borderism and monoracial microaggressions that are interactions meant to keep non-monoracial people in their place.[46] Authenticity policing is unique in that these interactions specifically center on the use of authenticity as a mechanism of intragroup power. Andrea's peers were policing Black authenticity in the forms of class, speech, and hair to interrogate her loyalty to Black people. Andrea also had conflicts about her hair within her own family. She says, "My hair is mixed. When I was little, I had an afro. Then when I got to a certain age my mother and my grandmother would fight about my hair. My mom wanted my hair to be braided like a Black girl, my grandma wanted my hair to be like a Latina girl, so there was always that conflict there in my family."[47] The significance of hair among African American women is documented in the literature in its relationship to Africa, enslavement, constructions of race, self-esteem, images of beauty, politics, identity, and the intersection of race and gender.[48] Andrea's hair became the battleground between her Mexican American mother who wanted her to have a Black hairstyle, and her Mexican American grandmother who desired a non-Black Latina aesthetic. Andrea's grandmother wanted her to wear her hair in a style that would authenticate her as Mexican American, not Black. Intrafamilial issues regarding racial/ethnic authenticity were common among Blaxicans' experiences, and sometimes resulted in estrangement with one's family.

Hip-hop was another marker of authenticity that was important particularly for Blaxican women. Erica, a woman from Indiana, described that "the
hardest thing about being Blaxican, is trying to live up to both standards."[49] Her
African American peers judged her in high school mostly because of the way she
danced. She says, "My name is Erica, and they would be like, 'Your name is Erica?
You're from Indiana? You talk like a White girl. You're half Mexican? You don't
speak Spanish good. You're not down with any of the Black people because you
don't know how to dance.' Or, 'You dance funny.' You dance a certain way and
it's not the right way. They doing the two-step, walk-it-out, and I'm like trying
to figure out who I am and I had a lot of negativity from both sides. I was never
Black enough and I was definitely never Mexican enough, ever."[50]

Erica felt pressure to dance a certain way to be accepted by her African
American peers as authentically Black. She was expected to know current hip-
hop dances such as the "two-step" and "walk-it-out." Blackness has increasingly
become synonymous with hip-hop culture.[51] Challenging Erica about her performance of hip-hop dances questions not only her racial/ethnic authenticity,
but also her gender and sexuality. Hip-hop and pornography have recently part-
nered in music videos to commodify Black women's bodies and illuminate constructions of Black femininity and masculinity.[52] Black women's excessive and
accessible heterosexuality as performed in hard-core and soft-core hip-hop acts
as a signifier that underlines the performance of Black hypermasculinity.[53] Thus,
policing Black authenticity around measures of hip-hop for Blaxican women was
about performing a certain kind of Black heterosexual femininity.

In contrast, Erica discusses how she feels around her Blaxican friends in
regards to dancing.[54] She says, "I don't have to worry about them saying, 'You're
not shaking your hips right.' Or, 'You're not two-steppin' right.' I don't have to
worry about them thinking I am not hip-hop enough to them. I love hanging out
with my Blaxican friends because there is not judgment there. They don't look
at you funny like, 'Oh, you're not doing this right.' Or 'You look silly when you
do it like that.' Pretty much when it comes to dancing that's where you get a lot
of hassle for how we dance. We can never dance good enough that's for sure."[55]

Blaxican women talked more about how hip-hop impacted their Black peers'
judgments of their identities in comparison to Blaxican men. Blaxican men talked
about hip-hop only in relation to how it made them closer to Black culture and
people. Eduardo from San Francisco says, "Sometimes when I am around Black people I feel like I am not Black enough, but I feel more comfortable for some reason
when I am around Black people than I do when I am around Mexicans. I look more
Mexican so it doesn't make any sense to me. But I think it is because I grew up into
hip-hop culture so I tend to be more familiar when I am around Black people."[56]

For Blaxican men, hip-hop also served as a measurement of Black authenticity, yet for men it was not about dancing. Rather, Blaxican men who were

familiar with hip-hop culture in the forms of dress, talk, mannerisms, gender expectations, and music felt a closer affinity to their Black side. Another study on mixed Mexican individuals also concluded that men felt pressure to conform to masculine expectations of Mexican men in the form of *machismo*.[57] The above examples are not exhaustive of how hair, skin color, and hip-hop are used as measures of gendered racial/ethnic authenticity that define Blackness. Rather, these examples represent some of the ways that Blaxicans experience authenticity policing by their African American peers that inspire agency to self-define a racial/ethnic identity that embraces the contradictions.

Discussion

Policing the boundaries of racial/ethnic authenticity through acceptance and exclusion around specific measures translates to an interrogation of loyalties to one non-White group. Thus, policing racial/ethnic boundaries is about protecting monoracial statuses as they were defined in the civil rights era and has gender implications. Stemming from the myth of White racial purity, racial categories are maintained through the taboo of miscegenation, or the mixing of racial groups through marriage, cohabitation, sex, and procreation. Expectations of authenticity are enacted to limit boundary crossing, and Blaxicans represent boundaries that have been crossed.[58] Policing of gendered racial/ethnic authenticity occurred most on women's bodies in comparison to Blaxican men. Blaxican participants witnessed their Mexican and Mexican American mothers being criticized, harassed, and ostracized for crossing racial lines, and at the same time Blaxican women were expected to conform to specific forms of femininity and were exoticized. Blaxicans were expected to erase or minimize their multiplicity in order to be viewed as authentically Black or authentically Mexican American. Participants were not willing to compromise one group over the other, and crafted an identity that blended both.

Dalmage discusses border patrolling by Whites and Blacks alike.[59] Individuals invested in maintaining the color line have patrolled the line on both sides. African Americans have policed the line for liberation, Whites to protect White privilege. Dalmage states, "Borders created to protect resources such as goods and power are kept in place by laws, language, cultural norms, images, and individual actions as well as by interlocking with other borders."[60] She highlights that Whites created the color line and are the only ones who have the institutional means to maintain the power granted in its maintenance. However, monoracial people of color continue to monitor the color line to the exclusion of multiracials of color. In fact, multiracial students of color who have been left out of student organizations modeled after traditional civil rights groups have created their own organizations nationwide.[61] Some view the power dynamics in the form

of authenticity policing within ethnic groups as counterproductive and insignifi-
cant to the advancement of coethnics' positions within the larger social and economic structure. In particular, Hunter states that light skin people of color are
typically not regarded as legitimate members of their ethnic communities yet
are advantaged in the labor market and in education.[62] Hunter claims that being
viewed as unauthentic by coethnic peers because of light skin color has only psychological and emotional consequences rather than material ones.[63]

Dalmage and Hunter are in agreement that managing racial/ethnic borders
benefits only Whites at the top of the racial social structure, and does little
to advance the position of non-White groups.[64] Nonetheless, the use of racial/
ethnic authenticity within and between racial/ethnic groups continues to occur
for social and political reasons and has particular histories. For example, African Americans patrol borders as a constant struggle for liberation from what the
color line imposes. Black border patrollers have an overriding concern about
being loyal to the race. Disloyalty implies weakness and acting in ways that are
complacent to the oppression of other African Americans.[65] Black and Mexican
American authenticity policing may suggest another way that the color line is
being maintained where monoracials are resisting a changing racial order that
is no longer the same Black/White dichotomous binary.

The issue of racial/ethnic authenticity for Blaxicans speaks to the potential
changes in the larger racial structure. Measurements about hair, skin color, hip-
hop, dancing, and Spanish implied specific race, class, and gender expectations
assumed essential to Blackness and what it means to be Mexican American.
Throughout their lives, Blaxicans experienced interactions with their Black and
Mexican American peers that informed them that they did not fit into these
particular constructs. The result of claiming authenticity to these two presumably stable and fixed categories is what prompted awareness of an in-between
state and influenced participants to self-define as Blaxican. Thus, the consequences of the use of authenticity as a form of exclusion of individuals who
desire to be a part of a fixed racial/ethnic group have the power of restructur-
ing the larger racial order and hierarchy. New racial/ethnic identities, whether
formally acknowledged or not, emerge out of the contradictions that surface
in claiming authenticity to two or more monoracial categories. These new categories of identity have the potential to change traditional racial hierarchies,
categories, and boundaries, particularly with the growth of multiracial populations.[66] In the case of Blaxicans, the social and psychological consequences of
not being viewed as racially or ethnically authentic force individuals to craft a
borderlands identity that blends both African American and Mexican American
historical sources.

My interviews suggest that Mexican Americans and African Americans are
invested for different reasons in policing racial/ethnic boundaries to maintain

the racial status quo in terms of the organization of collective identities. I found that African Americans and Mexican Americans pressure Blaxicans to choose loyalty to one non-White group, not both. Blaxicans must choose either a Black or Mexican American identity as a collective site for struggle against race and class oppression. Disloyalty for participants' African American peers suggests complacency with Black racial oppression. There is a higher investment in Black authenticity than there is in Mexican American authenticity. African Americans represent a smaller segment of the population in comparison to Latinas/os more broadly, and this is a factor in the desire to maintain numbers. The once legal and now socially accepted mechanism of the one-drop rule is specific to the United States and limits African Americans' mobility in the racial structure.[67] The one-drop rule was once imposed on African Americans to protect White supremacy and privilege, and has since been adopted by African Americans as a source of unity, community, and loyalty. African Americans have historically used identity politics as a location for struggle. In fact, African Americans view patrolling boundaries as troublesome yet necessary for liberation.[68]

Mexican Americans, on the other hand, occupy a more ambiguous position in the US racial hierarchy and have not been held to restrictive one-drop rules.[69] Although Mexican American identity is constructed within the backdrop of mestizaje, many Mexican Americans envision themselves as a singularized entity, even though attempts have been made at antiessentialism.[70] Also, Mexican American identity and culture is constantly reproduced via mass immigration and transnationalism, whereas Black identity is maintained without as much reproduction. Disloyalty to Mexican Americans in the form of appearing Black or not speaking Spanish represents a stepping down in racial status. For Mexican Americans, intermixing with Blacks is often looked down upon, and many participants' Mexican and Mexican American parents were criticized, ridiculed, and ostracized by their own families for marrying and having children with a Black partner. In contrast, multiethnic White Mexicans who appear White and do not speak Spanish are viewed as being assimilated to Whiteness.[71] This suggests Mexican Americans desire to maintain an intermediate position between White and Black, as was historically constructed and solidified during the civil rights era. Thus, monoracial groups of color use authenticity as a way of reinforcing and maintaining civil-rights-era racial constructions and order, not changing them because these have been the collective spaces in which people have organized against racial and class oppression. Articulations of Blaxican identities can represent for some a desire to distance from Blackness. On the contrary, Blaxican identities represent an embracing of being both Black and Mexican American simultaneously, and many participants articulated a political consciousness that brings together the historical sources of Black and Mexican American identity when trying to place their lives and experiences within a larger context. Rather than policing authenticity to force Blaxicans into the rigid socially constructed boundaries that define what it is to be Mexican American or Black, it would be more productive to use Blaxican consciousness as a conceptual tool to form Black-Brown coalitions. Similar to other identities, Blaxicans exist in a borderlands space, which is an intense place of struggle for liberation against oppressive constructs. Race-based civil-rights-era constructs aim to collectively organize to achieve group goals, and authenticity policing represents the desire to maintain rigid boundaries to protect these spaces of struggle. Blaxican identities are borderlands identities that are undefined and fluid, and push boundaries while embracing contradictions and ambiguities. Borderlands identities are also places of struggle that share the same goals of class and racial liberation that civil-rights-era identities do, but borderlands identities seek to accomplish goals of liberation by embracing common struggles, and by blending many historical sources at once. Therefore, viewing Blaxican identities from this perspective can be a place to learn how to build coalitions among African Americans and Mexican Americans to achieve similar goals.

NOTES

1. Andrea Avila, interview by author, Los Angeles, July 29, 2006, tape recorded. *Mayate* is a derogatory Spanish word whose literal translation is "black dung beetle," referring to African Americans.
2. Sarah Fenstermaker and Candice West, *Doing Gender, Doing Difference: Inequality, Power and Institutional Change* (New York: Routledge, 2002).
3. Marc P. Johnston and Kevin L. Nadal, "Multiracial Microaggressions: Exposing Monoracism in Everyday Life and Clinical Practice," in *Microaggressions and Marginality: Manifestation, Dynamics, and Impact*, ed. Derald Wing Sue (Hoboken, NJ: John Wiley, 2010), 123; Kevin L. Nadal, Yinglee Wong, Katie Griffin, Julie Sriken, Vivian Vargas, Michelle Wideman, and Ajayi Kolawole, "Microaggressions and the Multiracial Experience," *International Journal of Humanities and Social Science*, 7 (June 2011): 36; Heather M. Dalmage, "Discovering Racial Borders," in *Race in an Era of Change: A Reader*, ed. Heather M. Dalmage and Barbara Katz Rothman (New York: Oxford University Press, 2010), 95; Kelly F. Jackson, Thera Wolven, and Kimberly Aguilera, "Mixed Resilience: A Study of Multiethnic Mexican American Stress and Coping in Arizona," *Family Relations* 62 (January 2013): 212.
4. Melissa Herman, "Forced to Choose: Some Determinants of Racial Identification in Multiracial Adolescents." *Child Development* 75 (May 2004): 730.
5. Ibid., 730; Kerry Ann Rockquemore and David L. Brunsma, *Beyond Black: Biracial Identity in America* (Lanham, MD: Rowman & Littlefield, 2002); Barbara Tizard and Ann Phoenix, "The Identity of Mixed Parentage Adolescents," *Journal of Child Psychology and Psychiatry and Allied Disciplines* 36 (November 1995): 1399.
6. Kimberle Williams Crenshaw, "Mapping the Margins: Intersectionality, Identity Politics, and Violence Against Women of Color," *Stanford Law Review* 43 (July 1991): 1241; Patricia Hill Collins, *Black Feminist Thought: Knowledge, Consciousness, and the Politics of Empowerment* (New York: Routledge, 2000); bell hooks, *Feminist Theory: From Margin to Center* (Boston: South End, 2000).

7. Collins, *Black Feminist Thought*, 227.

8. Avila interview.

9. Edward Telles, Mark Q. Sawyer, and Gaspar Rivera-Salgado, *Just Neighbors? Research on African American and Latino Relations in the United States* (New York: Russell Sage Foundation, 2011), 1.

10. Horacio R. Ramírez, "Borderlands, Diasporas, and Transnational Crossings: Teaching LGBT Latina and Latino Histories," *OAH Magazine of History* 20 (March 2006): 39.

11. Gloria Anzaldúa, *Borderlands/La Frontera: The New Mestiza* (San Francisco: Aunt Lute Books, 1987), 101.

12. Ibid., 101.

13. Ibid., 99.

14. Ibid., 101.

15. Cecilia Menjívar, "Liminal Legality: Salvadoran and Guatemalan Immigrants' Lives in the United States," *American Journal of Sociology* 11 (January 2006): 999; Victor Turner, *The Forest of Symbols: Aspects of Ndembu Ritual* (Ithaca, NY: Cornell University Press, 1967).

16. Dalmage, "Discovering Racial Borders," 95.

17. The first generation is based on the immediate experience of identifying with parents from more than one racial/ethnic group. See more in G. Reginald Daniel, *Race and Multiraciality in Brazil and the United States: Converging Paths?* (University Park: Pennsylvania State University Press, 2006), 160.

18. Nicholas A. Jones and Amy Symens Smith, "The Two or More Races Population: 2000" (November 2001), http://www.census.gov/prod/2001pubs/c2kbr01-6.pdf.

19. Karen R. Humes, Nicholas A. Jones, and Roberto R. Ramirez, "Overview of Race and Hispanic Origin, 2010" (Washington, DC: US Census Bureau, 2011), http://www.census.gov/prod/cen2010/briefs/c2010br-02.pdf.

20. Sonya Rastogi, Tallese D. Johnson, Elizabeth M. Hoeffel, and Malcolm P. Drewery Jr., "The Black Population: 2010," http://www.census.gov/prod/cen2010/briefs/c2010br-06.pdf.

21. Kerry Ann Rockquemore, "Negotiating the Color-Line: The Gendered Process of Racial Identity among Black/White Multiracial Women," *Gender and Society* 16 (August 2002): 485.

22. Chester M. Pierce, "Is Bigotry the Basis of the Medical Problems of the Ghetto?," in *Medicine in the Ghetto*, ed. John C. Norman (New York: Meredith, 1969), 301.

23. Johnston and Nadal, "Multiracial Microaggressions," 123.

24. Nadal et al., "Microaggressions and the Multiracial Experience," 36.

25. Nicole Hodges, interview by author, Albuquerque, NM, August 3, 2006, tape recorded.

26. Maylei Blackwell, "Contested Histories: Las Hijas de Cuahtémoc, Chicana Feminisms, and the Print Culture in the Chicano Movement, 1968–1973," in *Chicana Feminisms: A Critical Reader*, ed. Gabriella. F. Arredondo, Aída Hurtado, Norma Klahn, Olga Nájera-Ramírez, and Patricia Zavella (Durham, NC: Duke University Press, 2003), 59.

27. Eliza Montes, interview by author, Los Angeles, January 2007, tape recorded.

28. Anita González, *Afro-Mexico: Dancing between Myth and Reality* (Austin: University of Texas Press, 2010), 25; Susan Thomas, *Cuban Zarzuela: Performing Race and Gender on Havana's Lyric Stage* (Urbana: University of Illinois Press, 2009).

29. Cynthia García Coll, Gontran Lamberty, Renee Jenkins, Harriet Pipes McAdoo, Keith Crnic, Barbara Hanna Wasik, and Heidie Vásquez García, "An Integrative Model for the Study of Developmental Competencies in Minority Children," *Child Development* 67 (October 1996): 1891; David Harris and Jeremiah J. Sim, "Who Is Multiracial? Assessing

the Complexity of Lived Race," *American Sociological Review* 67 (August 2002): 614; Ruth N. López Turley, "When Do Neighborhoods Matter? The Role of Race and Neighborhood Peers," *Social Science Research* 32 (March 2003): 61.

30. Julie Bettie, *Women without Class: Girls, Race and Identity* (Berkeley: University of California Press, 2003), 162.

31. Telles, Sawyer, and Rivera-Salgado, *Just Neighbors?*, 4.

32. González, *Afro-Mexico*, 27; José Vasconcelos, *The Cosmic Race/La Raza Cósmica*, trans. Didier T. Jaén (1979; repr., Baltimore: Johns Hopkins University Press, 1997).

33. Ian F. Haney López, *Racism on Trial: The Chicano Fight for Justice* (Cambridge, MA: Harvard University Press, 2003), 9.

34. Desire Campbell, interview by author, Las Cruces, NM, February 10, 2006, tape recorded.

35. Menudo is a traditional Mexican soup.

36. Corrido is a form of ballad or song in Spanish, usually about oppression, peasant life, or history.

37. Campbell interview.

38. Folklórico is a traditional dance style from Mexico reflecting cultures from various regions of the country.

39. Monica Bell, interview by author, Tucson, AZ, July 14, 2006, tape recorded.

40. González, *Afro-Mexico*, 116.

41. Ibid., 34.

42. Dalmage, "Discovering Racial Borders," 99.

43. Collins, *Black Feminist Thought*, 5.

44. Avila interview.

45. Joe Feagin and Hernán Vera, *White Racism* (New York: Routledge, 1995).

46. Dalmage, "Discovering Racial Borders," 95; Nadal et al., "Microaggressions and the Multiracial Experience," 36.

47. Avila interview.

48. Ingrid Banks, *Hair Matters: Beauty, Power, and Black Women's Consciousness* (New York: New York University Press, 2000).

49. Erica Donald, interview by author, Gary, IN, May 6, 2007, tape recorded.

50. Ibid.

51. Bettie, *Women without Class*, 130.

52. Mireille Miller-Young, "Hip-Hop Honeys and Da Hustlaz: Black Sexualities and the New Hip-Hop Pornography," *Meridians: Feminism, Race, Transnationalism* 8 (2008): 261; Crenshaw, "Mapping the Margins," 1241.

53. Tracy Denean Sharpley-Whiting, *Pimps Up, Ho's Down: Hip Hop's Hold on Young Black Women* (New York: New York University Press, 2007).

54. This is the only participant I interviewed who had Blaxican friends. All others knew Blaxicans only through family or virtually via the Internet.

55. Donald interview.

56. Eduardo Tijerina, interview by author, San Francisco, January 17, 2007, tape recorded.

57. Jackson, Wolven, and Aguilera, "Mixed Resilience," 212.

58. Natasha K. Warikoo, "Racial Authenticity among Second Generation Youth in New York and London," *Poetics* 35 (December 2007): 388.

59. Dalmage, "Discovering Racial Borders," 96.

60. Ibid., 94.

61. Ralina L. Joseph, *Transcending Blackness: From the New Millennium Mulatta to the Exceptional Multiracial* (Durham, NC: Duke University Press, 2012).

"YOU'RE NOT BLACK OR MEXICAN ENOUGH!"   143

62. Margaret L. Hunter, "The Persistent Problem of Colorism: Skin Tone, Status, and Inequality," *Sociology Compass* 1 (2007): 237.

63. Ibid.

64. Dalmage, "Discovering Racial Borders," 96; Hunter, "Persistent Problem of Colorism," 237.

65. Dalmage, "Discovering Racial Borders," 99.

66. G. Reginald Daniel and Josef Manuel Castañeda-Liles, "Race, Multiraciality, and the Neoconservative Agenda," in *Mixed Messages: Multiracial Identities in the "Color-Blind" Era*, ed. David Brunsma (Boulder, CO: Lynne Rienner, 2006), 125.

67. F. James Davis, *Who Is Black? One Nation's Definition* (University Park: Pennsylvania State University Press, 1991), 4.

68. Dalmage, "Discovering Racial Borders," 99.

69. Tomás Almaguer, *Racial Fault Lines: The Historical Origins of White Supremacy in California* (Berkeley: University of California Press, 1994); Haney López, *Racism on Trial*, 41.

70. Anzaldúa, *Borderlands/La Frontera*, 99.

71. Tomás R. Jiménez, "Negotiating Ethnic Boundaries: Multiethnic Mexican Americans and Ethnic Identity in the United States," *Ethnicities* 4.1 (2004): 75.

PART IV

Asian Connections

9

Bumbay in the Bay

The Struggle for Indipino Identity in San Francisco

MAHARAJ RAJU DESAI

You're not even a Filipino!" she points as her words shoot at me from across the room like an arrow. Once again, I'm being called out for my identity as an Indian Filipino (or Indipino). Once again, I have to justify my identity and explain why I am presenting at the Filipino American National Historical Society (FANHS) conference. Once my panel is over, she approaches me again and says, "So how are you a Filipino?" She critiques everyone else on my panel for what they *say*, but she critiques me on how I *look*. It is something I have unfortunately gotten used to and have experienced all my life. Many wonder how I can speak Tagalog or how I have family in the Philippines. Growing up, I recall people talking about me behind my back in high school and, more recently, how security at San Francisco International Airport always questions my visits to the Philippines. The friendly banter usually takes a little longer for me than everyone else as they try to ascertain whether I'm connected with some al-Qaeda cell in Mindanao or not. The FANHS conference is an interesting experience because here the voices of the *White* spouses of Filipinas are accepted wholeheartedly. At the same time, a fellow Filipino still questions and silences me. To clarify, I am of Indian and Filipino heritage. I am no different from other mestizos who are at this conference. Yet again, my existence is called into question. If I am viewed as an outsider in Filipino community spaces, where then do I (and others who are of mixed minority heritage) fit in?

Given these personal experiences, the lack of acknowledgment of Indipinos as part of the Filipino community, and that this mixed heritage community has a historical existence, it is clear that a conversation that centers the complexity of the Indipino experience is needed. This chapter provides an introductory exploration of the Indipino experience. I use the term "Indipino" because terms such as "Filipino Indian" or "Indian Filipino" do not convey the complexities of this identity, especially for those of us who also see ourselves as American. A critical mixed race scholar friend of mine, Teresa, gave me a shirt with the term "Indipino."[1] She herself, being Black and Filipino, had found identity with the term "Blacknpinay." Her hybridization of both facets of her ethnic identity is a practice that occurs in contemporary mixed race spaces. Scholar Rudy Guevarra coined the term "Mexipino" as a way to describe this blended community of people.[2] Teresa had found identity, comfort, and strength in Blacknpinay and had gifted me the term "Indipino" so that I could also find the same.

Indipino creates a space where I can simultaneously be Indian and Filipino without having to fit into anyone else's preconceived category of what either of those identities is. There is both a historical and a personal reasoning behind the term. "Indipino" is made up of two words: "Indi" (for Indian) and "Pino" (for Pilipino). Both words come from a colonial legacy and were created by the colonizers and placed on the indigenous populations. The words "Indian" and "Hindu" come from Indus and refer to the lands, people, and cultures east of the Indus River.[3] "Indian" was also later appropriated by Columbus and subsequent settler colonizers to misname the numerous indigenous nations of the Americas. Similarly, "Filipino" is a term that was initially applied to Spaniards born in the Philippine Islands. For the majority of Spanish occupation of the Philippines, the native people were referred to as Indios by the Spaniards.[4] "Filipino" has since become a term to refer to a native of the Philippine Islands as well as a citizen of the Republic of the Philippines. Among natives of the Philippines, "Filipino" has been Filipinized into "Pilipino" to match the native phonology. Although neither term was the original name of the local people, and although both terms have been misappropriated and misused, both have become a part of the identities of these respective peoples. Words hold our histories and tell our stories. We use terms that we call ourselves, and those help create our current identity. For instance, my Indipino family sees themselves as simultaneously Pilipino and Indian. When asked about their South Asian heritage, they will most commonly refer to themselves as Indian even though Punjabi may also be used. This is also because in a Pilipino context, *bumbay* and Indian are the only two words for a South Asian identity.[5] In her work, Leny Strobel argues the importance of naming as part of one's healing from our colonial histories.[6] We need to name ourselves and our world on our terms because these names we choose hold our histories and tell our stories. Indipino is a combination of these two names—Indian and Pilipino—that were forced upon us, but also rearticulated and rethought by us for ourselves.

I use this term to provide a more accurate understanding of the experiences and identities of this particular diasporic group. Currently there is no other term that accurately describes this particular community. Indians have been in the Philippines for a long time and have mixed with Filipinos, but only recently has a term emerged to name them. The traditional terms for South Asians in the Philippines, bumbay and Indian, connote the notion of a sojourner or inassimilable alien. These terms deny the deep history of connections between South Asia and the Philippines and create a binary that separates these "Indians" from Filipinos. I define Indipino as anyone with both South Asian and Filipino ancestry or culture. Historically, South Asians in the Philippines have primarily been Sindhi, Punjabi, or Madrasi (from the Sepoys who came to Manila between 1762 and 1764).[7] Indipino is a term that encompasses the experiences of these different groups within the Philippines in a singular context based on their being othered within Philippine society. This is different from Karen Leonard's term "Punjabi-Mexican," which focuses on a particular South Asian ethnic group. In her study on Punjabi-Mexican Americans, Leonard goes back and forth between the terms "Mexi-Hindu" and "Punjabi-Mexican."[8] The terms are dependent upon the context of who is doing the naming, when, and for what purpose. Also, the term "Hindu" implies a historical religious essentialism that ignores the extensive Sikh Punjabi community. Despite this, Karen Leonard's work does provide the opportunity for people with mixed South Asian heritage to have visibility. The difference with Indipino is that it relates to people with ethnic and cultural ties to both South Asian and Filipino culture. I prefer the term "Indipino" to "Punjabi-Filipino" or "Indian Filipino" because of the hyphenation and its connotation of splitting the self and community. In addition, the experiences of South Asians in the Philippines are distinct to other South Asian diasporic groups because of the unique colonial history of the Philippines under both the Spanish and American empires. The vast majority of other South Asian diasporic communities prior to World War II had been in British Commonwealth nations such as South Africa, Canada, and Malaysia.[9] In addition, migration to the Philippines was primarily voluntary, which is different from the history of forced coolie labor in places such as Guyana and Fiji. To me Indipino is an inclusive term that encompasses both people of mixed race and mixed culture, meaning I consider someone of Indian ancestry who grows up in the Philippines to also be Indipino.

My mom's entire family in the United States is Indipino, having both Punjabi and Filipino heritage. To me they have always looked Filipino because that is what I understood them to be growing up. We would all speak to our grandmother in Tagalog. It is also the language that our parents communicate to each other in and the language that we all grew up hearing first. I knew we all had Indian blood, too, but our culture, to me, seemed very Filipino. I decided to interview some of the only other Indipinos I knew, my cousins, in order to understand how they identify themselves and what their processes were like in the formation of those identities. None of us really grew up knowing anyone else with our mix outside of our family. How did this affect identity formation? Did they face the same discrimination that I did? Were they seen as Indian by the world, but when they looked in the mirror saw something else? How did this affect their sense of self and self-worth?

In the San Francisco Bay Area in the 1970s to 1990s, my cousins and I grew up in what was at the time the highest concentration of Filipinos in the United States.[10] However, my family's story starts much earlier with my grandfather's migration from Punjab to Manila in 1930. The Indian diaspora is more known in places like Great Britain, the United States, Canada, Singapore, Malaysia, Fiji, and Guyana, but the Indian diaspora in the Philippines is far less recognized.[11] Ajit Singh Rye states that the Indian community in the Philippines began to form after the American occupation of the islands in 1898.[12] These immigrants were coming to the Philippines from the regions of Sindh and Punjab in western India because discriminatory immigration policies in the United States and Canada made those destinations less accessible. Since the Philippines was a territory of the United States, it seemed like a viable location due to the possibility of better economic opportunities compared to those available in Sindh and Punjab.[13] In addition, the Philippines was also viewed as a stepping stone for Indian families to circumvent US immigration policy and eventually get to the United States. This Indian community is significant because migration to the Philippines was entirely voluntary and primarily happened before Indian independence from Britain. This is in stark contrast to other areas such as Guyana and Fiji, where forced migration through coolie labor and indentured servitude was the primary reason for large Indian populations.[14] The Philippines has one of the largest Punjabi and Sindhi populations of any country outside of former British Commonwealth nations in Southeast Asia.[15] The Philippines has an Indian community comparable to that of Thailand or Indonesia.[16] In fact, the famous Indian nationalist and freedom fighter, Subhas Chandra Bose, visited the Indian community in the Philippines prior to World War II to get support for the Indian independence movement.[17] However, there has been little research on the Indian community in the Philippines. This diasporic Indian community comprises Punjabi and Sindhi immigrants who migrated before the division of India and Pakistan.[18] The majority of the Punjabi immigrants to the Philippines were former soldiers in the British Army who were leaving Punjab due to land displacement and a lack of economic opportunity. It is interesting to note, however, that although these communities self-identify in terms of their nation of origin (Indian or Pakistani), the two communities intermingle in the Philippines and are viewed as one bumbay entity by Filipinos.[19] At the time of his arrival in Manila in 1930, my grandfather was one of 100 Punjabis out of a total of 500 Indians in the Philippines. By 1948, when India gained independence, there were still only a total of 677 Indians on record in the Philippines.[20]

My grandfather was one of the Punjabi migrants who occupied the lower social class of Indian migrants to the Philippines. Unlike their Sindhi counterparts who owned businesses, the Punjabi men in the Philippines were mainly engaged in merchant and money lending businesses.[21] The visible physical differences (darker skin color, turbans, beards, and taller stature) between these mainly Sikh Punjabi immigrant men and their Filipino counterparts led to many stereotypes of Indians or bumbay as they were called by Filipinos. Many Indians were called "5/6" because of the money lending businesses that many Punjabis owned that would charge six pesos for every five pesos borrowed. While this has become an Indian stereotype in the Philippines, it has also survived within the Filipino diaspora. I have been referred to as 5/6 by some of my Filipino students at the high school where I taught in San Francisco. What has been forgotten is the fact that the process of 5/6 predates the existence of an Indian community in the Philippines. In fact, this practice began by Chinese merchants in the Philippines during the Spanish colonial period. For example, the late president Corazon Aquino's family, the Cojuangcos, originally acquired wealth by lending money through 5/6 operations.[22] The Chinese have historical ties to the Philippines, as do Indians, and have been intermarrying with Filipinos for centuries. It is perhaps due to a large and sustained population of Chinese in the Philippines and their engagement in multiple merchant industries in addition to money lending that they were not referred as 5/6. However, there is a particular distrust of Indians as compared to the Chinese. While there is still anti-Chinese sentiment among many Filipinos, Chinese still have more social acceptance and economic access than do Indians. This distrust of Indians is a synthesis of classism and colorism that directly results from the colonial experience of Filipinos. Colonialism has left a hierarchy of civilization and power based on skin color in the Philippines where Whiteness is associated with beauty, wealth, and privilege.[23] Darkness is often associated with being native, savage, and other in the Philippines—it is something that many try to escape whether by bleaching their skin or through outmarriage.[24] The Chinese, having lighter skin, are more able to pass in Philippine society than are Indians. In addition, the Chinese, overall, have had more social mobility than Indians and dominate the Philippine economy through business ownership and wealth. Four of the five wealthiest Filipinos in 2015 were ethnically Chinese.[25] In addition, such major Philippine industries as ShoeMart, Philippine Airlines, Shangri-La, San Miguel, Tanduay, and Cebu-Pacific are Chinese owned.[26] It is this confluence of heightened visibility, ability to pass, and hierarchy of skin color and power that may be the reason why the Chinese are now exempt from the 5/6 stereotype while Indipinos have become the embodiment of the term. Some of these stereotypes are still seen in Philippine media today such as with the Deejay Bumbay character portrayed by Michael V on the comedy sketch show *Bubble Gang.*[27]

Another prevalent stereotype is the violent nature of Indian men. In fact, a common way to threaten mischievous children was to tell them that they would be taken away by the bumbay if they did not behave. These negative images of bumbays have remained in the Filipino consciousness.[28] In a conversation with a renowned Filipino American artist/director/producer, she stated that she grew up in the Philippines hearing adults mention the scary bumbays and how they kidnap bad children. She remembered her grandfather using the threat of the bumbay to keep her from misbehaving. One of my interviewees mentioned growing up hearing people associate bumbay with being *matapang*—meaning brave, but also violent or aggressive. These images and stereotypes are also what my mother and her siblings grew up with in Manila and had a direct influence on their identity and culture. Perhaps this is why we all grew up with only Tagalog and English. Everyone from the generation above mine seemed to have no connection to anything Indian except for tea and *roti*. There was a painting of the Taj Mahal and a picture of Guru Nanak that hung in my auntie's living room in San Francisco, but that was it. We mainly ate Filipino food and spoke about the Philippines.

Of the dozens of photo albums in our house, there were mainly pictures of the Philippines and America, except for one album of India. It almost seemed as if my mother and her siblings viewed Filipinos as better or more civilized than Indians, whom they often spoke about as backward. Their American education in the Philippines perpetuated a colonial agenda that privileged Whiteness and all things American. This assimilative school system would promote an Americanized Filipino identity and devalue a non-Western Indian identity. In an American colonial system, there is a connection between Whiteness and assimilation to American ideals, which are both equated with being civilized. Indian immigrants, who are neither fair-skinned nor as Americanized, are seen as the antithesis to civilization—hence this deep distrust of Indians in Philippine society. This, coupled with the anti-Indian stereotypes, would pressure them into valuing Filipino identity over Indian. The one thing I do remember, however, is the picture of my two cousins with our grandmother taken in Punjab in the 1970s. I wondered what it was like for them to grow up. They had both been born in Manila to a Filipina mother and an Indipino father. They came to America in the 1970s at a time when our family was getting in touch with their Indian roots and traveling to Punjab. I wondered if the way they grew up and the way they identified were different from my own experience. I decided to begin to explore the multiple and intersecting narratives of Indipina/o American experiences starting with my own family. I wanted to hear their stories and understand what the similarities and differences were between all our narratives and experiences. I interviewed four cousins who went to public schools in San Francisco and Daly City from at least fourth grade through high school in the late 1970s through early 1990s.

TABLE 9.1.

Interviewees, Age, and Birthplace

Name	Birthplace	Age
Teng	Manila, Philippines	49
Mary	Manila, Philippines	47
Lisa	San Francisco, CA	42
Ann	San Francisco, CA	36

In order to organize their responses, I build off the framework developed by Kerry Ann Rockquemore, David Brunsma, and Daniel Delgado that looks at multiracial identity formation through the multiple intersecting lenses of racial category, racial identification, and racial identity.[29] These three lenses can also be understood as institutional, interpersonal, and internalized. Racial category has to do with what arbitrary racial categories government and social institutions have created into which mixed people are forced to fit. Racial identification is the way that others judge what racial category the mixed person should identify with based on that person's perceived appearance. Racial identity is based on the way the mixed individual identifies himself or herself both racially and culturally. According to their theory, Rockquemore, Brunsma, and Delgado argue that these different lenses intersect and impact mixed race identity formation. In order to really understand the process of Indipino identity formation, it is important to look at all these different aspects and how they intersect.

Racial Category

South Asians do not generally fit into the general racial categories in America and have at different times been labeled as Caucasian, Asian, and even Black for various purposes. For example, in 1923, Bhagat Singh Thind argued in the US courts that Indians are considered Caucasoid and thereby should be eligible for American citizenship, which, at the time, was available only to free White people.[30] This stems from the multiple ethnic and physical differences among the many peoples who live in the vast region that makes up South Asia. Even as South Asians are considered part of the larger Asian American community, their faces and voices are often marginalized and eclipsed by the East Asian face of Asian America.[31] While Filipinos and other Southeast Asians are also marginalized within the Asian American community, South Asians were practically invisible especially in San Francisco during the 1980s and 1990s when I was growing up. I did not see many Indians in the media or in the community, especially in the San Francisco and Daly City areas. According to the US Census Bureau, between 2005 and 2009, the Filipino population was 5.5 times larger than that of South Asians in San Francisco and San Mateo counties. During that same time, the South Asian population in Santa Clara County was 1.24 times as large as that of Filipinos. In addition, in other suburban areas such as Fremont and Union City, the Filipino and South Asian populations were fairly equal for the same time period. During the 1980s and 1990s, those areas were not as connected to San Francisco as they are now. This was prior to the rise of Silicon Valley as a major commercial area, to which many South Asians migrated to work for the technology industry.[32]

For Teng and Mary, growing up in San Francisco at that time, they were not seen as fitting into any of the racial categories available (White, Black, Latino, or Asian). In the Philippines race operated differently than in the United States and they were viewed as Indian or other, since their features were not fully Filipino. Their responses about growing up in the Philippines describe an almost unspoken one-drop rule where they were viewed as bumbay despite being half Filipino as well.[33] However, in the United States they were viewed with ambiguity. Teng stated, "People didn't think of me as Filipino or Indian. They automatically assumed I was Mexican." Latino becomes the generic catchall racial category for Brown people who do not look quite Asian or Black enough. South Asians were this ambiguous Brown anomaly to the standard canon of races for many Americans at the time.[34] Mary had a similar experience. Upon her arrival in San Francisco she noticed, "People in the US are different. They categorize you as either White, Black, or Chinese. I didn't look like either one. I was categorized as Latino because I had the look." Even Ann, who was born and raised in Daly City, experienced similar racialization. She responded that people assumed she was Samoan or Latina throughout her childhood. This identification with a Latino (or Hispanic) racial category is significant because of the way that a Latino identity is treated within the larger framework of American government, especially through the US census. The United States recognizes that a Latino identity encompasses many different racial categories like Black, White, and Native American. This is similar to the way that Nazli Kibria describes the way race works within a South Asian framework. She argues that the South Asian identity actually encompasses multiple racial categories.[35] The migration experience, in which the new country essentializes South Asian identity into a monolithic category, derails the possibilities for multiplicity in racial categories. This is especially true of South Asians in both the Philippines and the United States, where the community was perceived as having very little intermarriage with the local population.[36] Bandana Purkayastha argues that South Asians tend to identify with their immigrant parents' country of origin because they do not fit into constructed ideas of Asian Americans, but this idea can be complicated when your parents are both immigrants from the Philippines.[37] If you identify with the Philippines as home because you do not fit into Asian America, but you are also viewed as an outsider within Filipino spaces, then where is home?

Racial Identification

Based on their physical appearance, the Indipinos in this study were constantly racialized in different ways. In fact, they would often describe their school experiences when reflecting on how their racial identities were viewed by others. Teng and Mary both recalled how classmates in the Philippines teased them because of their perceived racial-ethnic difference. Mary remembered them making fun of her during roll call because of her bumbay last name, Singh. Teng also described children making comments about her darker skin and pointed nose—features not typically associated with Filipinoness. Neither of them described these incidents as particularly negative; rather, they both made them sound routine. Ann also described the teasing she got from her relatives at home by saying, "My mom and aunt would say 'bumbay ka, you're Indian.' She would sometimes say 'you should have the red dot on your head.'" None of the respondents seemed to think that any of these incidents were extraordinary or particularly inflammatory. This may be an indication of how early these messages become normalized. Negative statements about Indianness, although meant in jest, do perpetuate this association with Indian culture and identity. Although these women all mentioned hearing similar statements, none indicated that they were said with malice or prejudice.

What is also interesting is that all of these women who are mixed Filipina describe their mixedness as being bumbay and not *mestiza*. The word "mestizo" or "mestiza" in the Philippines describes a quality of having mixed heritage, although it usually connotes a mixture of Filipino with Spanish, White American, or other European ancestry. Skin color comes into play because Filipinos of mixed heritage with dark skin are not viewed as mestizo or mestiza. Since the term also connotes beauty, the fact that Indipinos aren't seen as mestizo also means that they aren't necessarily seen as beautiful due to a hierarchy of skin color. While mestizos are embraced as Filipinos, these Indipinas were othered by the term bumbay, which almost superseded their identity as Filipinas. This experience is again different from that of the Chinese, who have their own terms for mixed Chinese Filipinos, *tsinoy* and *tsinay*.[38]

Aside from these instances of othering by Filipinos, participants also felt excluded from other Indian communities. Teng described how, as a young girl, she and her relatives would occasionally go to Punjabi functions at the Sikh temple in Fremont. She stated, "The Indians looked at us different because we weren't pure Indian and weren't raised in the culture." While Filipinos saw them as different based on physical appearance, the Indians othered them because of their lack of Indian cultural knowledge such as customs, religion, and language. There were other instances where having cultural knowledge allowed them to gain acceptance even though they weren't initially seen as part of that ethnic group. Lisa described her experiences in the Filipino club at her high school. She did not remember being treated differently by the Filipinos in that organization. She stated, "They knew I had Filipino in me and could understand the language." Her ability to understand Tagalog gave her more ability to fit in with the Filipinos in her high school while Teng's inability to speak or understand Punjabi alienated her from the Punjabis at the Sikh temple. Mixed race and mixed culture people often experience double negation where they have their identities policed and negated on both sides of their heritage by those who claim to have authority to determine who can and can't belong to that group.[39] This is somewhat different for people who are mixed with Asian and White who, in America, can generally claim their White identity without being questioned about being an authentic member of the group, while people with dual-minority mixes have to constantly prove their identities. Both of these phenomena are a result of the normalization of Whiteness and Americanness.

Even though all the women in this study can understand Tagalog and all but one can speak it fluently, that was not always enough for their peers to see them as Filipino. Despite having fluency in Tagalog, their physical appearance seemed to be a barrier in their acceptance in certain Filipino spaces. While some Filipino Americans have their identities quantified based on their ability to speak a Filipino language, Indipinos also have the additional barrier of their perceived difference based on appearance. Mixed heritage scholars argue that cultural knowledge such as language can be markers of identity, but that for mixed heritage people, the community still may not see these people as part of the community based on their physical difference.[40] Mary remembers that, in middle and high school, the majority of her friends were Filipina, but none of the Filipino boys would approach her romantically because, as she states, she "wasn't pure." In fact, more Latino boys hit on her than Filipinos. Teng and Lisa also described how people in high school would automatically assume they were Latina. Lisa even recalled an incident at her daughter's school a year ago when her daughter's classmate racialized her as Latina. She recalled, "A little boy at my daughter's school walked up to me and said he didn't know I could speak English because he thought I was Mexican." From their responses, it was clear that these types of microaggressions were very common, but they did not seem to faze the respondents—in fact, they seemed normal to them.[41] Ann remembered how classmates, upon hearing her ethnic mix, would ask her questions like "What do you eat? Do you have a red dot?" Lisa even stated that her boss told her he thought she was some kind of Latina when she first started. It seems these kind of external judgments are so common that they see them as part of their daily life.

Racial Identity

Growing up, I assumed that family members on my Indipino side primarily identified as Filipino. I assumed that since they all looked more Filipino than I, they never had to question their identities. The interview process showed how their identity formation was actually very similar to mine. Lisa describes her heritage as this: "The blood is Indian, but the heritage of the Philippines. My heritage is Filipino on both sides—food, language, religion, the way we do things." Mary explained this further when saying, "My family didn't teach us the Indian side, the culture. They didn't care about the culture. They were almost embarrassed of it. They didn't know and they didn't care to know. They were raised in the Philippines and they embraced that culture." Their parents' experiences of being Indian in the Philippines and the associated stereotypes and stigmas caused them to emphasize Filipino over Indian culture. This was passed down to their children in the form of notions of shame toward being too Indian. Ann stated, "When I was younger I was embarrassed to be Indian and Filipino. I remember hating being Indian when I was young." Indian was associated with something shameful or, at the very least, something less desirable than Filipino. Mixedness was not discussed even though it was all around. They all grew up understanding from about the age of five to seven that they were mixed.

Teng described how it was for her growing up. She remembered, "I think I had low self-esteem growing up. You just didn't quite belong to any group. My friends would say I look different or call me bumbay, but in my mind, that's all I knew." The hypervisibility of their mixed heritage, combined with the absence of dialogue around being mixed, had a significant impact on their individual identity formation. Lisa remembered an incident at a family party. She recalled, "I finally met a guy with my mix at a family party once. The guy was fascinated to meet another Filipino Indian. It was over twenty years before I met another person of my same mix." They had no knowledge that there were other Indipinos. In fact, the guy whom Lisa met was under the same impression—that he was the only Indipino out there. Ann eventually began to explore her Indian heritage more after finishing high school. She responded, "When I moved to Union City, I met a lot of Punjabis and got to learn the culture through friends. After that I was really comfortable in my skin." By learning about her Punjabi heritage, Ann began to appreciate that part of her heritage. Lisa, on the other hand, has always been proud to be mixed. She said, "I thought being mixed was cool—I prefer mixtures. It made me feel original because there aren't that many of us." What is interesting is that all four women had children with men of different ethnic groups. In fact, Mary, Teng, and to some extent Ann strictly dated non-Filipinos through high school because, as they explained, it was non-Filipino men who showed interest in them. Lisa is the only one to have children with a Filipino. Her husband is also of mixed race—mixed Filipino and White. Teng, who was racialized as Latina in high school, ultimately ended up with a Filipino spouse, but the father of her child is of mixed Latino ancestry. The other two women married Black men. This is significant because in this family, the women tend to date and marry people of other ethnic groups while the men tend to date and marry Filipinas. The racial identities that have been placed on them have definitely had an impact on how they see themselves and whom they choose as partners. When asked about their choice in partners, the women stated that they just chose the person they fell in love with. They never mentioned any intentional avoidance of Indian men. Teng did mention that when she went on a trip to Punjab with her grandmother there was an attempt made to arrange a marriage for her, but she refused. Other than that, there was no mention from any participant of any involvement with an Indian man, nor was there mention of their families pushing them to date either a Filipino or an Indian. In fact, it was the two women who dated and married Black men who described negative comments from family members toward their choice of partners. Perhaps they chose partners from communities that they had affinity with and who valued their mixed and Indian identities. None of the participants has dated an Indian. It may be due to their racialization as other or their being ostracized at times from other Filipinos, especially boys in high school, that led them to choose partners from other ethnic groups. Being seen as bumbay rather than mestizo created a subtle association of their physical features as other and not beautiful. It is very telling, however, that all of the participants as well as most of their family members never dated anyone Indian. Perhaps the comments they heard about being Indian influenced the way they saw Indians. This negative association with Indian features and bumbay stereotypes may also have negatively affected the way they viewed Indian men.

When asked how they identify today, all participants replied that they are ethnically Indian and Filipino or Indipino, but they see themselves as American culturally. Mary chose to distance herself from the Filipino group as she got older. She stated, "As I got older, I developed my own multicultural friends." It was in these diverse groups that she was able to find more acceptance without constantly having to validate her identity. To her, surrounding herself with a multicultural group of people felt like something very American. Teng, Lisa, and Ann all said that they felt neither Filipino enough nor Indian enough to really claim either culture. Instead, they felt that they were more American than anything else. This is significant, because for Teng, Mary, and Lisa Tagalog was their first language. In fact, Teng and Mary were both born in the Philippines and spent at least the first five years of their lives there. Teng, Mary, and Ann can still speak fluent Tagalog, yet they feel that they cannot fully claim Filipino as their culture. Teng and Mary are also the only ones in the entire family to have actually spent any time in Punjab—they both visited twice for two months at a time during high school. However, they do not feel like they can truly call themselves Indian. It seems that these Indipino women feel safest and most comfortable claiming American as their culture. Although they did not say it outright in the interviews, this hesitation to claim either ancestral culture can stem from the way their identities were always ambiguous. The negations that they got from both Filipinos and Indians may have made them hesitant to claim either identity. Based on their interviews, all participants ethnically identify as both Filipino and Indian, yet feel comfortable claiming only American as their culture. They distinguish a cultural identity of American from a Filipino and Indian (Indipino) ethnicity. Perhaps their assimilation in American society has caused them to consent to essentialized notions of what Filipino and Indian are. To them, being American is a confluence of race and class that is directly tied to being mixed, culture, and food. In addition, claiming this American identity may feel safer for them because they find comfort in the everyday practice of being American. In this sense, they have more access to American culture and are seen practicing it, so it feels more authentic to claim that culture as primary. They speak English, eat American foods, watch American media, and so on. They feel less likely to have their identities negated by claiming Americanness. This may be the result of the way that their identities were negated by both Indians and Filipinos or may also be the result of American xenophobia and their fear of being seen as other. In addition, American becomes emblematic of their mixed identity because of the construction of the American melting pot—especially since they all have children who are further mixed than they are.

Conclusion

This study was small and limited to the experiences of one Indipino family, however there were some significant findings. People from outside ethnicities often label double minority women who have ambiguous physical features as Latina. While the racial category of Asian comprises people of over one hundred different ethnic groups, Asians are often associated only with people of one specific East Asian look. The Latino category, in these instances, has been a catchall category for those who do not fit into the other racial categories. Even among Filipinos, there is the issue of the way that mixed heritage Filipinos of particular mixes, specifically non-European and dark-skinned, are seen differently than other mixed heritage Filipinos. The way that these women were consistently

referred to as bumbay as opposed to mestiza by other Filipinos is a clear indication of the racial hierarchy within Filipino consciousness. While there is a desire
to be labeled mestiza, people with darker-skinned, non-European mixes such as
Indian or Black often get labeled by their non-Filipino heritage. Separating those
with dark-skinned mixes from the term mestiza, which connotes beauty, reinforces a hierarchy of beauty where dark skin is deemed ugly and undesirable.
Furthermore, this negates claims to Filipino identity and the mixedness within
their heritages. Despite all this labeling, the women in this study have come out
with a strong sense of self and love for both aspects of their heritage. However,
when asked, they all claimed themselves to be more American than anything
else. This American identity functions as a safe space where they feel ownership
despite the fact that, historically, people of color consistently fight for the ability
to claim ownership of an American identity. For them being American is a synthesis of race and class that connects their mixed identity and their suburban
American lifestyle in opposition to assimilationist constructions of essentialized Filipino and Indian identities.

This study focused on children of mixed-heritage immigrant parents where
the mixing occurred in the Philippines. Further study on Indipinos would explore
identity formation within other families in sites where Filipino and Indian communities live in close proximity, such as Union City, Sacramento, Newark, and
Houston. In addition, there could be more focus on Indipinos who are first-
generation mixed—mixed children of parents who immigrated from India and
the Philippines, respectively. Their identity process should be different because
their Indian parents would not have experienced the stereotyping and prejudice
in the Philippines and would have more connection to Indian culture than the
parents of the participants in this study. It would also be significant to explore
mixed heritage children of Punjabi immigrants to the Philippines, like my family members, who have grown up in the more recent, post–Venus Raj era when
Indipinos are getting more visibility in the Philippine media.[42] Perhaps this
increased positive visibility may cause a shift in the perceptions and acceptance
of Indians in the Philippines and their mixed heritage children.

I intend this to be just the beginning of the study of Indipino identity formation. I know that in my family, this was probably the first time that any of us
actually stopped and reflected on our identify-formation process and experiences of growing up mixed. This process was very informative, insightful, and
curative for us. I know that these conversations will continue among us and
our other relatives who were not part of this study. I also hope this study sparks
other Indipinos and people of double-minority mixed heritage to explore similar conversations in their own families and communities.

NOTES

1. I want to thank Teresa A. M. Hodges for helping me with this work by sharing the term "Indipino" with me.

2. Rudy P. Guevarra Jr., *Becoming Mexipino: Multiethnic Identities and Communities in San Diego* (New Brunswick, NJ: Rutgers University Press, 2012).

3. Barbara Andaya, "Introduction to South and Southeast Asia" (course reader, University of Hawai'i at Manoa, 2014), 20.

4. Teodoro Agoncillo, *Introduction to Filipino History* (Quezon City: Garotech, 1974).

5. *Bumbay* is the Filipino pronunciation of the city of Bombay and the generic term used by Filipinos to mean an Indian person.

6. Leny M. Strobel, *Coming Full Circle: The Process of Decolonization among Post-1965 Filipino Americans* (Quezon City: Giraffe Books, 2001), 85–91.

7. Ajit Singh Rye, "The Indian Community in the Philippines," in *Indian Communities in Southeast Asia*, ed. Kernial Sandhu and A. Mami (Singapore: Institute of Southeast Asian Studies, 2001), 707–763.

8. Karen Leonard describes Mexi-Hindu as mixed heritage Mexican Indian families with a Punjabi father, Mexican mother, and mixed heritage children from California's Imperial Valley from the early twentieth century onward. Mexi-Hindu describes the mixed heritage families as well as the children themselves. See Karen I. Leonard, *Making Ethnic Choices: California's Punjabi Mexican Americans* (Philadelphia: Temple University Press, 1992).

9. Claude Markovitis, "Afterword: Stray Thoughts of a Historian on 'Indian' or 'South Asian' Diaspora(s)," in *Global Indian Diasporas: Exploring Trajectories of Migration and Theory*, ed. Gijsbert Oonk (Amsterdam: Amsterdam University Press, 2007), 266.

10. Benito M. Vergara Jr., *Pinoy Capital: The Filipino Nation in Daly City* (Philadelphia: Temple University Press, 2009), 2.

11. N. Gerald Barrier and Verne A. Dusenbery, eds., *Sikh Diaspora: Migration and the Experience beyond Punjab* (Columbia, MO: South Asia Books, 1989); Adesh Pal, ed., *Contextualizing Nationalism* (New Delhi: Creative Books, 2010); Pritam Singh and Shinder S. Thandi, eds., *Punjabi Identity in a Global Context*, 2nd ed. (New Delhi: Oxford University Press, 2000); Singh Rye, "Indian Community."

12. There was an initial group of Sepoy troops who settled in Cainta, Rizal, after they mutinied and left the British army that was occupying Manila in 1764. Singh Rye, "Indian Community," 713.

13. Ibid., 715–717.

14. Ibid., 714.

15. Indian Diaspora, "The Indian Diaspora Report for Southeast Asia" (August 18, 2000), http://indiandiaspora.nic.in/diasporapdf/chapter20.pdf.

16. Ibid.

17. Expat Insights, "Expat Insights YouTube Page" (August 4, 2010), https://www.youtube.com/watch?v=PbNqPqzjLMo.

18. Singh Rye, "Indian Community," 714–715.

19. Ibid.

20. Ibid., 718–719.

21. Ibid., 716.

22. Mentioned in a lecture in the Advanced Filipino Abroad Program (AFAP) from Ateneo de Manila University during a field excursion in Malolos, Bulacan, in July 2011.

23. Joanne L. Rondilla and Paul Spickard, *Is Lighter Better? Skin-Tone Discrimination among Asian Americans* (Lanham, MD: Rowman & Littlefield, 2007), 5.

24. Ibid., 79.

25. "Philippines' 50 Richest List," *Forbes*, March 2, 2015, http://www.forbes.com/philippines-billionaires/list/#tab:overall.

26. Ibid.

27. Jayjay Jimenez, "Michael V—DJ Bumbay," *YouTube* (July 26, 2009), https://www.youtube.com/watch?v=rlusQdYHfXk.

28. This is based on numerous conversations with family members, other members of the Filipino American community, and faculty at Ateneo de Manila University in Quezon City.

29. Kerry Ann Rockquemore, David Brunsma, and Daniel Delgado, "Racing to Theory or Retheorizing Race? Understanding the Struggle to Build a Multiracial Identity Theory," *Journal of Social Issues* 65 (2009): 13–34.

30. Ronald Takaki, *Strangers from a Different Shore: A History of Asian Americans* (New York: Little, Brown, 1998).

31. Nazli Kibria, "Not Asian, Black, or White? Reflections on South Asian American Identity," *Amerasia Journal* 22 (1996): 77–86.

32. US Census Bureau, "American Community Survey 5-Year Estimates," http://factfinder.census.gov/faces/nav/jsf/pages/searchresults.xhtml?refresh=t. Note: the data were found incorporating searches for Asian populations in the San Francisco Bay Area.

33. David Hollinger. "The One Drop Rule & the One Hate Rule," *Daedalus* 134 (Winter 2005): 18–19.

34. Bandana Purkayastha. *Negotiating Ethnicity: Second-Generation South Asian Americans Traverse A Transnational World* (New Brunswick, NJ: Rutgers University Press, 2005), 37.

35. Kibria, "Not Asian," 77–86.

36. Purkayastha, *Negotiating Ethnicity.*

37. Ibid., 37, 90–95.

38. Pronounced "chinoy" or "chinay." This term is a combination of *Intsik* (Chinese) and *Pinay* (Filipina) and also a play on the word *tisoy* or *tisay*, which is a contraction of *mestizo* and *mestizo.*

39. Silvia Bettez explored the experiences of mixed-race women, and many of them expressed similar sentiments of having aspects of their identity negated on both sides. See Bettez, "Mixed-Race Women and Epistemologies of Belonging," *Frontiers* 31 (2010): 142–165.

40. Maria P. P. Root, "Factors Influencing the Variation in Racial and Ethnic Identity of Mixed-Heritage persons of Asian Ancestry," in *The Sum of Our Parts: Mixed Heritage Asian Americans*, ed. Teresa Williams-León and Cynthia L. Nakashima (Philadelphia: Temple University, 2001), 86; Rondilla and Spickard, *Is Lighter Better?*, 35.

41. Robert Blauner, *Racial Oppression in America* (New York: Harper & Row, 1976).

42. Venus Raj was the winner of Binibining Pilipinas-Universe 2010. She is an actress, model, and television personality. She is of Indian and Filipino ancestry.

10

Hypervisibility and Invisibility of Female Haafu Models in Japan's Beauty Culture

KAORI MORI WANT

Japan's representative for the 2015 Miss Universe Pageant surprised many Japanese. The Miss Universe committee chose Ariana Miyamoto, a model, whose mother is Japanese and father is African American. The Japanese were surprised for two main reasons. First, Miyamoto is *haafu*, meaning half Japanese, who has part non-Japanese ancestry. Second, she has dark skin. Upon the announcement of Miyamoto's selection, there arose controversy among the Japanese. Some said that since Miss Universe is a representative of a nation's beauty, Miyamoto was not qualified because of her non-Japanese ancestry.[1] Her skin color was not overtly criticized, but the references to her not looking Japanese enough implied that her skin color was a problem.

While Miyamoto's haafu status was highly criticized, popular Japanese fashion magazines feature many haafu models. Most of them are half White and half Japanese or Asian. Japanese are accustomed to the presence of White female haafu models in Japan's beauty culture. White female haafu models embody beauty, which Japanese women admire. The Japanese have no problem viewing haafu models as the standard of beauty, yet Miyamoto shocked many Japanese because she challenged the general assumption of beauty. Miyamoto's presence was like an invisible ghost appearing in the daytime. Non-White female haafu models have been rendered invisible in Japan's beauty culture. In this chapter, I explore why they have been erased and how their presence challenges the Japanese perception of beauty.

In order to understand the invisibility of non-White female haafu models in Japan's beauty culture, this chapter first explains the overwhelming popularity of White female haafu models in Japan's beauty culture with a special focus on fashion and the cosmetics industry. I trace Japanese beauty history to see how

Japanese people came to valorize light skin and Caucasian facial features. Then, the chapter examines why non-White female haafu models in beauty culture are rendered invisible by applying the concepts of transnational lovely White ideology and local *kawaii* (cuteness) ideology, which is culturally specific to the Japanese context. This illustrates how two ideologies exclude non-White female haafu models from Japan's beauty culture.

This chapter uses the term "haafu" to describe mixed race/ethnic Japanese.[2] The word derived from the English word "half." Haafu generally means people with half Japanese and half non-Japanese heritage. For example, a person with a Japanese father and an African mother is haafu. Using the term "haafu" to express mixed race/ethnic Japanese is controversial because those of mixed race/ethnicity who were born and raised and live in Japan are considered fully Japanese.[3] However, the term treats those of mixed race/ethnicity as not Japanese enough. The term "haafu" has circulated in Japan, and mixed race/ethnic Japanese use the term to represent themselves.[4] This chapter uses the term while acknowledging its problems.

Popularity of White Female Haafu Models
in the Fashion and Cosmetics Industries

The social position of haafu is characterized by their hypervisibility and invisibility. They are hypervisible in the media. They have been popular as actors, singers, anchors, athletes, and models since the 1960s, a period that witnessed the emergence of many haafu stars such as Bibari Maeda, Linda Yamamoto, and Masao Kusakari, to name a few.

After the 1945 Japanese defeat in World War II, the Allied servicemen, mainly Americans, came to occupy the country with a mission of democratizing militaristic Japan. The General Headquarters of the Allied forces banned intimacy between Japanese women and American servicemen, and strengthened their nonfraternizing policy. Nevertheless, some servicemen had legitimate and illegitimate mixed race/ethnic children with Japanese women. Japanese women who had children with American servicemen were called *panpan* (prostitutes), even though they were not, and they were exposed to harsh prejudice.

Mixed race/ethnic children were also regarded as the offspring of prostitutes and discriminated against. Black mixed race children suffered more discrimination than White mixed race children because Japanese people looked down on dark skin.[5] Under this difficult social environment, many of these mixed race/ethnic children reached their teens or twenties in the 1960s. Having non-Japanese heritage gave them a unique physical difference that fascinated Japanese audiences. They became popular and achieved hypervisibility in show business. That period is referred to as the first haafu boom.[6] In fact, the term "haafu" is said to have originated with a once popular girl group, Golden Half, which consisted of four mixed race Japanese girls.[7]

Haafu entertainers remain popular today. While haafu entertainers in the 1960s were marred by the negative stereotype as being the illegitimate children of Japanese women and American servicemen, contemporary haafu entertainers are not susceptible to that kind of negative stereotype because the postwar stereotype of haafu is mostly just a memory. The negative stereotypes were wiped away with the strong influence of Western, especially American, culture. The 2000s witnessed the second haafu boom.[8] Japanese women admire haafu female celebrities' faces, which are characterized by big eyelids, long eyelashes, high noses, and full lips. The cosmetics industry has taken advantage of the haafu boom among Japanese women and produced haafu cosmetics, which allegedly make a typical flat Japanese face look haafu. They sell cosmetics such as lip creams, false eyelashes, eye shadow, and so on. Magazines also feature articles on how to produce a haafu-like face with makeup.

What is problematic about this popularity of haafu is that the admired face of haafu is half White and half Japanese. Non-White haafu, such as those who are part Black or part Brown, are virtually invisible in this phenomenon.[9] This does not mean that non-White haafu do not exist. Model agencies featuring non-Japanese and haafu models such as REMIX, Free Wave, and Zenith have non-White haafu models. For example, REMIX has a category of Black female models. Of the twenty-six Black models, seven seem to be haafu according to their ethnic profile. Yet, they are rarely seen in Japanese fashion magazines or the advertisements of cosmetics companies. While there are numerous White female haafu models in fashion magazines, it is rare to see non-White female haafu models. In this sense, non-White female haafu models are made to be invisible in Japan.

Another problem of the invisibility of non-White female models in Japan's beauty culture is that it is gender-specific. We can see some male haafu models regardless of skin color in Japanese fashion magazines. Having dark skin is seen as virile and acceptable for men in Japan. Yet dark skin is not regarded as a sign of female beauty because light skin has been traditionally a standard of beauty. The desire for White haafu beauty is thus gender-specific. With that, I also address the invisibility of non-White female models in Japan's beauty industry.

Analysis of the Japanese Fascination with Whiteness and Repulsion of Darkness

Japanese fashion magazines have many White female haafu models. For example, in September 2012 the fashion magazine *Runway* featured seven models, five of them White female haafu models, two others non-haafu Japanese.[10] The magazine did not use dark-skinned haafu models in this issue. A photo book, *Life as a Golden Half*, featured eleven haafu models, and all White female haafu models. The book cover declared that "the life of haafu models is shining! They are all girls' object of admiration."[11] White female haafu models are a fashion icon, whom Japanese women admire and emulate.

Some fashion magazines feature articles on how to create a White female haafu look. For example, the fashion magazine *Bea's UP* featured an article titled "Haafu Face Recipe" (see figure 10.1).[12] In this article, a cosmetician, Toshihito Tamura, demonstrates how to make a typical Japanese face look like haafu. The author writes, "All girls want to have big eyes, a face with chiseled features, small face, and full lips. They admire the haafu face. If you feel it is impossible to have the haafu face, Tamura will make your dreams come true."[13] Responding to Japanese girls' dreams, Tamura shows readers how to transform their face. The article shows a model who is surprised by her new look with haafu makeup who screams, "Wow!! Really!" From these magazines, we can see how the haafu face is admired by Japanese girls, and how popular it is.

The fascination with White female haafu models is not a recent phenomenon. As noted, when mixed race/ethnic children of Japanese women and American servicemen reached their teens and twenties in the 1960s, their physical difference attracted popularity in Japan's media, although a social environment that discriminated against them existed at the time. Many cosmetics companies have featured White female haafu models for their TV commercials to promote their products since the 1960s. Since cosmetics companies have created the trend for Japanese women, White female haafu faces have become the ideal face for Japanese women.

Hiroshi Wagatsuma and Toshinao Yoneyama trace the history of Japan's beauty culture and explain Japanese women's complex desire for light skin and Caucasian facial features. They contend that Japanese women's desire for Western beauty focuses on a desire for Caucasian facial features (not skin tone). Wagatsuma and Yoneyama write that Japanese women started using whitening powder in the Nara period (710–794) under the influence of Chinese culture. Since then, light skin has been a standard of female beauty in Japan.[14] Wagasuma and Yoneyama point out that Japanese women found Caucasian skin ugly because their skin was "not smooth, and had too many wrinkles."[15] They note that until the end of the Edo era (1603–1868), beautiful Japanese women had single eyelid eyes.[16] Caucasian faces were once regarded as monstrous because of their physical difference from the Japanese.[17] According to Wagasuma and Yoneyama, Japanese women's fascination with Caucasian face is a recent phenomenon. A Caucasian face was desired in Taisho era (1912–1926) when Western culture became popular.[18] The Japanese Westernization project in the mid-twentieth century influenced the standard of beauty, and the Caucasian face

FIGURE 10.1. "Haafu Face Recipe," *Bea's UP* (December 1, 2009): 52.

became idealized as a standard of female beauty. Light skin, which Japanese women admire, is derived not from Western influence, but from Chinese culture. Japanese women have been fascinated by Caucasian facial features, but not their skin. This is unique, in that Japanese beauty culture is not totally dominated by Western beauty ideology, as is the case in other countries.

Joanne Rondilla and Paul Spickard analyze the popularity of light skin in the cosmetics industry and demonstrate how it affects Filipino women's desire for light skin in their Is Lighter Better?. According to their analysis, transnational cosmetics companies such as L'Oreal and Esolis have use mixed race models with Asian and Caucasian heritage for their advertisements in the Philippines, trying to spread the lovely White ideology among Filipino women.[19] Wendy Chapkis explains what lovely White ideology is and writes, "Indeed, female beauty is becoming an increasingly standardized quality throughout the world. A standard so strikingly White, Western, and wealthy."[20] Under this ideology, women in the world strive to have light skin, Western facial features, and an affluent lifestyle.

The popularity of White female haafu models may be due to Japanese women's fascination with light skin and Caucasian facial features, influenced by lovely White ideology. Haafu have both traits—light skin and Caucasian facial features—that Japanese women admire. It seems that light skin and Caucasian facial features are the only prerequisites to become a popular White female haafu model. Julie Matthews analyzes the popularity of mixed race models in Asia and the West in her article "Eurasian Persuasions: Mixed Race, Performativity and Cosmopolitanism." She points out that their popularity rests on their "sameness and as much as difference."[21] Matthews analyzes the popularity of mixed race models in countries where Caucasians are the majority. Asianness marks difference, Whiteness sameness in her article. In Japan, the situation is opposite as Whiteness is the marker of difference. However, her analysis of the mixed race models as the embodiment of sameness and difference is useful in examining the popularity of White female haafu models in Japan. White female haafu models are different because they have Caucasian features but are the same as the general Japanese because most White female haafu models are part Japanese or part Asian. Their Asian heritage mitigates their difference. If cosmetic and fashion models are Caucasian women, they are physically too distant from Japanese women, and Japanese women cannot identify with those models. In fact, despite the fact that the Caucasian face has become popular, Wagatsuma and Yoneyama write that Japanese people still find the Caucasian face to be different from theirs and do not fully identify with it.[22] On the other hand, Japanese women may find White female haafu models possible to copy. Yet, White female haafu models cannot be popular just for having a Western and Japanese racial heritage. If so, any haafu could achieve success, which is not the case. I argue that alongside the transnational lovely White ideology, there is a local ideology that enables the popularity of White female haafu models in Japan: kawaii.

The Japanese beauty industry operates according to the concept of kawaii, which means cuteness. It is a culturally specific notion. A lovable woman in Japan must be kawaii. The definition of kawaii comes from Japanese people's feeling toward babies. Babies are soft, small, innocent, White, and vulnerable. Japanese women desire cosmetic products and clothing that can make them kawaii, meaning light, small, and vulnerable. They support models who can embody kawaii. Kawaii ideology excludes darkness from its scope because it favors lightness. The notion opposite to kawaii is ugliness and undesirability, which in many societies (including Japan) are associated with darkness. This may be one of the reasons that non-White female models are invisible in Japan's beauty culture. We will see how dark skin has been rendered undesirable in Japanese society by exploring the voices of non-White female haafu.

A Complex Social Gaze toward Dark Skin in Japan

As we have seen, while the Caucasian face and light skin are idealized in Japan, dark skin has been relegated to an undesirable position. Some scholars have explained why dark skin has been rejected by the Japanese. For example, John Russell examines the representations of Black people in Japanese literature and the mass media and concludes that Japanese people see Black people as "not human but animal, ugly, infantile, and different."[23] Wagatsuma and Yoneyama share a similar view of the Japanese perception of Black people. They contend that Japanese people regard Black people as "spooky, scary, dirty, animal-like, and different."[24] A similar view on dark skin is still seen in the media today. For example, Atsuhisa Yamamoto argues that Blackness is seen as "violent and criminal" by analyzing the criminal case of Rion Ito, a haafu with Black heritage. He belonged to a gang and was involved in the battering of a famous Kabuki actor in 2010, and became a target of mass media scandal. Yamamoto problematizes the mass media's association of Ito's crime with his Blackness.[25]

Some dark-skinned haafu recount their experiences of being exposed to a discriminatory social gaze toward their skin. From their voices, we can see the stereotypes inscribed on the dark-skinned haafu. Keiko Kozeki is a daughter of a Japanese mother and an African American serviceman father. She was born during the US occupation of Japan (1945–1952), and wrote of her experiences in a 1960s memoir. She experienced hardship in her upbringing. She was abandoned by both parents, was raised by poor stepparents, and had no access to education or a well-paid job. Most of all, she suffered from her dark skin. She writes, "When I was on a train one day, two university students talked to me. They said, 'Hi, Dakko-chan.' Dakko-chan was a popular plastic toy that featured a Black girl. When I did not respond, they said, 'Dakko-chan, would you like to have fun with us?' I did not know what Dakko-chan meant, but I knew they were making fun of me. They came close to me and said something offensive, so I slapped their faces. Then, they screamed 'Black' and 'prostitute's child' at me."[26] Dakko-chan was a popular toy in the 1960s. It had dark skin, full red lips, and big bulging eyes. Dakko means to be hugged in Japanese, implying physical intimacy. We could see that Kozeki's dark skin is exposed to the erotic desire of the university students through their metaphoric use of Dakko-chan and their insult with the word "prostitute's child." Kozeki's voice tells us that the Japanese associated female dark skin with sexual voluptuousness and low social status.

The problematic social gaze toward dark skin continued in the 1970s with the emergence of a girl's band that consisted of all Japanese and African American haafu, called Beauty Black Stones. In an article titled "Black Skin Japanese: Four Girls in Ecstasy," a band member, Kelly, described her experience as follows: "I have known that I am dark and haafu since I was a child. When I went to a public bath with my mother, I could not find where she was. I called her name, but she did not answer me. When I cried, she finally talked to me in a hush. I think she was ashamed of my skin color. When I grew up, I think about love, marriage, and sex, but my dark skin makes me feel gloomy."[27] Kelly's mother was ashamed of having a dark-skinned daughter, which hurt Kelly. She developed a sense of inferiority and could not think of her relationships or future positively. While the girls of the band talked honestly about their experiences as dark-skinned haafu, they were persistently asked about their sexual experiences by interviewer Tamiki Iguchi. Four girls encouraged themselves that dark-skinned Japanese were human beings and that they needed to fight against prejudice, but Iguchi emphasized their sexual experiences and called their musical ability "Negro's soul." He wrote of the stereotypes of dark-skinned women as erotic, tribal, and primitive. He wrote a quite sleazy article, which illustrates the conflicting power struggles between interviewer and interviewees. While four girls internalized the discriminatory Japanese gaze toward dark skin, they tried to overcome it and succeed as musicians. On the other hand, the interviewer slighted their voices and reduced the girls to cheap and erotic objects. From the accounts of Kozeki and Beauty Black Stones as well as scholars' analysis of dark skin, we see that dark skin is scorned in Japan.

Stephen Murphy-Shigematsu sums up the Japanese problematic attitudes toward skin color as follows: "The Japanese preference of White skin as a standard of beauty, and their prejudice to see the superiority of Caucasian's physical characteristics and American and Western cultures still remain in Japan. Black skinned Amerasians face harsher prejudice due to their skin color. Their skin is associated with the twisted images that African or African American cultures and races are inferior."[28] Light skin is admired and dark skin is spurned. Are Japanese perceptions of skin color so steadfast?

The representation of dark-skinned women has been gradually changing in contemporary Japanese mass media. Although some Africans and African American entertainers are popular for their outlandish behavior on TV, others achieve popularity for their sophisticated and intellectual deeds. An example of the former is Aja Kong. She is a female wrestler whose mother is Japanese and father is African American. She is popular for her ferocious makeup and violent performance in the wrestling ring. She is an example of the persistent stereotype of Black people as violent and barbaric. On the other hand, singers such as Thelma Aoyama and Chrystal Kay, both Black haafu, are represented as intellectual and sophisticated in the media. Both Aoyama and Chrystal Kay graduated from a very expensive international school and Sophia University, a prestigious Japanese university famous for its bilingual education. Aoyama and Kay's educational achievements and their fluency in English demonstrate their affluent upbringing and cultural capital. They are successful singers as well. They are not associated with negative stereotypes.

The changing perception toward dark skin has also been reported by mixed race people with Black heritage. Mitzi Carter and Aina Hunter are mixed race Americans with Black and Japanese heritage. They spent a period of time in Japan and reported positive experiences, problematizing the negative treatment of Blackness in academic writings such as that of John Russell. Carter and Hunter write,

> There is no doubt the invisible geographies of power that Russell is very conscious of exist and to ignore those is precarious. On the other hand, to also not give credence to the changing image of blackness is just as dangerous. If we have for so long said blacks do not have the means to their representation in Japan, but then dismiss the growing collection of narratives of blacks who have had positive experiences as tourists, temporary workers, or now living permanently in Japan, is to commit the same error that we accuse Japanese of doing—that is, dismissing any blacks as anomalies who or when they speak against the grain of the current models of blackness in Japan.[29]

Contemporary Japanese perception of skin color does not necessarily associate light skin with superiority and dark skin with inferiority. The experiences of White haafu and non-White haafu are becoming diverse. Murphy-Shigematsu explains that the experiences of haafu differ based on their social capital such as linguistic ability, level of education, social status of parents, and so on.[30] These aspects of social capital do not necessarily coincide with skin color. There are non-White people with high social capital and in high social classes. Skin color may coincide with social class, but other factors such as the presence of the father, education, and linguistic abilities seem to determine the social class of haafu in Japan. People with dark skin are therefore not as slighted in Japanese mass media as they used to be, although the fact that non-White people are still exposed to negative social experiences should not be dismissed. If non-White people are more accepted in contemporary Japan, why are non-White female haafu models invisible in Japan's beauty culture?

Kawaii Culture and the Invisibility of Non-White Female Haafu Models

As indicated earlier, there is a relationship between lightness and kawaii. For example, the haafu cosmetics company Jewerich declares on their home page that their products embody kawaii: "We are a new cosmetics brand with the theme of kawaii. We seek to make products that make the ideal eyes for girls."[31] Many Japanese fashion magazines and cosmetics companies sell products that make Japanese girls look kawaii. According to Inuhiko Yomota, kawaii is a unique notion specific to Japanese culture and difficult to translate into English.[32] This article uses the word "kawaii" without translation.

According to Hiroshi Nittono, Japanese female culture is characterized by their fascination with kawaii.[33] He writes that Japanese people find kawaii in concepts such as "petit, round, light, white, and transparency."[34] He contends that the feeling of kawaii is derived from the human feeling toward babies.[35] Women are more responsive to babies, and kawaii is therefore a more feminine feeling.[36] Kawaii objects are loved because of their pretty shape and baby-like nonaggressive behavior. Kawaii is found in the figure of Hello Kitty, produced by the toy company Sanrio.[37] Hello Kitty's real name is Kitty White. She was born in London, and her last name is very suggestive. Many of Sanrio's products, including My Melody, Little Twin Sisters, Cinnamon Role, and others, have Western roots.

White female haafu models share the traits of kawaii. They are White, are petit, and have big eyes. They are also regarded as infantile and nonaggressive. For example, in an article that analyzes the popularity of White female haafu celebrities and models, Miruo Shima writes, "They behave and talk in a childish manner but it is OK because they are haafu, meaning, they do not understand Japanese culture well. Haafu are not aggressive because they are part-Japanese. On the other side, foreigners are critical of Japanese people. . . . Haafu do not threaten Japanese like foreigners do."[38] A similar analysis can be found in other articles. Tomokazu Takashino writes that "haafu are not smart but they are very friendly."[39] We can see from these articles that Japanese people regard haafu as kawaii because they are infantile and nonthreatening. This is why they dominate Japan's beauty culture. On the other hand, if kawaii evokes baby-like vulnerability and femininity, then darkness evokes the opposite: aggressiveness and masculinity. This contrast is one of the reasons why non-White female haafu models are invisible—they cannot represent what Japanese women desire.

The fashion and cosmetics industries gain profits by catering to women's desires. Therefore, they use models who most appeal to the desire of Japanese women: White female haafu models. Non-White female haafu models are invisible because their darkness is not regarded as kawaii and they are not marketable in Japan's beauty culture. While Japanese women's desire for kawaii is manifested in the body of White female haafu models, the bodies of non-White female haafu models are suppressed as undesirable.

To summarize, non-White female haafu models may be invisible in Japan's beauty culture for various reasons. First, non-White female haafu models typically have darker skin. Unfortunately, dark skin is undesirable in Japan's beauty culture. Second, some do not have the Western female beauty traits that Japanese women admire. Last, some do not fit with kawaii concepts. Japan's beauty industries need models who have light skin, Western facial features, and kawaii characteristics. If non-White female haafu models want to succeed in Japan's fashion and cosmetics industries, they have to be kawaii. Unlike non-White female haafu models, White female haafu models are located at the intersection of transnational lovely White ideology and local kawaii ideology, on which the beauty industries can profit. Therefore, White female haafu models dominate Japan's beauty culture.

The hypervisibility of White female haafu has created the stereotype of haafu as kawaii, light, and Western. Non-White haafu are marginalized, reduced to non-kawaii status. They may feel inferior toward their own skin, non-Caucasian facial features, and cultural backgrounds. For example, a haafu who is in her twenties and whose mother is Thai and father is Japanese comments on her troubled feelings toward the haafu stereotype: "Most haafu in the media are Western haafu. . . . Western haafu are very pretty and attractive. Japanese people associate haafu with Western haafu. When I tell people I'm haafu, people are surprised. I'd like to say that anyone whose parents' nationalities are different is haafu, but I had inferiority of not looking like a pretty Western haafu. I one time wished to have an American mother so I could look different."[40] Her comments illustrate the association of haafu with kawaii and Caucasian facial features, and her incompatibility with these traits. The hypervisibility of White haafu gives non-White haafu a sense of inferiority because they feel excluded. Changing the representation of haafu in the media may be a way to overcome these feelings of inferiority. Especially for girls, the influence of beauty culture is huge. If it had more non-White haafu models, non-White haafu would be more confident in self-proclaiming that they are haafu too. This would contribute to challenging the stereotype of haafu and to exposing the reality of haafu, who are racially and ethnically diverse. How could the invisibility of non-White female haafu models be overcome?

Their invisibility is derived, as we have seen, partly from their relationship to the concept of kawaii. Kawaii does not contain darkness. According to

Nittono, however, what Japanese people find kawaii has changed with time: "Even the same generation of women find different objects kawaii. Fashion magazines redefine the meaning of kawaii one after another."[41] In short, there is a possibility that non-White female haafu models would be regarded as kawaii. If Japanese culture embraced darkness as kawaii, non-White female haafu models might be more visible in fashion magazines and the cosmetics industry. Yet, is it an ideal situation for them?

Kawaii is a unique cultural concept in Japan, but it is far from uncontroversial. For example, feminist scholar Chizuko Ueno points out that kawaii is a strategy for Japanese women to be loved and protected by men. Kawaii derives from baby's nonaggressive behaviors. The vulnerability of a baby evokes people's instinct to protect babies. Ueno contends that Japanese men are looking for a kawaii partner who satisfies their chauvinism. To respond to the men's desires, Japanese women strive to be kawaii. If they threaten men's chauvinism, they will not be loved by men. To be kawaii thus means to be nonthreatening to men's authority. Since women subject themselves to the desire of men by internalizing kawaii ideology, Ueno argues that kawaii puts women in a subservient second-class status made by a patriarchal society.[42] In short, as long as women try to be kawaii, they will be reduced to the subservient status desired by men. Under the dictates of kawaii ideology, Japanese women avoid non-kawaii traits such as darkness, aggressiveness, voluptuousness, and so on. Non-White female haafu models may embody these non-kawaii features, which have no market value in Japan. This may be a reason for their invisibility in Japan's beauty culture. Is there a possibility that Japan's beauty culture will accommodate non-White haafu female models who are incompatible with lovely White and kawaii ideology?

Conclusion

The Japanese fashion and cosmetics industries have used many White female haafu models, reflecting Japanese women's desire for light skin, Caucasian facial features, and kawaii. Non-White female haafu models are excluded from Japanese beauty culture because they do not have the qualities Japanese women desire. Their invisibility may be positively understood as their resistance to the lovely White and kawaii ideology. However, as long as they are invisible, their very existence is not acknowledged by Japanese society, negatively affecting their self-esteem.

As stated earlier, the Japan's 2015 Miss Universe contestant is Ariana Miyamoto. Although Miyamoto may have Western beauty, her dark skin counters kawaii ideology. Miyamoto's selection may be quite significant in changing the direction of female beauty in Japan because she proves that non-White haafu can represent Japan's female beauty. It may be difficult to create a new standard of beauty, completely free from the long-dominant lovely White ideology and kawaii, but with the circulation of diverse female representations, non-White haafu female models could become more visible in Japan's beauty culture.

Japan is often regarded as a racially and ethnically homogeneous nation, yet with the increasing rate of intermarriage, the haafu population is growing. The number of haafu has not been researched by any official institutions, so their population has to be inferred through the number of internationally married couples, whose children supposedly are haafu. According to Japan's National Institute of Population and Social Security Research, the number of international marriages was 21,448 in 2013.[43] Many of these couples are non-Japanese Asians married to Japanese (e.g., 39.8 percent of Japanese women married Chinese or Korean men; 58.2 percent of Japanese men married Chinese or Korean women).[44] From the statistics, it can be surmised that many haafu are people with non-White heritages. Yet the mass media overwhelmingly represent White haafu, which does not reflect the racial/ethnic diversity of haafu. To overcome the invisibility of non-White haafu in beauty culture, it would be important for non-White haafu female models to appear more frequently in fashion magazines and in the cosmetics industry's advertisements, which could gradually change Japanese consciousness of race and ethnicity. Their very existence in beauty culture could challenge the lovely White and kawaii ideology that is rampant in Japan, and could lead to the creation of an alternative female beauty, enabling all women to be proud of who they are regardless of skin color and facial features.

NOTES

1. Baye McNeil, "Meeting Miss Universe Japan, the Half Who Has It All," *Japan Times*, April 19, 2015, http://www.japantimes.co.jp/community/2015/04/19/general/meeting-miss-universe-japan.

2. This chapter roughly defines race as certain physical traits and ethnicity as cultural membership, but both are socially constructed concepts and are changeable with time and place.

3. Itsuko Kamoto, *Kokusaikekkon Ron?* [A theory on international marriage?] (Kyoto: Horitsu Bunkasha, 2008), 150–151.

4. Natalie Maya Miller and Marcia Yumi Lise, *The Hafu Project* (Japan: Hafu Project, 2010), 3.

5. Paul Spickard, *Mixed Blood: Intermarriage and Ethnic Identity in Twentieth-Century America* (Madison: University of Wisconsin Press, 1989),153.

6. Stephen Murphy-Shigematsu, *Amerajian no Kodomotachi: Shirarezaru Mainority Mondai* [Amerasian children: Unknown minority problems], trans. Junko Sakai (Tokyo: Shueisha, 2002), 101.

7. "Geinoukai wo Sekkensuru haafu Bijo" [Haafu beauties dominating show business], *Flash* (May 8, 2007): 29.

8. Hiro Endo, "Cool & Exotic: Haafu Girls Boom!" (May 30, 2007), http://allabout.co.jp/gm/gc/2027661.

9. This essay uses the terms "White" and "non-White" to express skin colors. These skin color classifications sometimes coincide with racial categories and/or geography. Whites are Caucasians. Blacks are people with African heritage. Browns are people with dark skin, but not as dark as Black people. Similar to the definitions of race and ethnicity, these color categories are also socially constructed concepts and are changeable with time and place.

10. *Runway* (September 29, 2012).

11. Superheadz, *Life as a Golden Half* (Tokyo: Powershovel, 2007), cover.

12. "Haafu Face Recipe," *Bea's UP* (December 1, 2009): 52.

13. Ibid., 52.

14. Hiroshi Wagatsuma and Toshinao Yoneyama, *Henken no Kouzou: Nihonjin no Jinshukan* [A structure of prejudice: Japanese racial views] (Tokyo: NHK Books, 1967), 20.

15. Ibid., 68.

16. Ibid., 26.

17. Ibid., 67.

18. Ibid., 37.

19. Joanne L. Rondilla and Paul Spickard, *Is Lighter Better? Skin-Tone Discrimination among Asian Americans* (Lanham, MD: Rowman & Littlefield, 2007).

20. Wendy Chapkis, *Beauty Secrets: Women and the Politics of Appearance* (Boston: South End, 1986), 37.

21. Julie Matthews, "Eurasian Persuasions: Mixed Race, Performativity and Cosmopolitanism," *Journal of Intercultural Studies* 28.1 (2007): 50.

22. Wagatsuma and Yoneyama, *Henken no Kouzou*, 89.

23. John Russell, *Nihonjin no Kokujinkan: Mondai ha Chibikuro Sambo dakedehanai* [Japanese perception of Black people: A problem is not only Chibikuro Sambo] (Tokyo: Shinhyoron, 1991), 4.

24. Wagatsuma and Yoneyama, *Henken no Kouzou*, 99.

25. Atsuhisa Yamamoto, "Haafu no Shintai Hyyosho ni okeru Danseisei to Jinshuka no Politics" [Masculinity on the physical representation of haafu and the politics of racialization] in *Haafu to ha dareka: Jinshu Konko, Media hyoushou, koushou jissen* [Who is haafu? Race mixture, media representation, negotiation], ed. Koichi Iwabuchi (Tokyo: Seikyuu, 2014), 114.

26. Keiko Kozeki, *Nihonnjinn Keiko: Aru Konketuji no Shuki* [Japanese Keiko: A memoir of a racially mixed girl] (Tokyo: Horupu, 1980), 59.

27. Tamiki Iguchi, "Kuroi Hada no Nihonjin: Yonin Musume ga Moetagiru Toki" [Black skin Japanese: Four girls in ecstasy], *Shukan Post* (February 17, 1972): 168–172.

28. Stephen Murphy-Shigematsu, *Amerajian no Kodomotachi: Shirarezaru Mainority Mondai* [Amerasian children: Unknown minority problems], trans. Junko Sakai (Tokyo: Shueisha, 2002), 95.

29. Mitzi Carter and Aina Hunter, "A Critical Review of Academic Perspectives of Blackness in Japan," in *Multiculturalism in the New Japan: Crossing the Boundaries Within*, ed. Nelson Graburn, John Ertl, and Kenji Tierney (New York: Berghahn Books, 2008), 197.

30. Stephen Murphy-Shigematsu, *When Half Is Whole: Multiethnic Asian American Identities* (Stanford: Stanford University Press, 2012), 129.

31. http://jewerich.jp/shopping.html.

32. Inuhiko Yomota, *Kawaii Ron* [Kawaii theory] (Tokyo: Chikuma Shinsho, 2006), 38.

33. Hiroshi Nittono, "Kawaii ni taisuru Koudoukagakuteki Apurochi" [A behavioral science approach to kawaii], *Ningenkagaku Kenkyu* 4 (2009): 19.

34. Ibid., 24.

35. Ibid., 29.

36. Ibid., 26.

37. Yomota, *Kawaii Ron*, 16.

38. Miruo Shima, "Haafu Tarento tairyo hassei no Naze" [Why are there so many haafu celebrities in show business?], February 14, 2012, http://news.livedoor.com/article/detail/6277751/.

39. Tomokazu Takashino, "Miwaku no Haagu Bijo Juukunin" [Nineteen exotic haafu beauties], *Playboy* (December 19, 2011): 6.

40. Koichi Iwabuchi, "Haafu toiu Category nikansuru Toujisha heno Kikitorichosa" [An interview with haafu on the category of haafu], in Iwabuchi, *Haafu to ha dareka*, 269–270.

41. Nittono, "Kawaii ni taisuru Koudoukagakuteki Apurochi," 29.

42. Chizuko Ueno, *Oiru Junbi* [Prepare to be old] (Tokyo: Gakuyo Shobo, 2005), 27–28.

43. National Institute of Population and Social Security Research, *Jinko no Doko: Nihon to Sekai Jinkoutoukei Shiryoshu 2015* [Demography trend: Japan and the world 2015] (Tokyo: Kosekitokei Kyokai, 2015), 105.

44. Ibid., 106.

11

Checking "Other" Twice

Transnational Dual Minorities

LILY ANNE Y. WELTY TAMAI

The cover of the November 12, 1953, issue of *Jet Magazine* asks in the title, "Do Japanese Women Make Better Wives?" Underneath the headline is a photograph of an interracially married couple, James and Teruko Miller. James Miller is Black and wears a military uniform and Teruko Miller is Japanese and wears a high-collared white blouse, and they both directly face the camera (see figure 11.1). The cover's subtext reads, "Indianapolis couple has found happily married life since wedding three years ago in Japan."[1] We can surmise that the magazine issue was intended to address the question of postwar interracial marriage of Black soldiers to Japanese women to the primarily Black readership of *Jet Magazine*. Why did they choose a Japanese woman to represent an ideal partner for Black men? Was the article inferring that perhaps Japanese women made better wives than Black women? Who were the mixed race children born to couples like James and Teruko?

Mixed race people born at the end of World War II made history quietly with their families and their communities. Wars and the military occupations that followed, coupled with increased migration across the Pacific, created a surge of interracial relationships, resulting in a midcentury multiracial baby boom. Easily identifiable by their mixed race features, they were the children of the enemy: in Japan they symbolized defeat and racial impurity, while in America they were seen as an extension of America's democratic intervention abroad and a symbol of the salvation that the United States offered Japan during the postwar occupation.[2] Their family lives varied. Some grew up with one or both of their biological parents, others were raised by extended family members. Due to choices made by their parents and policies instituted by states, many were left stateless, orphaned, raised by single mothers or by adoptive families. These multiracial American Japanese ushered in the legacy of transnational adoption

FIGURE 11.1. *Jet Magazine*, November 12, 1953.

and immigration of children from Asia. Their baby pictures peppered the postwar newspapers and magazines in Japan and the United States ranging from
Life, *Ebony*, and *Jet* to *Asahi Gurafu*.[3] The variety of the children's backgrounds
reflected the military's microcosm of American racial diversity.

This chapter focuses on the lesser known narratives of mixed race American Japanese who are dual minorities while highlighting the way in which
communities of color helped influence these mixed race families. Some dual

minorities had fathers who were Black, Latino, or Native American. Some grew up and remained in Japan or in Okinawa, while others came to the United States as young adults. Hundreds came as infants or young children and were adopted into American families. Leaving Japan to cross the Pacific Ocean meant arriving in their father's land to deal with a new set of rules surrounding race and the flux of a migrating identity. The stories span families, decades, time, and the Pacific. I connect the importance of oral history methodology with transpacific border crossing to address the issues of mixed race transnational adoption, migration, and marriage.

I examine both chronologically and thematically the ways in which the multiracial perspectives of dual minorities from two minority groups expand our understanding of the Japanese American community. The title of this chapter is a play on the selection of race boxes on official forms and documents, whereby dual-minority individuals might choose "other" twice. It refers to mixed race people whose racial background comes from parents who are both from two different minority ethnic groups. Upon further investigation, we gain new perspectives on the postwar mixed race experience. Specifically, I argue how interracial communities, families, and mixed race individuals challenged the default narrative of White normativity in the US military and in the postwar period, while also expanding our understanding of the transnational Black Pacific, or the diaspora of Blacks in the Pacific Rim. Using a variety of sources, including oral history interviews, autobiographies, archival material, magazines, and secondary sources, this chapter showcases the experiences of dual minorities within the context of a transnational community.

Decentering Whiteness through the Black Pacific

Decentering Whiteness requires intentionally searching for sources that provide a fuller history. In this chapter I showcase how the soft power of cartoons silenced images of Blacks by not including them. Moving beyond the mainstream story takes deliberate work because not only are the experiences of dual-minority mixed race individuals not prominent, but also the histories of their parents are often absent. However, within the context of mixed race studies, the experience of White-Japanese multiracials is a well-established narrative in the Pacific and in the United States.[4] Early on, scholars who focused on topics of mixed race Japanese individuals led the scholarship by including the voices of dual minorities.[5] From those stories of non-White mixed race individuals, we begin to uncover more about their parents and the historical circumstances which prevailed. If there were mixed race individuals who were Native American and Okinawan, Mexican and Okinawan, Black and Japanese, among other ethnic mixes, it is clear that the military was more ethnically diverse than presented in historical photos and books. In fact, numerous minorities served in the military, in addition to the individuals who served in segregated units, and we know this because of the backgrounds of the children. Interracially married couples and their children help to demonstrate the complexity of dual minorities and their place within migrant communities. This chapter contests the hegemony of Whiteness and its central position in our historical understanding of the post–World War II mixed race experience by examining mixed race migrant military communities through the lens of the transnational Black Pacific.

Postwar interracial couples and their communities were no different from the many mixed race families who crossed the Pacific before them. This chapter frames the postwar families within the historical context of mixed race communities beginning with immigrant Japanese groups who settled in the territory of Hawai'i and on the West Coast of the United States. Examining the early multiracial communities contextualizes their histories within the racial discourse.[6] Dual-minority individuals operated in a hybrid space that was layered with complex family histories. Examining multiracial communities also helps to build upon the scholarship of passing, which often privileges the narrative of White normativity.[7] It becomes evident that when given a choice, mixed race individuals did not always choose to be White. Unpacking the history of the pre–World War II mixed race Japanese communities sets the stage for the postwar communities and the racial climate that couples like James and Teruko Miller might have experienced.

Historicizing Mixed Race Communities

In the late nineteenth century, the first Japanese American families to settle in Hawai'i and the United States were interracial families with mixed race children.[8] These lesser known mixed race communities in the Japanese American context include the Gannenmono in the Kingdom of Hawai'i in 1868, the Wakamatsu Tea and Silk Farm Colony in Placerville, California, in 1869, and the first Japanese community outside of Portland in Multnomah County, which created the township of Orient, Oregon, in 1880. The first Japanese community that settled permanently came to the Kingdom of Hawai'i in 1868.[9] Like many sojourning immigrants, the majority of them were male laborers intending to stay briefly, earn money, and return to Japan as rich men. From the initial 153 laborers, only a handful remained and established families. Those who stayed married local Hawaiian women, created mixed families, and became the first Japanese settlers by remaining permanently in the community (see figure 11.2).[10]

FIGURE 11.2. Gannenmono Matsugoro Kuwata with his Hawaiian wife Meleana and family, circa 1899. They were the first Japanese American family to settle in Hawai'i. Kuwata was among the first of 153 laborers to leave Japan for Honolulu in 1868. *Source*: Bishop Museum, Honolulu, Hawai'i, NRC.1998.66.29.

The initial group from Japan who established roots on the US mainland were the members of the Wakamatsu Colony in Placerville, who arrived in San Francisco on May 20, 1869. With them they brought twenty thousand mulberry bushes and six million tea seeds with the intention of creating an agricultural community producing silk by settling and raising silkworms, which eat the leaves of the mulberry plant. Many of those initial pioneers returned to Japan after two years when the colony failed economically. However, among the few who stayed was Kuninosuke Masumizu (1849–1915), who married Carrie Wilson, the mixed race daughter of a Blackfoot Indian woman and a former Black slave. Their descendants, the Elebeck family, identify as African American and are aware of their mixed Japanese ancestry. In Gresham, Oregon, the first pioneering family from Japan who settled in 1880 was Miyo Iwakoshi and her Australian Scottish husband, Andrew McKinnon. They established a sawmill in East Multnomah County, and McKinnon named the township Orient after his wife. This European and Japanese family illustrates that the first family in Oregon also had mixed roots.[11]

These community studies reveal how circumstances like economics, opportunities, and wars resulted in the immigration of people to and from the United States.[12] The movement of people across the Pacific is more complicated than just push-and-pull factors between Asia and the Americas. The factors are not static. Economics, population decline, immigration legislation, wars, and a web of global industrial capital factored into the ebb and flow. The communities that sprang up as a result of interracial relationships and mixed race progeny did so because circumstances were favorable. The one-drop rule of hypodescent that operated to reinforce the master class and oppress the slave class did not always apply in cases with dual minorities because the racial hierarchy and ethnic landscape were simply different in the Pacific Rim.

Like the descendents of the initial Japanese American communities, mixed race individuals who are dual minorities force people to reconsider existing categories of race and mixed race. The scholarship that examines dual minorities in mixed race communities in greater detail includes Karen Leonard's *Making Ethnic Choices*, which examines mixed race Punjabi Mexicans in the Imperial Valley, and Rudy P. Guevarra Jr.'s *Becoming Mexipino*, on mixed race Mexican and Filipinos in San Diego.[13] For both Punjabi Mexicans and Mexipinos, one or both parents were immigrants and the children were dual minorities of Asian descent who were US citizens. Neither the Punjabi Mexicans nor the Mexipinos fit within the established Black-White binary but rather added additional layers by expanding and complicating our understanding of racial, marital, and religious diversity within dual mixed race communities.

Some mixed race American Japanese communities in the postwar context are families created by the military-industrial complex. Analogous to the migrant laborers to the United States, deployed military personnel and their families are also migrant laborers who created a racially mixed community within a militarized borderland on the US military bases. In Teresa Williams-León's study on mixed race military communities in Japan during the 1980s, very much like the aforementioned early mixed-race communities, we can see similar reasons for immigration and transpacific border crossing. For these families, labor and economics with the additional reason of military necessity catalyzed the immigration of this migrant labor force.[14] Especially following World War II and the American occupation of Japan, US military bases have been a mainstay in Japan and Okinawa, creating decades of hybrid and third-space communities of interracial families and mixed race children. New families enter when they have PCS (permanent change of station) orders to relocate to another duty location that may change from year to year, or every four years. Those communities have racial, cultural, and linguistic fluidity despite the electrified fences and limited access of the military bases. And much like the migrant mixed race families, they too experienced a process of acculturation.

Model Minority Wife

In "Do Japanese Women Make Better Wives?" *Jet Magazine* positioned Japanese women as model wives in contrast to what we can infer as Black women. There are parallels in the tone between this article and the William Petersen article,

"Success Story, Japanese-American Style," published in *New York Times Magazine* in 1966.[15] Petersen's article set into motion debates about Asian Americans, specifically Japanese Americans, as model minorities who achieved success in the United States despite barriers of racial discrimination. Combined, these texts perpetuate what I call the "model minority wife." The *Jet Magazine* article's framing of the argument that Japanese women might serve as model wives to Black men minimizes the position of Black women, if they choose not to think what their husbands wanted them to think. In short, *Jet Magazine* undermined Black womanhood. The article pits Japanese women against Black women, and indirectly blames Black wives for not being the model minority wife, much like Petersen's article praised Japanese Americans for being model minorities while questioning why Blacks did not achieve the same level of social and economic success.

Along with the Millers from the epigraph, another couple mentioned in the article, Bruce and Sayako Smith, reflect on their relationship as an African American husband and Japanese wife. Bruce states, "I like it when my wife waits on me hand and foot, gives me a massage when I come home from work, washes my back in hot water and turns down the bed so I can take a nap before dinner." Sayako responds, "I feel it is my duty to do my husband's bidding, . . . and if this makes me different from American women, then I don't know what to do about it because acting this way makes him happy. If he's happy, I am happy." The article continues, "As in her homeland, she [Sayako] regards her husband as No. 1 and herself as No. 2. Or as Mrs. Smith explains, 'I think only what I think Bruce wants me to think.'"[16] The Smiths and the Millers are two examples of families that have particularly defined gender roles as husband and wife. Do Japanese women make better wives when they take on a subordinate role within their marital relationship? Are Japanese wives better because they adapt to new relationships?

What is missing from this article is how these families actually functioned within the larger military communities, and specifically the Black military community. In reality, Black women were instrumental in helping Japanese women who were married to Black men get their bearings as new Americans in the United States. Japanese war brides who married Black soldiers acculturated to the new environment, learned how to be Americans, and navigated their households via the experiences of the Black community, not necessarily the White community. Interracially married couples who were in the military formed communities among themselves within the Black community both on and off the military base. For example, Curtiss Takada Rooks's parents met and married while his father served in the US Air Force in Japan. Although she was married to an African American man, Curtiss's Japanese mother learned how to be an American woman from Black women within the military community. Within the process of mastering American ways, many Japanese women learned how to be Black women first. Curtiss's mother learned how to cook many dishes typically served in Black households, and she established relationships by singing in the choir in their Baptist church.[17] According to *Jet Magazine*, the model wife might have been cast as a Japanese woman, however, it was Black women who modeled the behavior of Americans for Japanese women.[18]

Babysan's Soft Power

While *Jet Magazine* brought to light the experiences of Japanese women who were married to African Americans, another source from the period erased the presence of African American GIs entirely through the soft power of cartoon images. Bill Hume (1916–2009), a Navy reservist and cartoonist for the *Stars and Stripes* (the newspaper for the armed forces), published several illustrated paperback collections of his weekly comic strip, *Babysan*, following World War II (see figure 11.3).[19] Wildly popular, his books functioned as cultural guidebooks that explained the day-to-day incongruencies of Japanese customs to American GIs who had served in occupied Japan. His main character, Babysan, was a bright and lively Japanese woman who had many GI boyfriends and spoke like a fortune cookie. She wore tight-fitting shirts that revealed ample cleavage along with pencil skirts and *geta*, Japanese wooden clogs. Her hair bounced like that of a 1950s pinup model. The different scenarios in the books illustrate the hows and whys of the way Japanese culture might confuse the Americans occupying the country. In some settings she is talking to a group of American GIs, while in other settings she is having a conversation with one man. The men are always in their military uniforms, and they are always White.[20]

Part of the imagery within the exchange of cultural ideas of Americans in occupied Japan had to do with Bill Hume's depictions. The *Babysan* cartoons reinforced White normativity in the military. Hume colored the imaginations of a generation of soldiers through his cartoons. Seasoned servicemen in Japan could identify their own intimate relationships with Japanese women in the cartoons, and newly deployed servicemen learned about the culture of dating Japanese women. The reach of the books was broad, and their soft power was influential. The books were so popular that the publisher, Charles E. Tuttle Co., reprinted Hume's three books over a dozen times each, and in 1965 *Babysan's World: The Hume'n Slant on Japan* went into its twenty-fifth printing.

Hume's books were two-sided. On one hand, Hume took great care to explain particular aspects of Japanese society to confused Americans who had very little exposure to the idiosyncrasies of foreign mores. On the other hand, he sexualized Japanese women, omitted Black soldiers, reduced Japanese people to Asian caricatures, and made Japanese men a part of the scenery. As argued by historian Isaiah Walker, to sexualize the female and erase the male is a colonizing move.[21]

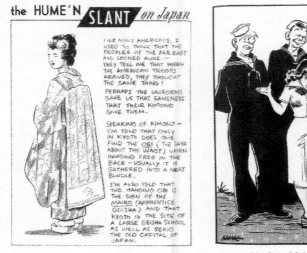 

FIGURE 11.3. Bill Hume, *Babysan's World: The Hume'n Slant on Japan* (Rutland, VT: Charles E. Tuttle Co, 1959).

Not only does this operate to reinforce colonialism, it also functions to center Whites via the erasure of Black and Japanese men. Babysan was an amalgamation of Japanese women in the mind of Bill Hume. Although the *Babysan* books discussed cultural questions and issues relating to interracial dating, Babysan was cast not as a future wife, but as a temporary girlfriend. As stated by Hume, "Babysan was a poor man's geisha."[22] But in fact, she was portrayed only as a White man's geisha.

Certainly, we can surmise that Hume did not include African American GIs in his cartoons because he was in a unit with only White men and the Black soldiers were in segregated units. However, Black men were part of the military and read the *Stars and Stripes*. Based on interviews, we know that Japanese women remarked that Black men were nicer to them than White men were.[23] Many Black soldiers dated and married Japanese women, and fathered mixed race children who were born during the US occupation of Japan and Okinawa. Black GIs and their children formed part of the transnational Pacific diaspora.[24]

Transnational Black Pacific

Concepts like the Atlantic World and the Black Atlantic engage regions that have connections and histories illustrating their relationship with Europe. Defined as the interaction of people within the empires that have bordered the Atlantic Ocean rim since the 1450s, the orientation of Atlantic World emphasizes the relationship to Europe. The Black Atlantic refers to the diaspora and culture of Blacks across the Atlantic World and into the Americas and the Caribbean.[25] Within that relationship exists an exchange of people, products, and culture that reinforces the metropole to the center, where the origins are often defined as European.

The Black Pacific refers to the consciousness of Blacks, their diaspora, and the connection to Asia via the Pacific Rim. The transatlantic slave trade and the forced removal of people from sub-Saharan Africa resulted in a wave of people of African descent mostly into the Americas. The Black Pacific parallels the Black Atlantic without the forced removal of people, but it includes the conscripted and voluntary military service of African Americans from the nineteenth century to the present in Asian nations. US military intervention in Asia and the Pacific has been a driving force for African Americans to cross the Pacific since the Spanish-American War.[26] Studies that center on the Pacific also work to decenter the Black-White binary because they must contend with Asia, thereby expanding our understanding of the changing and static dynamics of race and racism as well as existing social hierarchies. Other terms that emphasize the Black contribution specifically to Japan include Black Japan and Black Okinawa.[27] This chapter centers the narrative of Black Pacific by including the voices and stories of mixed race people and their parents who complicate this transpacific and transnational history.

Mixed race individuals and their families functioned within a transnational framework in the Pacific. The term "transnational" is defined as something that operates between and beyond national boundaries. However, the definition is more complicated than just border crossing or a company that has an office overseas. Transnational mixed race individuals need to be contextualized within their families and the larger global migration of labor, economics, capital, and colonialism.[28] Moreover, the US military is not only transnational but also global.[29] It operates globally in the name of democracy and defense within a sphere of colonialism. Service members are the migrant labor force who support the aims of the US government. The military fosters interracial relationships, which in turn create mixed race people. Their families transport culture back and forth between a transnational militarized borderland and the local community. As stated by Fernando Herrera Lima, "Transnational families are therefore vehicles—better yet, agents—for both material exchanges and the creation, re-creation and transformation of cultures."[30] Within this larger transnational framework, mixed race dual minorities must navigate being a person of color while also being a mixed race person of Asian descent. Sometimes this also includes an additional layer of identity as a transnational adoptee.

The postwar transnational adoption boom from East Asia to the United States began with a mixed race Black Japanese baby. Born in 1947, Demitoriasu, who later took on the name Damien, was also the first mixed race Black Japanese baby to come to the Elizabeth Saunders Home for Mixed-Blood Children. In fact, his adoption required an act of Congress for him to be able to enter the United States.[31] Miki Sawada, who was the headmistress of the Elizabeth Saunders Home, recalled the first mixed race Black and Japanese child who came to the orphanage:

> There was a boy named Deme chan. He was the first Black child that came to the Saunders Home. Underneath his long eyelashes were these big eyes that sparkled with intelligence. He struck me as a sociable and friendly child who was just starting to walk—by grabbing on to things and walking sideways. He wasn't the kind of kid to go and look for his parents, but maybe that was because he had not spent that much time with his birth mother. On his family register in the column that denotes the birthfather's whereabouts, it was written only as "unknown."
>
> At first we were calling him Demitoriasu (English pronunciation: Demetrius), but sometime later we started using the term of endearment of Deme chan and called him that.[32] For us [at the ESH] this was the first Black child and although we were particularly careful with him, he had no ill feelings, no cares or worries, and every day we raised him, he slept well and he ate well.[33]

His adoptive parents, the Tillman family, were a Black couple who were stationed in Japan while serving in the Air Force. They also adopted a mixed race Black Okinawan girl who became Damien's younger sibling.[34] Not only White families, but also Black families were actively adopting mixed race children from Japan.[35] Although the Tillmans had secured the adoption paperwork, due to the immigration laws restricting Asian immigration to the United States prior to the 1965 Immigration Act, they could not bring a baby from Japan, even if he was mixed race and had an American parent. Miki Sawada wrote to Congressperson Walter Judd from Minnesota to assist mixed race children with their immigration paperwork and to somehow bypass the legal restrictions. After much delay, her request was granted and Deme chan became the first mixed race transnational adoptee who immigrated to the United States, establishing a precedent for postwar adoptees from Asia.

While Black soldiers migrated west across the Pacific, some of their mixed race children migrated east to the United States as children and as adults in the decades following World War II. Keiko was born in 1947 in Sasebo, Nagasaki prefecture, to a Japanese mother and an African American father. In Sasebo, she had a difficult time growing up as Black and Japanese and spent a lot of time defending herself in fights with the neighborhood children.[36] When she was twenty years old, she married an African American man and came to the San Francisco Bay Area, where she has lived for over forty years (see figure 11.4).

After moving from Tokyo in 1967, Keiko and her family settled in the South Bay. She and her husband were married at a Japanese Christian Church, where they, among many Japanese Americans, are still members of the congregation. When Keiko's family had the opportunity to move north to Oakland, she recalled that she wanted to stay geographically closer to the Japanese American community rather than move where there was a greater concentration of African Americans. Her cultural home existed among the Japanese American community, and moving to a locale where African Americans lived was not necessarily a better fit for her. Keiko's decision to remain near the established Japanese American community illustrates how her choice challenges the narrative of the Black-White binary.

Nearly every year as an adult Keiko returns to visit her family in Japan, and inevitably she experiences microaggressions during those visits. Even though others assume from her appearance that she is foreign—and by default not Japanese—Keiko asserts her Japaneseness and decides what personal information she will share. When Keiko is complimented on her Japanese speech, local individuals remark, "Your Japanese is so good!" Keiko replies with, "Thank you. I've been to Japan a few times before." Clearly, Keiko positions herself in a way where she retains agency by not having to provide personal reasoning for her language ability, and also evades having to explain why her presumed foreign appearance and her native speech align.

FIGURE 11.4. Kassy and Keiko. *Source*: Era Bell Thompson, "Happy Ending: Grown-Up Brown Baby Finds Husband in Japan, a Home in the USA," *Ebony* (July 1968): 66.

Dual-minority individuals were not immune to shifts in racial formation, especially across borders. These racial encounters were situational and changed depending on age and historical period, illustrating the social constructed nature of race. Fredrick was born in postwar Japan to a Japanese mother and a Black father. He and his family moved to the United States when he was twelve years old. Fredrick and his mother spoke Japanese to each other, and coming to the States was a big change. On his blog he shared his experience as a mixed race person: "For me, in New Mexico, I got 'nigger' and 'Jap' and 'Gook' as well as 'Slant-eye' 'Fu-Manchu' and other comments and names about my being mixed-up, confused, impure. Later, primarily in the late 1960s into the 1970s, this turned to 'exotic' and 'you have beautiful skin.' Not as painful, but just as lonely (since I was not there but as a figure of their own racialized notions of people)."[37] Fredrick did not change anything about himself, but the way others perceived his racial identity was in flux over several decades.

The people who reinforced ethnic pride and defended dual minorities were not always from that same ethnic group. Curtiss was born to a Japanese mother and an African American father. His father was from North Carolina and came of age in postwar Japan where he served in the military. Japan was a place where Curtiss's father had status as a Black man, unlike in the South or other working-class places. Their family lived on military bases from Okinawa to Kansas. As a kid, Curtiss recalled using the term "gook" as a way to tease Asians. When his father got wind of this, he immediately corrected his son, reminding him, "You are gook. Your mother is a gook. Don't ever use that word again."[38] Curtiss's pride about being Japanese was fostered not only by his Japanese mother, but also by his African American father (see figure 11.5).

Black women helped Curtiss's mother get accustomed to the United States. As a result, her influence as a Japanese mother in the Rooks household expanded to include African American sensibilities. Curtiss recalled that his mother was involved in the women's choir at their Black Baptist church and had a circle of friends who were Black women from within the military community. He reflected on his family's food culture: "Perhaps the most fun mixture of culture came at the kitchen table. *Gohan* with every meal, turnip or mustard greens cooked slowly on Sunday afternoon, sweet potato pie at holidays, octopus or squid to freak out my Midwestern high school friends, and of course teriyaki chit'lins made our family cuisine our own."[39] To outsiders it may appear as a hybrid culture, but to their family, and many other families like theirs, this was the norm.

A transnational identity is complex and not devoid of misunderstandings by others. Elizabeth was born and raised in Okinawa and came to the United States to attend college. Her mother is Okinawan and her father is Black, and they met while her father was serving in the military in Okinawa. She has two half sisters, one who is Okinawan and Filipino, the other Okinawan and Puerto Rican. Elizabeth did not grow up with her father, and although she knew her biological mother, as an infant a childless couple unofficially adopted her. She often visited with her biological mother, but they never lived in the same household together. During college in Minnesota she met her future husband, an Ethiopian man who had fled persecution in his home country. After graduating from college in the United States, the two started their own family and made their home in mainland Japan. She remarked about her own identity and ethnic choices: "I wanted my children to know that they look like their parents."[40] Her children are bilingual in English and in Japanese. Although Elizabeth's background was clear to her, other people had difficulty understanding her mixed race background and cultural transnationalism.

The linguistic diversity in the transnational Black Pacific includes native English speakers, but also individuals for whom neither English nor Japanese is their first language. Saeko's father, who was an African American man from New York, had served in the US military in Okinawa, where he met her Okinawan mother.

FIGURE 11.5. The Rooks family, Manhattan, Kansas, ca. 1961. Courtesy of Curtiss Takada Rooks.

Saeko grew up in Okinawa and, along with Japanese, she was raised speaking Uchinaguchi, the indigenous language of Okinawa. "I am told that I am more Uchinaa than
most people in Okinawa, even though I am only half. My heart is Okinawan."[41] Similar
to Keiko's experience, locals in Okinawa praised Saeko because of her ability to speak
Japanese, despite the fact that she has lived there all of her life, and knows only limited English. Based on her appearance, they expect her to be a foreigner, or someone
who is currently serving duty on one of the military bases in Okinawa. As one would
presume, it is exhausting (and bordering on offensive) to be reminded of a perceived
linguistic and physical dissonance. Saeko repeats the same thing during these encounters: she is Okinawan, born and raised on the island, and has the linguistic authenticity as a native speaker of Uchinaguchi. Language is intimately tied to identity, and
on a larger scale, the languages that are connected to dual-minority identities have
many layers of meaning, despite appearing to be muted because of their mixed race
phenotype.

Conclusion

Decentering Whiteness takes work. It requires examining the default narrative
of White normativity, dismantling White hegemony by considering coexisting
narratives that are often marginalized or untold. Challenging White hegemony
includes expanding upon macro-level concepts like the Black Atlantic, by looking at Asia *west* across the Black Pacific to the Pacific Rim. In the search for these
stories, it is apparent that there are gaps in the sources when it comes to the
topic of dual minorities and their families.

This chapter has framed the stories of mixed race dual minorities in the
context of other historic mixed race families, illustrating how their experiences
are not all that rare. Postwar intermarried couples like James and Teruko Miller
were neither new nor revolutionary. There may have been only a few couples
in their local communities who looked like the Millers, however when contextualized historically, much like the Gannenmono, the Millers are the modern
example of people crisscrossing the Pacific, expanding the notion of the Black
Pacific, and challenging White normativity. Their mixed race children mir-
rored the experiences of Punjabi Mexicans and Mexipinos, and pushed boundaries of race and community too. By placing mixed race people like Damien,
Keiko, Fredrick, Curtiss, Elizabeth, and Saeko at the center of the discussion,
we begin to see the diversity in communities, in the ranks of the military, and
in the backgrounds of adoptees from Asia. We begin to examine race outside
the Black-White binary. We can expand the discussion of mixed race studies and
mixed race Asian Americans beyond those who are Asian and White.[42]

The sources and oral histories from the period show that at times Blacks
were blamed or absent. Black women were indirectly pitted against Japanese

women for not being model wives, while Black men were erased from the military narrative in cultural spaces. Black women jointly built and supported the African American military communities by providing domestic support for their nuclear families as well as for the Japanese women who had married into the Black community. War brides from Asia learned how to be American wives from the lead of Black women. These Japanese women were absorbed into the Black community, and were taught how to be American via Black America.

Cartoons have a soft cultural power, and the *Babysan* cartoon strip was no doubt influential because of its appeal and numerous reproductions. Through the cartoons and subsequent books, Bill Hume taught a generation of soldiers about Japan. But Hume completely left out Black soldiers from the cartoon strip. The omission of Black men in the cartoons reinforced White normativity for the readership. Although Hume's explanations of Japanese customs were culturally sensitive and sociologically crafted, at the same time he sexualized Japanese women by depicting them with curvy hips, large breasts, and cleavage. Calling out these biases and erasures is important to decenter Whiteness and draw attention to the sexualization of colonized bodies.[43]

The presence or absence of biological parents, the primary languages used, and the spaces where mixed race individuals grew up are factors that facilitated a transnational identity. Especially for individuals who are dual minorities, asserting their identity to others to address perceived dissonance often resulted in ethnic fatigue, as illustrated by the experiences of Keiko, Fredrick, and Saeko. Their transnational experiences required mixed race individuals to re-create a place and an identity even when they were not operating within the original environment. Military bases, new cities, and—for some—new families served as spaces where their identities waxed and waned. They navigated a transnational identity that changed depending upon where they lived, what languages they spoke, and how their status shifted with the changes in racial formation during the postwar period.

ACKNOWLEDGMENTS

This research was made possible through a Fulbright Fellowship through the Institute of International Education in Japan, and a Critical Mixed-Race Studies postdoctoral fellowship through the USC Shinso Ito Center for Japanese Religions and Culture. I would like to thank Jeff Dinkler for feedback on an earlier version of this chapter and acknowledge the suggestions I received from the editors of this volume, Joanne Rondilla, Rudy Guevarra, and Paul Spickard.

NOTES

1. "Do Japanese Women Make Better Wives?," *Jet Magazine*, November 12, 1953, 18–21. There is an aspect of pitting Japanese women against Black women to make the

comparison of a better partner, much in the same way William Petersen's article, "Success Story, Japanese-American Style," *New York Times Magazine* (January 9, 1966): 180, used Japanese Americans as an example of the model minority and pitted Blacks against Latinos.

2. The American occupation of Japan lasted from 1945 to 1952, while the American occupation of Okinawa was from 1945 to 1972.

3. Don Moser, "Japan's G.I. Babies: A Hard Coming-of-Age," *Life* (September 5, 1969): 40–47; Marc Crawford, "The Tragedy of Brown Babies Left in Japan," *Jet Magazine* (January 14, 1960): 14–17; Era Bell Thompson, "Japan's Rejected: Teen-agers Fathered by Negro Soldiers Face a Bleak Future in a Hostile Land," *Ebony* (September 1967): 42–54; Hiroshi Kozawa, "Suterareta konketsu no ko" [Abandoned mixed blood children], *Asahi Gurafu* [Asahi Picture News] (August 4, 1957): 8–9.

4. European colonialism resulted in people of mixed background, including English Chinese, Dutch Indonesians, and French Vietnamese. See Sui Sin Far (Edith Eaton), *Mrs. Spring Fragrance and Other Writings*, ed. Amy Ling and Annette White-Parks (Urbana: University of Illinois Press, 1995); Onoto Watanna (Winnifred Eaton), *A Half Caste and Other Writings* (Urbana: University of Illinois Press, 2002).

5. See Nathan Strong, "Patterns of Social Interaction and Psychological Accommodation among Japan's *Konketsuji* Population" (PhD diss., University of California, Berkeley, 1978). Strong's work pioneered the studies of multiracial people of Japanese descent. It examines Japanese and American (both White and Black) people in Japan and their social relationships. Christine Catherine Iijima Hall, "The Ethnic Identity of Racially Mixed People: A Study of Black-Japanese" (PhD diss., University of California, Los Angeles, 1980). Hall studied thirty multiracial Black Japanese in the Los Angeles area and the psychological aspects of their self-esteem, refuting previous literature that contended they had mental and psychological problems. George Kitahara-Kich, "Eurasians: Ethnic/Racial Identity Development of Biracial Japanese/White Adults" (PhD diss., Wright Institute, 1982), developed an identity development model. Michael C. Thornton, "A Social History of a Multiethnic Identity: The Case of Black-Japanese Americans" (PhD diss., University of Michigan, 1983); Thornton studied thirteen Black Japanese interracial couples in Kansas, Washington, DC, Michigan, and Massachusetts, and how the interracial family shaped the identity of their multiracial children. Stephen Murphy-Shigematsu, "The Voices of Amerasians: Ethnicity, Identity and Empowerment in Interracial Japanese Americans" (EdD diss., Harvard University, 1986); Murphy-Shigematsu studied Amerasian identity of multiracial Japanese Americans living in the US Midwest and Northeast. Teresa K. Williams-León, "International Amerasians: Third Culture Afroasian and Eurasian Americans in Japan" (MA thesis, University of California, Los Angeles, 1989); Williams studied bilingual multiracial Japanese Americans (both White and Black) who grew up with their nuclear families on and near the military bases in Japan. Paul Spickard, *Mixed Blood: Intermarriage and Ethnic Identity in Twentieth-Century America* (Madison: University of Wisconsin Press, 1989); Paul R. Spickard, "What Must I Be? Asian Americans and the Question of Multiethnic Identity," *Amerasia Journal* 23.1 (1997): 43–60. Examples in film include the 1959 movie *Konketsuji*, whose two child actors are Black and Japanese. In the arts, Velina Houston's critically acclaimed play *Tea* has characters who are dual minorities (1994). Media articles and stories of dual minorities during the postwar period do exist, but those disproportionately include examples of the tragic mulatto in the Asian and Asian American contexts.

6. G. Reginald Daniel, *More Than Black? Multiracial Identity and the New Racial Order* (Philadelphia: Temple University Press, 2002). Other examples of Black, White, and Native American multiracial communities include the Lumbees in North Carolina, the Melungeons in Tennessee and Kentucky, and the Ramapo mountain people around the border of New York and New Jersey. These communities are known as "triracial isolates."

7. Ingrid Dineen-Wimberly, "Mixed-Race Leadership in African America: The Regalia of Race and National Identity in the U.S., 1862–1916" (PhD diss., University of California, Santa Barbara, 2009); Allyson Hobbs, *A Chosen Exile: A History of Racial Passing in American Life* (Cambridge: Harvard University Press, 2014); Bliss Broyard, *One Drop: My Father's Hidden Life—A Story of Race and Secrets* (New York: Little, Brown, 2007).

8. Duncan Williams, "Key Moments in Japanese America's Mixed Race History, 1868–1945," in *Hapa Japan: Constructing Global Mixed Race and Mixed Roots Japanese Identities and Representations*, vol. 1, ed. Duncan Williams (Kaya Press, forthcoming 2017). In addition, these mixed families were presented in the exhibition "Visible and Invisible: A Hapa Japanese History" at the Japanese American National Museum in Los Angeles in 2011.

9. Ibid. See Figure 11.2. The first year of the Meiji period (1868–1912) was 1868, hence the name *gannen*, which refers to the first year (of the Meiji period) and *mono* meaning people.

10. Ibid.

11. Ibid.

12. Edna Bonacich and Lucy Cheng, "A Theoretical Orientation to International Labor Migration," in *Labor Immigration under Capitalism: Asian Workers in the United States before World War II*, ed. Bonacich and Cheng (Berkeley: University of California Press, 1984).

13. Rudy P. Guevarra Jr., *Becoming Mexipino: Multiethnic Identities and Communities in San Diego* (New Brunswick, NJ: Rutgers University Press, 2012); Karen I. Leonard, *Making Ethnic Choices: California's Punjabi Mexican Americans* (Philadelphia: Temple University Press, 1992). For additional scholarship that focuses on the Asian-Latino experience, see the *Journal of Asian American Studies*, special issue on Asian Pacific American experiences and Asian-Latino relations, 14.3 (October 2011).

14. Williams-León, "International Amerasians."

15. Petersen, "Success Story."

16. "Do Japanese Women Make Better Wives?," 20.

17. Curtiss Takada Rooks, telephone interview with Lily Anne Y. Welty Tamai, May 14, 2015.

18. Black women continued to provide a support system, even for mixed race American Japanese women from Japan well into the 1960s and 1970s. See Era Bell Thompson, "Happy Ending: Grown-Up Brown Baby Finds Husband in Japan, a Home in the USA," *Ebony* (July 1968): 63–68.

19. Bill Hume, *When We Get Back Home from Japan* (1953; repr., Tokyo: Koyoya, 1960); Bill Hume, *Babysan: A Private Look at the Japanese Occupation* (Rutland, VT: Charles E. Tuttle, 1958); Bill Hume, *Babysan's World: The Hume'n Slant on Japan* (Rutland, VT: Charles E. Tuttle, 1959). In addition to the *Stars and Stripes*, Bill Hume also drew cartoons for the *Navy Times* and the *Oppaman*.

20. Hume, *When We Get Back Home*; Hume, *Babysan*; Hume, *Babysan's World*.

21. Isaiah Helekunihi Walker, *Waves of Resistance: Surfing and History in Twentieth-Century Hawai'i* (Honolulu: University of Hawai'i Press, 2011), 90–92.

22. Robert Harvey, *Insider Histories of Cartooning: Rediscovering Forgotten Famous Comics and Their Creators* (Missoula: University Press of Mississippi, 2014).

23. John W. Dower, *Embracing Defeat: Japan in the Wake of World War II* (New York: Norton, 1999), 130.

24. Michael Cullen Green, *Black Yanks in the Pacific: Race in the Making of American Military Empire after World War II* (Ithaca, NY: Cornell University Press, 2010); Curtis James Morrow, *What's a Commie Ever Done to Black People? A Korean War Memoir of Fighting in the U.S. Army's Last All Negro Unit* (Jefferson, NC: McFarland, 1997).

25. Paul Gilroy, *The Black Atlantic: Modernity and Double-Consciousness* (Cambridge, MA: Harvard University Press, 1993) looks at Europe, Africa, and the Americas; Etsuko Taketani, *The Black Pacific Narrative: Geographic Imaginings of Race and Empire between the World Wars* (Hanover, NH: Dartmouth College Press, 2014); Vijay Prashad, *Everybody Was Kung Fu Fighting: Afro-Asian Connections and the Myth of Cultural Purity* (Boston: Beacon Press, 2001); Heike Raphael-Hernandez and Shannon Steen, eds., *AfroAsian Encounters: Culture, History, Politics* (New York: New York University Press, 2006).

26. Ingrid Dineen-Wimberly, "To 'Carry the Black Man's Burden': T. Thomas Fortune's Vision of African American Colonization of the Philippines, 1902–1903," *International Journal of Business and Social Science* 5.10 (2014): 69–74.

27. Mitzi Uehara Carter, "Mixed Race Okinawans and Their Obscure In-Betweenness," *Journal of Intercultural Studies* 35.6 (2014): 646–661; Ariko Ikehara, "Black-Okinawa and the MiXtory: Production of Mixed Spaces in Okinawa" (paper, University of Southern California Sawyer Seminar, April 26, 2014). For a historical overview of Black military personnel in Japan and Korea, see Green, *Black Yanks in the Pacific.*

28. Bonacich and Cheng, "Theoretical Orientation."

29. For Germany, see Heide Fehrenbach, *Race after Hitler: Black Occupation Children in Postwar Germany and America* (Princeton, NJ: Princeton University Press, 2005).

30. Fernando Herrera Lima, "Transnational Families: Institutions of Transnational Social Space," in *New Transnational Social Spaces: International Migration and Transnational Companies in the Early Twenty-First Century*, ed. Ludger Pries (New York: Routledge, 2001), 91.

31. US Congress House of Representatives, H.R. 711, introduced by Walter Judd, January 3, 1951.

32. *Chan* is an honorific title used for children or among very close friends. This is compared to *san*, which is the honorific title used with adults.

33. Miki Sawada, *Haha to ko no kizuna erizabesu sandazu homu no san ju nen* [A bond between a mother and a child: Thirty years of the Elizabeth Saunders home] (Kyoto: PHP Kenkyujo, 1980), 53–57.

34. Email correspondence with Lily Anne Y. Welty Tamai, June 22, 2009.

35. Mattie H. Briscoe, "A Study of Eight Foreign-Born Children of Mixed Parentage Who Have Been Adopted by Negro Couples in the U.S." (MA thesis, Atlanta University School of Education, 1956).

36. Coincidentally, Ariana Miyamoto, who was crowned the 2015 Miss Japan and will be representing Japan in the Miss Universe pageant, was born in Keiko's hometown of Sasebo, Nagasaki, in 1994 and is also Japanese and Black. After reading about Ariana, Keiko remarked, "Jidai ga kawatte yokatta [I'm so glad the times have changed]. It's

good for Japan. It's good for us." Keiko Clark, phone interview with Lily Anne Y. Welty Tamai, March 14, 2015.

37. Fredrick Cloyd, "Assimilating the Black Japanese—Japan and the US: Reflections" (September 3, 2013), https://waterchildren.wordpress.com/page/3/. See Fredrick Cloyd, *Dream of the Water Children* (New York: 2Leaf Press, forthcoming).

38. Curtiss Takada Rooks, "Reflections of a Suntanned Samurai: 25 Years of Hap(a)in' Around" (USC Mellon Sawyer Seminar, April 26, 2014).

39. Curtiss Takada Rooks, "On Being Japanese American," *Discover Nikkei* (October 26, 2007), http://www.discovernikkei.org/en/journal/2007/10/26/on-being-japanese-american.

40. Elizabeth Kamizato, interview with Lily Anne Y. Welty Tamai, December 23, 2007.

41. Kina Saeko, interview with Lily Anne Y. Welty Tamai, Chatan, Okinawa October 19, 2009.

42. Greg Robinson, "The Early History of Mixed-Race Japanese Americans," in Williams, *Hapa Japan.*

43. For further information on women, war, and colonialism, see Cynthia Enloe, *Bananas Beaches and Bases: Making Feminist Sense of International Politics* (Berkeley: University of California Press, 2000); Akemi Johnson, "The Body Politic: When US Soldiers Venture Abroad, Women's Bodies Can Become the Occupied Territories," *Nation* (April 28, 2014), http://www.thenation.com/article/179249/body-politic-when-us-soldiers-venture-abroad-womens-bodies-can-become-occupied-territ.

PART V

Reflections

12

Neanderthal-Human Hybridity and the Frontier of Critical Race Studies

TERENCE KEEL

Geneticists recently discovered we had sex with Neanderthals almost forty thousand years ago.[1] The "mixed" children we created would go on to reproduce with other humans, passing on a genetic legacy that continues to live on in the genomes of people today.[2] The categories we use to capture human becoming fail to describe the children of these early intraspecies unions. This is to say these mixed people don't fit neatly within our understanding of human ancestry and race. This is partly due to the fact that this was a "preracial" mixing event. Also at play was the fact that we have not accepted the full humanity of Neanderthals. Thus mixing with them generates some troubling conceptual problems for how we view the children we ostensibly made together.

When humans first slept with Neanderthals we had not fully diversified into the populations that scientists frequently define as "races" or the three major continental groups (i.e., African, Asian, European). By race here I am referring to the post-Enlightenment notion that humans belong to one of four homogenous populations that can be linked back to Africa, Asia, Europe, or the Americas. There were no people who fit this definition of race forty thousand years ago. The early humans who left Africa and first encountered Neanderthals in the Middle East were what scientists called the first anatomically modern humans, *Homo sapiens*. In less technical terms these were "simply humans," without a race and more or less identical to the people they left behind in Africa.

It would be tempting to call Neanderthals a race—perhaps one of the first "races" to be differentiated from other humans. We shared a common ancestor with them roughly between 560,000 and 765,000 years ago.[3] The small population that would eventually become Neanderthals left the mother continent and made their way into Europe by walking out of North Africa and across the Middle East somewhere between 270,000 and 440,000 years ago. They then trekked across Europe, settling as far west as Portugal, eventually becoming isolated from those of us who remained in Africa. This separation lasted for about 250,000 years, which according to scientists was long enough for both us and them to develop distinct biological and cultural characteristics.

Historically, scientists and the larger lay public have been unwilling to grant Neanderthals the status of being fully human; or at least human like the anatomically modern *Homo sapiens*. Neanderthals were thought to belong to a branch of the evolutionary tree that was entirely distinct from us. Indeed, they were believed to be so divergent biologically that procreation with humans was assumed to be impossible. Only in the past few decades have scientists reconstructed this vision and brought Neanderthals back into the human family.[4]

Were we to embrace them as fully human, the question of what *kind* of human they were would remain open for interpretation. Should we call them European? Perhaps, but certainly not in the sense that we would think of the French or Germans. Neanderthals occupied regions in Eastern Europe, and present-day Asian populations have on average 1.38 percent Neanderthal DNA in their genome.[5] This percentage is higher than the average amount of Neanderthal DNA in present-day Europeans, 1.15 percent.[6] Might we call Neanderthals Asian then? A compelling case could be made here, but again their timeline of existence puts them too far in the past to be classified under post-Enlightenment racial categories in the same way we use the concept of Asian to describe Han or Japanese populations.

Neanderthals are race-*less*—they have not been given membership in one of the four subpopulations that make up the so-called "human races." Racialization, as we know from Michael Omi and Howard Winant, is fundamentally an act carried on by "historically situated projects in which human bodies and social structures are represented and organized."[7] Yet history shows us that Neanderthals have not filled a large enough place within the Western scientific and cultural imaginary to become the focus of racializing projects and consequently earn the distinction of becoming one of the human races. The issue here is not merely one of biology but one of the politics of human belonging. People cannot claim being Neanderthal in the same way they can claim Mayan or Cherokee ancestry. Neanderthals have not passed along cultural practices that we recognize as sociologically (or "racially") unique and therefore legitimate in the sense of telling us something about the complexity our own (human) ancestry.

Thus it appears that enduring the processes that result in "being raced" provides the credentials for being human. Race, however, can serve this purpose only when we delimit the lives of people to specific moments in time.

Manipulate this timescale and human life becomes an undifferentiated mass of existence, making it impossible to distinguish ourselves from our great-grandchildren, Mesopotamians, chimpanzees, and amoebas.

The story of how humans became part Neanderthal presents us with an opportunity to think about mixing events that predate the emergence of "Whiteness" as an analytic category and therefore incorporate large evolutionary timescales into our thinking about human ancestry. Critical engagement with genetic science and human evolution prior to European colonial expansion has not been well represented within the field of race studies. The preference for working within more recent time frames of course reflects the unique political and social commitments of many scholars invested in exposing how the legacy of European colonialism, slavery, American imperialism, and Jim Crow shaped and constrained the conditions under which racial mixture in the "New World" took place. Scholars who study race and mixed people have gone to great lengths to demonstrate how monoraciality—a concept derived from the one-drop rule, which posits that individuals can truly belong to only one race—suppresses the lived experiences of people who possess and inhabit multiple ancestries.[8] In this essay I show how being part Neanderthal further exposes the fallacy of monoraciality largely because humans have never been pure. We have been mixing with people outside of our imagined lineage long before the so-called "races"—as we know them—existed and certainly before any notion of "Whiteness" could be projected onto our developmental past. In other words, we were mixed before we spread into the major continents of Europe and Asia. Being mixed is the ontological baseline for what it means to be human.

If we take this seriously, however, there remains a fundamental tension between knowledge about our biological selves and the pragmatic goals of mixed race scholarship. The latter has highlighted the experiences of multi-ethnics and especially first-generation mixed race people as exceptional—if not biologically then certainly socially and culturally. I use the story of Neanderthal-human hybridity to show how the seeds of this tension rest in our use of time to demarcate human belonging and in our cultured belief that human origins mark an exceptional moment of creation. The way beyond this tension involves keeping clear the distinction between claiming that mixed people are socially and politically unique rather than biological exceptions.

Deconstructing the Myth of the Neanderthal

Depictions of the Neanderthal as a hulking, primitive brute abound in popular culture. In 1953 there was the popular black-and-white film, *Neanderthal Man*, where a biologist develops a serum that reverts animals back to their primitive ancestors. After the biologist uses the formula himself, viewers witness his gruesome atavistic devolution into a Neanderthal, replete with protruding browridges, facial hair, and poor dental hygiene. In present-day popular culture Neanderthals are puns for car insurance commercials and the word of choice for describing misbehaving athletes and politicians. They also appear in children's movies such as DreamWorks Animation's film, *The Croods* featuring a primitive Neanderthal family whose life circumstances irreversibly change after their daughter falls for an anatomically modern human named "Guy."[9] It is clear that in our popular imagination calling someone a Neanderthal is not a compliment.

The common misperception that Neanderthals are either nonhuman or less than human can be traced back to initial studies of Neanderthals during the mid-nineteenth and early twentieth centuries. The first Neanderthal remains were discovered in 1856 deep inside a quarry mine in the Neander Valley of West Germany. Canyon workers found a remarkably narrow skullcap with protruding browridges and femur bones of such considerable weight and size that the first scientists who studied these remains believed this individual was certainly stronger and more robust than any known human.[10] But the question remained, was this human?

During the mid-nineteenth century an evolutionary account of human origins was not widely accepted by early paleontologists.[11] Throughout most of that century, the Christian idea that humans were direct and unique creations of God continued to filter scientific ruminations over the origins and development of our species.[12] Also at play was the idea that human groups were designed with traits that rendered them naturally adapted to their indigenous environments. This conception of human development, which had profound implications for how modern thinkers viewed racial groups, was also a carryover from Christian natural theology.[13] Darwin's evolutionary theory, however, suggested humans were neither created directly by God nor given all the traits they needed to survive. Instead, humans had adapted by developing new characteristics in response to a constantly changing environment. For evolutionists, human development was taken to be a linear progression up from primitive to more refined human types. Many scientists in the mid-nineteenth century, however, were slow to embrace this idea of human evolutionary development.[14] As a result, evolutionists and traditionalists quarreled over whether the skullcap, browridge, and leg bones found in the Neander Valley were archaic remnants of a long-disappeared species or merely the dead body of a recently deformed human.[15]

By the early twentieth century a new component to the debate over the Neanderthal had emerged. Not only were scientists and traditionalists at odds over whether Neanderthals were an ancient species, evolutionists also argued among themselves over whether humans had directly evolved from them.[16] The results of the latter dispute bear directly on the present-day misperception that Neanderthals were not fully human. In 1899 paleontologists discovered uniquely refined, but nonetheless ancient, human remains in Krapina (present-day Yugoslavia) that appeared to coexist with Neanderthals.[17] A similar discovery was made in the Grimaldi Caves on the French Mediterranean coast. Much like the fossils in Krapina, this "Grimaldi Man" possessed features strikingly similar to present-day humans, which included a smaller skull absent of brow-ridges and an upright posture. As additional fossils similar to Grimaldi Man were discovered throughout Western Europe, scientists in the early twentieth century would call this population the Cro-Magnons, which later in the twentieth century would be recognized as *Homo sapiens*, the first anatomically modern humans to launch a sustained expansion out of Africa, roughly forty thousand years ago.

Shortly after the start of the twentieth century the renowned French paleontologist Marcellin Boule compared Grimaldi Man to the first complete skeleton of a Neanderthal found in the caves of Chapelle-aux-Saints.[18] After this assessment Boule argued that Grimaldi Man, and the entire Cro-Magnon race to which he belonged, was more sophisticated, both biologically and culturally, than the Neanderthal. Not only did Cro-Magnons have an upright posture and a modern skull shape, their remains were found in caves across Western Europe that contained an elaborate tool culture and artwork that included engravings on stone and bone.[19] Neanderthals, on the other hand, were found in places that appeared to lack these cultural relics. Boule, along with many other paleontologists of his time, assumed that humans must have been the descendants of an ancient population that possessed signs of genius, innovation, and aesthetic sensibility at the very beginning of their existence. With their hulking physical structure and no discernible signs of culture, Boule argued that the woefully primitive Neanderthals were not the direct ancestors of modern humans. He believed instead that humans must have emerged from the Cro-Magnons who lived side by side with Neanderthals but ultimately won the evolutionary contest between the two groups. As the historian Michael Hammond argues, Boule effectively removed Neanderthals from the human family.[20]

This expulsion was compounded by French and British media depictions of Boule's work on the Neanderthal, which rendered them ape-like, savage beings, with only the slightest traces of humanity.[21] Cro-Magnons on the other hand fared well in broader cultural depictions as they were typically shown as being only a few steps removed from present-day humans. These contrasting images of the "primitive Neanderthal" versus the "refined Cro-Magnon" would be appropriated and interpreted in many different ways throughout Europe and the United States, but overwhelmingly they reinforced the idea that Neanderthals were less than fully human, if human at all.[22]

We continue to live with the distorted view of the "subhuman" Neanderthal as images of their primitiveness penetrate present-day media, popular culture, and even linguistic idioms. Neanderthals remain synonymous with "primitive brute," despite the fact that paleoanthropologists since the early 2000s have steadily recovered a fossil record that demonstrates Neanderthals possessed at least two separate tool cultures, performed ritual burials, experienced social stratification, developed abstract artwork, cooked their meat and created dishes using ground acorns, and even cultivated herbal remedies for indigestion and pain relief.[23] Geneticists also learned that Neanderthals carried in their genome variants of the FOXP2 gene involved in modern human language ability.[24] With these discoveries, scientists have welcomed Neanderthals back into the human family and consider them a sister species to modern humans who shared a common ancestor with us nearly 830,000 years ago.[25]

Our cultured perception about what it means to be human, not merely evolutionary processes, is what ultimately drove the Neanderthals into extinction. By this I mean that Neanderthals experienced a social death, which cost them the ability to be seen as human and therefore eligible to pass their inheritance down to us. Scientists in the nineteenth century studied the Neanderthal while still being committed to the Christian worldview that we were created in the image of God. This commitment drove scientists to cast Neanderthals from the family tree, as they were incapable of conceding that our earliest ancestors could lack the capacity for civilization, ingenuity, religion, and speech. So began the precipitous death of Neanderthals within the minds of experts and the popular social imagination. Belief in the ontological novelty of human creation prevented us, until recently, from considering not only that we were nearly identical to Neanderthals, but that their genes could live on in us, their human descendants.

The inability to think in large evolutionary timescales and our latent Christian hang-ups about what it means to be a member of our species are what lost the Neanderthal to history. In this regard, how we conceive of Neanderthals and mixed race people is beset by a similar set of problems. In both instances the time frames used to think about human becoming and the existential politics of being a recognized member of our species are the determining factors for embracing and legitimizing the lives of present-day people who claim a complex racial heritage.

Only *Some* of Us Are Part Neanderthal?

According to the most recent genetic studies, humans made contact with Neanderthals roughly forty thousand years ago in the Middle East as they migrated out of Africa. The group of humans (Eurasians) who exchanged DNA and culture with the Neanderthals would later become Asian and European. Initially, geneticists believed that Europeans and Asians possessed roughly the same amount of

Neanderthal ancestry (1–4 percent). Scientists therefore believed that Eurasians mated with Neanderthals before they branched into separate groups.[26] However more recent studies have lowered these percentages to an average of 1.15 percent for Europeans and 1.38 percent for East Asian populations.[27] To explain the different levels of Neanderthal DNA in Europeans, one team of geneticists proposed that Neanderthal genes were deleterious within humans. Therefore natural selection worked to remove these genes through a process of "purifying selection." Under this framework these geneticists claimed that East Asians were less effective at purifying their genome of harmful Neanderthal genes.[28] This model also assumed that there was only one major mating event between humans and Neanderthals, which took place before Eurasians branched into separate groups.[29] Geneticists have recently challenged this model, explaining instead that the different levels of Neanderthal DNA in Asians and Europeans are likely the result of multiple mating events between humans and Neanderthals, not of an inability of Asians to effectively eliminate harmful Neanderthal genes.[30] These same scientists also believe that the single mating event model could be plausible if Europeans mixed with other extinct humans, what they called a "ghost Eurasian population" that did not carry Neanderthal DNA and therefore diluted the percentage Neanderthal genes within Europeans.[31]

Geneticists continue to believe that Neanderthal ancestry is largely unique to the descendants of Eurasia. This includes Native Americans, Southeast Asians, Asian populations in the Pacific, populations in India, as well as Australian aboriginals.[32] Geneticists, however, did find very faint traces of Neanderthal ancestry in West Africans, with them possessing about 0.08 percent Neanderthal DNA.[33] Scientists from the Neanderthal Genome Project (NGP) initially theorized that Neanderthals did not return to Africa once they left the continent three hundred thousand years ago.[34] Only two hundred fifty thousand years later did they reunite with humans. Scientists now believe this meeting took place in Northeast Africa and across the Middle East as modern humans were migrating to Eurasia. Subsequent studies have corroborated this theory as geneticists learned that the Masai people in East Africa have significant traces of Neanderthal DNA.[35] This suggests that humans who came into contact with Neanderthals most likely returned to the northeastern regions of the continent where Neanderthal DNA would become diffuse among East Africans but not farther south or west in the continent.

What then does this discovery mean for African Americans? African Americans are recently admixed populations; this means their DNA includes European ancestry in addition to the DNA of other population groups. About 24 percent of African American DNA comes from Europe.[36] Thus African Americans are in theory part Neanderthal if the percentage of European DNA in their genome also carries Neanderthal genes. This is an important caveat as scientists have found that the location of Neanderthal DNA within members of the same population (for example Germans) varies widely.[37] In other words Neanderthal genes have not been passed down as a consistent block of genes within the human genome. So African Americans may or may not have Neanderthal ancestry; it all depends on where and how much Neanderthal DNA is found in their European ancestors.

Still, genetic studies following the 2010 draft sequence of the Neanderthal genome have consistently confirmed that West and South Africans carry very little Neanderthal DNA.[38] The picture we are left with is one where only the descendants of Eurasia are truly part Neanderthal. This includes populations who mixed with Europeans following the colonization of the "New World" as well as Asian populations who left the continent. Neanderthal ancestry, according to the subtext of this new genetic study, is not a story shared by all humans. Geneticists have created a new narrative about human evolution where West and South Africans have been left out of the recent drama of human promiscuity and biological change.

Our Ancestors Were Not Pure

The fact that humans and Neanderthals reproduced successfully means that there was enough genetic similarity between the two in order to have children. But does procreation imply that Neanderthals were also human? There appears to be no clear or simple answer to this question, largely because this distinction rests on how one defines what it means to belong to our species. Here we are stepping into philosophical territory where statistical representations of Neanderthal genes in humans clarify as much as complicate the issue. This is because Neanderthal variation, according to the NGP, appears to fall within the range of *acknowledged* human genetic variation. In other words, the Neanderthal genome is not consistently different from the human genome, given what we know about human variation. We are genetically similar because roughly 830,000 years ago we were members of the same population. The genomes of Neanderthals and present-day humans are also similar because we recently shared genes with each other when creating Neanderthal-human hybrids about 40,000 years ago.

However, some geneticists argue that all of this speculation about the genetic similarity and distance of Neanderthals to certain human populations is precisely that. Since its inception as a method of analysis, many geneticists have been critical of admixture technology and the attempt to infer the genetic ancestry of a population based upon the collection of traits known as single nucleotide polymorphisms (SNPs), which are variations in the DNA nucleotide base pair pattern of A-T-G-C.[39] These SNPs are thought to occur when one base pair switches to another nucleotide. Population geneticists interested in human difference claim that some populations carry a higher percentage of a collection of SNPs than other groups.[40] These SNPs have been given the technical term of an ancestry index marker (AIM) and are believed to tell researchers about the ancestral heritage of present-day people. In this most recent form of typological reasoning, geneticists claim to be capable of hypothesizing the various ancestries (genetic admixture) any given individual might possess.[41] The public has grown familiar with this technology due to the popularity of various television documentaries on human genetic ancestry as well as the increased affordability of direct-to-consumer DNA ancestry testing.[42] Biologists used SNPs and AIMs, along with other measures of genetic diversity, to locate Neanderthal genes within present-day racial groups.

Some scientists have been critical of this new method of reconstructing human ancestry largely because they believe geneticists interested in human difference fail to distinguish their work from the typological race studies of the nineteenth century.[43] Population geneticists Kenneth M. Weiss and Jeffrey C. Long, as well as computational biologist Brian W. Lambert, have been some of the most recent voices of opposition toward admixture technology and the use of computer software programs to calculate human ancestry. They have argued that contemporary geneticists inadvertently fall back onto racial typologies when they divide humans according to continental regions where specific genetic variations are assumed to have come into being. This has the effect of collapsing genetic ancestry due to gene flow with genetic ancestry due to environmental factors and other random changes that cause alleles to rise or fall in frequency. They affirm a view shared by other scientists that models of our genetic ancestry and lived human history represent two different things.[44] The former identifies a hypothesized continental origin based upon laboratory studies that carefully select a specific number of genetic traits, whereas the latter entails the lived experience of migration, mating, and cultural and environmental pressures that might cause a genetic trait to rise in frequency. This historical ancestry is remarkably complex and nearly impossible to know with any certainty.

According to Weiss and others, the trouble with admixture estimates is that the parental populations from which contemporary admixed individuals are thought to have descended are not alive to be sampled for the actual "parental" genetic markers.[45] Geneticists attempt to resolve this problem by sampling from contemporary populations, who then function as surrogates for the assumed parental groups in each continental region of interest.[46] Weiss and Lambert claim that this hypothetical representation of the origins of human diversity would be fine as a heuristic if not for the obvious fact that when the estimated parental populations are analyzed among themselves, their intragroup differences are as great and in some instances greater than intergroup comparisons.[47] In other words members within so-called present day races appear to be more different from each other than from people outside their racial group. Weiss, Long, and other geneticists stress that intragroup variation shows us how the *lived ancestry* of a population is more varied and more precarious than what can be modeled within a scientific laboratory using computer software. But in an effort to render this otherwise complex lived biological history quantitatively, they argue, geneticists who employ admixture technology assume that the parental populations of present-day people were the single carriers of a particular set of traits at some time in the past. According to Weiss and Long,

> Whether the investigator uses external information or makes estimates from the samples at hand, the parental populations are abstractions that conform to only the simplest kind of genetic structure. This structure places heavy emphasis on the idea that the world once harbored distinct and independently evolved populations that have now undergone admixture of an unstated type (often seeming to connote admixture due to colonial era migrations). The ideal markers for this kind of analysis are private to, and in high frequency in, only one of the putative parental populations, or at least display major differences in frequency among the putative parental populations.[48]

In other words, geneticists who develop models of our ancestors assume that they were pure given the frequency of certain SNPs when compared to other groups. However SNPs that have reached a high frequency within one population and not another are rare because the overwhelming majority of our genes are derived from a common ancestor. Weiss and Long argue that genetic variation across so called racial groups say more about the geographical conditions that forced certain alleles into high frequency than they reveal a moment of unique population differentiation.[49]

Despite this realization, many scientists continue to use SNPs to hypothesize moments in our evolutionary past when our ancestors were theoretically less mixed and more homogenous than we are now. This hypothetical reasoning—and the technology used to support this form of racial thought—organizes the heterogeneity of our mixed biological inheritance and re-creates the idea that present-day groups descended from idealistically pure ancestors. Moreover, this contemporary form of racial typology helps sustain the belief—derived from the Abrahamic faith traditions that shaped Western racial thinking—that the single most important moment within the life of a so-called racial group is its inception and differentiation from other members of our species.[50]

However, the genetic profile of present-day people is mixed with the ancestries of populations from around the globe. This mixture reflects the lived history of humans reproducing across geopolitical boundaries and in the case of Neanderthals with humans considered extinct. Humans are not pure biological units. We are instead mongrel creatures with the history of our mixed ancestors buried within our biology. Never has this been more clear than after the sequencing of the human, and now Neanderthal, genome.

Herein lies a crucial problem for the conceptualization and study of race. Unlocking the human genome has shown us that in the present moment all humans are thoroughly mixed. This heterogeneity, however, can be minimized or enhanced given, first, one's commitment to the idea that present-day people descend from "pure" races and, second, the time frame used to study human mixing and evolution.

We might call the first approach to race neo-polygenist in its orientation insofar as human difference comes to overshadow similarity shared across human groups. For example, geneticists interested in sorting the racial ancestry of present-day groups tend to limit their analysis to often no more than the past five to ten thousand years. Anything further back in time places humans in Africa during the time before large-scale "racial" differentiation is thought to have occurred. Thus looking back forty thousand years in the past won't tell you much about French or Native American ancestry.

The second approach to studying race we might call neo-monogenist. This approach gives primacy to the similarity shared across human groups, thereby creating a bulwark against the belief that humans fit neatly into biological divisions across the major continents. For example, if one were interested in showing the similarities that exist across human populations, one might look at the genetic structure of humans that was established earlier than five to ten thousand years ago. There one will find that the great majority of genetic diversity that humans currently carry can be traced back to Africa, before we spread across the different continents. Prior to thirty thousand years ago humans were equally genetically diverse, mixing throughout the African continent and carrying the genes of early human groups who either went extinct or were eventually absorbed by *Homo sapiens*. In other words, our ancestors were just like we are now: one large mixing population made up of highly genetically diverse people who do not easily fit into racialized groups.

Temporality, however, is an important factor not just for genetic science but also for scholars who study race and mixed people. Either we can view present-day mixed race people as ontologically distinct from their ancestors (the neo-polygenist approach) and therefore focus on specific kinds of mixture (e.g., Black/Latino, Asian/Black, East African/Swiss, etc.) within a delimited geopolitical time frame (e.g., post-European exploration, or post–*Loving v. Virginia*), or we can view present-day mixed race people as equally varied as their ancestors (the monogenist approach). The trouble with the neo-polygenist approach to conceptualizing present-day people is that it distorts the fact that relatively recent human mixing, say in the past five thousand years, pales in comparison to the amount of mixing that went into creating and consolidating the range of genetic variation (or what geneticists call substructure) that make us *Homo sapiens*. Scales of time matter when thinking about human diversity. Thus to say that mixed race people are biologically exceptional overestimates the significance of recent mixing events from an evolutionary perspective. It also inadvertently re-creates our past ancestors as if they were somehow pure. Humans now and in the past have always already been mixed. This is the all important lesson that must be learned from our evolutionary history. Mixed race people are not biologically unique nor exceptions to what it means to belong to our species.

Social versus Biological Timescales

The British American anthropologist Ashley Montagu wrote nearly sixty-five years ago that "in looking at the races of mankind today, what we see are largely the stages of development which they are in at our particular time. The varying manifestations of physical traits, which they exhibit, are not 'end-results' but bills of exchange, as it were, drawn on the bank of time, negotiable securities which can be turned into the coin of any realm with which it is sought to have biological relations."[51] Montagu's commentary on the 1950 UNESCO Statement on Race served as a warning to post–World War II scientists about the temporal and philosophical limits of using race to account for the causes of human variation. Implied in his analysis was the importance of viewing human populations as unstable biological entities that transcend the concepts we use to define them. Montagu believed this evolutionary vision of human biology was in jeopardy when scientists lost sight of the heuristic nature of racial categories and delimited the long process of human development to a specific moment of time. When this occurred, Montagu warned, it was fairly easy for scientists to believe race could explain something essential about the internal workings of human biology.

Montagu's poetic observation remains relevant for thinking about scales of time and the study of race. Specifically, it helps us see that a distinction needs to be made between sociopolitical timescales and biological timescales. We can think of sociopolitical timescales as referring to observations about human life and cultural heritage delimited by specific social and political periods of time. Many scholars of race work almost exclusively within sociopolitical timescales. For example, one might think of the lives of Black or Mexican Americans under the conditions of Jim Crow—a period lasting between the end of the nineteenth century and the end of the twentieth—as a sociopolitical timescale. Within this temporal framework, scholars of race might deploy specific concepts like Black, Negro, or Mexican, along with a host of other interpretive tools, to describe developments that shaped the cultural, political, and even biological (e.g., health, behavior, and reproductive practices) experiences of the people designated by these categories. To do work of this kind one must believe, at least provisionally, that the category "Black," or "Mexican," refers to a specific group of people under particular sociopolitical conditions. Race work of this sort is generally driven by a pragmatic goal—usually one that bears directly on the present needs of the observer—and therefore we are not in a position to doubt the racial categories being used. For example, one can't study or understand the effects of antimiscegenation laws during the 1920s over the lives of Black and Mexican people, without believing that indeed these people exist and that there were laws designed specifically against "Blacks" and "Mexicans."

Of course these people were not fully determined by their immediate sociopolitical conditions. They were much more than racial minorities stigmatized and targeted by the structural racism of their historical setting. They were also the carriers of a biogenetic history vastly older than the temporal limits placed on them by Jim Crow laws. This was a mixed biogenetic history far more varied and unstable than what the concept "Black" or "Mexican" could adequately capture. This complex biogenetic history makes up what might be called a biological timescale. This refers to processes of human development that have unfolded over periods of time that radically exceed the concepts (e.g., race) we use to capture human becoming. The effects of social life are capable of shaping and augmenting this human becoming. But our biogenetic history cannot be reduced to any given sociopolitical moment. When human becoming is placed on a biological timescale, race as we know it breaks down and the subjects we study blend into one another. One simply has to look at human genetic diversity over the course of the past forty thousand years. There we find that genetically all humans are 99.9 percent the same, that there are more intragroup differences inside so-called races than between different populations, and that the biogenetic history we carry does not correspond to the concepts we use to make sense of it. This is what was revealed after the sequencing of both the human and Neanderthal genomes. This is what it means to say there are no genes for race.

The tension between sociopolitical and biological timescales should serve as a reminder for those who study race and mixed race people that our constructions and racial heuristics can always be otherwise. On this point Montagu wrote, "[The] best we can do at the present time is to describe populations, and while our classifications may be interesting, we must be careful not to take them too seriously. The danger we must avoid is becoming either the *caretakers or the captives* of our own arbitrary classificatory schemes."[52] The fictions we create to make sense of human life within a given historical and political moment will always fail to capture the biogenetic mixture that resides within us. The key is to not believe that our racial fictions are reality.

We Are All Mongrel

Finding bits of Neanderthal in our genome forces us to acknowledge the opacity of the human past and challenges our cultured assumptions about our onto-logical uniqueness and the division between the human and the nonhuman world. For nearly 150 years scientists assumed that modern humans were free of Neanderthal ancestry. Yet as members of the NGP explain, not only was the discovery of Neanderthal DNA in present-day humans entirely unexpected, they also learned that there are potentially many other extinct early humans (such as a group they called Denisovans) whose DNA lives on in our genomes. Svante Paabo, one of the leading paleogeneticists on the NGP, explained, "This was an amazing finding. We had studied two genomes from extinct human forms [Neanderthal and Denisovan]. In both cases we had found some gene flow into modern humans. Thus, low levels of mixing with earlier humans seemed to have been the rule rather than the exception when modern humans spread across the world. This meant that neither Neanderthals nor Denisovans were totally extinct. A little bit of them lived on in people today."[53] We might say that all humans are mongrel, in the sense that it may be impossible to recover the many different early and more recent human ancestors who contributed to our genetic inheritance. In biological terms, mongrels are not merely organ-isms with a mixed heritage. They are beings where only part of their ancestry is known or recoverable. To say that we are all mongrel therefore is to acknowl-edge that our ancestry will never be fully known.

Of course to call ourselves human, and not merely advanced primates or even Neanderthals, implies that we know who and what makes us unique as a species. Securing this knowledge, however, remains one of the most elusive tasks in modern science. The unexpected discovery of Neanderthal DNA in the human gene pool belies the idea that human identity is unique, stable, and transparent to our inquiring minds.

At the same time, finding Neanderthal DNA in present-day humans puts on display how biological heterogeneity, or "being mixed," is in fact the default human ontological position. Humans were mixing before they became "races." At no point in our history has there been a member of our species not mixed with another human and nonhuman group. At a biological level, being mixed is the norm, not the exception, to human existence. "Purity," monoraciality, and indeed race itself are powerful human creations. For races exist only when thinking about human becoming within a specific moment in time while also assuming that this marks an ontologically novel or significant instance of human becoming. These temporal and conceptual constraints are at play when scientists assume human diversity can be reduced to fundamentally three ancestral groups. These assump-tions are also at play when we view mixed race people as biological exceptions to being human otherwise. In both cases we have yet to relieve ourselves of the burden of explaining human existence under the terms laid out before us by Christian natural theology, where life at its origination is believed to be onto-logically new and distinct. Our racial formations continue to venerate the myth of Adam and Eve.

But what does this mean for the field of mixed race studies, which has a political and social investment in recovering and advocating for the experi-ences of mixed people within a context where their existence is denied by the hegemony of monoracial norms?[54] Might conceding that all humans are mixed undermine these goals?

Here we arrive again at the tension between biological and social/cultural timescales, which I believe invites a healthy moment of self-reflexivity for those of us who study race. The vast scale of human evolutionary time—periods that involved countless mixing events—should push us to see that the temporal frameworks and concepts we use to study race are socially and politically useful fictions designed for present-day concerns. For example, when we capture the experiences of a first-generation multiethnic we must not lose sight of the fact that this is a temporally and socially delimited rendering of human becoming. These people are actually constituted by evolutionary processes that involve innumerable mixing events. Thus when we give preference to more recent mix-ing events (for example under the conditions of American colonialism or Jim Crow) it is crucial to remember that we are doing so for social and political rea-sons; we are creating heuristics designed to address needs and problems unique to these events and our present lives. In other words we are drawing attention to the novelty or exceptions that mixed race people represent for our social and political frames of reference. This is fundamentally different from claiming that mixed race people constitute biological exceptions to what it means to be human.

Of course there is always a danger that the work these heuristics perform may lead us into mistaking these fictions for reality, having us believe that mixed race people are in fact biologically unique. Keeping sight of the fact that human mixing predates race itself—that human evolutionary time escapes the frameworks we use to tame it—can create a bulwark against taking our own constructions too seriously.

Were we to push the frontier of our own social and political investments this might give us the language to talk about what it means to live within a liminal space between timescales that mark our immanent sociopolitical needs and biological timescales that are infinitely vaster than our concepts about race. To do this we must think more critically about human evolutionary history and how we belong to a species in a constant state of becoming and always already mixed. The death and resurrection of the Neanderthal show us that human evolutionary time is virtually meaningless until we give meaning to it. In this moment of rediscovering our Neanderthal inheritance we have an opportunity to yet again ponder what it means to be a perpetually mixed species that can be captured provisionally by sociopolitical framings but ultimately belongs to processes of becoming that exceed comprehension. Maybe then we could build a new set of heuristics around our past that reminds us that being mixed is fundamentally what it means to be human.

NOTES

1. Richard Green et al., "A Draft Sequence of the Neanderthal Genome," *Science* 328 (May 7, 2010): 710–722.
2. I am intentionally oversimplifying here to make the point that we are part Neanderthal and that there is considerably less distance between us than we have been socialized to believe. Neanderthals were much more than the few alleles that have persisted in the genomes of present-day people. It would be wrong to assume that their complex biological history, what I refer to later as a biological timescale, has been passed along to us in its entirety, or that an entire species can be reduced to a few genes.
3. Kay Prufer et al., "The Complete Sequence of a Neanderthal from the Altai Mountains," *Nature* 505 (January 2014): 45.
4. Green et al., "Draft Sequence of the Neanderthal Genome," 710.
5. Sriram Sankararaman et al., "The Genomic Landscape of Neanderthal Ancestry in Present-Day Humans," *Nature* 507 (March 2014): 354.
6. Ibid., 354.
7. Michael Omi and Howard Winant, *Racial Formation in the United States*, 3rd ed. (New York: Routledge, 2014).
8. G. Reginald Daniel, Laura Kina, Wei Ming Dariotis, and Camilla Fojas, "Emerging Paradigms in Critical Mixed Race Studies," *Journal of Critical Mixed Race Studies* 1.1 (2014): 13.
9. *The Croods*, directed by Kirk DeMico and Chris Sanders (Glendale, CA: DreamWorks, 2013).
10. Friedemann Schrenk and Stephanie Muller, *The Neanderthals* (New York: Routledge, 2009), 1.
11. Michael Hammond, "The Expulsion of Neanderthals from Human Ancestry: Marcellin Boule and the Social Context of Scientific Research," *Social Studies of Science* 12.1 (1982): 4–6.
12. Marianne Sommer, "Mirror, Mirror on the Wall: Neanderthal as Image and 'Distortion' in Early 20th-Century French Science and Press," *Social Studies of Science* 36.2 (2006): 210–215.
13. Terence Keel, "Religion, Polygenism, and the Early Science of Human Origins," *History of Human Sciences* 26.2 (2013): 3–32.
14. Sommer, "Mirror, Mirror on the Wall," 210–215.
15. Ibid., 210–215.
16. Hammond, "Expulsion of Neanderthals," 5–7.
17. Ibid., 5–7.
18. Ibid., 2.
19. Sommer, "Mirror, Mirror on the Wall," 214.
20. Hammond, "Expulsion of Neanderthals," 5–6.
21. Sommer, "Mirror, Mirror on the Wall," 216–225.

22. Ibid., 216–225.
23. See Karen Ruebens, "Regional Behavior among Late Neanderthal Groups in Western Europe: A Comparative Assessment of Late Middle Paleolithic Bifacial Tool Variability," *Journal of Human Evolution* 64.4 (October 2013): 341–362; William Rendu et al., "Evidence Supporting an Intentional Neanderthal Burial at La Chapelle-aux-Saints," *Proceedings of the National Academy of Sciences of the United States of America* 111.1 (January 2014): 81–86; Karen L. Privat, Tamsin O'Connell, and Michael Richards, "Stable Isotope Analysis of Human and Faunal Remains from the Anglo-Saxon Cemetery at Berinsfield, Oxfordshire: Dietary and Social Implication," *Journal of Archaeological Science* 29 (2002): 779–790; Joaquin Rodriguez-Vidal et al., "A Rock Engraving Made by Neanderthals in Gibraltar," *Proceedings of the National Academy of Sciences of the United States of America*, 111.37 (2014): 13301–13306; Amanda G. Henry et al., "Microfossils in Calculus Demonstrate Consumption of Plants and Cooked Food in Neanderthal Diets," *Proceedings of the National Academy of Sciences* 108.2 (2011): 486–491; Karen Hardy et al., "Neanderthal Medics? Evidence for Food, Cooking, and Medicinal Plants Entrapped in Dental Calculus," *Naturwissenschaften* 99.8 (2012): 617–626. Also, for a comprehensive discussion of the recent scientific discoveries about Neanderthal culture and their similarity to modern humans, see Dimitra Papagianni and Michael A. Morse, *The Neanderthals Rediscovered: How Modern Science Is Rewriting Their Story* (New York: Thames & Hudson, 2013).
24. Johannes Krause et al., "The Derived FOXP2 Variant of Modern Humans Was Shared with Neanderthals," *Current Biology* 17 (November 2007): 1–4.
25. Svante Paabo, *Neanderthal Man: In Search of Lost Genomes* (New York: Basic Books, 2014), 186–187.
26. Green et al., "Draft Sequence of the Neanderthal Genome."
27. Sankararaman et al., "Genomic Landscape of Neanderthal Ancestry," 354; Jeffrey D. Wall et al., "Higher Levels of Neanderthal Ancestry in East Asians Than in Europeans," *Genetics* 194.1 (2013): 199–209.
28. Sankararaman et al., "Genomic Landscape of Neanderthal Ancestry," 355–356.
29. Ibid., 356.
30. Benjamin Vernot and Joshua M. Akey, "Complex History of Admixture between Modern Humans and Neanderthals," *American Journal of Human Genetics* 96.3 (2015): 448–453.
31. Ibid., 450.
32. Sankararaman et al., "Genomic Landscape of Neanderthal Ancestry," 354.
33. Ibid., 354.
34. Green et al., "Draft Sequence of the Neanderthal Genome," 710–722.
35. Wall et al., "Higher Levels," 200–201.
36. Katarzyna Bryc et al., "The Genetic Ancestry of African Americans, Latinos, and European Americans across the United States," *American Journal of Human Genetics* 96.1 (2015): 42.
37. Green et al., "Draft Sequence of the Neanderthal Genome."
38. Matthias Meyer, et al., "A High-Coverage Genome Sequence from an Archaic Denisovan Individual," *Science* 338.6104 (2012): 222–226; Wall et al., "Higher Levels," 200; Sankararaman et al., "Genomic Landscape of Neanderthal Ancestry," 354.
39. Duana Fullwiley, "The Biologistical Construction of Race: 'Admixture' Technology and the New Genetic Medicine," *Social Studies of Science* 38.5 (2008): 701–702.
40. Ibid., 704–705.
41. Ibid., 701–706.

42. Henry T. Greely, "Genetic Genealogy: Genetics Meets the Marketplace," in *Revisiting Race in a Genomic Age*, ed. Barbara Keonig, Sandra Lee, and Sarah Richardson (New Brunswick, NJ: Rutgers University Press, 2008), 215–223; Kimberly Tallbear, "Native -American-DNA.com: In Search of Native American Race and Tribe," in Keonig, Lee, and Richardson, *Revisiting Race in a Genomic Age*, 235–252.

43. Kenneth M. Weiss and Brian W. Lambert, "Does History Matter? Do the Facts of Human Variation Package Our Views or Do Our Views Package the Facts?," *Evolutionary Anthropology* 19.3 (2010): 97.

44. Kenneth Weiss and Jeffrey Long, "Non-Darwinian Estimation: My Ancestors, My Genes' Ancestors," *Genome Research* 19.5 (May 2009): 706; Weiss and Lambert, "Does History Matter?," 97; Deborah Bolnick, "Individual Ancestry Inference and the Reification of Race as Biological Phenomenon," in Keonig, Lee, and Richardson, *Revisiting Race in a Genomic Age*, 80–82.

45. Weiss and Long, "Non-Darwinian Estimation," 706; Weiss and Lambert, "Does History Matter?," 97.

46. Weiss and Lambert, "Does History Matter?," 95.

47. Ibid., 95.

48. Weiss and Long, "Non-Darwinian Estimation," 705.

49. Ibid., 705.

50. Keel, "Religion, Polygenism."

51. Ashley Montagu, *A Statement on Race: An Extended Discussion in Plain Language of the UNESCO Statement by Experts on Race Problems* (New York: Henry Schuman, 1951), 56.

52. Ibid., 56–57.

53. Paabo, *Neanderthal Man*, 246–247.

54. Marc P. Johnston and Kevin L. Nadal, "Multiracial Microaggressions: Exposing Monoracism in Everyday Life and Clinical Practice," in *Microaggressions and Marginality: Manifestation, Dynamics, and Impact*, ed. Derald Wing Sue (Hoboken, NJ: John Wiley, 2010), 123–144.

13

Epilogue

Expanding the Terrain of Mixed Race Studies

What We Learn from the Study of Non-White Multiracials

NITASHA TAMAR SHARMA

Critical mixed race studies is an emerging field of study that is develop-ing with greater clarity. Yet it—like the experiences of multiracial people—struggles with underrecognition and misrepresentation. Part of this is demographic: self-declared multiracials were only 3 percent of the US popula-tion in 2013, representing 9.3 million Americans.[1] And part is institutional: many universities do not offer courses on multiracial experiences. The development of critical mixed race studies out of and away from mixed race studies further accounts for its low profile. Many scholars in mixed race studies have focused on the "what are you" question faced by "ethnically ambiguous" people and analyzed identity formation through first-person narratives. Critical mixed race studies presents more expansive and theoretically *critical* questions, methodologies, and politics that look, for instance, at multiracialism across the globe and at the rela-tionships of mixed race people to other communities of color. The essays in this volume fill a particular blind spot in mixed race studies: its tendency to privilege Whiteness by focusing on multiracials who are part White while neglecting dual (or more) minority mixed race people.

Red and Yellow, Black and Brown: Decentering Whiteness in Mixed Race Studies highlights the anxieties as well as intellectual and popular potential of criti-cal mixed race studies. The essays cohere around describing the definitions, experiences, and implications of multiracialism among people who do not iden-tify as being part White.[2] Chapters include personal stories of struggle growing up as Blasian (Houston and Mendoza Stickmon) and Indipino (Desai). Other chapters (Romo, Want) challenge stereotypes of multiracials that have included the "tragic mulatta" and the "happy hapa."[3] Verónica Castillo-Muñoz offers an important historiographical account of intermarriage among Indians, Mexicans,

Chinese, and Japanese in the Baja California borderlands at the turn of the nine-teenth century. The volume ends with Terence Keel's provocative examination of Neanderthal-*Homo sapiens* mixing approximately forty thousand years ago to retemporalize our ideas about *racial* mixing and racial *mixing*.

This book hosts essays that reify race and those that deconstruct the pro-cess of racialization. Some authors argue for the uniqueness of the mixed race experience, while others caution against exceptionalism. These voices reflect a variety of perspectives and methods about self-articulation, presenting a micro-cosm of the possibilities of—and continuing challenges to—disrupting and radically retheorizing race. Conversations across the chapters reveal the con-tradictions, obstacles, and possibilities of, on the one hand, advancing critical mixed race studies more widely into the academy and, on the other, impacting the popular (mis)understandings of multiracialism in the United States.[4] But we have much more work to do.

In this essay, I highlight what we can learn from these authors who have decentered Whiteness by centering the narratives and experiences of non-White multiracials. Decentering Whiteness means giving voice to non-Whites while recognizing the ways that racism has structured our lives. Ingrid Dineen-Wimberly's work presents interactions among the Makah that reflect the impact of White supremacy through the denigration of members with Afri-can ancestry. Experiences with racism can also be a powerful bond among non-Whites. Jessica Vasquez-Tokos explains how interminority alliances are forged through the shared yet distinct experiences non-Whites face with racialization and dispossession. What emerges are beautifully complex, some-times heartbreaking, and often empowering illustrations of life in the twenty-first century. This is the first volume to present these voices collectively, and its important intervention should not be missed.

Scholars in critical mixed race studies have urged us to pay greater atten-tion to several key areas. The first is to conduct more research on dual-minority multiracials. In *Becoming Mexipino*, Rudy Guevarra Jr.'s study of multiracial Mex-ican Filipinos in San Diego, California, he explains that "ours is a story that has existed for several hundred years and is a common experience . . . but no one has fully explored [either] this history" or "San Diego's Mexicans and Fili-pinos in relation *to* each other." This and other studies on mixed race people who are non-White work toward "rearticulating and moving beyond the black/white or white/other paradigm of race and mixed-race relations and focusing instead on the understudied histories of [non-White] mixed-race peoples . . . and the rich, complex ways identities are forged and maintained." This book is not just unique for its focus on non-White multiracials, but it is also theoreti-cally significant.[5]

Histories of Oppression Shape Non-White Interracial Unions

Antimiscegenation laws from as early as the 1600s were primarily concerned about the maintenance of White racial "purity" through the regulation of marriage between Whites and non-Whites and particularly with Blacks. As a result, marriage among non-Whites was not the focus of antimiscegenation laws. Within this context of the legal construction of race and the maintenance of racial boundaries between White and non-White, non-White multiracials do not necessarily signify the taboo that White/non-White unions holds in this nation. The research in this volume shows how dual minorities often seek histories of commonality as non-Whites who were subjected not only to these discriminatory laws, but also to the structuring systems of colonialism and slavery.

The shared non-White status of the interracial couples Jessica Vasquez-Tokos studied encouraged them to "generate a critique of racial and gender inequality in the United States." They cultivated "racial affinity" through their individual experiences with racism and an awareness of their communities' histories of native dispossession and anti-Mexican nativism, for example. As Vasquez-Tokos writes, "it was not critical to mirror one another's racial background in order to be on the racial periphery." These findings expand the focus in mixed race studies and the national press on interracial couples with one White partner that tend to make assumptions about proximity to Whiteness, passing, assimilation, and upward mobility. In these chapters, by contrast, we have non-White mixed couples whose relationships become "racial havens" and who together develop critiques of how racial power works in the United States. The implications of this shared racialized identity in a time shaped by the Black Lives Matter movement cannot be overstated.

This research is also critical for its attention to how racial intermarriage expands our understanding of gender dynamics and the intersection of race and gender as well as immigrant status: "The chief reasons my respondents gave for intermarriage with a member of another minority group are a nonwhite minority-minority connection and women's desire to escape patriarchy through out-marriage." These dynamics read differently in the research on Asian female and White male intermarriage within a context of war and framed by Orientalist notions of submissive and hyperfeminized Asian women.[6] The research on Black women with White male partners locates their racialized gender dynamics within the historical context of slavery while the rate of Black men's out-marriage is double that of Black women, sometimes explained through the racist stereotypes of the undesirability of Black women.[7]

Lily Anne Y. Welty Tamai shifts our focus on interminority tensions and attests to collaboration through her articulation of the role of Black communities and specifically of Black women in the acculturation process of Japanese wives of Black military husbands. While mainstream media may have tried to pit Japanese women as "model wives" against Black women, in practice the latter were central to Japanese women's everyday adjustment to life in the United States. Welty Tamai recounts how one Japanese wife "learned how to be an American woman from Black women within the military community" and that "Japanese women learned how to be Black women first." Through this focus on interminority relations, we shift away from the assumption that "assimilation" to American life happens through one's incorporation into White cultural norms and spaces. The experiences of non-White mixed race couples contest the assumption that people date interracially in order to access the privileges of Whiteness. Instead, we see the dynamics that take place within and across communities of color and the ways that people who illuminate the porousness of those borders often face "border patrolling."

Border Patrolling

Border patrolling, a concept Rebecca Romo draws from Heather Dalmage to describe the "issue of loyalty to race," emerges as a central trope in the experiences of dual minorities to a greater and more consistent effect than found in the literature on part White multiracials.[8] While each story is unique, the essays often revolve around the need to prove one's belonging. Racial logic that was once developed in order to monitor and control minority groups—such as the one-drop rule for Black people in the United States and blood quantum requirements for Native membership—are adopted by non-Whites in troubling and empowering ways. Non-White mixed race people face authenticity tests when others require them to have cultural capital in order to prove their belonging or are asked to choose one racial identity.

Romo describes how "Blaxicans . . . experienced rejection and prejudices directed toward them by African Americans" and also experienced "anti-Black sentiment coming from Latinas/os." Rather than rejecting both identities, this process moved Blaxicans to identify as both Black and Mexican. Maharaj Raju Desai interviewed Indipino family members who developed similar identities in the middle as a result of authenticity tests. They experienced "double negation," which included denigration from Filipinos based on colonial tropes of colorism and difference while also facing exclusion from Indian communities in the Bay Area. Authenticity policing and demands for proof of belonging are, as Romo argues, insults. However, she explains that border policing within the Black community is about one's commitment to Black liberation and loyalty to the race. Disloyalty signifies one's collusion with White racism in ways that oppress other Blacks. Authenticity holds slightly lower stakes among Mexican Americans who have had a relatively more flexible relationship within the US racial hierarchy. Thus, rather than simply casting these interminority tensions as analogous to White racism, Romo states that these practices "occur for social and political reasons and [have] particular histories." These actors face the dynamics of belonging to multiple communities of color that are distinct from those faced by part White multiracials who do not call upon multiple legacies of oppression. At the same time, these studies reveal what is unique for part Black multiracials.

Multiracial Blackness and the One-Drop Rule

One of the central insights emerging from the study of part Black non-White multiracials is the unevenness and flexibility of the often taken-for-granted ideology of the one-drop rule of hypodescent. A focus on Black and White multiracials who tend to identify as Black redoubles the strength of this racial logic. However, a different picture emerges when it comes to non-White Black multiracials. This volume acknowledges the multiplicity of being "Black and ___" in ways that reaffirm rather than disavow associations with Blackness. Multiracialism is not always only an assault on or escape from Blackness, and we see this *particularly* in the cases of people who are part Black dual minorities.[9]

How (or do) non-White multiracials who are part Black disrupt the one-drop rule of hypodescent? From the title of her essay, "Rising Sun, Rising Soul: On Mixed Race Asian Identity That Includes Blackness," to self-descriptions including "an Asian of African descent," Velina Hasu Houston's life story contests US racial logic. Houston does the unexpected: as an identifiably Black person. Rather, she centers her Japanese mother, herself in relation to eras in Japan, and her familiarity with Japanese communities in the United States. This disruption of the one-drop rule expands mixed race studies that focus on Black/White multiracials who generally identify as Black or as mixed, but not as White. Across these chapters, part Black multiracials identify as their multiple ancestries—do qualitative studies of Black/White multiracials reveal the same findings?

A global lens expands our understanding of the Black diaspora in Asia, including the Japan-raised children of Black and other non-White American men with Japanese women. Several chapters teach us about the Black, Latino, and Native American soldiers whose presence, according to Lily Anne Y. Welty Tamai, was larger than the record suggests, and whose experiences were more common than anomalous. Welty Tamai decenters both Whiteness and the United States through her focus on the Black Pacific to offer a different understanding of the Black diaspora. She writes, "The one-drop rule of hypodescent . . . did not always apply in cases with dual minorities because the racial hierarchy and ethnic landscape were simply different in the Pacific Rim." Kaori Mori Want's strongly contextualized interpretation of the experiences of part

Black haafu in Japan helps to disarticulate or, conversely, see the articulation of anti-Black racism and colorism that plagues communities across the globe.[10] She interprets the invisibility of non-White haafus in Japan's beauty culture through centuries-old notions of fairness and the development of kawaii culture, which privileges lightness, cuteness, and transparency and does not have space for darkness, which often suggests an aggressive sexuality or violence. Analyzing part Black haafu through Japan's historical and cultural lens means that their denigration or current valorization (or acceptance) is not simply reflective of changing notions of people of African descent. The shifting status and representation of part Black haafus are related to Japanese ideas about Black people, other non-Japanese people of color, and historical evaluations of lightness and darkness, or innocence and aggression.

This set of studies calls for a gender, generational, and geographic analysis of the variety of ways Blackness operates for men and women. The racial socialization of a young Indian and Black son of a family Cristina Ortiz interviewed highlights the strength of Black identities for multiracials of African ancestry. The family organized their socialization of their child through the lens of how he would be read by society (in this case, in Chicago)—as a Black man. The following chapter, Ingrid Dineen-Wimberly's analysis of her stepson, underscores the racial socialization of part Black minorities as Black men. Ortiz's and Vasquez-Tokos's findings are quite different from those of the families that Sharon Chang interviewed with one White parent who often didn't notice race, did not always think of their children as racialized, and didn't acknowledge their own Whiteness or its attendant privileges.[11]

Being Black and non-White opens us up to hearing and seeing a variety of ways of living and being for people of African descent that are not adequately explained by either the generations of European, African, and Native mixing or on the research of first-generation Black/White biracials. At the same time, it reaffirms the complexity of the one-drop rule as it specifically relates to people of African descent. Dineen-Wimberly explains why Blacks in the United States have adopted this racial logic: the one-drop rule lives on not only because of the legacy of slavery and Jim Crow segregation from which this logic emerged, but also as a source of strength and community. By recognizing one's part "as caretakers of a legacy" and identifying as (just) Black, part Black multiracials' identification as Black people "signals a loyalty to the complexity of the African American experience, both triumphant and oppressive." Do non-White and non-Black multiracials also experience the rule of hypodescent? Maharaj Raju Desai's work on Indipinos suggests that non-Black dual-minority biracials are not necessarily subjected to this ideology. However, they are often monoracially reinscribed as Latina/o. Racial misrecognition is also a common experience of Native and indigenous peoples.

Black and Indigenous

Dineen-Wimberly centers indigenous voices and examines the intersection of Blackness and indigeneity, while Verónica Castillo-Muñoz highlights the dynamics between Chinese, Mexican, mestizo, and indigenous people negotiating state priorities.[12] Dineen-Wimberly provides a compelling interpretation of the life story of Landon, a multigenerational multiracial who is Black, Indian, and other ancestries and has confronted anti-Black racism from both Mexicans and members of his Makah Tribe. At the same time, Dineen-Wimberly exposes "sanctioned acts of erasure," or what Patrick Wolfe has called "the elimination of the native" within the field such that "when an African American asserts indigenous ancestry, glares of disbelief and giggles often accompany such identification."[13] The general uniformity of anti-Black racism across non-Black communities, or what the author calls "the trouble with being mixed while Black," is troubling and is another example of how mixed race studies contributes to our understanding of anti-Blackness. People on the Makah reservation question Landon's native ancestry despite knowing his family name and his formal enrollment. People who are Native and White are still considered Native, yet Black ancestry seems to erase claims to indigeneity. In contrast, the author encourages us to honor "one's right to identify as one chooses."

Critical mixed race studies has much to contribute to current debates between and within Black studies and Native studies. Dineen-Wimberly's chapter charts the stakes of multiraciality for people of African descent and also the specific dynamics of multiracialism for native communities rooted in the history of genocide and current demographics and articulated through the blood quantum basis of access to land and resources. She asks, "With a limited number of tribal members, could emphasizing one's mixedness threaten the survival of the Makah?" Ultimately, Landon expresses an identification with his various backgrounds, paralleling the identities of several of the other authors who discuss blended or multiple identities.

Not Either/Or but Both/And: Fused Identities

Repeated across these texts is not an either/or but a both/and articulation of self expressed through terms like "Blaxican," "Blackapina," and "Indipino." Like Velina Hasu Houston, Janet Mendoza Stickmon reflects on her life experiences, describing a shift from thinking of herself as composed of "inauthentic" halves to a blended whole. She expresses this latter identity through the term "Blackapina"; Desai calls it "Indipino."

Romo's exceptional study of forty Blaxicans responds explicitly to the question: what do non-White multiracials tell us that is different from those who are part White? She explains that Blaxicans "articulate a connection to two separate histories of racial oppression. Rather than choose between two racial/ethnic minority identities, Blaxicans choose both." The authenticity policing ("border patrolling") they face from both Blacks and Mexicans leads them to "craft an in-between identity that embraces both of their backgrounds." This diverges from White/minority biracials for whom phenotype impacts proximity to Whiteness and who are generally, in this racially structured society, pushed to identify with their non-White background. In addition, unlike part White mixed race people, Black Mexicans come from groups that "have been socially, economically, and politically disadvantaged for generations." Despite, or perhaps because of, these histories, non-White multiracial identity is a source of strength, whereby when White is not an option, "choosing both [identities] is less likely to be viewed as trying to climb the racial hierarchy" and thus can reflect a "non-hierarchical valuation of one group over the other," argues Romo.

The complicated expectations that multiracials face in a monoracial world, according to Romo, actually can restructure "the larger racial order and hierarchy." This happens as, subjected to two sets of authenticity tests, Blaxicans maintain authenticity to both and therefore find themselves in an "in-between state." Thus, and perhaps ironically, boundary maintenance that presumes monoracialism leads some multiracials to craft "new racial/ethnic identities" that "emerge out of the contradictions that surface in claiming authenticity to two or more monoracial categories." Romo's findings are significant in no small part due to her strong sample and insightful analysis.

The Problem with Mixed Race Methods

Critical mixed race studies is equipped to engage methods beyond the introspective self-narrative or the interview format of personal contacts. It can also historicize multiracialism, not as a new phenomenon, but as a product of colonialism, imperialism, militarism, genocide, and migrations preceding them.[14] And yet few scholars engage their projects in this way.

This volume reveals both the multidisciplinary nature of the scholarly study of mixed race people and the diverse members of its chorus, including artists and activists alongside academics. The contributions reflect an unresolved tension between public and academic understandings about race and personhood. They also point to the methodological tendencies (weaknesses?) within this field, including small sample sizes, a focus on self-narration, and interviews with family members. How can we take into account the uniqueness and particularity of individual life stories—including those that reaffirm experiences of being betwixt and between, marginalized, and navigating strife-filled lives—that so many researchers attempt to combat? What do we make of academics who say that the examples of liminality, ambiguity, and negotiation are not unique to the multiracial experience, whereas the life stories insist otherwise? How do we communicate between these visions and experiences and draw the links between life stories and theoretical concepts? One way is to present them alongside one another, as they are here, without having to reconcile their contradictions and their vastly different approaches.

Multiracialism is an area with the potential not only to represent an underrepresented population, but to also retheorize race and attend to the multivalence of racism, including monoracism.[15] We can do this by studying non-normative (family, racial, sexual) formations through an intersectional lens. For instance, what is the nexus of multiracial identity with queer identities?[16] Romo's forty participants allow her to see the *intersectional* and patterned nature of non-White multiracial identity formation—community members monitored Blaxicans not only for their racial or cultural knowledge, but also along class and gender expectations. Blaxican women felt that "issues surrounding identity [signified through debates over hair, skin color, and hip hop for instance] were more difficult and frequent for women than for Blaxican men," including their experiences with being sexually exoticized. We also see a difference between the monoracial and multiracial experiences as the latter navigate the challenges and strengths of expectations of minority women across two communities.

These chapters provide a robust, antiracist, theoretical, and unique response to questions of belonging, identity, race, family, culture, and our shared futures. They do this by providing a microscopic view, through oral histories and self-reflective narratives, of individuals treading the boundaries between communities. Following their paths shows us the circumscribing power of constructed boundaries—maintained by those within and outside of these communities. Supplementing these narratives with larger scale and longitudinal research projects will allow us to make more generalizable statements about the implications of mixed race.

The When and Where of the Multiracial: The Future of Critical Mixed Race Studies

If certain mixed race encounters are used by the popular media to signify the future (the end of racism!), then some have been relegated to the past, silenced, or erased. Houston describes the extinction of a generation and offers a different temporal and somber rather than celebratory reading of mixed race. Castillo-Muñoz's important historiographical account of intermarriage among Indians, Mexicans, Chinese, and Japanese in the Baja California borderlands at the turn of the nineteenth century contests depictions of racial mixing as new. Her focus on the shaping conditions of labor insists upon an economic—and not just racial—analysis of multiracialism. The shift in focus from "what are you" to "when" and "where are you" marks an exiting direction in our field.[17] It is what locates Keel's study of "how humans became part Neanderthal" and his call to "incorporate large evolutionary timescales into our thinking about human ancestry" as a central part of this project. Keel's focus on Neanderthal-human mating highlights the incompleteness of statements about race that arise from a presentist framework.[18] He reminds us that the "fallacy of monoraciality [is] largely because humans have never been pure." Simply stated, he writes that "being mixed is the ontological baseline for what it means to be human." However this line of thinking comes close to the argument that "we are all mixed and so no one is mixed (race)," which discredits the experiences of mixed race people. As Ronald Sundstrom has argued, there is a mixed race identity unique from the monoracial experience because mixed race people say there is.[19]

Critical mixed race studies can learn from this temporal shift to a longer history of mixing by distinguishing between what Keel terms sociopolitical timescales and biological timescales. That means that multiracials can be socially significant today, but we are not biologically exceptional. Ultimately, Keel shores up historical evidence to imagine an alternative future, reminding us that "the key is to not believe that our racial fictions are reality." The essays in this collection redefine "mixed race" and illustrate the productivity and failure of nomenclature (what is "mixed"? what is "race"?). Larger questions raised by the contributors beg for expanded methods and a broader scope with regard to place and time. This reorientation may combat the inward-looking myopia that often describes contemporary mixed race studies in the United States. A historical and expansive approach to mixed race also stopgaps the tendency of always ending on the future—a note forward, a promise of evolution and progress, the explicit vision or implied hint that in the future we will all be more mixed, and therefore better off. New work in critical mixed race studies reminds us that we must look not only back, but also beyond.

NOTES

1. Pew Research Center, "Multiracial in America: Proud, Diverse and Growing in Numbers" (June 11, 2015), 29, http://www.pewsocialtrends.org/2015/06/11/multiracial-in-america/.

2. The focus on non-White multiracials adds to the foundational texts in this area. Some of the earlier works on dual minorities focused on identity formation and include Teresa Kay Williams, "The Theater of Identity: (Multi-)race and Representation of Eurasians and AfroAsians," in *American Mixed Race: The Culture of Microdiversity*, ed. Naomi Zack (Lanham, MD: Rowman & Littlefield, 1995), 79–96; and the following chapters in Teresa Williams-León and Cynthia L. Nakashima's *The Sum of Our Parts: Mixed Heritage Asian Americans* (Philadelphia: Temple University Press, 2001): Cynthia Nakashima,

"Servants of Culture: The Symbolic Role of Mixed-Race Asians in American Discourse," 35–48; Christine Iijima Hall and Trude Turner, "The Diversity of Biracial Individuals: Asian-White and Asian-Minority Biracial Identity," 81–92; Michael Thornton and Harold Gates, "Black, Japanese, and American: An Asian American Identity Yesterday and Today," 93–106. For a more comprehensive list, see Steven Riley's remarkable website: www.mixedracestudies.org. Recent book-length work includes Rudy P. Guevarra Jr., *Becoming Mexipino: Multiethnic Identities and Communities in San Diego* (New Brunswick, NJ: Rutgers University Press, 2012).

3. For more on these stereotypes, see Lori Pierce, "Six Queens: Miss Ka Palapala and Interracial Beauty in Territorial Hawai'i," in *War Baby/Love Child: Mixed Race Asian American Art*, ed. Laura Kina and Wei Ming Dariotis (Seattle: University of Washington Press, 2013).

4. An example of a representation of multiracials that has become widely viewed by the mainstream is Kip Fulbeck's multimedia exhibit *The Hapa Project*. Fulbeck offers a book, website, and photographic museum exhibit centered on over twelve hundred portraits of people who "self-identified as hapa" (www.thehapaproject.com). This multimedia project that began in 2001 has increased national attention to the controversial use of the Hawaiian word "hapa" and the overall profile of mixed race people. For critical responses to this project and the term "hapa," see Wei Ming Dariotis, "Hapa: The Word of Power," *Hyphen Magazine* (December 3, 2007); Brandon Ledward, "On Being Hawaiian Enough: Contesting American Racialization with Native Hybridity," *Hulili: Multidisciplinary Research on Hawaiian Well-Being* 4.1 (2007): 107–143; Kina and Dariotis, *War Baby/Love Child*; Colleen Daniher, "Exhibiting 'Hapas' in the Twenty-First Century: 'The Hapa Project' in RACE: Are We So Different? and *War Baby/Love Child*" (presentation, Association for Asian American Studies, Evanston, IL, April 2015). Other mainstream representations of the growing multiracial population in the United States include *National Geographic*'s 2013 photo gallery "The Changing Face of America," which, like Fulbeck's, features portraits of multiracial faces (http://ngm.nationalgeographic.com/2013/10/changing-faces/schoeller-photography).

5. Rudy P. Guevarra, Jr., *Becoming Mexipino: Multiethnic Identities and Communities in San Diego* (New Brunswick, NJ: Rutgers University Press, 2012): 4, 5, 7, emphasis original.

6. See Yen Le Espiritu, *Asian American Women and Men: Labor, Laws, and Love* (Thousand Oaks, CA: Sage, 1997).

7. See Patricia Hill Collins, *Black Feminist Thought: Knowledge, Consciousness, and the Politics of Empowerment* (New York: Routledge, 2000).

8. Heather M. Dalmage, *Tripping On The Color Line: Black-White Multiracial Families in a Racially Divided World* (New Brunswick, NJ: Rutgers University Press, 2000).

9. The multiracial movement's push in the 1990s for the US census to allow people to mark more than one category led to some civil rights groups' concerns that the numbers of Black Americans would decrease, thereby impacting race-based federal funding. Some scholars have also contended that multiracialism can be a form of anti-Blackness and may appeal to those people attempting to move away from their African ancestry. See Jared Sexton, *Amalgamation Schemes: Antiblackness and the Critique of Multiracialism* (Minneapolis: University of Minnesota Press, 2008); Minkah Makalani, "Rejecting Blackness and Claiming Whiteness: Antiblack Whiteness in the Biracial Project," in *White Out: The Continuing Significance of Racism*, ed. Ashley Doane and Eduardo Bonilla-Silva (New York: Routledge, 2003).

10. Joanne L. Rondilla and Paul Spickard, *Is Lighter Better? Skin-Tone Discrimination among Asian Americans* (Lanham, MD: Rowman & Littlefield, 2007).

11. Sharon Chang, *Raising Mixed Race: Multiracial Asian Children in a Post-racial World* (New York: Routledge, 2015).

12. Andrew Jolivette, *Louisiana Creoles: Cultural Recovery and Mixed-Race Native American Identity* (New York: Lexington Books, 2007). See also Nitasha Sharma, "Pacific Revisions of Blackness: Blacks Address Race and Belonging in Hawai'i," *Amerasia Journal* 37.3 (2011): 43–60.

13. Patrick Wolfe, "Settler Colonialism and the Elimination of the Native." *Journal of Genocide Research* 8.4 (2006): 387–409.

14. Minelle Mahtani, *Mixed Race Amnesia: Resisting the Romanticization of Multiraciality* (Vancouver: University of British Columbia Press, 2014).

15. According to Eric Hamako, monoracism is "*the systemic privileging of things, people and practices that are racialized as 'single-race' and/or 'racially pure' (e.g., 'Monoracial') and the oppression of things, people, and practices that are racialized as being of more than one-race (e.g., 'Multiracial,' 'Mixed-Race,' 'Multiethnic, etc.)*"; Eric Hamako, "Improving Anti-racist Education for Multiracial Students" (PhD diss., University of Massachusetts, Amherst, 2014), 81, emphasis original. See also Marc P. Johnston and Kevin L. Nadal, "Multiracial Microaggressions: Exposing Monoracism in Everyday Life and Clinical Practice," in *Microaggressions and Marginality: Manifestation, Dynamics, and Impact*, ed. Derald Wing Sue (Hoboken, NJ: John Wiley, 2010), 123–144.

16. There has been some work on the intersection of (bi)raciality and (bi)sexuality, including George Kitahara Kich, "In the Margins of Sex and Race: Difference, Marginality, and Flexibility," 263–276, and Karen Maeda Allman, "(Un)natural Boundaries: Mixed Race, Gender, and Sexuality," 277–290, both in *The Multiracial Experience: Racial Borders as the New Frontier*, ed. Maria P. P. Root (Thousand Oaks, CA: Sage, 1996). See also "Bi Bi Girl," in Stephen Murphy-Shigematsu, *When Half is Whole: Multiethnic Asian American Identities* (Stanford, CA: Stanford University Press, 2012).

17. At the 2014 Critical Mixed Race Studies roundtable panel, Minelle Mahtani presented the question "Where are you?" while panelist Daniel McNeil posed the question "When are you?"

18. See Mahtani, *Mixed Race Amnesia.*

19. Ronald Sundstrom, "Being and Being Mixed Race," *Social Theory and Practice* 27.2 (2001): 285–307.

ACKNOWLEDGMENTS

Many people helped in the building of this book. We owe a great debt to the many scholars of critical mixed race studies whose names appear in the endnotes and bibliography, and to the Critical Mixed Race Studies Association, at whose meeting we first presented much of this work. Among the people who contributed to that occasion who were not able to join us in the volume but whose fine minds helped us arrive at our destination are Evelyn Alsultany, Niccole Coggins, Kevin Escudero, Camilla Fojas, Teresa Hodges, Sally Howell, Mark James, Laura Kina, Becky King-O'Riain, Joo Young Lee, LeiLani Nishime, Juliana Pegues, Zeli Rivas, and Michael Thornton. We especially want to thank the individual contributors to this volume for their outstanding work, and Nitasha Sharma for bringing the volume together with her thoughtful and insightful epilogue.

Thanks are due to our home institutions, Arizona State University and the University of California, Santa Barbara. They have provided us happy homes for scholarly work, access to fine libraries, and the company of stimulating colleagues, especially in the Asian Pacific American Studies Program at ASU and the Departments of Black Studies, Asian American Studies, and History at UCSB. Leslie Mitchner and her colleagues at Rutgers University Press have been model editors and abettors of our intellectual enterprise.

Our families have been ridiculously supportive of this project, as of so many others over the years. Joanne L. Rondilla would like to thank her Arizona community and students at ASU and UC Berkeley for reminding her that the work we do matters. *Maraming salamat* to her family for their unwavering support. Finally, she would like to thank her husband Jose Ureta for managing to love her, even when she's hundreds of miles away. Rudy Guevarra Jr.

would like to thank his family and friends for their continued love and support over the years, and his students who never cease to inspire him. Paul Spickard thanks Anna Lucky Louise Spickard for unswerving engagement and encouragement of his work, and for not neglecting the great achievements of her own.

BIBLIOGRAPHY

Acevedo, Gabriel. "Hispanics and Their Perceptions of Family Dynamics: An Extension and Test of Group Reference Theory." *Journal of Comparative Family Studies* 40 (2009): 387–414.

Acuña, Rodolfo. *Occupied America: A History of Chicanos.* 7th ed. New York: Longman, 2011.

Adams, David Wallace. *Education for Extinction: The American Indian Boarding School Experience, 1875–1928.* Lawrence: University Press of Kansas, 1995.

Agoncillo, Teodoro. *Introduction to Filipino History.* Quezon City: Garotech, 1974.

Aguilar, Camín Héctor, and Meyer Lorenzo. *In the Shadow of the Mexican Revolution.* Trans. Luis Alberto Fierro. Austin: University of Texas Press, 1996.

Aguirre Bernal, Celso. *Compendio Histórico Biográfico de Mexicali 1539–1966.* Mexicali: Mexicali, B. CFA, 1966.

Agustin, José. *Trajicomedia Mexicana.* Vol. 1. Mexico: Editorial Planeta Mexicana, 1990.

Ahn, Ji-Hyun. "Rearticulating Black Mixed-Race in the Era of Globalization: Hines Ward and the Struggle for Koreanness in Contemporary South Korean Media." *Cultural Studies* 28.3 (2014): 391–417.

Alba, Richard D., and Victor Nee. *Remaking the American Mainstream: Assimilation and Contemporary Immigration.* Cambridge, MA: Harvard University Press, 2003.

"The A List 1997." *A Magazine* (January 31, 1998): 50.

Allman, Karen Maeda. "(Un)natural Boundaries: Mixed Race, Gender, and Sexuality." In Root, *Multiracial Experience*, 277–290.

Almaguer, Tomás. *Racial Fault Lines: The Historical Origins of White Supremacy in California.* Berkeley: University of California Press, 1994.

Alonzo, Ana Maria. *Thread of Blood: Colonialism, Revolution, and Gender on Mexico's Northern Frontier.* Tucson: University of Arizona Press, 1995.

Alvarez, Robert R., Jr. *Familia: Migration and Adaptation in Baja and Alta California, 1800–1975.* Berkeley: University of California Press, 1987.

Anderson, Benedict. *Imagined Communities: Reflections on the Origin and Spread of Nationalism.* Rev. ed. London: Verso, 1991.

Andrews, David, and C. L Coles. "America's New Son: Tiger Woods and America's Multiculturalism." In *Sports Stars: The Cultural Politics of Sporting Celebrity*, ed. David Andrews and Steven Jackson. New York: Routledge, 2001. Pp. 70–86.

Andrews, Matthew M. "(Re)examining (Multi)racial Identity: Black-Filipino Multiracials in the San Francisco-Bay Area." *Berkeley McNair Research Journal* 13 (2005): 27–38.

Anguiano, María Eugenia. *Agricultura y Migración en el Valle de Mexicali.* Tijuana: El Colegio de la Frontera Norte, 1995.

Anzaldúa, Gloria. *Borderlands/ La Frontera: The New Mestiza.* San Francisco: Aunt Lute Books, 1987.

Asante, Molefi Kete. "Racing to Leave the Race: Black Postmodernists Off-Track." *Black Scholar* 23.3–4 (1993): 50–51.

Azoulay, Katya Gibel. *Black, Jewish, and Interracial.* Durham, NC: Duke University Press, 1997.

Bald, Vivek. *Bengali Harlem and the Lost Histories of South Asian America.* Cambridge, MA: Harvard University Press, 2013.

Balderrama, Francisco E., and Raymond Rodriguez, *Decade of Betrayal: Mexican Repatriation in the 1930s.* Albuquerque: University of New Mexico Press, 1995.

Baldoz, Rick. *The Third Asiatic Invasion: Empire and Migration in Filipino America, 1898–1946.* New York: New York University Press, 2011.

Baldwin, Mark, and John Holmes. "Salient Private Audiences and Awareness of the Self." *Journal of Personality and Social Psychology* 52.6 (1987): 1087–1098.

Ball, Edward. *Slaves in the Family.* New York: Ballantine, 1998.

Banks, Ingrid. *Hair Matters: Beauty, Power, and Black Women's Consciousness.* New York: New York University Press, 2000.

Barrier, N. Gerald, and Verne A. Dusenbery, eds. *Sikh Diaspora: Migration and the Experience beyond Punjab.* Columbia, MO: South Asia Books, 1989.

Basson, Lauren L. *White Enough to Be American? Race Mixing, Indigenous People, and the Boundaries of State and Nation.* Chapel Hill: University of North Carolina Press, 2008.

Bean, Frank, and Jennifer Lee. "Plus ça change . . . ? Multiraciality and the Dynamics of Race Relations in the United States." *Journal of Social Issues* 65.1 (2009): 205–219.

"Beauty Queen Brings Light to Japan's Racial Issues." *CBS News* (April 13, 2015)

Becker, Marjorie. *Setting the Virgin on Fire: Lázaro Cardenas, Michoacán Peasants, and the Redemption of the Mexican Revolution.* Berkeley: University of California Press, 1995.

Beltrán, Mary, and Camilla Fojas, eds. *Mixed Race Hollywood.* New York: New York University Press, 2008.

Bendick, Marc, Charles W. Jackson, Victor A. Reinoso, and Laura E. Hodges. "Discrimination Against Latino Job Applicants: A Controlled Experiment." *Human Resource Management* 30.4 (1991): 469–484.

Bettez, Silvia C. "Mixed-Race Women and Epistemologies of Belonging." *Frontiers* 31 (2010): 142–165.

Bettie, Julie. *Women without Class: Girls, Race and Identity.* Berkeley: University of California Press, 2003.

Bier, Lisa. *American Indian and African American People, Communities and Interactions: An Annotated Bibliography.* Westport, CT: Praeger, 2004.

Blackwell, Maylei. "Contested Histories: Las Hijas de Cuahtémoc, Chicana Feminisms, and the Print Culture in the Chicano Movement, 1968–1973." In *Chicana Feminisms: A Critical Reader*, ed. Gabriella. F. Arredondo, Aída Hurtado, Norma Klahn, Olga Nájera-Ramírez, and Patricia Zavella. Durham, NC: Duke University Press, 2003. Pp. 59–89.

Blauner, Robert. *Racial Oppression in America.* New York: Harper & Row, 1976.

Blumenbach, Johann Friedrich. *The Anthropological Treatises of Johann Friedrich Blumenbach.* London: Longman, 1865.

Boime, Eric. "Beating Plowshares into Swords: The Colorado River Delta, the Yellow Peril, and the Movement for Federal Reclamation, 1901–1928." *Pacific Historical Review* 78.1 (2009): 27–53.

Bolnick, Deborah. "Individual Ancestry Inference and the Reification of Race as Biological Phenomenon." In Keonig, Lee, and Richardson, *Revisiting Race in a Genomic Age*, 70–87.

Bonacich, Edna, and Lucy Cheng, eds. *Labor Immigration under Capitalism: Asian Workers in the United States before World War II.* Berkeley: University of California Press, 1984.

Bonilla-Silva, Eduardo, and David Embrick. "Black, Honorary White, White: The Future of Race in the United States?" In Brunsma, *Mixed Messages*, 33–48.

Booker, James. "All about People." *New Voice of New York* (August 5, 2004): 3.

Bourdieu, Pierre. *Outline of a Theory of Practice.* Cambridge: Cambridge University Press, 1977.

Bowechop, Janine. "Preface." In *Voices of a Thousand People*, by Patricia Erikson, with Helma Ward and Kirk Wachendorf. Lincoln: University of Nebraska Press, 2005. Pp. xi–xiii.

Boykin, A. Wade, and Forrest D. Toms. "Black Child Socialization: A Conceptual Framework." In *Black Children: Social, Educational, and Parental Environments*, ed. Harriette Pipes McAdoo and John Lewis McAdoo. Thousand Oaks, CA: Sage, 1985. Pp. 33–51.

Brace, C. Loring. *"Race" Is a Four-Letter Word: The Genesis of a Concept.* New York: Oxford University Press, 2005.

Branch, John. "Ward Helps Biracial Youths on Journey toward Acceptance." *New York Times* (November 9, 2009).

Briscoe, Mattie H. "A Study of Eight Foreign-Born Children of Mixed Parentage Who Have Been Adopted by Negro Couples in the U.S." Master's thesis, Atlanta University School of Education, 1956.

Brooks, James F. *Captives and Cousins: Slavery Kinship, and Community in the Southwest Borderlands.* Chapel Hill: University of North Carolina Press, 2002.

——, ed. *Confounding the Color Line: The Black-Indian Experience in North America.* Lincoln: University of Nebraska Press, 2002.

Brown, Judith. *Global South Asians: Introducing the Modern Diaspora.* Cambridge: Cambridge University Press, 2006.

Brown, Tiffany L., and Ambika Krishnakumar. "Development and Validation of the Adolescent Racial and Ethnic Socialization Scale (ARESS) in African American Families." *Journal of Youth and Adolescence* 36.8 (2007): 1072–1085.

Broyard, Bliss. *One Drop: My Father's Hidden Life—A Story of Race and Secrets.* New York: Little, Brown, 2007.

Brunsma, David. "Interracial Families and the Racial Identification of Mixed Race Children: Evidence from the Early Childhood Longitudinal Study." *Social Forces* 84.2 (2005): 1131–1157.

——, ed. *Mixed Messages: Multiracial Identities in the "Color-Blind" Era.* Boulder, CO: Lynne Rienner, 2006.

Bryc, Katarzyna, Eric Y. Durand, J. Michael Macpherson, David Reich, and Joanna L. Mountain. "The Genetic Ancestry of African Americans, Latinos, and European Americans across the United States." *American Journal of Human Genetics* 96.1 (2015): 37–53.

Butler, Judith. *Bodies That Matter: On the Discursive Limits of "Sex."* New York: Routledge, 1993.

——. *Gender Trouble: Feminism and the Subversion of Identity.* New York: Routledge, 1990.

Byrd, Jodi. *The Transit of Empire: Indigenous Critiques of Colonialism.* Minneapolis: University of Minnesota Press, 2011.

Cannon, Mardelo. "Cannon's Comments: Black Men Doing Their Thing Deserve More Respect." *Sacramento Observer* (August 3, 2006): D1–D2.

Cardoso, Lawrence A. *Mexican Emigration to the United States, 1897–1931: Socio-economic Patterns.* Tucson: University of Arizona Press, 1980.

Carter, Greg. *The United States of the United Races: A Utopian History of Racial Mixing.* New York: New York University Press, 2013.

Carter, Mitzi Uehara. "Mixed Race Okinawans and Their Obscure In-Betweenness." *Journal of Intercultural Studies* 35.6 (2014): 646–661.

Carter, Mitzi, and Aina Hunter. "A Critical Review of Academic Perspectives of Blackness in Japan." In *Multiculturalism in the New Japan: Crossing the Boundaries Within*, ed. Nelson Graburn, John Ertl, and Kenji Tierney. New York: Berghahn Books, 2008. Pp. 188–198.

Carter, Richard. "Tiger Woods' Maudlin Mea Culpa Was a Stone-Cold Sham." *New York Amsterdam News* (February 25, 2010): 10.

Caughy, Margaret O'Brien, Patricia J. O'Campo, and Carles Muntaner. "Experiences of Racism among African American Parents and the Mental Health of Their Preschool-Aged Children." *American Journal of Public Health* 94.12 (2004): 2118–2124.

Chang, Jason Oliver. "Racial Alterity in a Mestizo Nation." *Journal of Asian American Studies* 14.3 (2011): 331–359.

Chang, Sharon. *Raising Mixed Race: Multiracial Asian Children in a Post-racial World*. New York: Routledge, 2015.

Chapkis, Wendy. *Beauty Secrets: Women and the Politics of Appearance*. Boston: South End, 1986.

Charmaz, Kathy. *Constructing Grounded Theory*. Thousand Oaks, CA: Sage, 2014.

———. "'Discovering' Chronic Illness: Using Grounded Theory." *Social Science and Medicine* 30.11 (1990): 1161–1172.

Charmaz, Kathy, and Richard G. Mitchell. "Grounded Theory in Ethnography." In *Handbook of Ethnography*, ed. Paul Atkinson, Amanda Coffey, Sarah Delamont, John Lofland, and Lyn Lofland. Thousand Oaks, CA: Sage, 2001. Pp. 160–174.

Chavez, Leo R. *The Latino Threat: Constructing Immigrants, Citizens, and the Nation*. Stanford, CA: Stanford University Press, 2008.

Chee, Alexander. "Where I'm Starting From: A Biracial Writer Navigates the Muddy Waters of Identity." *A Magazine* (September 30, 2000): 50.

Chen, Liliana, Tomio Geron, Karen Lam, Daniel Ou, and Angelo Ragaza. "The 25 Most Influential Asian Americans." *A Magazine* (January 31, 1997): 53.

Chevalier, Jack. "Tiger Explains His Inner Peace." *Philadelphia Tribune* (July 19, 2002): 1C.

Child, Brenda J. *Boarding School Seasons: American Indian Families*. Lincoln: University of Nebraska Press, 2000.

Childs, Erica Chito. *Navigating Interracial Borders: Black-White Couples and Their Social Worlds*. New Brunswick, NJ: Rutgers University Press, 2005.

Chong, Kelly H. "Relevance of Race: Children and the Shifting Engagement with Racial/Ethnic Identity among Second-Generation Interracially Married Asian Americans." *Journal of Asian American Studies* 16.2 (2013): 189–221.

Chou, Rosalind, Kristen Lee, and Simon Ho. "Love Is (Color)blind: Asian Americans and White Institutional Space at the Elite University." *Sociology of Race and Ethnicity* 1.2 (2015): 302–316.

Christensen, Casey. "Mujeres Publicas: American Prostitutes in Baja California, 1910–1930." *American Historical Review* 82 (May 2013): 215–247.

Clark, Emily. *The Strange History of the American Quadroon: Free Women of Color in the Revolutionary Atlantic World*. Chapel Hill: University of North Carolina Press, 2013.

Cleaver, Jack. "Kleaver's Klippins: 'Innocent' Things People 'Happen' to Say." *Los Angeles Sentinel* (May 7, 1997): A7.

———. "Kleaver's Klippins: Tiger Woods' Success Brings Problems." *Los Angeles Sentinel* (April 30, 1997): A7.

Cloyd, Fredrick. "Assimilating the Black Japanese—Japan and the US: Reflections." September 3, 2013. https://waterchildren.wordpress.com/page/3/.

———. *Dream of the Water Children*. New York: 2Leaf Press, forthcoming.

———. "Two Players Levelling the Playing Field." *International Examiner* (July 1, 1998): 14.

Cochran, John, Mitchell Chamlin, Leonard Beeghley, and Melissa Fenwick. "Religion, Religiosity, and Nonmarital Sexual Conduct: An Application of Reference Group Theory." *Sociological Inquiry* 74.1 (2004): 102–127.

Coleman, Brett R. "Being Mixed and Black: The Socialization of Mixed-Race Identity." PhD diss., University of Illinois at Chicago, 2012.

Coleman, Major G. "Job Skill and Black Male Wage Discrimination." *Social Science Quarterly* 84.4 (2003): 892–906.

Coleman, Monyca. "Tiger Woods: The Hype Continues." *Indianapolis Recorder* (May 3, 1997): B7.

Collins, Patricia Hill. *Black Feminist Thought: Knowledge, Consciousness, and the Politics of Empowerment*. New York: Routledge, 2000.

———. *Fighting Words: Black Women and the Search for Justice*. Minneapolis: University of Minnesota Press, 1998.

———. "Learning from the Outsider Within." *Social Problems* 33.6 (1986): 14–32.

Collins, Rebecca. "For Better or Worse: The Impact of Upward Social Comparison on Self-Evaluations." *Psychological Bulletin* 119.1 (1996): 51–69.

Colson, Elizabeth. *The Makah Indians: A Study of an Indian Tribe in Modern American Society.* 1953. 2nd ed., Westport, CT: Greenwood, 1977.

Conde, Carlos. "Mahatma Gandhi Is Tiger Woods—He Wished." *Hispanic Outlook in Higher Education* (May 17, 2010): 5.

Consejo Nacional para la Cultura y las Artes: Centro Cultural Tijuana. China en las Californias. Tijuana: Conaculta, 2002.

Cope, Douglas. *The Limits of Racial Domination in Colonial Mexico City.* Madison: University of Wisconsin Press, 1993.

Cornell, Stephen, and Douglas Hartmann. *Ethnicity and Race: Making Identities in a Changing World.* Rev. ed. Thousand Oaks, CA: Pine Forge Press, 2007.

Coronado, Marc, Rudy P. Guevarra, Jr., Jeffrey Moniz, and Laura Furlan Szanto, eds. *Crossing Lines: Race and Mixed Race across the Geohistorical Divide.* Santa Barbara: University of California, Santa Barbara, Multiethnic Student Outreach, 2003.

Crawford, Marc. "The Tragedy of Brown Babies Left in Japan." *Jet Magazine* (January 14, 1960): 14–17.

Crawford, Susan E., and Ramona Alaggia. "The Best of Both Worlds? Family Influences on Mixed Race Youth Identity Development." *Qualitative Social Work* 7.1 (2008): 81–98.

Crenshaw, Kimberlé Williams. "Mapping the Margins: Intersectionality, Identity Politics, and Violence Against Women of Color." *Stanford Law Review* 43 (July 1991): 1241–1299.

Creswell, John W. *Qualitative Inquiry and Research Design: Choosing among Five Approaches.* Thousand Oaks, CA: Sage, 2012.

Crippen, Cheryl, and Leah Brew. "Intercultural Parenting and the Transcultural Family: A Literature Review." *Family Journal* 15.2 (2007): 107–115.

Crow Dog, Mary, and Richard Erdoes. *Lakota Woman.* New York: Harper Perennial, 1990.

Crowe, Jerry. "Ward Learned by Mom's Example." *Los Angeles Times* (February 4, 2006).

Curry, George. "Why Tee Off on Tiger?" *Michigan Chronicle* (December 30, 2009): A6.

DaCosta, Kimberly. *Making Multiracials: State, Family, and Market in the Redrawing of the Color Line.* Stanford, CA: Stanford University Press, 2007.

Dagbovie, Sika. "Star-Light, Star-Bright, Star Damn Near White: Mixed-Race Superstars." *Journal of Popular Culture* 40 (March 2007): 217–237.

Dalmage, Heather M. "Discovering Racial Borders." In *Race in an Era of Change: A Reader*, ed. Heather M. Dalmage and Barbara Katz Rothman. New York: Oxford University Press, 2010. Pp. 94–101.

——, ed. *The Politics of Multiracialism: Challenging Racial Thinking.* Albany: State University of New York Press, 2004.

——. *Tripping on the Color Line: Black-White Multiracial Families in a Racially Divided World.* New Brunswick, NJ: Rutgers University Press, 2000.

Dang, Janet, and Jason Ma. "1999 the Year in Review." *Asianweek* (January 12, 2000): 3.

Daniel, G. Reginald, ed. *Journal of Critical Mixed Race Studies.* Santa Barbara: University of California, Santa Barbara, 2014.

——. *More Than Black? Multiracial Identity and the New Racial Order.* Philadelphia: Temple University Press, 2002.

——. "'Passers and Pluralists': Subverting the Racial Divide." In Root, *Racially Mixed People in America*, 91–107.

——. *Race and Multiraciality in Brazil and the United States: Converging Paths?* University Park: Pennsylvania State University Press, 2006.

Daniel, G. Reginald, and Josef Manuel Castañeda-Liles. "Race, Multiraciality, and the Neoconservative Agenda." In Brunsma, *Mixed Messages*, 125–146.

Daniel, G. Reginald, Laura Kina, Wei Ming Dariotis, and Camilla Fojas. "Emerging Paradigms in Critical Mixed Race Studies." *Journal of Critical Mixed Race Studies* 1.1 (2014): 6–65.

Daniel, G. Reginald, and Hettie V. Williams, eds. *Race and the Obama Phenomenon: The Vision of a More Perfect Multiracial Union.* Jackson: University Press of Mississippi, 2014.

Daniels, Douglas Henry. *Pioneer Urbanites: A Social and Cultural History.* Berkeley: University of California Press, 1991.

Daniher, Colleen. "Exhibiting 'Hapas' in the Twenty-First Century: 'The Hapa Project' in RACE: Are We So Different? and *War Baby/Love Child*." Presentation at the Association for Asian American Studies conference, Evanston, IL, April 2015.

Dariotis, Wei Ming. "Hapa: The Word of Power." *Hyphen Magazine* (December 3, 2007).

Davis, F. James. *Who Is Black? One Nation's Definition.* University Park: Pennsylvania State University Press, 1991.

Dawson, Michael C. *Behind the Mule: Race and Class in African-American Politics.* Princeton, NJ: Princeton University Press, 1994.

Deaux, Kay. *To Be an Immigrant.* New York: Russell Sage Foundation, 2006.

Deere, Carmen Diana. *Household and Class Relations: Peasants and Landlords in Northern Peru.* Berkeley: University of California Press, 1990.

Deere, Carmen Diana, and Magdalena Leon. *La Mujer y la Política Agraria en America Latina.* Mexico City: Siglo Veintiuno Editores, 1986.

De Genova, Nicholas. *Working the Boundaries: Race, Space, and "Illegality" in Mexican Chicago.* Durham, NC: Duke University Press, 2005.

De Genova, Nicholas, and Ana Ramos-Zayas. *Latino Crossings: Mexicans, Puerto Ricans, and the Politics of Race and Citizenship.* New York: Taylor & Francis, 2003.

Denzin, Norman K., and Yvonna S. Lincoln. *The Qualitative Inquiry Reader.* Thousand Oaks, CA: Sage, 2002.

Derman-Sparks, Louise, Carol Tanaka Higa, and Bill Sparks. "Children, Race and Racism: How Race Awareness Develops." *Interracial Books for Children Bulletin* 11.3–4 (1980): 3–15.

Derr, Erik, and Melissa London. "Pioneer Gala: The Stuff That Dreams Are Made Of." *Northwest Asian Weekly* (May 16, 1997): 1.

De Smit, Nicolette. "Mothering Multiracial Children: Indicators of Effective Interracial Parenting." PhD diss., McGill University, 1997.

DeSouza, Carole. "Against Erasure: The Multiracial Voice in Cherrie Moraga's Loving in the War Years." In *Mixing It Up: Multiracial Subjects*, ed. SanSan Kwan and Kenneth Speirs. Austin: University of Texas Press, 2004. Pp. 181–206.

Diguet, León. "La Basse-Californie d'après." *Annales de Geographie* 9.45 (1900): 243–250.

Dineen-Wimberly, Ingrid. "Mixed-Race Leadership in African America: The Regalia of Race and National Identity in the U.S., 1862–1916." PhD diss., University of California, Santa Barbara, 2009.

———. "To 'Carry the Black Man's Burden': T. Thomas Fortune's Vision of African American Colonization of the Philippines, 1902–1903." *International Journal of Business and Social Science* 5.10 (2014): 69–74.

Dominguez, Virginia. *White by Definition: Social Classification in Creole Louisiana*. New Brunswick, NJ: Rutgers University Press, 1986.

Dower, John W. *Embracing Defeat: Japan in the Wake of World War II*. New York: Norton, 1999.

Dowling, Julie A. *Mexican Americans and the Question of Race*. Austin: University of Texas Press, 2014.

Du Bois, W.E.B. *The Souls of Black Folk*. Chicago: A.C. McClurg, 1903. Reprint, New York: Dover, 1994.

Duleep, Harriet Orcutt, and Seth Sanders. "Discrimination at the Top: American-Born Asian and White Men." *Industrial Relations* 31.3 (1992): 416–432.

Duncan, H. Robert. "The Chinese and the Economic Development of Northern Baja California, 1889–1929." *Hispanic American Historical Review* 74.4 (1994): 615–647.

Dwyer, John. *The Agrarian Dispute: The Expropriation of American-Owned Rural Land in Post Revolutionary Mexico*. Durham, NC: Duke University Press, 2008.

Dyer, Richard. *White—Essays on Race and Culture*. New York: Routledge, 1997.

"Earning His Stripes: Tiger Woods Emerges Victorious in Invitational Playoff, Captures His First Win on the Professional Golf Tour." *Asianweek* (October 17, 1996): 9.

Edgar, Adrienne Lynn. *Tribal Nation: The Making of Soviet Turkmenistan*. Princeton, NJ: Princeton University Press, 2004.

Edmonston, Barry, and James P. Smith. *The New Americans: Economic, Demographic, and Fiscal Effects of Immigration*. Washington, DC: National Academies Press, 1997.

Edwards, Penny, Debjani Ganguly, and Jacqueline Lo, eds. "Mixed Race around the Globe." Special issue of *Journal of Intercultural Studies* 28.1 (2007): 1–155.

Elam, Michele. *The Souls of Mixed Folk: Race, Politics, and Aesthetics in the New Millennium*. Stanford, CA: Stanford University Press, 2011.

Endo, Hiro. "Cool & Exotic: Haafu Girls Boom!" May 30, 2007. http://allabout.co.jp/gm/gc/2027661.

Enloe, Cynthia. *Bananas Beaches and Bases: Making Feminist Sense of International Politics*. Berkeley: University of California Press, 2000.

Espinoza, José Angel. *El Ejemplo de Sonora*. Mexico City, 1932.

Espiritu, Yen Le. *Asian American Women and Men: Labor, Laws, and Love*. Thousand Oaks, CA: Sage, 1997.

Etzioni, Amatai. "A Look at . . . Racial Identity: Let's Not Be Boxed in by Color." *Washington Post* (June 8, 1997): C03.

Fackler, Martin. "Biracial Beauty Queen Challenges Japan's Self-Image." *New York Times* (May 29, 2015).

Farley, Reynolds, and John Haaga, eds. *The American People: Census 2000*. New York: Russell Sage Foundation, 2005.

Fatimilehin, Iyabo A. "Of Jewel Heritage: Racial Socialization and Racial Identity Attitudes amongst Adolescents of Mixed African–Caribbean/White Parentage." *Journal of Adolescence* 22.3 (1999): 303–318.

Feagin, Joe R. *Racist America: Roots, Current Realities, and Future Reparations.* New York: Routledge, 2000.

Feagin, Joe, and Debra Van Ausdale. *The First R: How Children Learn Race and Racism.* Lanham, MD: Rowman & Littlefield, 2001.

Feagin, Joe, and Hernán Vera. *White Racism.* New York: Routledge, 1995.

Fehrenbach, Heide. *Race after Hitler: Black Occupation Children in Postwar Germany and America.* Princeton, NJ: Princeton University Press, 2005.

Fenstermaker, Sarah, and Candice West. *Doing Gender, Doing Difference: Inequality, Power and Institutional Change.* New York: Routledge, 2002.

Festinger, Leon. "A Theory of Social Comparisons." In Hyman and Singer, *Readings in Reference Group Theory and Research,* 123–146.

Firman, John, and Ann Gila. *Psychosynthesis: A Psychology of the Spirit.* Albany: State University of New York Press, 2002.

Fitzpatrick, Michael, and Tim Macfarlan, "'I've Been Called N****r and Had Trash Thrown at Me': First Mixed Race Miss Japan Hits Out at the 'Spasmodic Vomit of Racial Abuse' She's Suffered Because Father Is African-American." *Daily Mail* (April 1, 2015).

Fojas, Camilla, and Rudy Guevarra, Jr. *Transnational Crossroads: Remapping the Americas and the Pacific.* Lincoln: University of Nebraska Press, 2012.

Forbes, Jack D. *Africans and Native Americans: The Language of Race and the Evolution of Red-Black Peoples.* 2nd ed. Urbana: University of Illinois Press, 1993.

Fowler-Salamini, Heather, and Mary Kay Vaughan, eds. *Women of the Mexican Countryside, 1850–1990: Creating Spaces, Shaping Transitions.* Tucson: University of Arizona Press, 1994.

Frankenberg, Ruth. *White Women, Race Matters: The Social Construction of Whiteness.* Minneapolis: University of Minnesota Press, 1993.

French, William E., and Katherine Elaine Bliss. *Gender, Sexuality and Power in Latin America since Independence.* Lanham, MD: Rowman & Littlefield, 2007.

Frey, William H. "America's Diverse Future: Initial Glimpses at the U.S. Child Population from the 2010 Census." Washington, DC: Brookings Institution, April 2011.

Fulbeck, Kip. *Paper Bullets.* Seattle: University of Washington Press, 2001.

———. *Part Asian, 100% Hapa.* San Francisco: Chronicle Books, 2006.

Fullwiley, Duana. "The Biologistical Construction of Race: 'Admixture' Technology and the New Genetic Medicine." *Social Studies of Science* 38.5 (2008): 695–735.

Funderburg, Lise. *Black, White, Other: Biracial Americans Talk about Race and Identity.* New York: Morrow, 1994.

García Coll, Cynthia, Gontran Lamberty, Renee Jenkins, Harriet Pipes McAdoo, Keith Crnic, Barbara Hanna Wasik, and Heidie Vásquez García. "An Integrative Model for the Study of Developmental Competencies in Minority Children." *Child Development* 67 (October 1996): 1891–1914.

Garduño, Everardo. *La Disputa por la Tierra . . . La Disputa por la Voz: Historia Oral del Movimiento Agrario en el Valle de Mexicali.* Mexicali: Universidad Autónoma de Baja California, 2004.

Gates, Henry Louis, Jr. "High Cheekbones and Straight Black Hair? 100 Amazing Facts about the Negro: Why Most Black People Aren't 'Part Indian,' Despite Family Lore." *Root* (April 21, 2014).

http://www.theroot.com/articles/history/2014/04/whymostblackpeoplearentpartind
iahtml.

——. "We Come from People." In *Finding Your Roots with Henry Louis Gates, Jr.* KOCE, October 28, 2014. DVD.

Geiger, Andrea. *Subverting Exclusion: Transpacific Encounters with Race, Caste and Borders, 1885–1928*. New Haven, CT: Yale University Press, 2011.

"Geinoukai wo Sekkensuru haafu Bijo" [Haafu beauties dominating show business]. *Flash* (May 8, 2007): 29–33.

Gen, Rilan. "Keshouhin Sangyo no Gyoukai Kouzou Bunseki: Michael Porter no Itsutu no Kyousou Youin Bunseki to tomoni" [An analysis of the cosmetic industry's structure: Michael Porter's analysis of five factors of industry competition]. *Gendai Shakai Bunka Kenkyuu*, no. 40 (December 2007): 89–102.

Gilroy, Paul. *The Black Atlantic: Modernity and Double-Consciousness*. Cambridge, MA: Harvard University Press, 1993.

Gladwell, Malcolm. *The Tipping Point: How Little Things Can Make a Big Difference*. New York: Little, Brown, 2000.

Glaser, Barney G., and Anselm L. Strauss. *The Discovery of Grounded Theory: Strategies for Qualitative Research*. Hawthorne, NY: Aldine de Gruyter, 1967.

Glass, Ronald David, and Kendra R. Wallace. "Challenging Race and Racism: A Framework for Educators." In Root, *Multiracial Experience*, 341–358.

Glick, Clarence E. *Sojourners and Settlers: Chinese Migrants in Hawaii*. Honolulu: University of Hawaiʻi Press, 1980.

Gobineau, Arthur, Comte de. *The Inequality of Races*. 1853–1855. Reprint, New York: Howard Fertig, 2010.

Golash-Boza, Tanya. "Dropping the Hyphen? Becoming Latino(a)-American through Racialized Assimilation." *Social Forces* 85.1 (2006): 27–56.

Golash-Boza, Tanya Maria, and Pierrette Hondagneu-Sotelo. "Latino Immigrant Men and the Deportation Crisis: A Gendered Racial Removal Program." *Latino Studies* 11.3 (2013): 271–292.

Gómez, Laura E. *Manifest Destinies: The Making of the Mexican American Race*. New York: New York University Press, 2007.

Gómez Estrada, José Alfredo. *La Gente del delta del Rio Colorado: Indigenas, colonizadores y ejidatarios*. Mexicali: Universidad Autonoma de Baja California, 2000.

Gómez Izquierdo, José. *El Movimiento Antichino en México 1871–1934: Problemas del Racismo y del Nacionalismo Durante la Revolución Mexicana*. Mexico City: Instituto Nacional de Antropología e Historia, 1991.

González, Anita. *Afro-Mexico: Dancing between Myth and Reality*. Austin: University of Texas Press, 2010.

Gonzalez, Cruz Edith. "La Inversión Francesa en la Minería Durante el Porfiriato." Thesis, Universidad Veracruzana, Xalapa, Veracruz, 1985.

González, Freddie. "Chinese Dragon and Eagle of Anahuac: The Local, National, and International Implications of the Ensenada Anti-Chinese Campaign of 1934." *Western Historical Quarterly* 44.1 (2013): 48–68.

González, Gilbert G. *Labor and Community: Mexican Citrus Worker Villages in Southern California County 1890–1950*. Chicago: University of Illinois Press, 1994.

Gonzalez, Juan. *Harvest of Empire: A History of Latinos in America*. New York: Viking, 2000.

Gordon, Lewis. *Her Majesty's Other Children: Sketches of Racism from a Neocolonial Age*. Lanham, MD: Rowman & Littlefield, 1997.

Gordon-Reed, Annette. *The Hemingses of Monticello: An American Family*. New York: Norton, 2008.

Gould, Stephen Jay. *The Mismeasure of Man*. Rev. ed. New York: Norton, 1996.

Grant, Madison. *The Passing of the Great Race; or, The Racial Basis of European History*. New York: Charles Scribner's Sons, 1916.

"A Great Golfer, but One Poor Role Model." *Philadelphia Tribune* (December 20, 2009), 12A.

Greely, Henry T. "Genetic Genealogy: Genetics Meets the Marketplace." In Keonig, Lee, and Richardson, *Revisiting Race in a Genomic Age*, 215–223.

Green, Michael Cullen. *Black Yanks in the Pacific: Race in the Making of American Military Empire after World War II*. Ithaca, NY: Cornell University Press, 2010.

Green, Richard, Johannes Krause, Adrian W. Briggs, Tomislav Maricic, Udo Stenzel, Martin Kircher, et al. "A Draft Sequence of the Neanderthal Genome." *Science* 328 (May 7, 2010): 710–722.

Greene, Beverly. "Sturdy Bridges: The Role of African American Others in the Socialization of African American Children." *Women and Therapy* 10 (September 1990): 205–225.

Grieco, Elizabeth M., and Rachel C. Cassidy. "Overview of Race and Hispanic Origin, 2000." Vol. 8. Washington, DC: US Census Bureau, 2001.

Grillo, Trina, and Stephanie M. Wildman. "Obscuring the Importance of Race." In *Critical White Studies: Looking behind the Mirror*, ed. Richard Delgado and Jean Stefancic. Philadelphia: Temple University Press, 1997. Pp. 619–626.

Guevarra, Rudy P., Jr. *Becoming Mexipino: Multiethnic Identities and Communities in San Diego*. New Brunswick, NJ: Rutgers University Press, 2012.

———. "Burritos and *Bagoong*: Mexipinos and Multiethnic Identity in San Diego, California." In Coronado et al., *Crossing Lines*, 73–96.

Guillermo, Emil. "EMIL AMOK! Call Me Tiffany." *Filipino Express* (December 22, 1996): 11.

———. "EMIL AMOK: The First Annual Emilamok Awards." *Filipino Express* (January 4, 1998): 11.

———. "EMIL AMOK! Tiger's Bold New World." *Filipino Express* (April 27, 1997): 11.

Gupta, Akhil, and James Ferguson. "Beyond 'Culture': Space, Identity, and the Politics of Difference." *Cultural Anthropology* 7 (February 1992): 6–23.

Gutierrez, David. *Walls and Mirrors: Mexican Americans, Mexican Immigrants, and the Politics of Ethnicity*. Berkeley: University of California Press, 1995.

"Haafu Face: Be Like Rola." *RyuRyu* (September 2, 2014): 14–15.

"Haafu Face Recipe." *Bea's UP* (December 1, 2009): 55–59.

Hackett, Gail, and Angela Byars. "Social Cognitive Theory and the Career Development of African American Women." *Career Development Quarterly* 44 (June 1996): 322–339.

Haefelin, Sandora. *Haafu ga Bijin nante Mousou Desukara: Komatta Junjapa tono Tatakai no Hibi* [It is an illusion that haafu are beautiful: Struggles with the Japanese]. Tokyo: Chuoshinsho Laclef, 2012.

Haizlip, Shirlee Taylor. *The Sweeter the Juice: A Family Memoir in Black and White*. New York: Free Press, 1995.

Hall, Christine Catherine Iijima. "The Ethnic Identity of Racially Mixed People: A Study of Black-Japanese." PhD diss., University of California, Los Angeles, 1980.

Hall, Christine Iijima, and Trude Turner. "The Diversity of Biracial Individuals: Asian-White and Asian-Minority Biracial Identity." In Williams-León and Nakashima, *Sum of Our Parts*, 81–92.

Hall, Stuart. *Representation: Cultural Representations and Signifying Practices*. Newbury Park, CA: Sage, 1977.

Hamako, Eric. "Improving Anti-racist Education for Multiracial Students." PhD diss., University of Massachusetts, Amherst, 2014.

Hamann, Donald, and Linda Walker. "Music Teachers as Role Models for African American Students." *Journal of Research in Music Education* 41 (Winter 1993): 303–314.

Hammond, Michael. "The Expulsion of Neanderthals from Human Ancestry: Marcellin Boule and the Social Context of Scientific Research." *Social Studies of Science* 12.1 (1982): 4–6.

Han, Brian. "Hines Ward: The Legend Goes On." *Korea Times* (October 23, 2014).

Haney López, Ian F. *Racism on Trial: The Chicano Fight for Justice.* Cambridge, MA: Harvard University Press, 2003.

Hannula, Don. "State Indians Worse Off Than Negroes." *Seattle Times* (July 26, 1968): 9.

Haraway, Donna. "Situated Knowledges: The Science Question in Feminism and the Privilege of Partial Perspective." *Feminist Studies* 14.3 (1988): 575–599.

Hardy, Karen, Stephen Buckley, Matthew J. Collins, Almundena Estalrrich, Don Brothwell, Les Copeland, et al. "Neanderthal Medics? Evidence for Food, Cooking, and Medicinal Plants Entrapped in Dental Calculus." *Naturwissenschaften* 99.8 (2012): 617–626.

Harmon, Alexandra. *Indians in the Making: Ethnic Relations and Indian Identities around Puget Sound.* Berkeley: University of California Press, 1998.

Harris, David, and Jeremiah J. Sim. "Who Is Multiracial? Assessing the Complexity of Lived Race." *American Sociological Review* 67 (August 2002): 614–627.

Hart, John Mason. *Empire and Revolution: The Americans in Mexico since the Civil War.* Berkeley: University of California Press, 2002.

———. *Revolutionary Mexico.* Berkeley: University of California Press, 1987.

Harvey, Robert. *Insider Histories of Cartooning: Rediscovering Forgotten Famous Comics and Their Creators.* Jackson: University Press of Mississippi, 2014.

Henderson, Susie. "Tiger Woods Raised the Bar, Winnings in Sport of Golf." *Los Angeles Sentinel* (September 5, 2001): B1.

Henderson, Timothy. *The Word in the Wheat: Rosalie Evans and Agrarian Struggle in the Puebla-Tlaxcala Valley of Mexico, 1906–1927.* Durham, NC: Duke University Press, 1998.

Henry, Amanda G., Alison S. Brooks, and Dolores R. Piperno. "Microfossils in Calculus Demonstrate Consumption of Plants and Cooked Food in Neanderthal Diets." *Proceedings of the National Academy of Sciences* 108.2 (2011): 486–491.

Herman, Melissa. "Forced to Choose: Some Determinants of Racial Identification in Multiracial Adolescents." *Child Development* 75 (May 2004): 730–748.

Herrera Carrillo, Pablo. *Reconquista y Colonización del Valle de Mexicali y Otros Escritos Paralelos.* Mexicali: Universidad Autónoma de Baja California, 2002.

Herrera Lima, Fernando. "Transnational Families: Institutions of Transnational Social Space." In *New Transnational Social Spaces: International Migration and Transnational Companies in the Early Twenty-First Century,* ed. Ludger Pries. New York: Routledge, 2001. Pp. 77–93.

Hesse, Barnor. "Racialized Modernity: An Analytics of White Mythologies." *Ethnic and Racial Studies* 30.4 (2007): 643–663.

Heyman, Josiah. *Life and Labor on the Border: Working People of Northeastern Sonora, Mexico, 1886–1986.* Tucson: University of Arizona Press, 1991.

Hidalgo, Danielle Antoinette, and Carl L. Bankston. "Blurring Racial and Ethnic Boundaries in Asian American Families: Asian American Family Patterns, 1980–2005." *Journal of Family Issues* 31.3 (2010): 280–300.

Hilden, Patricia Penn. *When Nickels Were Indians: An Urban, Mixed-Blood Story.* Washington, DC: Smithsonian, 1995.

Hobbs, Allyson. *A Chosen Exile: A History of Racial Passing in American Life.* Cambridge, MA: Harvard University Press, 2014.

Hollinger, David. "The One Drop Rule & the One Hate Rule." *Daedalus* 134 (Winter 2005): 18–28.

Honig, Bonnie. *Democracy and the Foreigner.* Princeton, NJ: Princeton University Press, 2001.

hooks, bell. *Feminist Theory: From Margin to Center.* Boston: South End, 2000.

Horton, Hayward Derrick. "Racism, Whitespace, and the Rise of the Neo-Mulattoes." In Brunsma, *Mixed Messages,* 117–121.

Houston, Velina Hasu. *Tea.* New York: Dramatists Play Service, 2007.

Hubbard, Rebecca R. "Afro-German Biracial Identity Development." PhD diss., Virginia Commonwealth University, 2010.

Hu-DeHart, Evelyn. "China Towns and Borderlands: Inter-Asian Encounters in the Diaspora." *Modern Asian Studies* 46.2 (2012): 425–451.

———. "La Comunidad China." *Revista Ciguatan,* no. 17 (1988): 16.

Hughes, Diane. "Correlates of African American and Latino Parents' Messages to Children about Ethnicity and Race: A Comparative Study of Racial Socialization." *American Journal of Community Psychology* 31.1–2 (2003): 15–33.

Hughes, Diane, and Lisa Chen. "The Nature of Parents' Race-Related Communications to Children: A Developmental Perspective." In *Child Psychology: A Handbook of Contemporary Issues,* ed. Lawrence Balter and Catherins S. Tamis-LeMonda. Philadelphia: Psychology Press, 1999. Pp. 467–490.

———. "When and What Parents Tell Children about Race: An Examination of Race-Related Socialization among African American Families." *Applied Developmental Science* 1.4 (1997): 200–214.

Hughes, Diane, James Rodriguez, Emilie P. Smith, Deborah J. Johnson, Howard C. Stevenson, and Paul Spicer. "Parents' Ethnic-Racial Socialization Practices: A Review of Research and Directions for Future Study." *Developmental Psychology* 42.5 (2006): 747–770.

Hume, Bill. *Babysan: A Private Look at the Japanese Occupation.* Rutland, VT: Charles E. Tuttle, 1958.

———. *Babysan's World: The Hume'n Slant on Japan.* Rutland, VT: Charles E. Tuttle, 1959.

———. *When We Get Back Home from Japan.* 1953. Reprint, Tokyo: Koyoya, 1960.

Humes, Karen, Nicholas A. Jones, and Roberto R. Ramirez. "Overview of Race and Hispanic Origin, 2010." Washington, DC: US Census Bureau, 2011. http://www.census.gov/prod/cen2010/briefs/c2010br-02.pdf.

Hunter, Margaret L. "The Persistent Problem of Colorism: Skin Tone, Status, and Inequality." *Sociology Compass* 1 (2007): 237–254.

———. *Race, Gender and the Politics of Skin Tone.* New York: Routledge, 2005.

Hyman, Herbert. "Introduction." In Hyman and Singer, *Readings in Reference Group Theory and Research,* 3–21.

Hyman, Herbert, and Eleanor Singer, eds. *Readings in Reference Group Theory and Research.* New York: Free Press, 1968.

Ifekwunigwe, Jayne O., ed. *"Mixed Race" Studies: A Reader.* New York: Routledge, 2004.

Iguchi, Tamiki. "Kuroi Hada no Nihonjin: Yonin Musume ga Moetagiru Toki" [Black skin Japanese: Four girls in ecstasy]. *Shukan Post* (February 17, 1972): 168–172.

Ikehara, Ariko. "Black-Okinawa and the MiXtory: Production of Mixed Spaces in Okinawa." Paper, University of Southern California Sawyer Seminar, April 26, 2014.

Iwabuchi, Koichi, ed. *Haafu to ha dareka: Jinshu Konko, Media hyoushou, koushou jissen* [Who is haafu? Race mixture, media representation, negotiation]. Tokyo: Seikyuu, 2014.

———. "Haafu toiu Category nikansuru Toujisha heno Kikitorichosa" [An interview with haafu on the category of haafu]. In Iwabuchi, *Haafu to ha dareka*, 243–284.

Jackson, Kelly F., Thera Wolven, and Kimberly Aguilera. "Mixed Resilience: A Study of Multiethnic Mexican American Stress and Coping in Arizona." *Family Relations* 62 (January 2013): 212–225.

Jenkins, Richard. *Rethinking Ethnicity: Arguments and Explorations.* New York: Russell Sage Foundation, 1997.

Jiménez, Tomás R. "Negotiating Ethnic Boundaries: Multiethnic Mexican Americans and Ethnic Identity in the United States." *Ethnicities* 4.1 (2004): 75–97.

Johnson, Akemi. "The Body Politic: When US Soldiers Venture Abroad, Women's Bodies Can Become the Occupied Territories." *Nation* (April 28, 2014). http://www.thenation.com/article/179249/body-politic-when-us-soldiers-venture-abroad-womens-bodies-can-become-occupied-territ.

Johnson, Kevin R. *How Did You Get to Be Mexican? A White/Brown Man's Search for Identity.* Philadelphia: Temple University Press, 1999.

———, ed. *Mixed Race America and the Law.* New York: New York University Press, 2003.

Johnston, Marc P., and Kevin L. Nadal. "Multiracial Microaggressions: Exposing Monoracism in Everyday Life and Clinical Practice." In Sue, *Microaggressions and Marginality*, 123–144.

Jolivette, Andrew. *Louisiana Creoles: Cultural Recovery and Mixed-Race Native American Identity.* New York: Lexington Books, 2007.

———, ed. *Obama and the Biracial Factor: The Battle for a New American Majority.* Bristol: Policy Press, 2012.

Jones, Bernie D. *Fathers of Conscience: Mixed-Race Inheritance in the Antebellum South.* Athens: University of Georgia Press, 2009.

Jones, Lisa. *Bulletproof Diva: Tales of Race, Sex, and Hair.* New York: Doubleday, 1994.

Jones, Nicholas A., and Jungmiwha Bullock. "The Two or More Races Population: 2010." C2010BR-13. Washington, DC: US Census Bureau, 2012.

Jones, Nicholas A., and Amy Symens Smith. "The Two or More Races Population: 2000." November 2001. http://www.census.gov/prod/2001pubs/c2kbr01-6.pdf.

Joseph, Gilbert, and Timothy Henderson, eds. *The Mexican Reader.* Durham, NC: Duke University Press, 2000.

Joseph, Gilbert, and Daniel Nugent, eds. *Everyday Forms of State Formation: Revolution and the Negotiations of Rule in Modern Mexico.* Durham, NC: Duke University Press, 1994.

Joseph, Ralina L. *Transcending Blackness: From the New Millennium Mulatta to the Exceptional Multiracial.* Durham, NC: Duke University Press, 2012.

Kamoto, Itsuko. *Kokusaikekkon Ron?* [A theory on international marriage?]. Kyoto: Horitsu Bunkasha, 2008.

Kano, Mikiyo. "Racially Mixed Children Problems and the Creation of the Myth of the Homogeneous Nation." In *Occupation and Gender*, ed. Center for Peace and Culture Research at Keisen Women's University. Tokyo: Impact, 2007. Pp. 213–260.

Kaplan, Amy, and Donald Pease, eds. *Cultures of United States Imperialism.* Durham, NC: Duke University Press, 1994.

Katz, William Loren. *Black Indians: The Hidden Heritage.* New York: Simon & Schuster, 1985.

Keel, Terence. "Religion, Polygenism, and the Early Science of Human Origins." *History of Human Sciences* 26.2 (2013): 3–32.

Kelly, Herbert. "Two Functions of Reference Groups." In Hyman and Singer, *Readings in Reference Group Theory and Research*, 199–206.

Kelsky, Karen. *Women on the Verge: Japanese Women, Western Dreams.* Durham, NC: Duke University Press, 2001.

Kemper, Theodore. "Reference Groups, Socialization, and Achievement." In *Social Psychology: Readings and Perspectives,* ed. Edward Borgata. Chicago: Rand McNally, 1969. Pp. 297–312.

Kennedy, Randall. *Interracial Intimacies: Sex, Marriage, Identity, and Adoption.* New York: Pantheon, 2003.

Kerig, Dorothy Pierson. "Yankee Enclave: The Colorado River Land Company and Mexican Agrarian Reform in Baja California, 1902–1944." PhD diss., University of California, Irvine, 1989.

Kibria, Nazli. "Not Asian, Black, or White? Reflections on South Asian American Identity," *Amerasia Journal* 22 (1996): 77–86.

Kich, George Kitahara. "In the Margins of Sex and Race: Difference, Marginality, and Flexibility." In Root, *Multiracial Experience,* 263–276.

Kim, Mee-Ae. "Immigrants, Workers, Pioneers: The Chinese and Mexican Colonization Efforts, 1890–1930." PhD diss., Washington State University, 2000.

Kina, Laura, and Wei Ming Dariotis, eds. *War Baby/Love Child: Mixed Race Asian American Art.* Seattle: University of Washington Press, 2013.

King, Michelle, and Karen Mulron. "The Effects of Television Role Models on the Career Aspirations of African American Junior High School Students." *Journal of Career Development* 23 (Winter 1996): 111–125.

King-O'Riain, Rebecca, Stephen Small, Minelle Mahtani, Miri Song, and Paul Spickard, eds. *Global Mixed Race.* New York: New York University Press, 2014.

Kitahara-Kich, George. "Eurasians: Ethnic/Racial Identity Development of Biracial Japanese/White Adults." PhD diss., Wright Institute, 1982.

Knight, Alan. *The Mexican Revolution.* 2 vols. Cambridge: Cambridge University Press, 1986.

———. "The Working Class and the Mexican Revolution, c. 1900–1920." *Journal of Latin American Studies* 16 (1984): 51–79.

Koenig, Barbara A., Sandra Soo-Jin Lee, and Sarah S. Richardson, eds. *Revisiting Race in a Genomic Age.* New Brunswick, NJ: Rutgers University Press, 2008.

Kozawa, Hiroshi. "Suterareta konketsu no ko" [Abandoned mixed blood children]. *Asahi Gurafu* [Asahi Picture News] (August 4, 1957): 8–9.

Kozeki, Keiko. *Nihonnjinn Keiko: Aru Konketuji no Shuki* [Japanese Keiko: A memoir of a racially mixed girl]. Tokyo: Horupu, 1980.

Krause, Johannes, Carles Lalueza-Fox, Ludovic Orlando, Wolfgang Enard, Richard E. Green, Hernán A. Burbano, et al. "The Derived FOXP2 Variant of Modern Humans Was Shared with Neanderthals." *Current Biology* 17 (November 2007): 1–4.

Lacy, Tim. "Another Viewpoint: 'The New Kid.'" *Afro-American* (April 1, 2006): B8.

———. "The Masters Tournament." *Afro-American Red Star* (April 5, 2008): C7.

"Latest Wood's Drama Affecting Money, Re-opening Race Dialogue within Black Community." *Jacksonville Free Press* (December 10, 2009): 5.

Lazarre, Jane. *Beyond the Whiteness of Whiteness: Memoir of a White Mother of Black Sons.* Durham, NC: Duke University Press, 1996.

Ledward, Brandon. "On Being Hawaiian Enough: Contesting American Racialization with Native Hybridity." *Hulili: Multidisciplinary Research on Hawaiian Well-Being* 4.1 (2007): 107–143.

Lee, Erika. *At America's Gates: Chinese Immigration during the Exclusion Era, 1882–1943.* Chapel Hill: University of North Carolina Press, 2003.

———. "The Yellow Peril: Asian Exclusion in the Americas." *Pacific Historical Review* 76.4 (2007): 537–562.

Lee, Jennifer, and Frank D. Bean. "America's Changing Color Lines: Immigration, Race/Ethnicity, and Multiracial Identification." *Annual Review of Sociology* 30 (2004): 221–242.

———. *The Diversity Paradox: Immigration and the Color Line in Twenty-First Century America.* New York: Russell Sage Foundation, 2010.

———. "Reinventing the Color Line: Immigration and America's New Racial/Ethnic Divide." *Social Forces* 86.2 (2007): 561–586.

Lee, K. W. "Arirang Passage: New Ethnic Americans." *Korea Times* (February 25, 1997): 12.

Lee, Sharon, and Barry Edmonston. "Hispanic Intermarriage, Identification, and U.S. Latino Population Change." *Social Science Quarterly* 87.5 (2006): 1263–1279.

Lee, Traci G. "Biracial Miss Universe Japan Faces Backlash." *MSNBC* (March 26, 2015), http://www.msnbc.com/msnbc/biracial-miss-universe-japan-faces-backlash.

Lee Mancilla, Manuel. *Viaje al Corazón de La Península: Testimonio de Manuel Lee Mancilla.* Mexicali: Instituto de la Cultura de Baja California, 2000.

Leksander, Susan. "Psychosynthesis and Multiracial Clients: Diversity and Integration of Multiple Selves." San Francisco: California Institute of Integral Studies, 2007.

Leonard, Karen I. *Making Ethnic Choices: California's Punjabi Mexican Americans.* Philadelphia: Temple University Press, 1992.

Lesane-Brown, Chase L. "A Review of Race Socialization within Black Families." *Developmental Review* 26.4 (2006): 400–426.

Leslie, Kent Anderson. *Woman of Color, Daughter of Privilege: Amanda America Dickson, 1949–1893.* Athens: University of Georgia Press, 1995.

Lim, Julia. "Chinos and Paisanos: Chinese Mexican Relations in the Borderlands." *Pacific Historical Review* 79.19 (2010): 50–85.

Lin, Monica, Virginia Kwan, Anna Cheung, and Susan Fiske. "Stereotype Content Model Explains Prejudice for an Envied Outgroup: Scale of Anti-Asian American Stereotypes." *Personality and Social Psychology Bulletin* 31 (January 2005): 34–47.

Linnaeus, Carolus. *Systema naturae per regna tria naturae, secundum classes, orgines, genera, species, cum characteribus, differentiis, synonymis.* Stockholm: Holmiae, 1758.

Littke, Jim. "Tiger Woods: Just a Young Black Man in a Green Jacket." *Los Angeles Sentinel* (April 23, 1997): A3.

Lomawaima, K. Tsianina. *They Called It Prairie Light: The Story of Chilocco Indian School.* Lincoln: University of Nebraska Press, 1995.

López Turley, Ruth N. "When Do Neighborhoods Matter? The Role of Race and Neighborhood Peers." *Social Science Research* 32 (March 2003): 61–79.

Lorey, E. David, ed. *United States-Mexico Border Statistics since 1900.* Los Angeles: UCLA Latin American Center, 1990.

———. *The U.S.–Mexico Border in the 20th Century.* Wilmington, DE: Scholarly Resources, 1999.

Magaña, Mario Alberto. *China en las Californias.* Consejo Nacional para la Cultura y las Artes. Tijuana: CONACULTA, 2001.

Mahtani, Minelle. *Mixed Race Amnesia: Resisting the Romanticization of Multiraciality.* Vancouver: University of British Columbia Press, 2014.

Makalani, Minkah. "Rejecting Blackness and Claiming Whiteness: Antiblack Whiteness in the Biracial Project." In *White Out: The Continuing Significance of Racism*, ed. Ashley Doane and Eduardo Bonilla-Silva. New York: Routledge, 2003. Pp. 81–94.

Mann, Eberhard, and J. A. Waldron. "Intercultural Marriage and Child Rearing." In *Adjustment in Intercultural Marriage*, ed. John F. McDermott, Wen-Shing Tseng, and Thomas Maretzki. Honolulu: University of Hawai'i Press, 1977. Pp. 62–80.

Marbury, Ja'Nitta. "Racial Socialization of Biracial Adolescents." PhD diss., Kent State University, 2006.

Markovitis, Claude. "Afterword: Stray Thoughts of a Historian on 'Indian' or 'South Asian' Diaspora(s)." In *Global Indian Diasporas: Exploring Trajectories of Migration and Theory*, ed. Gijsbert Oonk. Amsterdam: Amsterdam University Press, 2007. Pp. 263–274.

Marks, Jonathan. *Human Biodiversity: Genes, Race, and History*. New York: Aldine de Gruyter, 1995.

Marquez, John. *Black-Brown Solidarity: Racial Politics in the New Gulf South*. Austin: University of Texas Press, 2013.

Marr, Carolyn J. "Assimilation through Education: Indian Boarding Schools in the Pacific Northwest." University of Washington Digital Collections, n.d. https://content.lib .washington.edu/aipnw/marr.html#bibliography.

Marriott, Michel. "Multiracial Americans Ready to Claim Their Own Identity." *New York Times* (July 20, 1996): A1.

Marterso, Daniel, with Funada-Classen. *The Japanese in Latin America*. Urbana: University of Illinois Press, 2004.

Martínez, María Elena. *Genealogical Fictions: Limpieza de Sangre, Religion and Gender in Colonial Mexico*. Palo Alto, CA: Stanford University Press, 2008.

Martinez, Oscar. *Border Boom Town: Ciudad Juarez since 1848*. Austin: University of Texas Press, 1978.

———. *Fragments of the Mexican Revolution: Personal Account from the Border*. Albuquerque: University of New Mexico Press, 1984.

———, ed. *U.S.-Mexico Borderlands: Historical and Contemporary Perspectives*. Wilmington, DE: Jaguar Books on Latin America, 1996.

Mason, Jennifer. *Qualitative Researching*. London: Sage, 2002.

Matthews, Julie. "Eurasian Persuasions: Mixed Race, Performativity and Cosmopolitanism." *Journal of Intercultural Studies* 28.1 (2007): 41–54.

McBride, James. *The Color of Water: A Black Man's Tribute to His White Mother*. New York: Riverhead, 1996.

McClurg, Laurie. "Biracial Youth and Their Parents: Counseling Considerations for Family Therapists." *Family Journal* 12.2 (2004): 170–173.

McIntosh, Peggy. "White Privilege: Unpacking the Invisible Knapsack." In *Race, Class, and Gender in the United States*, ed. Paula Rothenberg. New York: Macmillan, 1988. Pp. 188–192.

McKelvey, Robert S. *Dust of Life: America's Children Abandoned in Vietnam*. Seattle: University of Washington Press, 1999.

McNeil, Baye. "Meeting Miss Universe Japan, the Half Who Has It All." *Japan Times* (April 19, 2015). http://www.japantimes.co.jp/community/2015/04/19/general/meeting -miss-universe-japan.

McWilliams, Carey. "Introduction." In *America Is in the Heart*, by Carlos Bulosan. 1946. Reprint, Seattle: University of Washington Press, 1973. Pp. vii–24.

Memmi, Albert. *The Colonizer and the Colonized*. Boston: Beacon Press, 1967.

Mendoza Stickmon, Janet C. "Barack Obama: Embracing Multiplicity—Being a Catalyst for Change." In Daniel and Williams, *Race and the Obama Phenomenon*, 62–83.

———. *Crushing Soft Rubies—A Memoir*. Oakland: Broken Shackle, 2014.

Menjívar, Cecilia. "Liminal Legality: Salvadoran and Guatemalan Immigrants' Lives in the United States." *American Journal of Sociology* 11 (January 2006): 999–1037.

Menjívar, Cecilia, and Leisy J. Abrego. "Legal Violence: Immigration Law and the Lives of Central American Immigrants." *American Journal of Sociology* 117.5 (2012): 1380–1421.

Menon, Sridevi. "Disrupting Asian America: South Asian American Heritage as Strategic Sites of Narration." *Alternatives: Global, Local, Political* 31 (July–September 2006): 345–366.

Merton, Robert K. "Continuities in the Theory of Reference Groups and Social Structure." In Merton, *Social Theory and Social Structure*, 335–440.

———, ed. *Social Theory and Social Structure*. New York: Free Press, 1968.

Merton, Robert K., and A. S. Kitt. "Contributions to the Theory of Reference Group Behavior." In *Studies in the Scope and Method of the American Soldier*, ed. Robert Merton and Paul Lazarsfeld. Glencoe, IL: Free Press, 1950. Pp. 40–106.

Merton, Robert K., and Alice S. Rossi. "Contributions to the Theory of Reference Group Behavior." In Merton, *Social Theory and Social Structure*, 279–335.

Meyer, Matthias, Marie-Theres Gansauge, Heng Li, Fernando Racimo, Swapan Mallick, Joshua G. Schraiber, et al. "A High-Coverage Genome Sequence from an Archaic Denisovan Individual." *Science* 338.6104 (2012): 222–226.

Miller, Natalie Maya, and Marcia Yumi Lise. *The Hafu Project*. Japan: Hafu Project, 2010.

Miller-Young, Mireille. "Hip-Hop Honeys and Da Hustlaz: Black Sexualities and the New Hip-Hop Pornography." *Meridians: Feminism, Race, Transnationalism* 8 (2008): 261–292.

Mitarai, Rocky Kiyoshi. "Hate Crime in Japantown." *Mavin* 1.3 (1999): 41–42.

Mitchell, Stephanie, and Patience Schell, eds. *The Women's Revolution in Mexico, 1910–1953*. Lanham, MD: Rowman & Littlefield, 2007.

Mizuo, Junichi. *Keshohin no Brandoshi: Bunmeikaika kara Global marketing e* [Brand history of cosmetics: From Westernization to global marketing]. Tokyo: Chuko Shinsho, 1998.

Modleski, Tania. *Feminism without Women: Culture and Criticism in a "Postfeminist" Age*. New York: Routledge, 1991.

———. *Old Wives' Tales and Other Women's Stories*. New York: New York University Press, 1998.

Montagu, Ashley. *A Statement on Race: An Extended Discussion in Plain Language of the UNESCO Statement by Experts on Race Problems*. New York: Henry Schuman, 1951.

Moran, Rachel F. *Interracial Intimacy: The Regulation of Race and Romance*. Chicago: University of Chicago Press, 2001.

Morrow, Curtis James. *What's a Commie Ever Done to Black People? A Korean War Memoir of Fighting in the U.S. Army's Last All Negro Unit*. Jefferson, NC: McFarland, 1997.

Moser, Don. "Japan's G.I. Babies: A Hard Coming-of-Age." *Life Magazine* (September 5, 1969): 40–47.

Mukazhanova, Karina. "The Politics of Multiple Identities in Kazakhstan." In *Multiple Identities: Migrants, Ethnicity, and Membership*, ed. Paul Spickard. Bloomington: Indiana University Press, 2013. Pp. 265–289.

Mumford, Esther Hall. *Seattle's Black Victorians, 1852–1901*. Seattle: Ananse Press, 1980.

Mumford, Kevin J. *Interzones: Black/White Sex Districts in Chicago and New York in the Early Twentieth Century*. New York: Columbia University Press, 1997.

Murguia, Edward. *Chicano Intermarriage: A Theoretical and Empirical Study*. San Antonio, TX: Trinity University Press, 1982.

Murphy-Shigematsu, Stephen. *Amerajian no Kodomotachi: Shirarezaru Mainority Mondai* [Amerasian children: Unknown minority problems]. Trans. Junko Sakai. Tokyo: Shueisha, 2002.

———. "The Voices of Amerasians: Ethnicity, Identity and Empowerment in Interracial Japanese Americans." EdD diss., Harvard University, 1986.

———. *When Half Is Whole: Multiethnic Asian American Identities*. Stanford, CA: Stanford University Press, 2012.

Murray, Carolyn B., Julie E. Stokes, and Jean Peacock. "Racial Socialization of African American Children: A Review." In *African American Children, Youth and Parenting*, ed. R. L. Jones. Hampton, VA: Cobb and Henry, 1999. Pp. 209–230.

Nadal, Kevin L., Marie-Anne Issa, Katie E. Griffin, Sahran Hamit, and Oliver B. Lyons. "Religious Microaggressions in the United States: Mental Health Implications for Religious Minority Groups." In Sue, *Microaggressions and Marginality*, 287–312.

Nadal, Kevin L., Julie Sriken, Kristin C. Davidoff, Yinglee Wong, and Kathryn McLean. "Microaggressions within Families: Experiences of Multiracial People." *Family Relations* 62.1 (2013): 190–201.

Nadal, Kevin L., Yinglee Wong, Katie Griffin, Julie Sriken, Vivian Vargas, Michelle Wideman, and Ajayi Kolawole. "Microaggressions and the Multiracial Experience." *International Journal of Humanities and Social Science* 7 (June 2011): 36–44.

Nagle, Jill. "Framing Radical Bisexuality: Toward a Gender Agenda." In *Bisexual Politics: Theories, Queries and Visions*, ed. Naomi Tucker. Binghamton, NY: Haworth Press, 1995. Pp. 305–314.

Nakashima, Cynthia L. "An Invisible Monster: The Creation and Denial of Mixed-Race People in America." In Root, *Racially Mixed People in America*, 162–178.

———. "Servants of Culture: The Symbolic Role of Mixed-Race Asians in American Discourse." In Williams-León and Nakashima, *Sum of Our Parts*, 35–48.

Nakashima Brock, Rita. "Cooking without Recipes—Interstitial Integrity." In *Off the Menu—Asian and Asian North American Women's Religion and Theology*, ed. Rita Nakashima Brock, Jung Ha Kim, Kwok Pui-lan, and Seung Ai Yang. Louisville: Westminster John Knox Press, 2007. Pp. 125–144.

Nash, Gary B. *Forbidden Love: The Secret History of Mixed-Race America*. New York: Holt, 1999.

———. *Red, White and Black: The Peoples of Early America*. Englewood Cliffs, NJ: Prentice Hall, 1974.

National Institute of Population and Social Security Research. *Jinko no Doko: Nihon to Sekai Jinkoutoukei Shiryoshu 2015* [Demography trend: Japan and the world 2015]. Tokyo: Kosekitokei Kyokai, 2015.

Navarro, Mireya. "When You Contain Multitudes." *New York Times* (April 24, 2005): A1.

Nemoto, Kumiko. *Racing Romance: Love, Power, and Desire among Asian American/White Couples*. New Brunswick, NJ: Rutgers University Press, 2009.

"Newly Crowned Miss Universe Is One-Quarter Korean." *Korea Times* (June 24, 1997): 32.

Nicoli, José Patricio. *El Estado de Sonora: Yaquis y Mayos*. Mexico City: Imprenta de Francisco Díaz de León, 1885.

Nittono, Hiroshi. "Kawaii ni taisuru Koudoukagakuteki Apurochi" [A behavioral science approach to kawaii]. *Ningenkagaku Kenkyu* 4 (2009): 19–35.

Nobles, Wade. *Seeking the Sakhu: Foundational Writings for an African Psychology*. Chicago: Third World Press, 2006.

Obama, Barack. *Dreams from My Father: A Story of Race and Inheritance*. Tokyo: Kodansha, 1995.

Ocampo, Anthony C. "Are Second-Generation Filipinos 'Becoming' Asian American or Latino? Historical Colonialism, Culture and Panethnicity." *Ethnic and Racial Studies* 37.3 (2014): 425–445.

Olcott, Jocelyn. *Revolutionary Women in Post Revolutionary Mexico*. Durham, NC: Duke University Press, 2005.

Olcott, Jocelyn, Mary Kay Vaughan, and Ana Gabriela Cano, eds. *Sex in Revolution: Gender, Politics, and Power in Modern Mexico*. Durham, NC: Duke University Press, 2006.

Olumide, Jill. *Raiding the Gene Pool: The Social Construction of Mixed Race*. London: Pluto Press, 2002.

Omi, Michael, and Howard Winant. *Racial Formation in the United States: From the 1960s to the 1990s*. 2nd ed. New York: Routledge, 1994.

——. *Racial Formation in the United States.* 3rd ed. New York: Routledge, 2014.

Ong, Aihwa. *Buddha Is Hiding: Refugees, Citizenship, the New America.* Berkeley: University of California Press, 2003.

——. *Flexible Citizenship: The Cultural Logics of Transnationality.* Durham, NC: Duke University Press, 1999.

Ota Mishima, María Helena. *Siete Migraciones Japonesas en México 1890–1978.* Mexico City: El Colegio de México, 1982.

Paabo, Svante. *Neanderthal Man: In Search of Lost Genomes.* New York: Basic Books, 2014.

Pal, Adesh, ed. *Contextualizing Nationalism.* New Delhi: Creative Books, 2010.

Papagianni, Dimitra, and Michael A. Morse. *The Neanderthals Rediscovered: How Modern Science Is Rewriting Their Story.* New York: Thames & Hudson, 2013.

Parmasad, Ken. "Searching for Continuity: The Ancestral Impulse and Community Identity Formation in Trinidad." *Caribbean Quarterly* 30 (September–December 1994): 22–29.

Passel, Jeffrey S., Gretchen Livingston, and D'Vera Cohn. "Explaining Why Minority Births Now Outnumber White Births." Washington, DC: Pew Research Center, May 17, 2012. http://www.pewsocialtrends.org/2012/05/17/explaining-why-minority-births-now-outnumber-white-births/.

Payne, Les. "Who Would Qualify for Slavery Reparations?" *Jacksonville Free Press* (August 9, 2007): 4.

Peña Delgado, Grace. *Making the Chinese Mexican: Global Migrations, Localisms and Exclusion in the Mexico-U.S. Borderlands.* Stanford, CA: Stanford University Press, 2012.

Perdue, Theda. *"Mixed Blood" Indians: Racial Construction in the Early South.* Athens: University of Georgia Press, 2010.

——. "Native Americans, African Americans and Jim Crow." In Tayac, *IndiVisible*, 21–33.

Petersen, William. "Success Story, Japanese-American Style." *New York Times Magazine* (January 9, 1966): 180.

Peterson-Renault, Melissa. "'Makah': Melissa Peterson and the Makah Cultural and Research Center." In *Native People of the Olympic Peninsula: Who We Are, by the Olympic Peninsula Intertribal Cultural Advisory Committee*, ed. Jacilee Wray. Norman: University of Oklahoma Press, 2002. Pp. 151–167.

Pew Research Center. "Multiracial in America: Proud, Diverse and Growing in Numbers." June 11, 2015. http://www.pewsocialtrends.org/2015/06/11/multiracial-in-america/.

Philips, A. Denis. "El Moviemiento Anti-Chino in Sonora, Mexico." *Ethnohistory* 26.1 (1979): 65–80.

Pierce, Chester M. "Is Bigotry the Basis of the Medical Problems of the Ghetto?" In *Medicine in the Ghetto*, ed. John C. Norman. New York: Meredith, 1969. Pp. 301–314.

Pierce, Lori. "Six Queens: Miss Ka Palapala and Interracial Beauty in Territorial Hawai'i." In Kina and Dariotis, *War Baby/Love Child*, 111–115.

Pieterse, Jan Nederveen. *White on Black: Images of Africa and Blacks in Western Popular Culture.* New Haven, CT: Yale University Press, 1995.

Pleiss, Mary, and John Feldhusen. "Mentors, Role Models, and Heroes in the Lives of Gifted Children." *Educational Psychologist* 30 (Summer 1995): 159–169.

Portes, Alejandro, and Rubén G. Rumbaut. *Legacies: The Story of the Immigrant Second Generation.* Berkeley: University of California Press, 2001.

Prashad, Vijay. *Everybody Was Kung Fu Fighting: Afro-Asian Connections and the Myth of Cultural Purity.* Boston: Beacon Press, 2001.

Privat, Karen L., Tamsin O'Connell, and Michael Richards. "Stable Isotope Analysis of Human and Faunal Remains from the Anglo-Saxon Cemetery at Berinsfield, Oxfordshire: Dietary and Social Implication." *Journal of Archaeological Science* 29 (2002): 779–790.

Prufer, Kay, Fernando Racimo, Nick Patterson, Flora Jay, Sriram Sankararaman, Susanna Swayer, et al. "The Complete Sequence of a Neanderthal from the Altai Mountains." *Nature* 505 (January 2014): 45.

Pulido, Laura. *Black, Brown, Yellow and Left: Radical Activism in Los Angeles.* Berkeley: University of California Press, 2006.

Purkayastha, Bandana. *Negotiating Ethnicity: Second-Generation South Asian Americans Traverse a Transnational World.* New Brunswick, NJ: Rutgers University Press, 2005.

Qian, Zhenchao, and José A. Cobas. "Latinos' Mate Selection: National Origin, Racial, and Nativity Differences." *Social Science Research* 33.2 (2004): 225–247.

Ragaza, Angelo. "Service with a Style." *A Magazine* (September 30, 1997): 13.

Ramírez, Horacio R. "Borderlands, Diasporas, and Transnational Crossings: Teaching LGBT Latina and Latino histories." *OAH Magazine of History* 20 (March 2006): 39–42.

Raphael-Hernandez, Heike, and Shannon Steen, eds. *AfroAsian Encounters: Culture, History, Politics.* New York: New York University Press, 2006.

Rastogi, Sonya, Tallese D. Johnson, Elizabeth M. Hoeffel, and Malcolm P. Drewery Jr. "The Black Population: 2010." http://www.census.gov/prod/cen2010/briefs/c2010br-06.pdf.

Regis, Humphrey. "Mass Communication and Cultural Domination: The Reimportation/Reexportation Framework." *Journal of African Communications, Special Monograph Edition* 6 (2004): 3–67.

Rendu, William, Cédric Beauval, Isabel Crevecoeur, Priscilla Bayle, Antoine Balzeau, Thierry Bismuth, et al. "Evidence Supporting an Intentional Neanderthal Burial at La Chapelle-aux-Saints." *Proceedings of the National Academy of Sciences of the United States of America* 111.1 (January 2014): 81–86.

Rénique, Gerardo. "Race, Region, and Nation: Sonora's Anti-Chinese Racism and Mexico's Postrevolutionary Nationalism, 1920s–1930s." In *Race and Nation in Modern Latin America*, ed. Nancy P. Appelbaum, Anne S. McPherson, and Karin Alejandra Rosenblatt. Chapel Hill: University of North Carolina Press, 2003. Pp. 211–236.

Renker, Ann M. "Makah Tribe: People of the Sea and the Forest." University of Washington Digital Collections, n.d. https://content.lib.washington.edu/aipnw/renker.html.

Reuter, Edward Byron. *The Mulatto in the United States, Including a Study of the Role of Mixed-Blood Races throughout the World.* 1918. Reprint, New York: Negro Universities Press, 1969.

———. *Race Mixture: Studies in Intermarriage and Miscegenation.* 1918. Reprint, New York: Negro Universities Press, 1969.

Revoyr, Nina. *Southland.* New York: Akashic, 2003.

Richeson, Jennifer, and Maureen Craig. "Intra-minority Intergroup Relations in the Twenty-First Century." *Daedalus* 140 (February 2011): 166–175.

Rivas Hernandez, Ignacio. "La Industria." In *Historia General de Baja California Sur I. La Economia Regional*, ed. Deni Trejo Barajas and Edith Gonzalez Cruz. La Paz: Universidad Autónoma de Baja California, 2002. Pp. 287–326.

Roberts, Dorothy. *Killing the Black Body: Race, Reproduction, and the Meaning of Liberty.* New York: Vintage, 1999.

Roberts, Sam. "Minorities in the US Set to Become Majority by 2042." *New York Times* (August 14, 2008).

Robinson, Greg. "The Early History of Mixed-Race Japanese Americans." In Williams, *Hapa Japan*, vol. 1.

Rockquemore, Kerry Ann. "Negotiating the Color-Line: The Gendered Process of Racial Identity among Black/White Multiracial Women." *Gender and Society* 16 (August 2002): 485–503.

Rockquemore, Kerry Ann, and David L. Brunsma. *Beyond Black: Biracial Identity in America.* Lanham, MD: Rowman & Littlefield, 2002.

Rockquemore, Kerry Ann, David L. Brunsma, and Daniel Delgado. "Racing to Theory or Retheorizing Race? Understanding the Struggle to Build a Multiracial Identity Theory." *Journal of Social Issues* 65 (2009): 13–34.

Rockquemore, Kerry Ann, and Tracey A. Laszloffy. *Raising Biracial Children.* Lanham, MD: AltaMira, 2005.

Rodríguez, Abelardo. *Memoria Administrativa. Del Gobierno del Distrito Norte de la Baja California 1924–1927.* 1927. Reprint, Mexico City: Universidad Autónoma de Baja California, 1993.

Rodríguez, Clara E. *Changing Race: Latinos, the Census, and the History of Ethnicity in the United States.* New York: New York University Press, 2000.

Rodriguez, Gregory. "The Nation: Who Are You?" *New York Times* (June 3, 2001).

Rodriguez-Vidal, Joaquin, Francisco d'Errico, Francisco Giles Pacheco, Ruth Blasco, Jordi Rosell, Richard P. Jennings, et al. "A Rock Engraving Made by Neanderthals in Gibraltar." *Proceedings of the National Academy of Sciences of the United States of America* 111.37 (2014): 13301–13306.

Romero, Robert Chao. *The Chinese in Mexico.* Tucson: University of Arizona Press, 2010.

Romo, Rebecca. "Blaxican Identity: An Exploratory Study of Blacks/Chicanas/os in California." Paper, National Association for Chicana and Chicano Studies Annual Conference, San Jose, CA, 2008.

Rondilla, Joanne L., and Paul Spickard. *Is Lighter Better? Skin-Tone Discrimination among Asian Americans.* Lanham, MD: Rowman & Littlefield, 2007.

Rooks, Curtiss Takada. "On Being Japanese American." *Discover Nikkei* (October 26, 2007). http://www.discovernikkei.org/en/journal/2007/10/26/on-being-japanese-american/.

Root, Maria P. P. "A Bill of Rights for Racially Mixed People." In Root, *Multiracial Experience*, 3–14.

———. "Experiences and Processes Affecting Racial Identity Development: Preliminary Results from the Biracial Sibling Project." *Cultural Diversity and Mental Health* 4.3 (1998): 237–247.

———. "Factors Influencing the Variation in Racial and Ethnic Identity of Mixed-Heritage persons of Asian Ancestry." In Williams-León and Nakashima, *Sum of Our Parts*, 61–70.

———. *Love's Revolution: Interracial Marriage.* Philadelphia: Temple University Press, 2001.

———, ed. *The Multiracial Experience: Racial Borders as the New Frontier.* Thousand Oaks, CA: Sage, 1996.

———, ed. *Racially Mixed People in America.* Newbury Park, CA: Sage, 1992.

Root, Maria P. P., and Matt Kelly, eds. *Multiracial Child Resource Book: Living Complex Identities.* Seattle: MAVIN Foundation, 2003.

Rosaldo, Renato. *Culture and Truth: The Remaking of Social Analysis.* Boston: Beacon Press, 1993.

Rosenfeld, Michael J., and Byung-Soo Kim. "The Independence of Young Adults and the Rise of Interracial and Same-Sex Unions." *American Sociological Review* 70.4 (2005): 541–562.

Roth, Philip. *The Human Stain.* New York: Houghton Mifflin, 2000.

Roth, Wendy D. "The End of the One-Drop Rule? Labeling of Multiracial Children in Black Intermarriages." Paper, Sociological Forum, 2005.

Ruebens, Karen. "Regional Behavior among Late Neanderthal Groups in Western Europe: A Comparative Assessment of Late Middle Paleolithic Bifacial Tool Variability." *Journal of Human Evolution* 64.4 (October 2013): 341–362.

Ruiz, Ramón. *The People of Sonora and Yankee Capitalists.* Tucson: University of Arizona Press, 1988.

Ruiz, Vicki. "Citizen Restaurant: American Imaginaries, American Communities." *American Quarterly* 60.1 (2008).

———. *From Out of the Shadows: Mexican Women in Twentieth-Century America*. New York: Oxford University Press, 1998.

Russell, John. *Nihonjin no Kokujinkan: Mondai ha Chibikuro Sambo dakedehanai* [Japanese perception of Black people: A problem is not only Chibikuro Sambo]. Tokyo: Shinhyoron, 1991.

Said, Edward. *Orientalism*. New York: Random House, 1978.

Sanchez, George J. *Becoming Mexican American: Ethnicity, Culture, and Identity in Chicano Los Angeles, 1900–1945*. New York: Oxford University Press, 1993.

Sankararaman, Sriram, Swapan Mallick, Michael Dannemann, Kay Prüfer, Janet Kelso, Svante Pääbo, Nick Patterson, and David Reich. "The Genomic Landscape of Neanderthal Ancestry in Present-Day Humans." *Nature* 507 (March 2014): 354–357.

Saunt, Claudio. *Black, White, Indian: Race and the Unmaking of an American Family*. New York: Oxford University Press, 2005.

Sawada, Miki. *Haha to ko no kizuna erizabesu sandazu homu no san ju nen* [A bond between a mother and a child: Thirty years of the Elizabeth Saunders home]. Kyoto: PHP Kenkyujo, 1980.

Schantz, Eric. "From the Mexicali Rose to the Tijuana Brass: Vice Tours of the United States-Mexico Border 1910–1965." PhD diss., University of California, Los Angeles, 2001.

Schiavone Camacho, Julia María. *Chinese Mexicans: Transpacific Migrations and the Search for a Homeland 1910–1960*. Chapel Hill: University of North Carolina Press, 2012.

———. "Crossing Boundaries, Claiming a Homeland: The Mexican Chinese Transpacific Journey to Becoming Mexican, 1930–1960." *Pacific Historical Review* 78.4 (2009): 245–577.

Schirmer, Daniel, and Stephen Shalom, eds. *The Philippines Reader*. Boston: South End, 1987.

Schoeller, Martin, photographer. "The Changing Face of America." *National Geographic* (2013). http://ngm.nationalgeographic.com/2013/10/changing-faces/schoeller-photography.

Schrenk, Friedemann, and Stephanie Muller. *The Neanderthals*. New York: Routledge, 2009.

Scott, Shaun, producer and director. "The End of Old Days." Seattle Civil Rights & Labor History Project, January 3, 2015. http://depts.washington.edu/civilr/film_end_days.htm.

Secretaria de Economía. *Compendio Estadístico México: Dirección General de Estadística*. 1948.

———. *Séptimo Censo General de Población*. *México: Dirección General de Estadística*. 1950.

Segura, Dense, and Patricia Zavella, eds. *Women and Migration in the U.S. Mexico Borderlands*. Durham, NC: Duke University Press, 2007.

Senna, Danzy. *Caucasia*. New York: Riverhead, 1998.

Sexton, Jared. *Amalgamation Schemes: Antiblackness and the Critique of Multiracialism*. Minneapolis: University of Minnesota Press, 2008.

Shah, Hemant, and Michael Thornton. *Newspaper Coverage of Interethnic Conflict: Competing Visions of America*. Thousand Oaks, CA: Sage, 2004.

Sharfstein, Daniel J. *The Invisible Line: Three American Families and the Secret Journey from Black to White*. New York: Penguin, 2011.

Sharma, Nitasha. "Pacific Revisions of Blackness: Blacks Address Race and Belonging in Hawai'i." *Amerasia Journal* 37.3 (2011): 43–60.

Sharpley-Whiting, Tracy Denean. *Pimps Up, Ho's Down: Hip Hop's Hold on Young Black Women*. New York: New York University Press, 2007.

Shiao, Jiannbin Lee, and Mia H. Tuan. "'Some Asian Men Are Attractive to Me, but for a Husband . . .': Korean Adoptees and the Salience of Race in Romance." *Du Bois Review* 5.2 (2008): 259–285.

Shima, Miruo. "Haafu Tarento tairyo hassei no Naze" [Why are there so many haafu celebrities in show business?]. February 14, 2012. http://news.livedoor.com/article/detail/6277751/.

Shipek, Florence C., ed. *Autobiography of Delfina Cuero.* Menlo Park, CA: Ballenas Press, 1991.

Singh, Anand. "South African Indian Migration in the Twenty-First Century: Towards a Theory of 'Triple Identity.'" *Asian Identity* 9 (June 2008): 5–16.

Singh, Pritam, and Shinder S. Thandi, eds. *Punjabi Identity in a Global Context.* 2nd ed. New Delhi: Oxford University Press, 2000.

Singh Rye, Ajit. "The Indian Community in the Philippines." In *Indian Communities in Southeast Asia,* ed. Kernial Sandhu and A. Mami. Singapore: Institute of Southeast Asian Studies, 2001. Pp. 707–763.

Smedley, Audrey. *Race in North America: Origin and Evolution of a Worldview.* Boulder, CO: Westview, 1999.

Smith, Andrea. "Soul Wound: The Legacy of Native American Schools." *Amnesty International Magazine* (March 26, 2007). http://www.amnestyusa.org/node/87342.

Sollors, Werner, ed. *Interracialism: Black-White Intermarriage in American History, Literature, and Law.* New York: Oxford University Press, 2000.

Sommer, Marianne. "Mirror, Mirror on the Wall: Neanderthal as Image and 'Distortion' in Early 20th-Century French Science and Press." *Social Studies of Science* 36.2 (April 2006): 207–240.

Song, Miri. "Introduction: Who's at the Bottom? Examining Claims about Racial Hierarchy." *Ethnic and Racial Studies* 27.6 (November 2004): 859–877.

Spencer, Jon Michael. *The New Colored People: The Mixed-Race Movement in America.* New York: New York University Press, 2000.

Spencer, Rainier. *Challenging Multiracial Identity.* Boulder, CO: Lynne Rienner, 2006.

———. *Spurious Issues: Race and Multiracial Identity Politics in the United States.* Boulder, CO: Westview Press, 1999.

Spicer, Edward H. *Cycles of Conquest: The Impact of Spain, Mexico, and the United States on the Indians of the Southwest 1533–1960.* Tucson: University of Arizona Press, 1962.

———. *The Yaquis: A Cultural History.* Tucson: University of Arizona Press, 1980.

Spickard, Paul. "Does Multiraciality Lighten? Me-Too Ethnicity and the Whiteness Trap." In Winters and DeBose, *New Faces in a Changing America,* 289–300.

———. *Mixed Blood: Intermarriage and Ethnic Identity in Twentieth-Century America.* Madison: University of Wisconsin Press, 1989.

———. *Race in Mind: Critical Essays.* Notre Dame, IN: University of Notre Dame Press, 2015.

———. "What Must I Be? Asian Americans and the Question of Multiethnic Identity." *Amerasia Journal* 23.1 (1997): 43–60.

Spickard, Paul, and W. Jeffrey Burroughs, eds. *We Are a People: Narrative and Multiplicity in Constructing Ethnic Identity.* Philadelphia: Temple University Press, 2000.

Spickard, Paul, Rowena Fong, and Patricia L. Ewalt. "Undermining the Very Basis of Racism: Its Categories." *Social Work* 40.5 (1995): 725–728.

Steinberg, Stephen. *Turning Back: The Retreat from Racial Justice in American Thought and Policy.* Boston: Beacon Press, 2001.

Stephen, Lynn. "Viva Zapata! Generation, Gender, and Historical Consciousness in the Reception of Ejido Reform in Oaxaca." Transformation of Rural Mexico Series no. 6. San Diego: University of California, San Diego, Center for U.S. Mexican Studies, 1994.

———. *Women and Social Movement in Latin America: Power from Below.* Austin: University of Texas Press, 1997.

Stern, Norton B. *Jewish Refuge and Homeland.* Los Angeles: Dawson's Book, 1973.

Stevenson, Howard C. "Validation of the Scale of Racial Socialization for African American Adolescents: Steps toward Multidimensionality." *Journal of Black Psychology* 20.4 (1994): 445–468.

St. John, Rachel. *Line in the Sand: A History of the U.S.-Mexico Border*. Princeton, NJ: Princeton University Press, 2011.

Stoler, Ann. *Race and the Education of Desire: Foucault's History of Sexuality and the Colonial Order of Things*. Durham, NC: Duke University Press, 1995.

Stonequist, Everett V. *The Marginal Man: A Study in Personality and Culture Conflict*. 1937. Reprint, New York: Russell and Russell, 1961.

Strobel, Leny M. *Coming Full Circle: The Process of Decolonization among Post-1965 Filipino Americans*. Quezon City: Giraffe Books, 2001.

Strong, Nathan. "Patterns of Social Interaction and Psychological Accommodation among Japan's *Konketsuji* Population." PhD diss., University of California, Berkeley, 1978.

Sturm, Circe. *Blood Politics: Race, Culture, and Identity in the Cherokee Nation of Oklahoma*. Berkeley: University of California Press, 2002.

Sue, Christina, and Edward Telles. "Assimilation and Gender in Naming." *American Journal of Sociology* 112.5 (2007): 1383–1415.

Sue, Derald Wing, ed. *Microaggressions and Marginality: Manifestation, Dynamics, and Impact*. Hoboken, NJ: John Wiley, 2010.

Sue, Derald Wing, Christina M. Capodilupo, Gina C. Torino, Jennifer M. Bucceri, Aisha Holder, Kevin L. Nadal, and Marta Esquilin. "Racial Microaggressions in Everyday Life: Implications for Clinical Practice." *American Psychologist* 62.4 (2007): 271–286.

Sue-A-Quan, Trev. *Cane Reapers: Chinese Indentured Immigrants in Guyana*. Vancouver: Riftswood, 1999.

Sui Sin Far. *Mrs. Spring Fragrance and Other Writings*. Urbana: University of Illinois Press, 1995.

Sundstrom, Ronald. "Being and Being Mixed Race." *Social Theory and Practice* 27.2 (2001): 285–307.

———. *The Browning of America and the Evasion of Social Justice*. New York: State University of New York Press, 2008.

Superheadz. *Life as a Golden Half*. Tokyo: Powershovel, 2007.

Sussman, Robert Wald. *The Myth of Race: The Troubling Persistence of an Unscientific Idea*. Cambridge, MA: Harvard University Press, 2014.

Takahashi, Kosuke. "Multiracial Miss Universe Japan Symbolizes the Country's Transformation." *Huffington Post Japan* (May 8, 2015). http://www.huffingtonpost.com/2015/05/08/multiracial-miss-universe_n_7205026.html.

Takaki, Ronald. *Strangers from a Different Shore: A History of Asian Americans*. New York: Little, Brown, 1998.

Takashino, Tomokazu. "Miwaku no Haafu Bijo Juukunin" [Nineteen exotic haafu beauties]. *Playboy* (December 19, 2011): 6–10.

Taketani, Etsuko. *The Black Pacific Narrative: Geographic Imaginings of Race and Empire between the World Wars*. Hanover, NH: Dartmouth College Press, 2014.

Talbot, Donna M. "Exploring the Experiences and Self-Labeling of Mixed-Race Individuals with Two Minority Parents." *New Directions for Student Services*, no. 123 (2008): 23–31.

Tallbear, Kimberly. "Native-American-DNA.com: In Search of Native American Race and Tribe." In Keonig, Lee, and Richardson, *Revisiting Race in a Genomic Age*, 235–252.

Tayac, Gabrielle, ed., *IndiVisible: African-Native American Lives in the Americas*. Washington, DC: Smithsonian, 2009.

Taylor, Quintard. *The Forging of a Black Community: Seattle's Central District from 1870 through the Civil Rights Era*. Seattle: University of Washington Press, 1994.

Taylor, Robert. "Are you Black, Black Enough and Who Decides?" *Jacksonville Free Press* (May 14, 2009): 7.

Taylor, Steve. "The Diasporic Pursuit of Home and Identity: Dynamic Punjabi Transnationalism." *Sociological Review* 62 (2014): 276–294.

Telles, Edward, Mark Q. Sawyer, and Gaspar Rivera-Salgado. *Just Neighbors? Research on African American and Latino Relations in the United States.* New York: Russell Sage Foundation, 2011.

Thai, Ted, photographer. *Time Magazine*, special issue (November 18, 1993).

Thapar, Romila. *The Penguin History of Early India: From Origins to AD 1300.* New Delhi: Penguin Books, 2002.

"13-Year-Old Blazes Lane in Olympic Swimming." *Asianweek* (March 14, 2008): 17.

Thomas, Anita Jones, and Suzette L. Speight. "Racial Identity and Racial Socialization Attitudes of African American Parents." *Journal of Black Psychology* 25.2 (1999): 152–170.

Thomas, Susan. *Cuban Zarzuela: Performing Race and Gender on Havana's Lyric Stage.* Urbana: University of Illinois Press, 2009.

Thompson, Era Bell. "Happy Ending: Grown-Up Brown Baby Finds Husband in Japan, a Home in the USA." *Ebony Magazine* (July 1968): 63–68.

———. "Japan's Rejected: Teen-agers Fathered by Negro Soldiers Face a Bleak Future in a Hostile Land." *Ebony Magazine* (September 1967): 42–54.

Thornton, Michael. "Policing the Borderlands: White- and Black-American Newspaper Perceptions of Multiracial Heritage and the Idea of Race, 1996–2006." *Journal of Social Issues* 65.1 (2009): 105–127.

———. "A Social History of a Multiethnic Identity: The Case of Black-Japanese Americans." PhD diss., University of Michigan, 1983.

Thornton, Michael, and Harold Gates. "Black, Japanese, and American: An Asian American Identity Yesterday and Today." In Williams-León and Nakashima, *Sum of Our Parts*, 93–106.

Thornton, Michael, and Hemant Shah. "US News Magazine Images of Black-Asian American Relationships, 1980–1992." *Communication Review* 1.4 (1996): 497–519.

Thornton, Michael, and Atsushi Tajima. "A 'Model' Minority: Japanese Americans as References and Role Models in Black Newspapers, 2000–2010." *Communication and Critical/Cultural Studies* 11 (April 2014): 139–157.

"3-Year-Old Golf Wonder Boy for Real—A Tiger Woods to Be?" *Filipino Reporter* (September 24, 1998): 30.

"A Tiger Who Shows Many Stripes and Teaches Lessons of Many Colors." *Afro-American Red Star* (April 26, 1997): A4.

"Tiger Woods' True Color." *Northwest Asian Weekly* (January 3, 2003): 2.

Tizard, Barbara, and Ann Phoenix. *Black, White, or Mixed Race?* New York: Routledge, 1993.

———. "The Identity of Mixed Parentage Adolescents." *Journal of Child Psychology and Psychiatry and Allied Disciplines* 36 (November 1995): 1399–1410.

Tout, Otis. *The First Thirty Years in Imperial Valley California.* San Diego: Otis Tout Publisher, 1931.

Toya, Riina. *Ginza to Shiseido: Nihon wo Modern ni shita Kaisha* [Ginza and Shiseido: A company that made Japan modern]. Tokyo: Shinchosensho, 2012.

Turley, Ruth N. L. "When Do Neighborhoods Matter? The Role of Race and Neighborhood Peers." *Social Science Research* 32 (March 2003): 61–79.

Turner, Victor. *The Forest of Symbols: Aspects of Ndembu Ritual.* Ithaca, NY: Cornell University Press, 1967.

Ualieva, Saule K., and Adrienne L. Edgar. "In the Laboratory of Peoples' Friendship: Mixed People in Kazakhstan from the Soviet Era to the Present." In King-O'Riain et al., *Global Mixed Race*, 68–90.

Ueno, Chizuko. *Oiru Junbi* [Prepare to be old]. Tokyo: Gakuyo Shobo, 2005.

Urry, John. *Reference Groups and the Theory of Revolution*. London: Routledge and Kegan Paul, 1973.

US Census Bureau. "Population Estimates, American Community Survey, Census of Population and Housing, State and County Housing Unit Estimates, County Business Patterns, Nonemployer Statistics, Economic Census, Survey of Business Owners, Building Permits." December 2, 2015. http://quickfacts.census.gov/qfd/states/00000.html.

US Congress. "Federal Measures of Race and Ethnicity and the Implications for the 2000 Census." Hearings before the Subcommittee on Government Management, Information and Technology of the House Committee on Government Reform and Oversight, 105th Congress. Washington, DC: Government Printing Office, 1997.

Vasconcelos, José. *The Cosmic Race/La Raza Cósmica*. Trans. Didier T. Jaén. 1979. Reprint, Baltimore: Johns Hopkins University Press, 1997.

——. *La Raza Cósmica*. Los Angeles: California State University, Los Angeles, Centro de Publicaciones Department of Chicano Studies, 1979.

Vasquez, Jessica M. "Gender across Family Generations: Change in Mexican American Masculinities and Femininities." *Identities* 21.5 (2014): 532–550.

——. *Mexican Americans across Generations: Immigrant Families, Racial Realities*. New York: New York University Press, 2011.

Vasquez, Jessica M., and Christopher Wetzel. "Tradition and the Invention of Racial Selves: Symbolic Boundaries, Collective Authenticity, and Contemporary Struggles for Racial Equality." *Ethnic and Racial Studies* 32.9 (2009): 1557–1575.

Velásquez Gutierrez, Margarita. *Políticas Sociales, Transformación Agraria Ia Participación de las Mujeres en el Campo: 1920–1988*. Cuernavaca Morelos: UNAM, entro Regional de Investigaciones Multidisciplinarias, 1992.

Velásquez Leon, Heather. *Baja California, Manual de Estadísticas Básicas del Estado de Baja California*. Mexico City: Mexico SPPP, Gobierno del Estado, 1982.

Velásquez Morales, Catalina. *Baja California un Presente con Historia*. Baja California: Universidad Autónoma de Baja California, 2000.

——. *Los Imigrantes Chinos en Baja California, 1920–1937*. Mexicali: Universidad Autónoma de Baja California, 2001.

——. "Organización y Ascenso en los Chinos de Baja California (1920–1937)." In *China en las Californias*, ed. Centro-Cultural-Tijuana. Tijuana: Conacutla, 2004. P. 112.

Vergara, Benito M., Jr. *Pinoy Capital: The Filipino Nation in Daly City*. Philadelphia: Temple University Press, 2009.

Vernot, Benjamin, and Joshua M. Akey. "Complex History of Admixture between Modern Humans and Neanderthals." *American Journal of Human Genetics* 96.3 (2015): 448–453.

Wachs, Stewart. "Reel Life & Real Life: Film-maker Regge Life on Identity & the Joys and Trials of Being Intercultural." *Perspectives on Asia: Kyoto Journal*, no. 40 (Spring 1999): 14–19.

Wagatsuma, Hiroshi, and Toshinao Yoneyama. *Henken no Kouzou: Nihonjin no Jinshukan* [A structure of prejudice: Japanese racial views]. Tokyo: NHK Books, 1967.

Walker, Isaiah Helekunihi. *Waves of Resistance: Surfing and History in Twentieth-Century Hawai'i*. Honolulu: University of Hawai'i Press, 2011.

Wall, Jeffrey D., Melinda A. Yang, Flora Jay, Sung K. Kim, Eric Y. Durand, Laurie S. Stevison, et al. "Higher Levels of Neanderthal Ancestry in East Asians Than in Europeans." *Genetics* 194.1 (2013): 199–209.

Walter, Meade Adalberto. *El Valle de Mexicali*. Mexicali: Universidad Autónoma de Baja California, 1996.

Wang, Oliver. "Notes on the Run: Lost in the Woods." *International Examiner* (June 3, 1997): 8.

Warikoo, Natasha K. "Racial Authenticity among Second Generation Youth in New York and London." *Poetics* 35 (December 2007): 388–408.

Watanna, Onoto [Winnifred Eaton]. *A Half Caste and Other Writings*. Urbana: University of Illinois Press, 2002.

Watarae, Tamaki. "Haafu ni naru Nikkeijin Brajirujin Josei" [Nikkei Brazilians play a role of haafu]. In Iwabuchi, *Haafu to ha dareka*, 178–197.

Waters, Mary C. *Ethnic Options: Choosing Identities in America*. Berkeley: University of California Press, 1990.

Webb, Arthur. "What Does Being African American Mean—Who Said So?" *Tri-State Defender* (October 15, 2005): 4A.

Weiss, Kenneth M., and Brian W. Lambert. "Does History Matter? Do the Facts of Human Variation Package Our Views or Do Our Views Package the Facts?" *Evolutionary Anthropology* 19.3 (2010): 92–97.

Weiss, Kenneth M., and Jeffrey Long. "Non-Darwinian Estimation: My Ancestors, My Genes' Ancestors." *Genome Research* 19.5 (May 2009): 703–710.

West, Candice, and Don H. Zimmerman. "Doing Gender." *Gender and Society* 1 (June 1987): 125–152.

West, Dorothy. *The Wedding*. New York: Doubleday, 1995.

Westdale, Virgil, with Stephanie A. Gerdes. *Blue Skies and Thunder: Farm Boy, Pilot, Inventor, TSA Officer, and WW II Soldier of the 442nd Regimental Combat Team. Memoirs of a Japanese American*. New York: iUniverse, 2010.

Wetzel, Christopher. *Gathering the Potawatomi Nation: Revitalization and Identity*. Norman: University of Oklahoma Press, 2015.

Wickberg, Edgar. "The Chinese Mestizo in Philippine History." *Journal of South Asian History* 5.1 (1964): 62–100.

Wiencek, Henry. *The Hairstons: An American Family in Black and White*. New York: St. Martin's, 1999.

Wilber, Ken. *A Brief History of Everything*. 2nd ed. Boston: Shambhala, 1996.

Wilkerson, Isabel. *The Warmth of Other Suns: The Epic Story of America's Great Migration*. New York: Random House, 2010.

Will, George. "Melding in America." *Washington Post* (October 5, 1997): C07.

Williams, Alvarez de. *The Cocopah People*. Phoenix: Indian Travel Series, 1974.

Williams, Duncan, ed. *Hapa Japan: Constructing Global Mixed Race and Mixed Roots Japanese Identities and Representations*. 2 vols. Los Angeles: Kaya Press, Forthcoming.

———. "Key Moments in Japanese America's Mixed Race History, 1868–1945." In Williams, *Hapa Japan*, vol. 1.

Williams, Gregory Howard. *Life on the Color Line*. New York: Penguin, 1995.

Williams, Teresa. "The Theater of Identity: (Multi-)race and Representation of Eurasians and AfroAsians." In Zack, *American Mixed Race*, 79–96.

Williams-León, Teresa K. "International Amerasians: Third Culture Afroasian and Eurasian Americans in Japan." MA thesis, University of California, Los Angeles, 1989.

Williams-León, Teresa K., and Cynthia L. Nakashima, eds. *The Sum of Our Parts: Mixed Heritage Asian Americans*. Philadelphia: Temple University Press, 2001.

Williamson, Joel. *New People: Miscegenation and Mulattoes in the United States*. New York: Free Press, 1980.

Winters, Loretta I., and Herman L. DeBose, eds. *New Faces in a Changing America: Multiracial Identity in the 21st Century*. Thousand Oaks, CA: Sage, 2003.

Wiseman, Paul. "Ward Spins Biracial Roots into Blessing." *USA Today* (April 10, 2006).

Wolfe, Patrick. "Settler Colonialism and the Elimination of the Native." *Journal of Genocide Research* 8.4 (2006): 387–409.

Wong, Bill. "Yellow Pearls: An American Tiger." *Asianweek* (April 24, 1997): 6.

———. "Yellow Pearls: Tiger's Fans." *Asianweek* (February 13, 1997): 6.

Wright, Marguerite. *I'm Chocolate, You're Vanilla: Raising Healthy Black and Biracial Children in a Race-Conscious World*. San Francisco: Jossey-Bass, 1998.

Yamamoto, Atsuhisa. "Haafu no Shintai Hyyosho ni okeru Danseisei to Jinshuka no Politics" [Masculinity on the physical representation of haafu and the politics of racialization]. In Iwabuchi, *Haafu to ha dareka*, 114–142.

Yancey, George. "Racial Justice in a Black/Nonblack Society." In Brunsma, *Mixed Messages*, 49–62.

"The Year of the Tiger." *Atlanta Inquirer* (May 3, 1997): 6.

Yomota, Inuhiko. *Kawaii Ron* [Kawaii theory]. Tokyo: Chikuma Shinsho, 2006.

Young, Elliot. *Alien Nation: Chinese Migration in the Americas from the Coolie Era to World War II*. Chapel Hill: University of North Carolina Press, 2014.

Yu, Henry. "Tiger Woods at the Center of History: Looking back at the Twentieth Century through the Lens of Race, Sports, and Mass Consumption." 2003. https://www.history.ubc.ca/documents/faculty/yu/Tiger_Woods_Center.pdf.

Yudell, Michael. *Race Unmasked: Biology and Race in the 20th Century*. New York: Columbia University Press, 2014.

Zack, Naomi, ed. *American Mixed Race: The Culture of Microdiversity*. Lanham, MD: Rowman & Littlefield, 1995.

———. *Race and Mixed Race*. Philadelphia: Temple University Press, 1994.

NOTES ON CONTRIBUTORS

VERÓNICA CASTILLO-MUÑOZ earned her PhD in history at the University of California, Irvine. She is an Assistant Professor of History at the University of California, Santa Barbara. Formerly a University of California President's Postdoctoral Fellow at UC San Diego, she is the author of two articles on labor and migration in the US-Mexico borderlands. Her book, *The Other California: Land, Identity, and Politics on the Mexican Borderlands*, was published by the University of California Press.

MAHARAJ RAJU DESAI received his MA in Asian American studies from San Francisco State University and is pursuing a PhD in education at the University of Hawai'i at Mānoa. He is also a part-time lecturer in the Department of Philippine Studies at City College of San Francisco. His research interests include critical pedagogy, ethnic studies, youth participatory action research, language learning, critical literacy, critical mixed race studies, and Philippine studies.

INGRID DINEEN-WIMBERLY earned her PhD in history at the University of California, Santa Barbara. She is a tenured Lecturer in History at the University of La Verne, Point Mugu Campus. She is the author of several articles on mixed race issues and African American history and of *The Allure of Blackness among Mixed Race Americans, 1862–1916* (forthcoming).

RUDY P. GUEVARRA JR. holds a PhD in history from the University of California, Santa Barbara. He is Associate Professor of Asian Pacific American Studies at Arizona State University. He is author or editor of three books and several articles on racial complexity. Among his books are *Becoming Mexipino: Multiethnic Identities and Communities in San Diego* (2012) and *Transnational Crossroads: Remapping the Americas and the Pacific* (2012). His current project is *Aloha Compadre: Latina/os in Hawai'i, 1832–2010*. He won the Early Career Award from the Association for Asian American Studies as well as a Ford Foundation Dissertation Fellowship and a UC Berkeley Chancellor's Postdoctoral Fellowship, among other honors.

VELINA HASU HOUSTON earned her MFA at the University of California, Los Angeles and PhD at the University of Southern California. She is Professor of Theatre, Resident Playwright, and Director of the Master of Fine Arts in Dramatic Writing program at the University of Southern California. She is the winner of many prizes, fellowships, and international honors including the Loving Prize from the Mixed Roots Film and Literary Festival, and her plays, more than thirty in number, have been performed in theaters across the United States, in several countries in Europe and Asia, and on television. Among her recent plays are *Tea, With Music*; *The DNA Trail*; and *The Intuition of Iphigenia*.

TERENCE KEEL holds a PhD from Harvard University and is an Assistant Professor of History and Black Studies at the University of California, Santa Barbara. He works at the intersection of racial studies, history, religious studies, and the history of science. He is the author of several articles on the history of racial ideas, the human genome, and the relationships between *Homo nenderthalensis* and *Homo sapiens*, as well as the book *The Religious Pursuit of Race: How Christianity Shaped Modern Scientific Ideas about Human Difference*, which will be published by Stanford University Press.

JANET C. MENDOZA STICKMON is Professor of Humanities at Napa Valley College. She holds two master's degrees, in ethnic studies from University of California, Berkeley and also from the Graduate Theological Union in Berkeley. She is the author of several book chapters and two books, *Midnight Peaches, Two O'clock Patience—A Collection of Essays, Poems, and Short Stories on Womanhood and the Spirit* (2012) and *Crushing Soft Rubies—A Memoir* (2004).

KAORI MORI WANT earned a PhD at the State University of New York–Buffalo. She is Associate Professor teaching Asian American culture and literatures in the Department of English at Konan Women's University in Japan. She is the author of several articles on mixed race, interracial, and international couples, and racial hierarchies in Japan.

CRISTINA M. ORTIZ is a PhD candidate in social work at the University of Chicago and Assistant Professor of Sociology at St. Norbert College. She is the author of several articles on multiraciality and transracial adoption. Her dissertation is titled "An Exploration of Parental Racial Socialization in Dual-Minority Multiracial Families."

REBECCA ROMO earned her PhD in sociology from the University of California, Santa Barbara. She is Assistant Professor of Sociology at Santa Monica College and a former American Sociological Association Minority Fellow. She is the author of *Blaxican Borderlands: Living Race and Identity in Black and Brown* (forthcoming from University of Nebraska Press).

JOANNE L. RONDILLA's PhD is in ethnic studies from the University of California, Berkeley. She is a long-term Lecturer in Asian Pacific American Studies at Arizona State University. She is author or editor of several articles and two books: Pacific Diaspora: Island Peoples in the United States and Across the Pacific (2004) and Is Lighter Better? Skin-Tone Discrimination among Asian Americans (2007). Her current project is Colonial Faces: Beauty and Skin Color Hierarchy in the Philippines and the United States.

NITASHA TAMAR SHARMA earned her PhD in anthropology at the University of California, Santa Barbara. She is Associate Professor of African American Studies and Asian American Studies, as well as McCormick Professor of Teaching Excellence, at Northwestern University. She is the author of many articles and of Hip Hop Desis: South Asian Americans, Blackness, and a Global Race Consciousness (2010). Her current projects are Hidden Hapas: Multiracial Blacks and Blackness in Hawai'i and New Politics of Race in Hawai'i.

PAUL SPICKARD has a PhD in history from the University of California, Berkeley. He is Professor of History and Affiliate Professor of Black Studies, Asian American Studies, Religious Studies, East Asian Studies, and Middle Eastern Studies at the University of California, Santa Barbara. He is author or editor of nineteen books and fourscore articles on race, migration, and related topics in the United States, the Pacific, Northeast Asia, and Europe. He has received the Loving Prize from the Mixed Roots Film and Literary Festival, the Richard Yarborough Mentoring Award from the American Studies Association, the Robert Perry Mentoring Award from the National Association for Ethnic Studies, the Outstanding Book on Human Rights Award from the Gustavus Myers Center, and other honors. Among his recent books are Multiple Identities: Migrants, Ethnicity, and Membership (2013), Global Mixed Race (2014), and Race in Mind: Critical Essays (2015). His current projects include Growing Up Ethnic in Germany and Shape Shifters: Journeys across Terrains of Race and Identity.

JESSICA VASQUEZ-TOKOS has a PhD in sociology from the University of California, Berkeley. She is Associate Professor of Sociology at the University of Oregon. She is a former Ford Foundation Postdoctoral Fellow at the University of Southern California. She is the author of many articles and the book Mexican Americans across Generations: Immigrant Families, Racial Realities (2011).

LILY ANNE Y. WELTY TAMAI earned her PhD in history at the University of California, Santa Barbara. A former postdoctoral fellow at the University of California, Los Angeles and the University of Southern California, she is History Curator at the Japanese American National Museum in Los Angeles. She is the author of several articles and book chapters on mixed race American Japanese and related topics. She is the author of Military-Industrial Intimacy: Mixed-Race American-Japanese, Eugenics, and Transnational Identities (forthcoming from University of Nebraska Press).

INDEX

Printed in the United States
By Bookmasters